Slovakia in History

Until the dissolution of Czechoslovakia, Slovakia's identity seemed inextricably linked with that of the former state. This book explores the key moments and themes in the history of Slovakia from the Duchy of Nitra's ninth-century origins to the establishment of independent Slovakia at midnight 1992–1993. Leading scholars chart the gradual ethnic awakening of the Slovaks during the Reformation and Counter-Reformation and examine how Slovak national identity took shape with the codification of standard literary Slovak in 1843 and the subsequent development of the Slovak national movement. They show how, after a thousand years of Magyar–Slovak coexistence, Slovakia became part of the new Czechoslovak state from 1918 to 1939, and shed new light on its role as a Nazi client state as well as on post-war developments leading up to full statehood in the aftermath of the collapse of communism in 1989. There is no comparable book in English on the subject.

MIKULÁŠ TEICH is Emeritus Fellow of Robinson College, Cambridge, and Honorary Professor, Vienna University of Technology (Technische Universität Wien). His publications include work on the history of chemistry, biomedical sciences and biotechnology; social, economic and national aspects of scientific and technical developments; and Slavica.

DUŠAN KOVÁČ is Vice-President of the Slovak Academy of Sciences and President of the Slovak National Committee of Historians. His previous publications include *Dějiny Slovenska* (History of Slovakia, 1998).

MARTIN D. BROWN is an assistant professor of international history at Richmond, the American International University in London. His previous publications include *Dealing with Democrats. The British Foreign Office's Relations with the Czechoslovak Émigrés in Great Britain, 1939–1945* (2006).

Slovakia in History

Edited by

Mikuláš Teich, Dušan Kováč
and Martin D. Brown

CAMBRIDGE
UNIVERSITY PRESS

CAMBRIDGE UNIVERSITY PRESS
Cambridge, New York, Melbourne, Madrid, Cape Town,
Singapore, São Paulo, Delhi, Tokyo, Mexico City

Cambridge University Press
The Edinburgh Building, Cambridge CB2 8RU, UK

Published in the United States of America by Cambridge University Press, New York

www.cambridge.org
Information on this title: www.cambridge.org/9780521802536

© Cambridge University Press 2011

First published 2011

A catalogue record for this publication is available from the British Library

Library of Congress Cataloguing in Publication Data
Slovakia in history / edited by Mikuláš Teich, Dušan Kovác, Martin D. Brown.
    p.   cm.
    Includes bibliographical references and index.
    ISBN 978-0-521-80253-6 (Hbk.)
    1. Slovakia–History.   2. National characteristics, Slovak.   3. Slovakia–
Politics and government.   I. Teich, Mikuláš.   II. Kovác, Dušan.
III. Brown, Martin D.   IV. Title.
    DB2763.S56 2010
    943.73–dc22

                                                                                2010022615

ISBN 978-0-521-80253-6 Hardback

Contents

Figures

Illustrations 1, 2, 5 and 6 from Institute of
Historical Studies of the Slovak Academy of Sciences.

Illustrations 3 and 4 from D. Kováč, *Dějiny Slovenska* (1998).

Illustrations 7, 8, 9, 10, 11, 12, 13, 14, 15, 16, 17, 18 and 19
reproduced with kind permission of ČTK Photobank/
Multimedia.

Maps

Notes on contributors

ELISABETH BAKKE is an associate professor and heads the bachelor programme in European studies at the University of Oslo. She studied political science and specialises in the politics and political history of Central Europe, especially Czechoslovakia. Her publications deal with questions of national identity, national self-determination, Czech–Slovak relations, and ideology and the concept of Czechoslovakism.

MICHAEL BARNOVSKÝ was a historian at the Institute of Historical Studies, Slovak Academy of Sciences. His research was concerned with the history of Slovakia after the Second World War, particularly the period of 'controlled democracy' in the years 1945–1948. On this theme he published his principal work, *Na ceste k monopolu moci. Mocenskopolitické zápasy na Slovensku v rokoch 1945–1948* (On the road to monopoly power. Power-political struggles in Slovakia in the years 1945–1948 (Bratislava, 1991)).

MARTIN D. BROWN is an assistant professor of international history at Richmond, the American International University in London, a Fellow of the Royal Historical Society and a member of the steering committee of the British–Czech–Slovak Historians' Forum. His most recent book, *Dealing with Democrats. The British Foreign Office's Relations with the Czechoslovak Émigrés in Great Britain, 1939–1945* (Frankfurt am Main, 2006), deals with British foreign policy formation and decision-making during the Second World War and in particular relations with the Czechoslovak government-in-exile. A Czech-language translation was published in October 2008. He is currently researching British foreign policy during the era of détente, leading up to the Helsinki Final Act of 1975.

VALERIÁN BYSTRICKÝ is a historian at the Institute of Historical Studies, Slovak Academy of Sciences. From 1998 to 2006 he was director of the institute. He has published widely in the area of Balkan studies. Lately his professional interests centre on the history of the Second

Czechoslovak Republic, concerning the period between the First
Republic and the emergence of the Slovak state in 1939. The results
of this research were recently published in *Od autonómie k vzniku
slovenského štátu* (From autonomy to the emergence of the Slovak state
(Bratislava, 2008)).

VILIAM ČIČAJ is a historian at the Institute of Historical Studies,
Slovak Academy of Sciences, and chairman of the Slovak Historical
Association. His field of interest is the early modern history of
Slovakia, especially religious disturbances at the time of Reforma-
tion and Counter-Reformation.

EVA FRIMMOVÁ is a historian at the Institute of Historical Studies,
Slovak Academy of Sciences. She is the author of books and articles
dealing with humanism and the Renaissance on the territory of contemporary Slovakia, especially in the area of literature and book
culture.

ĽUDOVÍT HARAKSIM was a historian at the Institute of Historical
Studies, Slovak Academy of Sciences, before 1970. He was then
obliged to give up his academic activities and worked in a museum
without the possibility of publishing. In 1990 he was able to return
to the Institute of Historical Studies. His research concentrated on
Slavic historical studies, including Slavic reciprocity, political and
ideological Panslavism, and Slovak–Russian and Slovak–Ukrainian
relations in the nineteenth century.

IVAN KAMENEC is a historian at the Institute of Historical Studies,
Slovak Academy of Sciences. His main area of interest is the history
of the Slovak state (1939–1945). He authored a short history of the
Slovak state (1992) and a biography of Jozef Tiso (1998). The main
part of his research is dedicated to the holocaust of Slovak Jews. On
this theme he has published numerous articles and the book *Po stopách
tragédie* (On the track of tragedy (Bratislava, 1991)).

DUŠAN KOVÁČ is Vice-President of the Slovak Academy of Sciences and
President of the Slovak National Committee of Historians. In the
years 1990–1998 he was director of the Institute of Historical Studies,
Slovak Academy of Sciences. His main field of interest is the history
of Central Europe in the nineteenth and twentieth centuries. He is the
author of numerous books and articles dealing with the problems of
nationalism, nationalistic political agendas, Czech–Slovak relations
and national minorities in Central Europe. His books include *Dějiny
Slovenska* (History of Slovakia (Prague, 1998, 2006)).

EVA KOWALSKÁ is a historian at the Institute of Historical Studies, Slovak Academy of Sciences. Her field of research is social and cultural history of the eighteenth century, problems of 'enlightened absolutism', and the reforms of Maria Teresa and Joseph II, including the Slovak Protestant movement in connection with the beginning of Slovak nationalism. Her principal work in this field is *Evanjelické a.v. spoločenstvo v 18. storočí* (Lutheran community in the eighteenth century (Bratislava, 2001)).

NATALIA KRAJČOVIČOVÁ is a historian at the Institute of Historical Studies, Slovak Academy of Sciences. She is the author of several works on the history of the First Czechoslovak Republic, including the Slovak autonomist agenda and Czech–Slovak relationships in the years 1918–1939. She has also published on the history of the Slovak and Czechoslovak agrarian movement, the Agrarian Party and land reform. Her biography of the Slovak agrarian-liberal politician Emil Stodola was published in 2007.

MIROSLAV LONDÁK heads the Department of Contemporary History at the Institute of Historical Studies, Slovak Academy of Sciences. His special interest is the contemporary economic history of Slovakia. With Stanislav Sikora and Elena Londáková he authored *Predjarie. Politický, ekonomický a kultúrny vývoj 1960–1967* (Before Spring. Political, economic and cultural development in Slovakia 1960–1967 (Bratislava, 2002)). Recently he published *Rok 1968 a ekonomická realita na Slovensku* (The year 1968 and economic reality in Slovakia (Bratislava, 2007)).

ELENA LONDÁKOVÁ is a research fellow at the Institute of Historical Studies, Slovak Academy of Sciences. Her field of interest is the history of culture in Slovakia after the Second World War. In articles and monographs she has analysed controversial developments in culture and cultural politics during the Communist dictatorship. With Stanislav Sikora and Miroslav Londák she published *Predjarie. Politický, ekonomický a kultúrny vývoj 1960–1967* (Before Spring. Political, economic and cultural development in Slovakia 1960–1967 (Bratislava, 2002)).

JÁN LUKAČKA is an associate professor at Comenius University, Bratislava, and head of the Department of Medieval History, Institute of Historical Studies, Slovak Academy of Sciences. He has published numerous articles on the early history of the Kingdom of Hungary (1000–1526), with an emphasis on ethnic Slovak society and its social and cultural development.

JAN PEŠEK is a research fellow at the Institute of Historical Studies, Slovak Academy of Sciences. His field of research is the Communist totalitarian system in Slovakia, persecution in the early years of the totalitarian Communist regime, and the system and structure of the totalitarian machinery in Czechoslovakia. His works include (with Michal Barnovský) *Štátna moc a cirkvi na Slovensku 1948–1953* (State power and churches in Slovakia 1948–1953 (Bratislava, 1997)) and biographical sketches of representatives of the Communist totalitarian regime: Jan Pešek, *et al., Aktéry jednej éry na Slovensku 1948–1989* (Actors of one era in Slovakia 1948–1989 (Bratislava, 2003)).

VILÉM PREČAN is professor of history at Charles University, Prague, and head of the Czechoslovak Documentation Centre, Prague. His main area of interest is contemporary Czech and Slovak history. After the military occupation of Czechoslovakia in August 1968 he co-edited documents of the occupation *Sedm pražských dnů 21.–17.srpen 1968* (translated as *The Czech Black Book* (1969)) which led to his political persecution. He was obliged to leave the Institute of History of the Czechoslovak Academy of Sciences. In 1976 he emigrated to Germany where he established the Czechoslovak Documentation Centre of Independent Literature. After returning to Czechoslovakia, he headed the newly established Institute of Contemporary History from 1990 to 1998. Among other works, he has published two volumes of documents on the Slovak National Uprising and three volumes of documents on Charter 77.

JAN RYCHLÍK is professor of history at Charles University, Prague. His main area of research is Slovak history and history of Czech–Slovak relations. He has published two volumes on relations between Czechs and Slovaks in the twentieth century: *Češi a Slováci ve 20. století. Česko-slovenské vztahy 1914–1945* (Czechs and Slovaks in the twentieth century. Czech–Slovak relations 1914–1945 (Bratislava, 1996)) and *Češi a Slováci ve 20. století. Česko-slovenské vztahy 1945–1992* (Czechs and Slovaks in the twentieth century. Czech–Slovak relations 1945–1992 (Bratislava, 1998)). On the division of Czechoslovakia in 1993, he has published *Rozpad Československa* (Disintegration of Czechoslovakia (Bratislava, 2002)).

VLADIMÍR SEGEŠ is a historian at the Institute of Military History, Slovak Ministry of Defence, Bratislava. His field of interest is medieval military history and history of towns in medieval Upper Hungary, including the history of law and criminality. This theme is the subject of his recent book *Prešporský pitaval. Zločin a trest v stredovekej*

Bratislave (Preßburg's criminal cases. Crime and punishment in medieval Bratislava (Bratislava, 2005)).

STANISLAV SIKORA is a research fellow at the Institute of Historical Studies, Slovak Academy of Sciences. His field of interest is the period of the Prague Spring 1968. He has published articles on the reform process from the mid 1960s in Slovakia. With Miroslav Londák and Elena Londáková he has co-authored *Predjarie. Politický, ekonomický a kultúrny vývoj na Slovensku v rokoch 1960–1967* (Before Spring. Political, economic and cultural development in Slovakia 1960–1967 (Bratislava, 2002)).

MICHAL ŠTEFANSKÝ is a research fellow at the Institute of Military History, Slovak Ministry of Defence, Bratislava. His interests centre on contemporary political and military history, in particular the year 1968, the period of 'normalisation' (1969–1989) and the 'velvet revolution' in 1989, which are dealt with in numerous publications, including books and articles.

JÁN STEINHÜBEL is a medievalist at the Institute of Historical Studies, Slovak Academy of Sciences. His main field of research is the early medieval history of Central Europe, especially the Duchy of Nitra, Great Moravia and the beginnings of the Kingdom of Hungary. His principal work is *Nitrianske kniežatstvo* (Duchy of Nitra (Bratislava, 2004)).

ŠTEFAN ŠUTAJ is professor of history at the University of Prešov, Slovakia, and a research fellow at the Institute of Humanities and Social Sciences, Slovak Academy of Sciences. He heads the Slovak section of the Slovak–Hungarian Historical Commission. He is the author of numerous monographs and studies on ethnic-national minorities in Slovakia after the Second World War, especially the Magyar minority.

MIKULÁŠ TEICH is Emeritus Fellow of Robinson College, Cambridge, and Honorary Professor, Vienna University of Technology (Technische Universität Wien). His publications include work on the history of chemistry, biomedical sciences and biotechnology; philosophical and methodological aspects of the history of science and technology; social, economic and national aspects of scientific and technical developments; the history of scientific institutions; and Slavica.

JOSEF ŽATKULIAK is a historian at the Department of Contemporary History of the Institute of Historical Studies, Slovak Academy of

Sciences. His main area of interest centres on Czech–Slovak federalisation and its beginnings in 1968. His principal work in this field is *Federalizácia československého štátu 1968–1970. Vznik československej federácie roku 1968* (Federalisation of the Czechoslovak state 1968–1970. Beginning of the Czech–Slovak Federation in 1968 (Prague and Bratislava, 1996)).

Acknowledgements

It is a great pleasure to offer thanks to colleagues and friends who gave helpful comments and suggestions in the early/later stages of the project: Dr Gertrude Enderle-Burcel, Professor Andrea Komlosy, Professor Michael Mitterauer, Dr Albert Müller, Dr Milan Otáhal and Dr Joachim Whaley. We think warmly of William Davies for his early encouragement and are grateful to Michael Watson, his successor at Cambridge University Press, for his unwavering support of the project. Thanks are also due to Chloe Howell of Cambridge University Press for aiding with presswork and to Karen Anderson Homes for carefully copy-editing the text. We thank Angela Spindler-Brown for her assistance in sourcing photographs from the Czech Republic archives. We would also like to thank the anonymous reviewer at CUP for his/her comments.

We remember with deep sorrow Michal Barnovský (1937–2008) and Ľudovít Haraksim (1928–2008), who died before the publication of the book.

We thank the Institute of Geographical Studies of the Slovak Academy of Sciences for the map of the Slovak Republic (by Magister Róbert Pazúr). We are indebted to the Institute of Historical Studies of the Slovak Academy of Sciences for making it possible to draw on its archives, including illustrations and maps (by Michal Kostovský) from *A Concise History of Slovakia* (edited by Elena Mannová). Dušan Kováč is most grateful to the British Academy for generous financial support, which enabled him to travel to Britain and participate in direct editorial consultations.

Once again Mikuláš Teich offers public gratitude to Professor Alice Teichova who helped in many different ways – his debts to her are incalculable.

Map 1 Slovak Republic

POLAND

HIGH TATRAS

Poprad

Stará
L'ubovňa

Bardejov

Svidnik

Medzilaborce

Liptovský
Mikulas

Kežmarok

Topľa

Cndava

Laborec

Liptovský
Hrádok

Poprad

Levoča

Prešov

Snina

TATRAS

Spišská
Nová Ves

Hornád

Vranov nad
Topľou

Humenné

Brezno

SLOVAK ORE MOUNTAINS

Tisovec

Revúca

Rožňava

Košice

Michalovce

Ipeľ

Trebišov

Uh

UKRAINE

Rimavská
Sobota

Fiľakovo

HUNGARY

| 0 | 20 | 40 | 60 | 80 | 100 km |

| 0 | 10 | 20 | 30 | 40 | 50 | 60 miles |

1 Slovakia, the Slovaks and their history

Dušan Kováč

I

In January 1993 the Slovak Republic became an independent state after the division of Czecho-Slovakia into two states. With an area of 49,000 km^2 and population of 5.3 million, it is one of the smaller European states. The capital of Slovakia is Bratislava with a population of half a million people.[1] The world at large began to take an interest in Slovakia, the Slovaks, and their culture and history only after 1993. Since the history of the Slovaks developed within the framework of the Kingdom of Hungary until 1918, and then within Czechoslovakia, not only the amateur, but also the expert public may ask what the history of Slovakia is. Does such a history really exist?

In fact, Slovakia and the Slovaks have long been a subject of historical scholarship. If we could trace the development of Hungarian historiography, we would find that since various chroniclers were of Slovak ethnic origin (not least Ján of Turiec, the most eminent), Slovakia and especially the Slovak ethnic group have attracted interest. This tradition continued in humanist and Baroque historiography, since the territory of present-day Slovakia formed a substantial part of Habsburg Hungary during this period. The rest of Hungary was under Turkish domination. Interest in Slovakia and the Slovaks was heightened in the period of the Enlightenment, mainly thanks to the formally written defences (*apologias*) of the Slovaks (the earliest-known example is that of Ján Baltazár Magin from 1723) (Fig. 3), which used historical arguments. Also influential was the activity of the distinguished scholar of Slovak origin Matej (Matthias) Bel, who devoted a significant part of his outline of Hungarian history (*Hungariae antiquae et novae prodromus*, 1723) to the development

---

[1] Bratislava has been the official name of the city only since 1919. Prior to that point the name was only used by Slovak nationalists. This name was derived from the first-known written reference to the castle *Brezalauspurch*. The Latin name was Posonium, the German Preßburg, the Slovak Prešporok, and the Magyar Pozsony, the official name within the Kingdom of Hungary.

of the Slovak ethnic group. The first attempt at a systematic account of the history of the Slovaks appeared in 1780, in the form of Juraj Papánek's *Historia gentis Slavae*. From the end of the eighteenth century, the history of the Slovaks and of Slovakia became the subject of systematic interest.

In the formation of modern Slovakia, history played a key role: the record of a 'glorious past' became a key instrument of national agitation. This history was, however, often simply invented and mythological (using inadequate terms such as 'Old Slovaks' for the period of the eighth and ninth centuries, renaming Great Moravia as Great Slovakia, giving a Slovak identity to the rulers of the region in the Middle Ages and so on).

II

How does recent Slovak historiography tackle what it variously calls Slovak history or the history of Slovakia? This concept has two dimensions: territorial and ethnic. In the territorial sense, the subject of Slovak history is the territory of present-day Slovakia. This means that Slovak historiography, in conjunction with archaeology, devotes attention to the pre-Slavic period, and that it also takes an interest in the ethnic groups that lived in this territory both before and after Slavic settlement, which occurred in the fifth century. These two aspects are, understandably, not identical, and only their synthesis forms the subject called the history of Slovakia.

The past, perceived in this way, as a type of national master narrative, can be found in some works, which are mostly in Slovak and therefore not very accessible to the wider public. In the 1960s, the first attempts were made to produce an academic, synthetic history of Slovakia. This work was unfinished, terminating at the end of the nineteenth century.[2] Twenty years later there emerged a history of Slovakia in seven volumes.[3] Both these synthetic works are, of course, very strongly marked by the time of their creation. After 1989 only two short volumes were produced.[4]

---

[2] Ľ. Holotík and J. Tibenský (eds.), *Dejiny Slovenska I* [History of Slovakia, vol. I] (Bratislava, 1961); J. Mésároš (ed.), *Dejiny Slovenska II* [History of Slovakia, vol. II] (Bratislava, 1968).

[3] S. Cambel (ed.), *Dejiny Slovenska I–VII* [History of Slovakia, vols. I–VII] (Bratislava, 1985–1992).

[4] D. Kováč, *Dějiny Slovenska* [History of Slovakia] (Prague, 1998, 2007); E. Mannová (ed.), *A Concise History of Slovakia* (Bratislava, 2000).

III

In the Hungarian period, Slovakia had no administrative frontiers. The Kingdom of Hungary was divided into counties (Latin: *comitatus*, Slovak: *župa*, or *stolica*), which did not take the ethnic situation into account. The Slovaks called their country 'Slovensko' (Slovakia) – the term appears in written documents from as early as the fifteenth century but it was not precisely defined. At the time when the first Slovak political programmes were conceived, it was only an ill-defined region 'between the Tatras and the Danube', that is, the region called 'Upper Hungary' in Magyar literature.

The administrative frontiers of Slovakia were created by the formation of the Czechoslovak Republic in 1918 and confirmed by peace treaties. Since then, Slovakia has existed as an independent administrative territory. Until 1993 this territory was part of the Czechoslovak Republic, which, according to the 1920 constitution and further constitutions until 1968, was a centralised state. Slovakia was regarded as an independent unit – it had its own ministry from 1918 to 1927, and a Land Office (Krajinský úrad) headed by a Land President after 1927 – but it did not have its own legislative assembly, government or other autonomous bodies.

The brief period of the so-called Second Republic from October 1938 to March 1939 was an exception: the post-Munich Czecho-Slovakia in practice changed into a confederative, tripartite state (Bohemia and Moravia-Silesia; Slovakia; Carpatho-Ruthenia). From 1939 to 1945, the Slovak Republic existed as an independent state under German tutelage. However, the borders of this satellite and vassal of Nazi Germany were not identical to those of present-day Slovakia. The greatest change concerned regions in southern Slovakia, which were handed over to Hungary on Hitler's orders, following the Vienna Arbitration of November 1938. In 1943, before the Slovak National Uprising, a new resistance parliament with the name Slovak National Council was constituted. This institution, together with the Board of Commissioners, which formed a sort of embryonic Slovak government, continued to exist after the war. However, the centralist model was also gradually applied in post-war Czechoslovakia, and the Slovak autonomous authorities became impotent appendages of the central authorities in Prague. Communist totalitarianism, established in Czechoslovakia in February 1948, strengthened this centralisation.

A Czechoslovak federation was formally created during the Prague Spring of 1968. The Slovak Republic was formed, with the Slovak National Council as its parliament and a Slovak government. However, after the Warsaw Pact invasion, the federation did not really function. The Slovak authorities continued to operate formally but policies depended on the decisions of the centralised Communist Party, which was not federalised, and in the end on Moscow which was against any decentralisation or autonomy in the satellite states. The question of the political and administrative division of the state was reopened after 1989. The discussions about the name of the state – whether to write Czecho-Slovakia with a hyphen or Czechoslovakia without one – and about the division of responsibilities between the central government and the two national governments within the framework of the federation ended in 1993 with the division of the state. The quarrel about how to write the state name, which received the ironical sobriquet of the 'hyphen war', observed from outside seemed to be rather comical, but in reality it reflected the different perception of the common Czech–Slovak statehood by the majority of the Czech society on the one hand and majority of the Slovak society on the other.

The division of Czecho-Slovakia was undertaken in a peaceful manner, which was appreciated by the international community. Nevertheless, the two states currently enjoy a very good relationship and mutual co-operation. The Slovak Republic is a member of many international organisations, including the United Nations (UN) and, after some difficulties during the problematic Vladimír Mečiar government, has been a member state of the European Union (EU) since 2004.

IV

The Slovaks began to emerge as a modern nation at the same time as other developed European nations, as part of the spread of European nationalism from the end of the eighteenth century. In the first phase, activity began among the educated strata, who concentrated on cultivating their own language. In the Kingdom of Hungary, Latin was the official language and to a large extent also the literary language up to the early nineteenth century. As a result of Slovaks' linguistic closeness with the Czechs, the idea that the Czechs and Slovaks formed one Czechoslovak nation existed in this period, mainly among Slovak Protestants. However, the Czechs and Slovaks were separated by different historical development. The Czechs developed historically in the Kingdom of Bohemia, while Slovakia formed part of the Hungarian Lands of the Crown of Saint Stephen from the eleventh century. There were periods when the two kingdoms had a common monarch, and this situation became permanent from 1526 onwards.[5] Nevertheless they

---

[5] The year 1526 marks the beginning of the Habsburg monarchy. From this date the Habsburgs were not only princes of the Austrian Lands, but (usually) also Holy Roman Emperors, as well as kings of Bohemia (with Moravia and Silesia) and of Hungary (with Croatia).

always represented independent entities with distinct internal features. Thus, when the Czechs and the Slovaks reached the stage when they were formulating their own political programmes, their differing histories meant that they developed individual plans and aims.

From the middle of the nineteenth century, the political programme of the Slovaks aimed to achieve cultural and political-territorial autonomy within the framework of the Kingdom of Hungary. This demand was put in the document *The Demands of the Slovak Nation* during the Revolution of 1848. The *Memorandum of the Slovak Nation* of 1861 contained the same demand. Until the First World War, the Slovaks accepted allegiance to the Crown of Saint Stephen of Hungary, but demanded autonomous rights as an independent nation. They appealed to natural rights but also referred to their national historical development.

The political programme of the Slovaks changed only in the years of the First World War when all the relevant currents of Slovak political life accepted the programme of Czech–Slovak statehood, which came to fruition when the Czechoslovak Republic was established in 1918. In the following years, Slovak political goals fluctuated between acceptance of the centralist model and demands for autonomy within the framework of Czechoslovakia. Paradoxically, even in the 1992 parliamentary elections, immediately before the break-up of Czechoslovakia, the small Slovak National Party (with 8 per cent of the vote) was the only Slovak political party advocating an independent Slovak state.

V

The question of the ethno-genesis of the Slovaks is an important one in Slovak historiography. Written documents and especially archaeological evidence clearly demonstrate that the Slovaks are the direct descendants of the 'Old Slavs', who lived in the Carpathian basin from the fifth century. The term 'Old Slavs' does not exist in historical documents, and it emerged in the literature in order to distinguish between these earlier Slavs, who were undifferentiated both ethnically and linguistically, and contemporary separate nations who speak Slavic languages.[6]

---

[6] The expression 'Slavs' (*Slovania* in Slovak, *Slavyane* in Russian) derived from *slovo* – 'word' in Slovak and Russian. A Slav was able to communicate, to speak – in contrast to the dumb, mute person: *nemý* in Slovak, *nemoi* in Russian. Thus the designation for a German – who could neither understand nor be understood by Slovaks – is *Nemec* in Slovak, *Nemets* in Russian (*német* in Magyar).

The Old Slavs arrived in the Carpathian basin and the Danube region during the so-called migration period. The territory of Slovakia in that time already had a rich history. There is evidence of settlement of people of the Neanderthal type more than 100,000 years ago. Many prehistoric peoples lived on the territory of Slovakia. The Danube was a boundary of the Roman Empire (*limes romanus*). At the time of the Slavic settlement, the country was very thinly populated. The Slavs were very numerous and not very differentiated in language. Their first organisational units were tribes. The territory of Slovakia was probably part of the Slavic tribal union known as Samo's Empire.[7] In the territory of Slovakia itself, Nitra became the centre of another Slavic tribal union under the leadership of Duke Pribina. This Duchy of Nitra became part of the state known from the sources as Great Moravia (*Vel'ká Morava, Moravia magna*). At the beginning of the tenth century, after the fall of Great Moravia, the territory of present-day Slovakia gradually became part of the Hungarian state. Ethnic development or differentiation continued among the Slavs. The state framework of the Kingdom of Hungary was important for the development of the Slovaks. The frontiers of the state separated them from the ethnically related Western Slavs – the Poles and Czechs – and resulted in the Slovaks evolving into an individual ethnic entity. The multi-ethnic Kingdom of Hungary contained Southern Slavs (Croats and Serbs) and Eastern Slavs (Ruthenes), but the Slovaks were the only Western Slavs. In Latin sources they continued to be called Slavi (*Sclavi*), but in Hungary in the Middle Ages this term already unambiguously denoted the Slovaks, since the other ethnic groups had their own specific names in Latin. The native language with its numerous dialects gradually internalised the words 'Slovák' and 'Slovensko' in the Middle Ages. These designations were retained most frequently in geographical names.

The Magyars called the Slovaks *Tóts* and the German colonists called them *Wends* (*Winds*). From the Middle Ages, there were ethnic conflicts in Hungary mainly along ethnic boundaries and in towns. The rulers generally resolved them justly, without ethnic prejudice, as documented in the *Privilegium pro Slavis* (Fig. 2), issued in 1381, by which King Louis I the Great granted the burghers of Slovak origin in Žilina parity representation in the town council with Germans. Sharp ethnic conflicts flowed mainly from the fact that the ethnic groups living in Hungary – Magyars, Germans, Slovaks, Croats, Serbs, Romanians and others – were linguistically and culturally very different. As a result, ethnic homogenisation of

---

[7] Samo is described as a Frankish merchant who led the Slavs against the Avars. He was elected ruler in 623 and died in 658.

the country could not succeed, and the Kingdom of Hungary remained a multi-ethnic state until its dissolution in 1918.

The specific situation in the Kingdom of Hungary, including occasional polemics between scholars, created conditions for the formation of a national ideology by the early eighteenth century, that is, before the ideas of the Enlightenment and the later works of Herder and Hegel had begun to exert an influence. From the middle of the nineteenth century the formation of the Slovaks as a separate nation in the ethnic, linguistic and cultural senses was supported by the general acceptance of a standardised Slovak literary language. Politically, the process of nation formation ended in the 1930s.

VI

Thus, Slovak history is the history of a nation but also the history of states. Until 1918 the Slovaks shared a state history with the other nations of the Kingdom of Hungary, and after 1918 with the Czechs and the national minorities in Czechoslovakia. Slovak national history cannot be separated from these state frameworks. On the other hand, there is a specific history of the Slovak people, including the history of Slovakia as a territory. Once in the early period of the Kingdom of Hungary, the Duchy of Nitra formed a sort of separate 'third of the kingdom' administered by a prince – the heir to the throne. In the fourteenth century, in the period of feudal fragmentation, this territory became the domain of important magnates – the Omodej family and Matúš (Matthew) Csák. In the sixteenth and seventeenth centuries, in the period of the Turkish invasion, the territory of Slovakia formed a substantial part of Habsburg Hungary. Reflecting these traditions and the consciousness of ethnic difference, Slovak representatives produced a national ideology over the course of the eighteenth and nineteenth centuries; from the middle of the nineteenth century they added a national political programme. Even in the unitary Czechoslovak Republic, Slovakia's territorial integrity was not in doubt.

VII

What, then, are the dominant features or key points of Slovak historical development?

(1) Great Moravia is the oldest important milestone in Slovak tradition. The arrival of the missionaries Cyril and Methodius in Great Moravia is still commemorated with a state holiday in the Slovak Republic. The Slovaks rightly identify with the tradition of Great

Moravia and its cultural heritage because its inhabitants are clearly their ancestors. However, since the differentiation among the Slavs was only beginning in the ninth century, Great Moravia is actually a Slavic tradition, with which the Czechs (Moravians) also identify. It is associated with the invention of the Slavic script and the Slavic liturgy by Cyril and Methodius, which form a general, Slavic-wide heritage still highly regarded by the Eastern Slavs. As to Slovak history, this period constitutes a significant stage in the process of Slovak ethno-genesis. But the evolution of Slovaks into their own ethnic group occurred in the Hungarian era of Slovak history.

(2) After 1526 the Kingdom of Hungary became part of the Habsburg monarchy. As the Turks ruled the greater part of Hungary, Habsburg Hungary consisted effectively of the present territory of Slovakia with Bratislava as the capital and coronation town. This proved to be of great consequence for the history of the territory as well as for the history of the Slovak ethnic group. Humanist and later Baroque literature and the struggle of the Reformation and Counter-Reformation faithfully reflect the process of gradual ethnic awakening of the Slovaks against the background of power and ideological battles.

(3) The process of the formation of the Slovak nation began at the end of the eighteenth century and culminated in the codification of standard literary Slovak in 1843 and the creation of a Slovak political programme in 1845–1848. The peak of this process was the armed uprising of the Slovaks during the Revolution of 1848–1849. In the following years of harsh Magyarisation in the Kingdom of Hungary, the small Slovak cultural and political elite failed in its agitation for cultural and political autonomy, and thus this process came to an end only after 1918.

(4) The years of the First Czechoslovak Republic (1918–1938) constitute the period of the completion of the formation of the Slovaks as one of the European nations. Moreover, it is also a time of remarkable cultural and educational growth in the whole society.

(5) The Slovak National Uprising of 1944 is undoubtedly the peak in the history of the twentieth century. In the shape of one of the largest armed undertakings to the German rear, it proved that the Slovaks had not come to terms with the domination of their country by Nazi Germany nor with the totalitarian regime set up by the domestic collaborationist government.

The reader will find each of these key points dealt with in this book. The history of Great Moravia is not the subject of a separate chapter, because this history has a wider (not only Slovak) context and is sufficiently known from other literature.[8] However, the contribution by Ján Steinhübel considers the administrative and political continuity of the Duchy of Nitra from the pre-Great Moravian period to the beginnings of the Hungarian state. Ján Lukačka addresses the question of the continuity of the aristocracy from the Great Moravian period to the period of the Kingdom of Hungary. The rise of towns is treated by Vladimír Segeš, who offers a further examination of medieval society, as the territory of present-day Slovakia constituted the most urbanised part of the Kingdom of Hungary. Humanism, the Reformation and Counter-Reformation are considered by Eva Frimmová (cultural-historical aspects) and Viliam Čičaj (political and confessional aspects).

The reader will find the process of formation of the Slovak nation regarding its ideological and political programmatic sides analysed by contributions from Eva Kowalská, Ľudovít Haraksim and Dušan Kováč. Natália Krajčovičová and Valerián Bystrický devote attention to the period 1918–1939. The inquiry of Elisabeth Bakke into Czechoslovakism is also centred on this period even though its concerns go beyond it. Vilém Prečan writes about the Slovak National Uprising, while Ivan Kamenec and Jan Rychlík throw light on its wider internal and external context. For an understanding of contemporary Slovak society and the processes occurring in it, the period after the Second World War is very important. Therefore several concluding studies are devoted to this period, including chapters by Michal Barnovský, Jan Pešek, Stanislav Sikora, Jozef Žatkuliak, Michal Štefanský, and Miroslav Londák and Elena Londáková. The problems of the Magyar minority, discussed by Štefan Šutaj, also lie largely within this period.

Slovakia in History is, like the previous volume *Bohemia in History* (1998, edited by Mikuláš Teich), not a continuous, systematic and chronological Slovak national narrative, but it contains key issues and themes chosen and selected from Slovakia's past and analysed and worked out in detail by specialists. While it is inevitable that facts and events in some chapters of a multi-authored collection will overlap, this structure enables each chapter to be read separately.

VIII

Professional Slovak historiography is still a relatively young science. During the period when many European nations laid down firm foundations for knowledge of their past, that is, in the course of the

---

[8] For works in English, see G. J. Kovtun, *Czech and Slovak History: An American Bibliography* (Washington, DC, 1996), ch. 6, pp. 87–94.

nineteenth century and especially in its second half, Slovak historiography remained on an amateur level and lacked a systematic approach to researching Slovak society. In the nineteenth century the eminent Slovak Slavist Pavol Jozef Šafárik worked as a professional historian outside Slovakia, mainly in Prague. At the beginning of the twentieth century, the professional archivist Pavol Križko was engaged in researching regional history. Historical research was also undertaken by 'nationalistic enthusiasts' – priests, jurists, journalists and so on, that is, by Slovak intellectuals without professional academic contacts.

In objective terms, this was caused by the unsatisfactory conditions in the Kingdom of Hungary and affected more than just Slovak historiography. The Slovaks lacked any real national cultural infrastructure; by 1918 there were fewer than 300 elementary schools and no *gymnasia* (secondary schools preparing pupils for university) offering instruction in Slovak. The foundations of professional Slovak historiography began to be laid only after the birth of Czechoslovakia, when Comenius University was created in Bratislava. The founding in 1942 of the Slovak Academy of Sciences and Arts, in which historiography was well represented, led to further progress in historical research. In 1953 the Slovak Academy of Sciences, including the Institute of History, was founded and became the central research institution in the field of history. More university departments, professional archives and museums were gradually established.[9]

Many of the problems with which Slovak historiography struggles have their roots in the past. For example, Slovak archivists have not yet completed one of their basic tasks – the publication of documents concerning Slovak history. Therefore, many basic sources are accessible only to a narrow circle of specialists who are able to engage in archival work. The interested public has no chance of confronting the various ideologised or mythical constructions produced by publicists and some historians. A comprehensively researched account of Slovak history

---

[9] For more information, see Dušan Kováč, Adam Hudek and Frank Hadler (eds.), *Vademecum. Contemporary History – Slovakia. A Guide to Archives, Research Institutions, Libraries, Associations and Museums* (Bratislava and Berlin, 2008); E. Mannová and D. P. Daniel (eds.), *A Guide to Historiography in Slovakia* (Bratislava, 1995). For older literature, see V. Jankovič and A. Škorupová, *Bibliografia k dejinám Slovenska. Literatúra vydaná do roku 1965* [Bibliography of Slovak history. Literature published up to 1965] (Bratislava, 1997). After 1989, see A. Sedliaková, *Historiografia na Slovensku 1990–1994* [Historiography in Slovakia 1990–1994] (Bratislava, 1995); Sedliaková, *Slovenská historiografia 1995–1999. Výberová bibliografia* [Slovak historiography 1995–1999. Selected bibliography] (Bratislava, 2000); Sedliaková, *Slovenská historiografia 2000–2004. Výberová bibliografia* [Slovak historiography 2000–2004. Selected bibliography] (Bratislava, 2006).

appeared only in the 'Marxist' period. There was no comparable positivist or alternatively oriented work to challenge it. We also find the shadow of the past in the interpretive conceptions in Slovak history.

If we go back to the beginning of Slovak historiography, we find that the first historical works arose from the need to defend the Slovak nation and its past. Such works therefore had an unambiguously apologetic character. Various institutions and parts of society still demand apologias or praise for the antiquity and the historical uniqueness of the Slovaks even from professional historians. Historians resist this pressure but at least some parts of society are still not willing to accept historiography as a professional branch of academia.

Since the beginnings of Slovak professional historiography fall into the period after 1918, this historiography was also to some extent marked by the times of its origin. In this period Slovak historiography came to be shaped by the concept of a unitary Czechoslovak history. It was under this influence that Slovak history lost its independent dynamic and became a kind of regional appendage to Czech history. The result was that the Slovaks were 'deprived' of their Hungarian historical heritage. An application of this principle to the period after 1918 would mean 'depriving' them of their Czecho-Slovak historical heritage as well. There is a danger of reducing Slovak history to the history of Slovak dissent in Hungary and in Czechoslovakia.

One problem for Slovak historiography is Marxism, or rather so-called Marxism-Leninism. After 1948, Marxist methodology became compulsory for Slovak historiography. The problem lay not in Marxism as such, but in the very dogmatic form known as Marxism-Leninism, which was hardly compatible with Marx's work. This so-called method of research was imposed on all active historians by the political authorities, and supervision over historiography was conducted by uneducated Party officials, who reduced Marxism to simplified theorems which they simply inflicted on historiography. This hegemonic intervention had an even more serious effect on Slovak historiography than on that of some neighbouring countries because it began to be applied before Slovak historians could lay adequate foundations for a professional field. To put it differently: before various interpretative currents and schools could arise naturally, Slovak historical scholarship was laid on the Procrustean bed of this form of Marxism-Leninism.

From the 1950s, an ever deepening paradox could be observed: with the Institute of History at the Slovak Academy of Sciences in the forefront, a good institutional basis for historical scholarship arose and developed in Slovakia. Professionally well-trained historians entered the field of historiography. However, the institution was involved in ever deepening conflicts with the regime's efforts to impose a one-sided interpretation of the historical process. But it would be a mistake to dismiss all of Slovak historiography after 1948 as entirely worthless. High-quality works were produced. However, they did not originate thanks to a favourable political situation but rather in spite of unfavourable conditions. Well-regarded works could be produced in sub-fields that did not receive the attention of the ruling Communist Party.

The greatest problems lay in interpretation of the history of the twentieth century. Even in cases where historiography crossed the politically created limits on scholarly discourse in meetings and conferences of specialists, the results were not published and they did not come to the attention of society as a whole and certainly were not mentioned in school textbooks. While historiography created some space for itself in the 1980s, textbooks remained stuck in the 1950s. A widening abyss opened up between historiography and the historical consciousness of society.

After 1989, Slovak historiography was faced with a new situation: hopeful, encouraging, but at the same time immensely demanding.[10] It could not overcome all the handicaps immediately. Concentrated effort and a longer-term perspective were required. The demanding nature of the tasks required realisation of the need to proceed gradually and work out a systematic programme for their achievement. The first task faced by Slovak historians after November 1989 was the removal of obvious problems (most commonly concerning, as noted, the history of the twentieth century), which the professional community knew about but had not been able to come to terms with publicly. This task was completed relatively rapidly. New works were published, the Institute of Historical Studies of the Slovak Academy of Sciences organised a series of lectures for teachers and the public, and new educational texts and textbooks were produced. The task of removing other distortions, ones which had resulted from the one-sided interpretation of the historical process, was more complicated. This one-sidedness affected both the older and the more recent periods of history, and concerned questions

---

[10] See D. Kováč, 'Die slowakische Historiographie nach 1989. Aktiva, Probleme, Perspektiven', *Bohemia* 37 (1) (1996), 169–74; E. Kowalská, 'Neue Wege zur Bewältigung der Geschichte der Slowakei in den 1990er Jahren', in A. Ivaniševič, A. Kappeler, W. Lukan, and A. Suppan (eds.), *Klio ohne Fesseln? Historiographie im östlichen Europa nach dem Zusammenbruch des Kommunismus* (Vienna, 2002), pp. 287–98; E. Hrabovec, 'Zehn Jahre nach der Wende. Slowakische Historiographie: Ein schwieriger Weg zur Selbstverortung', in Ivaniševič, *et al.* (eds.), *Klio ohne Fesseln?*, pp. 299–314. For a more general observation on post-Communist historiography, see D. Kováč, 'Paradoxa und Dillemata der postkommunistischen Geschichtsschreibung', in the same work, pp. 15–42.

such as the periodisation of history, the interpretation of the historical process as the history of class struggle, and the history of socio-economic formations supplanting one another. Research began to place greater emphasis on a deep analysis of society in its historical development. The traditional emphasis on politics did not provide an adequate basis for identifying social changes. It is paradoxical, but social history is actually the discipline that has been held back the most, and it is still sometimes necessary to restate first principles. This particularly applies to the history of the working class, even though the workers' movement was seemingly one of the most preferred disciplines after 1948. Research on elites and on various social groups (children, women and old people) did not attract historians. The redirecting of research that has arisen from political changes – into the study of the history of everyday life, the development of civil society, ethno-historical stereotypes and the history of towns and regions – is already bringing results.

In spite of these problems and limitations, Slovak historiography has already made great strides. Free academic research was not completely stopped even in the period of Communist totalitarianism. Several findings of Slovak historical science are valuable for the understanding not only of Slovak history but also for the history of Central Europe in general. However, these findings are relatively little known to experts abroad. This is partly a result of the long-lasting isolation of Slovak historiography from world historiography but is also, to a large extent, due to the simple fact that the majority of works of Slovak historians exist only in Slovak, and thus are accessible only to a narrow circle of interested persons.

After the establishment of the independent Slovak Republic in 1993, an entirely understandable and growing interest in Slovakia as a country, and thus also in its history, has emerged on the part of professional historians and political scientists, including teachers and students, who are interested in Central Europe. This led us to decide to make available in this book to the international public some of the results of modern research into Slovak history; most contributors are Slovaks (together with two Czechs and one Norwegian colleague). We offer it to all who are interested in the history of Slovakia and the Slovaks. In English, 'Slavonic' and 'Slavic' are often used interchangeably; as a rule in this book we use the latter. Except for rulers and other well-known figures, we have not generally Anglicised first (given) names.

Finally, I would like to explain how we use the terms 'Hungary', 'Hungarian', 'Magyar', 'Czechoslovakia' and 'Czecho-Slovak' (with a hyphen). There is confusion in the majority of literature about the use of the terms 'Hungarian' and 'Magyar', and they are often used as synonyms. We employ 'Hungary' and 'Hungarian' as political terms denoting the state and its citizenship and 'Magyar' as an ethnic, linguistic and cultural category. So we do not use the expression 'Hungarian language' but consequently only the 'Magyar language' and so on. This distinction is necessary for the proper interpretation of Slovak history, because for many centuries Slovaks as well as Magyars were inhabitants of Hungary, which was always a multi-ethnic state; however, Slovaks were never Magyars, and the two spoke different languages. 'Czechoslovakia' was the official name of a common Czech–Slovak state with two exceptions. From October 1938 to March 1939 the official name of the state was the Czecho-Slovak Republic (Czecho-Slovakia). After 1991 the name of the state in documents written in Slovak was 'Czecho-Slovakia', in documents written in Czech 'Czechoslovakia' (without a hyphen). The official name was the 'Czech and Slovak Federative Republic'.

2   The Duchy of Nitra

Ján Steinhübel

The territory of contemporary Slovakia was first inhabited by Slavs from about the end of the fifth century AD. These peoples arrived in the territory of Slovakia from the north, passing through gaps in the Carpathian mountains. Their settlements stretched down to the Danube river in the south. Traces of their simple square houses of wood and straw, dug into the ground, complete with a small stone hearth in the corner, grain storage pits and cremation graves with pottery of the 'Prague type' are found across the plains and basins of southern Slovakia.[1]

In the second half of the seventh century, the developments in Moravia and Slovakia were not paralleled in the rest of the Western Slavic world. But they were comparable to the other Slavic settlements across the Carpathian basin, where Slavic duchies grew in strength. One of these, Carinthia, lay in the shadow of the eastern Alps, on the upper courses of the Drava, Mur and Ens rivers. Another was Slavonia, on the middle course of the Sava, separated from the Avar khanate by the marshy lower course of the Drava. The remnants of material culture here, characterised by cast bronze objects from the skeleton graves of the second half of the seventh and eighth centuries, are similar to those found across the whole Carpathian basin.[2] By this stage the Slovaks were already part of the multi-ethnic Kingdom of Hungary, where they would remain for a thousand years; thus the ethno-genesis of the Slovaks, and their evolution into a separate nation, was to be a lengthy process.

---

[1] G. Fusek, 'Archeologické doklady k najstaršiemu slovanskému osídleniu Slovenska' [Archaeological evidence of the earliest Slavic settlement of Slovakia], *Slavica Slovaca*, 28 (1993), 30–5; Fusek, *Slovensko vo včasnoslovanskom období* [Slovakia in the early Slavic period] (Nitra, 1994), pp. 93, 118.

[2] K. Vinski-Gasparini and S. Ercegovic, 'Ranosrednjovjekovno groblje u Brodskom Drenovcu' [An early medieval cemetery at Brodsky Drenovec], *Vjesnik Arheološkog Muzeja u Zagrebu*, 1 (1958), 129–61; P. Zs. Pach (ed.), *Magyarország története* [History of Hungary], vol. I/1 (Budapest, 1984), pp. 320 (map), 335.

Pribina's duchy

The structures of ducal power among Slavonians and Croats relied on an army, a system of fortresses and the duke's own retinue which, when combined together, formed the basis of a developing state. The same can be said about the Duchy of Moravia and the Duchy of Nitra. The Frankish invasions during 791–803 and Slavic attacks lasting until 811 destroyed the Avar khanate.[3] After the disintegration of the Avar realm, the territory of the Carpathian basin was divided between its powerful neighbours. Charlemagne (742–814) conquered Pannonia, and the Bulgarian khan Krum (802–814) added the eastern part of the Avar realm – Transylvania and the Tisa basin – to his empire.[4] The whole northern part of the Carpathian basin, separated from the Bulgarian Tisa basin by the Nógrád and the Buk mountains, and from the Frankish frontier marches in Pannonia by the Danube, now belonged to the Duchy of Nitra in south-western Slovakia ruled by Pribina (d. 860).

Military engagements with the Avars lasted another twenty years (791–811), affecting both Moravia and Nitra. The rulers of both areas, predecessors of Dukes Mojmír (d. 846) and Pribina, surrounded themselves with powerful military retinues during the constant wars with the Avars. Throughout Moravia and in Slovakia solidly fortified hillforts were constructed.[5] These not only defended the surrounding population and their properties in wartime, but also secured the administration and defence of the whole territory. They were centres of ducal power that constituted a defensive system of a developing state. When the dukes of Moravia and Nitra had united the ethnically and geographically demarcated territories of old Moravia and Nitra and freed themselves from Avar overlordship, they were left with large retinues of professional warriors, accustomed to war and without sufficient means of support from domestic resources. The solution was territorial expansion. A more extensive territory with a larger number of peasant-farmers would be able to support more warriors. Thus Duke Mojmír of Moravia invaded Nitra, possibly in 833, and expelled Pribina.[6] By uniting the two duchies he created what has become known as Great Moravia.

---

[3] J. Steinhübel, *Veľkomoravské územie v severovýchodnom Zadunajsku* [Great Moravian territory in north-east Transdanubia] (Bratislava, 1995), pp. 9–11, 22–3.

[4] V. N. Zlatarski, *Istorija na balgarskata daržava prez srednite vekove* [History of the Bulgarian state in the Middle Ages] (Sofia, 1918), vol. I, p. 421; P. Panajotov, *Srednovekovna balgarska istorija* [Medieval Bulgarian history] (Sofia, 1992), p. 57.

[5] T. Štefanovičová, *Osudy starých Slovanov* [Fortunes of the Old Slavs] (Martin, 1989), pp. 70–7, 82–4.

[6] H. Wolfram (ed.), *Conversio Bagoariorum et Carantanorum. Das Weißbuch der Salzburger Kirche über die erfolgreiche Mission in Karantanien und Pannonien* (Vienna, Cologne and Graz, 1979), vol. X, pp. 50–1.

Great Moravia and Nitra

Mojmír's Moravia was named after the Morava river, referred to as the Marus by Pliny the Elder and Tacitus.[7] Since the Byzantine missionary Methodius (815–885) had been granted the title archbishop of Moravia, his residence could have also been called Moravia.[8] The title of a bishop or archbishop was usually taken from the place of residence (town or castle) and only exceptionally from the name of the country as a whole, because not only could one country contain several bishoprics (for example, in Bavaria), but also one bishopric could encompass several countries (for example, the Salzburg Diocese). We can identify Methodius's see with the dynastic seat of the Mojmírs in present-day Mikulčice, a town built by the Moravians in the second half of the seventh century.[9] The castle's faubourg at Mikulčice was occupied by the ducal retinue, which owned the fifty-four iron and bronze spurs with hooks found there.[10] In about 800, the ruling duke rebuilt and extended the castle. A strong timber and earth wall faced with stone replaced the previous wooden palisades.[11] The river and castle gave their name to the whole country ruled by the Mojmírs. It is possible that the name of the Nitra river (then Nitrava) was transferred to the ducal castle built on a rocky hill in one of its meanders.[12] That is, just as the country and castle of Morava took their name from the Morava river,

---

[7] J. Dobiáš, *Dějiny československého území před vystoupením Slovanů* [History of the Czechoslovak territory before the appearance of the Slavs] (Prague, 1964), pp. 7, 11.

[8] 'Methodius was allowed to leave by the blessed Pope Hadrian and proceeded to Pannonia, with all his pupils, to the town of Moravia he held as his archbishopric': D. Bartoňková, L. Havlík, Z. Masařík, J. Ludvikovský and R. Večerka (eds.), *Magnae Moraviae fontes historici*, vol. II (Brno, 1967), p. 254; L. E. Havlík, *Morava v 9.–10. století. K problematice politického postavení sociální a vládní struktury a organizace* [Moravia in the ninth to tenth centuries. Problems of the political situation of social and governmental structure and organisation] (Prague, 1978), pp. 18–19; Havlík, *Kronika o Velké Moravě* [The chronicle about Great Moravia] (Brno, 1993), pp. 142, 150, 156–7; Havlík, *Svätopluk Veliký, král Moravanů a Slovanů* [Svätopluk the Great, King of the Moravians and Slavs] (Brno, 1994), pp. 34–8.

[9] D. Třeštík, '"Trh Moravanů" – ústřední trh staré Moravy' ["The market of the Moravians" – the central market of Old Moravia], *Československý časopis historický*, 21 (1973), 879–84.

[10] J. Poulík, *Mikulčice. Sídlo a pevnost knížat velkomoravských* [Mikulčice. Seat and fortress of dukes of Great Moravia] (Prague, 1975), pp. 42–5, 135–6; Poulík, 'Svědectví výzkumů archeologických o Velké Moravě' [Testimony of archaeological research on Great Moravia], in Poulík and B. Chropovský (eds.), *Velká Morava a počátky československé státnosti* [Great Moravia and the beginnings of Czechoslovak statehood] (Prague and Bratislava, 1985), pp. 13, 19–20, 56, 60–1.

[11] Poulík, *Mikulčice*, pp. 48, 52–4.

[12] Wolfram, *Conversio*, vol. XI, pp. 52–3; P. Bednár, 'Nitriansky hrad v 9. storočí' [Nitra Castle in the ninth century], *Pamiatky a múzeá*, 3 (1995), 65–7.

so the Nitrava river gave its name to the castle on its banks and to the whole domain ruled by the duke of Nitra.

Possibly as early as 833, the Duchy of Nitra belonged to the Great Moravian state as an autonomous ducal demesne (*údel*). Up to 871, it was headed by Svätopluk I (871–894), nephew of the Great Moravian duke Rastislav (846–870).[13] The ecclesiastical organisation of Great Moravia also respected the distinct position of the Duchy of Nitra. A bishopric was founded in 880 with Viching as bishop.[14] Before his death Svätopluk I divided Great Moravia between his sons. The younger son, Svätopluk II (in all probability duke of Nitra, 894–899), was subordinated to his older brother Mojmír II. Svätopluk II, goaded and supported by the margrave of the Eastern Mark Aribos, unsuccessfully rebelled against his brother in 898–899.[15] Great Moravia later played an important role in the emerging historical/national consciousness of the Slovaks. This historical tradition is related to the first important Slavic state on the present territory of Slovakia, to its Christianisation and to the flowering culture of that time.

The rise of the Hungarian state

After the break-up of Great Moravia (c. 907), the Old Magyars conquered the territory of Slovakia, and its future fate was determined by events within the Carpathian basin. From about 920, Slovakia fell under the strategic control of Old Magyar military garrisons.[16] We know this from the evidence of the oldest graves and small burial grounds of Magyar horsemen that extend north as far as Skalica, Hlohovec, Nitra, Levice, Lučenec and Michal'any.[17] Thus the garrisons of Old Magyar

---

[13] In 869 historical sources record the 'regnum Zuentibaldi nepotis Rastizi'. See D. Bartoňková, L. Havlík, Z. Masařík and R. Večerka, *Magnae Moraviae fontes historici*, vol. I (Brno, 1964), p. 77.

[14] See D. Bartoňková, L. Havlík, I. Hrbek, J. Ludvíkovský and R. Večerka, *Magnae Moraviae fontes historici*, vol. III (Brno, 1969), pp. 205–6.

[15] Bartoňková *et al.*, *Magnae Moraviae*, vol. I, pp. 124–6.

[16] A. Ruttkay, 'Problematika historického vývoja na území Slovenska v 10.–13. storočí z hl'adiska archeologického bádania' [The problem of historical development in the territory of Slovakia in the tenth to thirteenth centuries in the light of archaeological research], in Poulík and Chropovský (eds.), *Velká Morava*, pp. 156–7; L. E. Havlík, 'Velká Morava v kontextu evropských a obecných dějin' [Great Moravia in the context of European and world history], *ibid.*, pp. 196–7; M. Hanuliak, 'Gräberfelder der slawischen Population im 10. Jahrhundert im Gebiet der Westslowakei', *Slovenská archeológia*, 40 (1992), 280–1.

[17] Ruttkay, '*Problematika*'.

horsemen controlled the centre of the land from their base at Nitra, which had once ruled the whole duchy.

Apart from the old Duchy of Nitra, further Magyar duchies emerged in the Carpathian basin, with their centres in the castles of Marosvár (later Csanád, now Cenad),[18] Alba Iulia (Gyulafehérvár),[19] Bihar[20] and Esztergom.[21] The dynasty of Árpád ruled the Duchy of Nitra from perhaps 971. During the reign of the Hungarian duke Géza (c. 971–997), whose capital was Esztergom, his younger brother Michael was subordinate duke of Nitra (c. 971–995).[22] After the violent death of Michael, for which his brother Géza was probably responsible,[23] Géza's son Stephen ruled in Nitra (c. 995–997).[24]

The medieval chronicler Anonymus wrote of a Polish–Hungarian war at the beginning of the eleventh century. According to his account, Duke Boleslaw the Brave – who became the first Polish king – defeated the Hungarians 'and subjugated to his rule the whole of their land as far as the Danube'.[25] Boguchwal and other Polish chroniclers mention various Slavic dukes who acknowledged Polish sovereignty. They also mention Duke Wladislaus (Ladislas) from the House of Árpád and that his lands bordered the Tisa, Danube and Morava rivers.[26] Thus Michael's son Ladislas the Bald inherited his father's former duchy thanks to help from his powerful Polish cousin Boleslaw, and he had to acknowledge Boleslaw's sovereignty.

The Hungarian–Polish chronicle describes the southern and eastern frontiers of the Duchy of Nitra during its union with Poland. The Danube formed the southern frontier as far as Esztergom. From there, the frontiers went east to the Nógrád and the Buk mountains and to the bend of the Tisa. In the east the Zemplín castle and Slánské mountains formed the frontier. From there the frontier line followed the Ondava mountains to the junction of the Hungarian, Polish and Ruthenian

[18] Pach, *Magyarország története*, vol. I/1, pp. 764–9.
[19] *Ibid.*, pp. 725–6, 764–9.
[20] *Ibid.*, p. 622.
[21] *Ibid.*, pp. 741, 745.
[22] Sz. Vajay, 'Großfürst Geysa von Ungarn Familie und Verwandtschaft', *Südostforschungen*, 21 (1962), 54–6, 64–6, 68.
[23] *Ibid.*, 55–6.
[24] Pach, *Magyarország története*, vol. I/1, pp. 746–9.
[25] Cf. 'Numquid non ipse Hungaros frequentius in certamine superavit, totamque terram eorum usque Danubium suo dominio mancipavit': A. Bielowski (ed.), *Monumenta Poloniae historica*, vol. I (Warsaw, 1960), p. 399.
[26] Cf. 'Wladislai pars Ungariae, que inter fluvios Czissam, Danubium et Moravam constitit': A. Bielowski (ed.), *Monumenta Poloniae historica*, vol. II (Warsaw, 1961), p. 479.

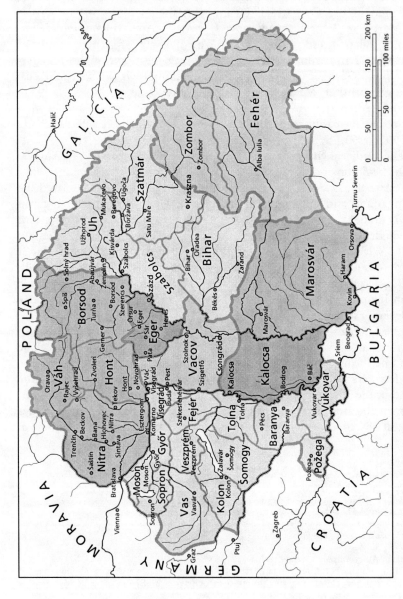

Map 2 The Kingdom of Hungary in the year 1000

frontiers on the main ridge of the Carpathians.[27] Thanks to these Polish chroniclers we can delineate the historic frontiers of the Duchy of Nitra. Its territorial extent corresponded roughly to that of contemporary Slovakia.

King Stephen I the Saint

King Stephen of Hungary (997–1038) lost control of the Duchy of Nitra soon after his coronation. According to the Hungarian–Polish chronicle, 'three months after the coronation', that is, at the end of March or beginning of April 1001, the two sides began diplomatic negotiations. Boleslaw the Brave offered Stephen peace. Stephen proposed a meeting with Boleslaw on the Hungarian–Polish frontier. The king of Poland accepted the proposal:

When his whole army was assembled, he came to meet the king before Esztergom, and here on the frontier between Poland and Hungary he established his camp ... On the next day when the sun rose, they met and exchanged the kiss of peace, and with joined hands they went to the Esztergom Cathedral, which was then newly built in honour of the sainted martyr Vojtech [Adalbert] of Poland and Hungary. When all this was successfully completed, all the Polish soldiers from the greatest to the least were rewarded and the prince [Boleslaw] was given gifts. After this they separated.[28]

After the death of Ladislas the Bald (before 1030), his younger brother Vazul inherited the Duchy of Nitra. However, he did not enjoy his inheritance for long. In January 1030, King Mieszko II of Poland invaded Saxony. As he plundered the region, a rebellion broke out in Poland, fomented by his brothers Bezprim and Otto. Prince Jaroslav the Wise of Kiev attacked from the east and captured Belz.[29] The power of the Polish king suddenly began to disintegrate. It was probably at this time that King Stephen of Hungary gained control of Nitra, while Duke Oldřich of Bohemia (1012–1034) took over Moravia. Mieszko II could not help the Polish garrisons in the castles of Moravia,[30] because he was

---

[27] Cf. 'Nam termini Polonorum ad litus Danubii ad civitatem Strigoniensem terminabantur. Deinde in Agriensem civitatem ibant, demum in fluvium, qui Tizia nominatur, cadentes, regirabant iuxta fluvium, qui Cepla nuncupatur usque ad castrum Salis ibique inter Ungaros, Ruthenos et Polonos finem dabant': E. Szentpétery (ed.), *Scriptores rerum Hungaricarum tempore ducum regumque stirpis Arpadianae gestarum*, vol. II (Budapest, 1938), pp. 310–11.

[28] *Ibid.*

[29] G. Labuda, *Mieszko II król polski (1025–1034). Czasy przełomu w dziejach państwa polskiego* [The Polish king Mieszko II (1025–1034). Turning points in the history of the Polish state] (Cracow, 1992), pp. 67–77.

[30] B. Bretholz (ed.), *Monumenta Germaniae historica* (Berlin, 1923), vol. II, p. 75.

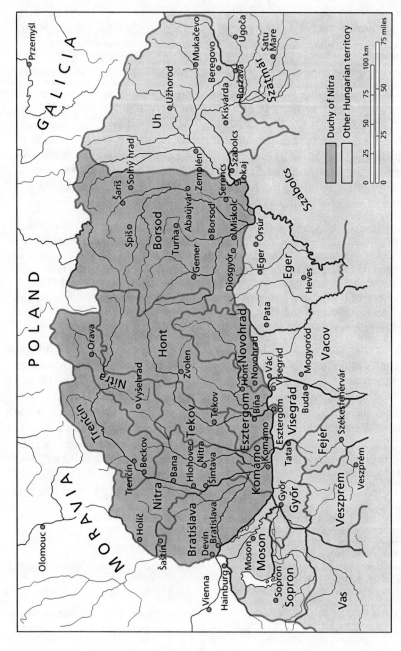

Map 3 The Duchy of Nitra in the eleventh century

fighting at home against his brothers, and he expected further attacks by the Russians and Germans, who took further territory away from Poland in the following year, 1031.[31]

King Stephen imprisoned Prince Vazul in Nitra Castle. Vazul's three sons, Levente, Andrew and Béla, together with their cousin Domoslav (son of Ladislas the Bald), fled to Bohemia after Vazul was blinded in prison.[32] At the court of Duke Oldřich of Bohemia, the four members of the House of Árpád met King Mieszko II of Poland, who also found political asylum there at the end of 1031. When Mieszko gained power in Poland for the second time (1032–1034), he received Vazul's three sons at his court.[33] Their older cousin Domoslav, who could rely on Czech support, remained with Prince Oldřich. The youngest, Béla, married Mieszko's daughter Rycheza and stayed in Poland.[34] Levente and Andrew went to Kiev.[35]

The Duchy of Nitra under the rule of King Stephen's successors

At the beginning of September 1042, a large German and Czech army crossed the Hungarian frontier. This was a response to the previous threat from King Samuel Aba of Hungary (1041–1042), and a Hungarian invasion of the Eastern Mark and the Mark of Carinthia.[36] King Henry III of Germany listened to the advice of Duke Břetislav I of Bohemia, and led his whole army to the north bank of the Danube. After capturing Hainburg and Bratislava 'he devastated the country north of the Danube' as far as the Hron river, and twice defeated the Hungarians when they attempted to counter-attack. Consequently, the inhabitants (*incolae*) of nine counties (castle districts) north of the Danube submitted to Henry through special embassy (*missa legatione*). However, they emphatically refused to acknowledge the recently deposed king of Hungary, Peter Orseolo (1038–1041),

---

[31] G. Labuda, *Utrata Moraw, panstwo polskie w XI wieku. Studia z dziejów polskich i czechoslowackich I* [The loss of Moravia suffered by the Polish state in the eleventh century. Studies in Polish and Czechoslovak history I] (Wrocław, 1960), pp. 114–18, 124.

[32] E. Szentpétery (ed.), *Scriptores rerum Hungaricarum tempore ducum regumque stirpis Arpadianae gestarum*, vol. I (Budapest, 1937), pp. 320–1, 334–7; Vajay, 'Großfürst Geysa', 99–100.

[33] Szentpétery (ed.), *Scriptores*, vol. I, p. 334.

[34] *Ibid.*, pp. 334–5.

[35] *Ibid.*, p. 335.

[36] L. B. ab Oefele (ed.), *Annales Altahenses maiores ad a. 1042. Scriptores rerum Germanicarum in usum scholarum ex Monumentis Germaniae historicis recusi* (Hannover, 1891), pp. 29–31; B. Krzemieńska, *Břetislav I* (Prague, 1986), pp. 311–13.

who accompanied Henry. Thereupon, the German king listening to the Czech duke 'received the submission of the nine counties. At the entreaty of Břetislav and with the agreement of the inhabitants, he gave them to the nephew of King Stephen [*fratrueli Stephani regis*], who came with this duke.'

The inhabitants of the nine northern counties, whose representatives appeared before Henry III, were 'provinciales', that is inhabitants of one province. It was a 'country [*partem*]', which accepted a new 'duke [*ducem*]', that is a duchy, or more precisely the old Duchy of Nitra 'fortified by rivers and marshes in the south'.[37] So we know that the swollen Danube constituted the border, which separated it from the rest of Hungary.

Who then was this nephew, or more precisely the 'brother's son' (*fratruelis*), who came to Slovakia in Břetislav's retinue? Heriman's chronicle, the Altaich, and the Hildesheim Annals, from which information about these events is sourced, do not mention his name. King Stephen had no brothers, only two male cousins, Ladislas the Bald and Vazul, both of whom were already dead. Therefore, the *fratruelis* was probably one of their sons. However, they were more distant nephews, twice removed from Stephen. Levente, Andrew and Béla could not have been with Břetislav in September 1042 because they had left Bohemia ten years before. Domoslav was the only one among the four living members of the House of Árpád who could have gone on this expedition with Břetislav. He was also the eldest and so had the most right to rule in Hungary or at least in part of it. The nine Nitra counties wished Domoslav to be their duke. He was the son of the former duke of Nitra, Ladislas the Bald, so they regarded him as the rightful heir. Břetislav supported their wish and advised Henry to agree.

Henry and Břetislav did not have to criss-cross the whole duchy to its furthest points with their armies in order to secure the region. By conquering the most important part of the territory, including Nitra, they won control of the whole duchy and could end their military operation at the Hron river. This area included not just the territory they directly occupied in south-west Slovakia, from Bratislava to the Hron; all nine counties of the Duchy of Nitra submitted to their rule. These were the large castle districts, spread across the whole territory of the duchy, from the Morava and Danube to the Tisa and the Slanské

---

[37] *Annales Altahenses maiores ad a. 1042*, pp. 31–2; W. Trillmich and R. Buchner, *Herimanni Augiensis Chronicon (Hermann von Reichenau Chronik) ad a. 1042* (Berlin, 1961), pp. 674–5; Vajay, 'Großfürst Geysa', 65–7, 99–100; Krzemieńska, *Břetislav I*, pp. 313–17.

mountains, as recorded by the Polish chroniclers. Thus Domoslav's duchy did not end at the Hron, but extended far beyond the territory directly affected by Henry's and Břetislav's campaign.[38]

According to the later testimony given by the Bavarian chronicler Aventinus (who wrote in the sixteenth century utilising sources now lost), the new duke was presented with 2,000 Bavarian and Czech soldiers by Henry and Břetislav. Aventinus's report appears to be quite credible, although we cannot confirm it absolutely.[39] However, Duke Domoslav did not remain in Nitra for long. After the withdrawal of the victorious armies, King Samuel Aba of Hungary expelled him, and he had to flee back to Bohemia.[40]

In September 1046, the House of Árpád victoriously returned to Hungary. Vazul's son Andrew was able to utilise the opposition of Hungarian magnates to foreigners as well as the great pagan uprising, which had already brought down the second reign of Peter Orseolo (1044–1046), to achieve his aim. Nor did Andrew's older brother, Levente, stand in the way of his accession to the Hungarian crown. Levente remained a pagan until his death – he did not desire the throne and died the following year.[41] Apart from Andrew and Levente, two other descendants of Árpád had returned to Hungary. They were Andrew's older cousin, Domoslav, who came back from exile in Bohemia, and a younger brother, Béla, who was still waiting in Poland. Domoslav was the eldest living member of the House of Árpád, so he had a claim to the throne, which Andrew had to respect. We do not know whether he participated in Peter's fall, or whether he returned to Hungary only after Andrew's victory in 1046. He did not become king and contented himself with the Duchy of Nitra, which he had briefly ruled four years before. Domoslav, Duke of Nitra (Damaslaus *dux*, 1046–1048), granted property to the monastery at Pécsvárad, and King Géza II confirmed his donation in 1158.[42] Domoslav must have

---

[38] The military defeat of the king of Hungary in a single battle near Menfö on 5 July 1044, and the subsequent occupation of his seat at Székesfehérvár, decided the struggle for the whole kingdom. Cf. *Annales Altahenses maiores ad a. 1044*, pp. 34–7; Krzemieńska, *Břetislav I*, pp. 322–4. At this moment, the victorious German king controlled not just the directly occupied part of Transdanubia, but the whole kingdom, which he could hand over to his ally Peter Orseolo. The country contained no organised force capable of successful resistance. A similar situation occurred on a smaller scale in the Duchy of Nitra in September 1042.

[39] Krzemieńska, *Břetislav I*, p. 316.

[40] Trillmilch and Buchner, *Herimanni Augiensis Chronicon*, pp. 674–5.

[41] Szentpétery (ed.), *Scriptores*, vol. I, pp. 336–44.

[42] G. Györffy (ed.), *Diplomata Hungariae antiquissima I* (Budapest, 1992), pp. 77–8.

died by 1048, since in that year King Andrew I (1046–1061) gave the now vacant duchy to his younger brother Béla.

Andrew I summoned Béla from Poland in 1048, and after deliberation 'divided the country into three parts, two of which remained in the possession of the king, while the third went to the duke'.[43] Béla's autonomous duchy (*ducatus*) extended from the Morava river to the border of Transylvania. It was composed of two parts: Nitra, where his elder cousin Domoslav, father Vazul, uncle Ladislas the Bald and grandfather Michael had ruled before him, and neighbouring Bihar, extending from the upper Tisa in the north to the Körös river in the south, from the Transylvanian borders in the east to the Tisa river in the west. Béla was a sovereign lord of his demesne. This is testified by ducal half-denarii – they had the words *BELA DVX* engraved on them – as well as by the previously mentioned *Hungarian Chronicle*.[44] Béla probably had the coins struck at his ducal seat in Nitra.[45] New fortifications were added to Nitra castle, in the form of a strong timber and earth wall with chambered construction built, according to archaeologists, on the remains of the Great Moravian rampart of the middle of the eleventh century, and these could have been the work of Duke Béla. When Béla became king of Hungary (1060–1063), he left the Duchies of Nitra and Bihar unoccupied. He died while marching against Emperor Henry IV, who invaded Hungary in September 1063. Henry IV placed Andrew's son Solomon (1063–1074) on the vacant throne.[46] Béla's three sons, Géza, Ladislas and Lampert, fled to Poland, and asked King Boleslaw II the Bold for help, as their father had done before them. Boleslaw interrupted a war in Russia and, immediately after the emperor withdrew, invaded Hungary and defeated Solomon, who then retreated to the strongly fortified Moson castle on the western frontier of the kingdom.[47]

[43] Szentpétery, *Scriptores*, vol. I, pp. 344–5; Gy. Kristó, *A XI. századi hercegség történet Magyarországon* [Ducal history in Hungary in the eleventh century] (Budapest, 1974), pp. 60–2.

[44] J. Hlinka, Š. Kazimír and E. Kolníková, *Peniaze v našich dejinách* [Money in our history] (Bratislava, 1976), pp. 140–1, 165–6, 170; Hlinka, 'Nálezy mincí na Slovensku z 11. až začiatku 14. storočia a ich historicko-numizmatická analýza' [Finds of coins in Slovakia from the eleventh century to the beginning of the fourteenth and their historical-numismatic analysis], *Slovenská numizmatika*, 10 (1989), 157, 160–1; Hlinka, 'New Notions About the Hungarian Mintage Development of the Eleventh–Fourteenth Centuries Related to the Territory of Slovakia', in *Actes du XIe Congrès International de Numismatique organisé à l'occasion du 150e anniversaire de la Société Royale de Numismatique de Belgique Bruxelles, 8–13 septembre 1991* (Louvain la Neuve, 1993), vol. III, pp. 196–8.

[45] Bednár, 'Nitriansky hrad', 66.

[46] Szentpétery (ed.), *Scriptores*, vol. I, pp. 361–3.

[47] *Ibid.*, pp. 362–3.

The Polish chronicler Boguchwal provides important testimony about the expedition of Boleslaw II against Solomon: 'Then he invaded Hungary, wanting to renew the frontier of the Kingdom of Poland on the Danube, Tisa and Morava rivers.' After the Polish victory, the new king of Hungary had no choice: 'King Solomon, acknowledging his defeat, not only gave up fighting but also renounced the part of his kingdom lying beyond the above mentioned rivers, considering himself fortunate that he could stay in the other part of the kingdom beyond the Danube'.[48] The part of the Kingdom of Hungary lying between the Danube, Tisa and Morava rivers, which Solomon had to give up, corresponds to the Duchy of Nitra, as already subordinated to Boleslaw the Brave in 1001. The territory of the Duchy of Nitra, established long before its incorporation into the Kingdom of Hungary, therefore did not change for a long time. The Polish king did not keep Nitra but handed it over to his ally and relative Géza. Solomon feared Duke Géza and the powerful Polish army, so he remained in Moson, near the German frontier, where he could expect help. Bishop Dezider, who advised Géza, negotiated the peace: 'He should leave the kingdom to Solomon although he is too young, and he, Géza should be content with the duchy his father ruled before him.' Duke Géza listened to the bishop, and the sons of Béla made peace with Solomon at Györ on 20 January 1064. Solomon remained king, Duke Géza kept Nitra, and his younger brother Ladislas was satisfied with Bihar, while the youngest, Lampert, not possessing a domain of his own, stayed on at Géza's court.[49]

The half-denarii of Duke Géza, probably struck at Nitra, had a higher silver content than royal coins. In contrast to King Solomon, who withdrew coins from circulation and replaced them with new ones containing less silver, Géza did not change the value of his coins. Géza's half-denarii bear his second name Duke Magnus, *DVX MAGNUS*, on the obverse. The reverse bears the alternative name for Hungary,

---

[48] Cf. 'Post hoc Hungariam adiit, volens metas regni Poloniae in Danubio, Czyssawa et Morawa fluviis habere. Cui Salamon rex Hungarorum cum suo exercitu in montanis Russiae et Hungariae, ad suum regnum volens prohibere ingressum, occurit. Sed plurimis de suo exercitu in eisdem concludendo. Et cernens sibi et suae genti imminere periculum pacem praecatur, centum milia auri talenta offerens Boleslao, ut ab impugnatione sui desistat. Cui rex Boleslaus respondit: "Polonos, inquit, non aurum habere, sed aurum habentibus imperare delectat; turpius enim, ait vinci pretio, quam proelio." Victum itaque rex Salamon se cognoscens, tam bello quam parte sui regni, inter fluvios praedictos consistente, cessit; felicem se reputans, in alia parte regni, ultra Danubium, posse manere"': Bielowski (ed.), *Monumenta Poloniae historica*, vol. II, pp. 486–7.

[49] Szentpétery, *Scriptores* (ed.), vol. I, pp. 362–3; Kristó, *A XI. századi*, pp. 62–3.

PANONAI, as do other Hungarian coins from the eleventh century.[50]
Duke Ladislas of Bihar did not issue coins.

In January 1074, Solomon assembled military units from thirty counties in the royal part of Hungary. Since Solomon's thirty counties constituted two-thirds of the whole Kingdom of Hungary, the ducal third must have included fifteen counties and the whole kingdom of forty-five counties. After the previous divisions, Solomon was determined to destroy the power of the two dukes. Duke Ladislas of Bihar and his younger brother Lampert sought help abroad, while Duke Géza of Nitra chose to remain in Ladislas's Duchy of Bihar. In February 1074, Solomon broke the armistice, crossed the frozen Tisa river at Kemej, and defeated the weak Bihar army, commanded by Géza in the absence of Ladislas. In the battle near Kemej, Géza had only four units from the four Bihar counties, in contrast to Solomon's thirty units.[51] If we omit the four Bihar counties from the fifteen counties that composed the ducal third of Hungary, we find that Géza's Duchy of Nitra then had eleven counties.[52]

Géza and the remnants of his army left Bihar and withdrew to Vác, where he met Duke Otto of Olomouc and his own brother Ladislas to whom he handed over the remnants of the Bihar army (*bihoriensi agmine*). Géza placed himself at the head of the assembled Nitran units. While pursuing Géza, Solomon heard about the meeting of the three dukes at Vác. He therefore turned towards Pest and camped at Rákos. The army of the dukes then left its camp at Vác and established a new camp at Cinkota near Pest. Between the royal and ducal armies stood the Mogyoród hill. Ladislas commanded the Bihar army on the left wing; Géza with the Nitran forces (*in nitriensi agmine*) occupied the centre, with Otto's Moravians on the right. King Solomon was completely defeated in the battle on 14 March 1074. He fled with the remnants of his forces to Moson castle on the western frontier of Hungary, where he waited for German help. The dukes entered the royal seat of Székesfehérvár and posted garrisons in Kapuvár, Babót, Székesfehérvár and other important fortresses in the royal part of Hungary.[53] Géza became king of Hungary (1074–1077), and left Bihar and his own Nitra to his brother Ladislas, who held this position until Géza died in 1077. Then

---

[50]   Hlinka *et al.*, *Peniaze*, pp. 140–1, 165–6, 170–1; Hlinka, 'Nálezy', 57, 160–1; Hlinka, 'New Notions', pp. 196–8.

[51]   Szentpétery, *Scriptores* (ed.), vol. I, pp. 383–4.

[52]   Kristó, *A XI. századi*, pp. 85–86; Kristó, *A vármegyek kialakulása Magyarországon* [The development of the counties in Hungary] (Budapest, 1988), pp. 197–200. The Duchy of Nitra had two more counties in 1074 than it did in 1042. These clearly originated by dividing larger counties into smaller ones.

[53]   Szentpétery, *Scriptores* (ed.), vol. I, pp. 385–91.

Ladislas became king of Hungary (1077–1095); not intending to share his reign over Hungary, he retained the Duchies of Nitra and Bihar.[54] After Ladislas's death the elder son of Géza I, Koloman, became king (1095–1116) while his younger brother Álmos (1095–1108) became the last duke of Nitra and Bihar. In 1108 Koloman removed Álmos by capturing and blinding him and later his son Béla. The blind Álmos was sent to the monastery at Demes.[55]

Thus the year 1108 marked the end not only of the Árpád autonomous ducal demesne, but also of the history of the Duchy of Nitra. After Pribina – over the course of two and a half centuries – descendants from the Mojmír and Árpád families had followed each other as dukes. Up to 1108 Nitra was an autonomous duchy, a clear political entity, which laid the territorial and historical foundations of Slovakia.

[54] After becoming king of Hungary in 1077, Ladislas in particular did not intend to share power in the country with the deposed Solomon, or to allow anybody to rule in Nitra as duke. Cf. Ladizlaus, 'quarto anno regni sui pacificatus est cum Salamone, donans ei stipendia ad regales expensas sufficienta. Optimates autem regni futura pericula ballice cladis caute precaventes non patiebantur regnum partiri cum Salomone, ne novissima fierent peiora prioribus': Szentpétery (ed.), *Scriptores*, vol. I, pp. 407; Kristó, *A XI. századi*, pp. 93–4.
[55] Szentpétery (ed.), *Scriptores*, vol. I, pp. 420–3, 427–30; Kristó, *A XI. századi*, pp. 108–24.

3   The beginnings of the nobility in Slovakia

Ján Lukačka

Before and after Great Moravia

Across the territory of Slovakia the stratification of society, characteristic of early feudal society in Western and Central Europe, began to take place shortly before the Great Moravian period, at the beginning of the ninth century.[1] This process was connected with the evolution of Pribina's Duchy of Nitra, the first example of a demonstrable Slavic state north of the middle Danube. The predecessors of Duke Pribina utilised the defeat inflicted on the Avars by the Frankish king Charlemagne and his son Pipin in the final decade of the eighth century to further their political goals. With an armed retinue they quickly exploited the Avars' weakened position and, in a short time, created the territorial basis of the Duchy of Nitra in south-western Slovakia. The town of Nitra became its political and economic centre. Professional warriors of varied origin made up the duchy's armed retinue. The majority certainly descended from the former tribal aristocracy loyal to the ruling duke. Some could have come from the free strata of the mass of the people. The duke chose individuals who demonstrated above-average military abilities and loyalty to the ruling dynasty.

The creation of a territorial organisation, based on fortified hillforts and adjoining countryside, is also characteristic of the process of medieval state formation. Several members of the retinue were placed in these hillforts to secure the administration of the territory and collect the agreed tribute in the name of the duke. Pribina's Nitrans quickly began to expand their power base, especially to the east and south-east where their actions did not encounter any serious opposition. Around 825, Pribina married a Christian from the Bavarian Wilhelm family, and he agreed to the Christianisation of his domain. This process culminated

---

[1] For the best source on this subject, see K. Štulrajterová (ed.), *Najstaršie rody na Slovensku* [The oldest families in Slovakia] (Martin, 1994).

in the building of the first Christian church at Nitra and its solemn consecration by Archbishop Adalram of Salzburg in 828.

The natural process of building up Nitran statehood was interrupted by the unexpected invasion of Mojmír I from the neighbouring Duchy of Moravia in about 833. After his defeat, Duke Pribina was forced to leave the country together with a large part of his retinue and seek help from the Franks.[2] Other members of the Nitran upper ranks accepted Moravian rule and were allowed to remain.

After the military power of Great Moravia had been broken in a battle with the Old Magyars, probably in Transdanubia (905–906), members of the Great Moravian leading strata took advantage of this altered situation and joined them in plundering expeditions into Western Europe. An alliance with the Magyars enabled them to survive and maintain positions of domination in the territory of Slovakia not yet permanently occupied by the Magyars, but which constituted the Magyar sphere of interest. Archaeological finds of Old Magyar horsemen's graves from the first half of the tenth century testify to this development. Their distribution shows that Magyar military settlements did not extend beyond the line Bratislava–Trnava–Hlohovec–Nitra–Levice–Lučenec–Moldava nad Bodvou–Trebišov, that is, they were located in the southern part of Slovakia.[3]

To the north of this line, not only did the older settlement structures survive, so did the territorial-administrative organisations, led by native magnates. The renowned historian Daniel Rapant first suggested the existence of a local Slovak elite after the fall of Great Moravia some time ago. At first, his theory was basically a matter of intuition, as in the early 1950s he could not support his claim with any concrete historical or archaeological evidence. It was only following systematic investigations of the aristocratic manors at Ducové near Piešt'any, and later also at Nitrianska Blatnica, by Alexander Ruttkay in the 1970s that Rapant's hypothesis was unambiguously confirmed.[4] These activities also provided a more precise chronology for the gradual incorporation

---

[2] After his defeat, about 833, Pribina was accompanied into exile by the greater part of his retinue. We have a list of its leading members, compiled in 850 on the occasion of the consecration of a church at his seat in the Duchy of Lower Pannonia. They are listed prior to the German nobles. See R. Marsina (ed.), *Pramene k dejinám Slovenska* [Sources on the history of Slovakia], vol. II (Bratislava, 1999), p. 142.

[3] A. Točík, *Die altmagyarischen Gräberfelder in der Südwestslowakei* (Bratislava, 1968).

[4] A. Ruttkay, *Ducové. Vel'komoravský velmožský dvorec a včasnostredoveké pohrebisko* [Ducové. A Great Moravian high aristocratic manor and an early medieval cemetery] (Nitra, 1975). The thesis of the existence of a Slovak noble rank can also be supported by examining parallel developments in Moravia, where a local leading stratum maintained its position during the tenth century. Duke Spytihněv of Bohemia eliminated its

of the territory of south-western Slovakia into the organisational framework of the emerging Hungarian state.

According to the testimony of these archaeological finds, the Old Magyars crossed the Danube and military units began to settle in south-western Slovakia in the 920s. The first ordinary Magyar settlers, mixing with local population, appeared in the course of the 930s and 940s. The Magyar historian, György Györffy, supposes that the Árpád dynasty had already taken possession of the Duchy of Nitra by the beginning of the tenth century. However, the oldest Magyar narrative sources state that the Old Magyar chieftain, Lél, who clearly did not come from the Árpád family, had originally occupied Nitra and sojourned in the area between it and Hlohovec.[5] In 955, Lél together with warriors Bulcsu and Súr participated in a plundering expedition into German lands where they suffered a catastrophic defeat on the banks of the Lech river. The leaders were captured and later executed. Their territories were then taken over by the Árpáds. Thus the Duchy of Nitra became part of the domain of the House of Árpád. More specifically, it was Árpád's grandson, Taksony, who started the process of integrating the fragmented tribal territories into a larger unit. His sons Géza and Michael continued his work beyond the 970s. The elder son Géza became the grand duke, while his younger brother Michael gained Nitra as an autonomous demesne (údel).

The intensive effort of the emerging Hungarian state to penetrate deeper into the mountain valleys and basins of the Carpathians should be viewed in the light of Michael's activities as head of the Nitra autonomous demesne. He clearly had to break the resistance of the native nobles, among whom the ancestors of the Poznans in north-western Slovakia and the Hunts in south-central Slovakia held leading positions. However, the confrontation ended with the representatives of these families accepting the suzerainty of Duke Michael and entering into his service, while retaining part of their family domains.[6]

---

prominent representatives for somewhat trivial reasons in 1055. See B. Bretholz, *Chronik der Böhmen des Cosmas von Prag* (Berlin, 1923), pp. 105–6.

[5] E. Szentpétery (ed.), *Scriptores rerum Hungaricarum tempore ducum regumque stirpis Arpadianae gestarum*, vol. I (Budapest, 1937), pp. 166–7.

[6] A variety of opposing views exist on the origins of these noblemen. Hungarian historiography recognises their non-Magyar origin; in agreement with the chronicler Simon of Kéza, they are regarded as Germans (Swabians). Slovak historians, especially J. Hodál, convincingly demonstrated their domestic (Slovak) origin in his extensive study. See J. Hodál, 'Pôvod, sídla a hodnost' predkov rodu Hunt-Pázmány' [The origin, seats and rank of the ancestry of the Hunt-Pázmány family], *Historický sborník Matice slovenskej*, 4 (1946), 136–64.

The Poznans and the Hunts

We do not know exactly when the Poznans converted to Christianity, but churches found within their fortified manors (Ducové, Nitrianska Blatnica and Visegrád) were operating during this period. Indeed, the Poznans took over the neglected Benedictine monastery below the Zobor hill, overlooking Nitra, in the last quarter of the tenth century and became its secular patrons. They revived the monastic community and granted it various properties from their land holdings.[7]

The Poznans and Hunts remained in the service of Duke Michael until his early death about 995, when he was killed, apparently, on the orders of his elder brother Géza. Géza's son Stephen became the new duke of the Nitra autonomous demesne. He was accompanied to Nitra by his Bavarian wife, Gizela, and a large German retinue. Stephen and his wife became zealous Christian missionaries, who concerned themselves with restoring the half-ruined episcopal church of St Emeram and establishing a provostry at Nitra castle. For a brief time between 995 and 997, close personal relations were established between the young Stephen and the local Poznan and Hunt magnates. The strength of these contacts was tested in 997 when Grand Duke Géza died, and Kopány (a member of a minor Árpád branch based at Somogy) claimed the title and launched a rebellion against the young Stephen. In his time of greatest need, Duke Stephen turned to the *duces provinciales* Poznan and Hunt who both remained loyal. These representatives of two important aristocratic families, together with their armed retinues, significantly augmented Stephen's military strength; his main striking force consisted of German knights from his wife's retinue. Stephen expressed his unlimited confidence in Poznan and Hunt by making both *duces* his bodyguards. The allied armies eventually defeated the rebellious Kopány near Veszprém.[8]

In the period after the defeat of Kopány, Poznan and Hunt became extremely powerful at the grand ducal court in Esztergom. Young Stephen granted them further property in the Duchy of Nitra, especially in the southern regions. He also gave them part of the property of the defeated Kopány in Somogy.[9] Poznan and Hunt remained close to Stephen and had significant influence on his

---

[7] The striking connection between the property of the abbey and the properties of the Hunt–Poznan family in south-western Slovakia also testifies to this fact. Apart from this, various documents from the twelfth century to the beginning of the fourteenth show that members of this family were the collective patrons of Zobor abbey.

[8] Szentpétery (ed.), *Scriptores rerum Hungaricarum*, vol. II (Budapest, 1938), pp. 381–2.

[9] These holdings, located in the south of the Kingdom of Hungary, still belonged to descendants of the Hunt and Poznan families in the thirteenth and fourteenth centuries.

decision-making, an influence they retained after Stephen was crowned the first king of Hungary in 1000.[10]

The Poznan and Hunt lineages

Poznan and then his son Bukven retained the position of county sheriff (*župan*) of Nitra[11] for a number of years, and were among the leading nobles at the court of the Nitran demesne rulers, as were Hunt and his descendants.[12]

From the eleventh century, the Poznans and Hunts each developed in two family lines. The first line contained the direct descendants of the original *duces provinciales*, who had the right to use the designations 'de genere Poznan' and 'de genere Hunt' respectively and, approximately from the middle of the twelfth century, after the fusion of the previously separate families – 'de genere Hunt-Poznan'. Apart from the original family properties, and the estates granted by the first kings of the House of Árpád, significant positions at the royal court and patronage over the monasteries of Zobor and Bzovík were traditionally inherited through this direct line.

Apart from the main lineage, extended Poznan and Hunt family affiliations also existed, but these relatives did not share in the extensive new grants. They gained comparatively large holdings with five to seven settlements within the framework of the original family properties. Over the course of the twelfth century, these families settled as separate units, which were later named after their residences or regions. In the thirteenth century, they had already lost awareness of a common origin with the direct descendants of Poznan and Hunt.

The oldest genealogical data about the closer and extended Poznan affiliations are preserved in the so-called Zobor charters, dating from 1111–1113. The first of these mentions twelve Nitran nobles, who had to confirm by oath the rights granted to the monastery of Zobor by King Stephen I. At least four of these nobles came from the Poznan family. Characteristically, they had all held the office of sheriff of Nitra for some time. The first to be mentioned was Una, the second Bacha. Another two witnesses were the brothers Deda and Cace, the sons of Bukven.[13]

---

[10] For example, Hunt and Poznan are mentioned as witnesses in the foundation charter of St Martin's Abbey at Pannonhalma in 1002 (*astantibus ducibus videlicet Poznano, Cuntio, Orzio*). See R. Marsina (ed.), *Codex diplomaticus et epistolaris Slovaciae* (Bratislava, 1971), vol. I, p. 47, no. 50.

[11] *Comes* in Latin, *ispán* in Magyar.

[12] J. Steinhübel, 'Uhorské kráľovstvo a Nitrianske kniežatstvo' [The Kingdom of Hungary and the Duchy of Nitra], *Historický časopis*, 48 (2000), 15f.

[13] Marsina (ed.), *Codex*, p. 63, no. 68.

According to all indications, these two noble elders (both were over eighty at the time the charter was issued) were grandsons of Poznan. Evidence for this conclusion is provided by the continuing frequent use of these names in the direct Poznan line throughout the thirteenth century. This line undoubtedly included the *principes regni*, Moyses and Cosma, who were sought by Abbot Godfrid of Zobor in 1113 to testify regarding the property of the monastery.[14] We know for certain that Cosma came from the Poznan family and was one of the leading Hungarian magnates. In 1123, during an expedition to Galicia he led the great nobles' opposition to King Stephen II. Moyses was probably his brother or possibly a cousin. They were descendants of Deda and Cace. Cosma apparently held a higher rank at the king's court, while Moyses was sheriff of Nitra for a long time at the beginning of the twelfth century. Cosma and Moyses probably lived until the middle of the twelfth century. The majority of the most important aristocratic families in south-western Slovakia were descended from them.[15]

The surviving written sources also give us relatively detailed information about the fate of Hunt's descendants. *Dux provincialis* Hunt left two sons Bína and Lambert, who further increased the land holdings of the family. They gained generous grants from Saint Stephen, the first king of Hungary and his successors, due to their family links with the ruling Árpád dynasty.

About 1090, Hunt's grandson Lampert II married a sister of Saint Ladislas I. The charter from Lampert II and his son Nicholas (before 1132) founding the Benedictine abbey of Bzovík is an extraordinarily valuable source of information about the properties of the Hunt family. The list of granted properties in the charter strictly distinguishes between three types of property. The first type is the so-called hereditary property of the family (*hereditarium*); the second, those properties obtained by purchase from other owners; and the third, properties granted to individual members of the family by the kings of Hungary or rulers of Nitra.[16] It is worth noting that hereditary property of pre-Hungarian origin prevailed among the family possessions.

The Miškovecs and the Radvan-Bogats

Information on status and property, similar to that regarding the Poznans and Hunts, is also available for other families, especially those

---

[14] *Ibid.*, p. 65, no. 69.
[15] For example, among others, the counts of Svätý Jur and Pezinok, the Forgách family, the lords of Sek, Šišov and Hradná.
[16] Marsina (ed.), *Codex*, pp. 71–2, no. 74.

from the eastern parts of the former Duchy of Nitra. This material concerns old aristocratic families known as the Miškovecs and the Radvan-Bogats. Older Magyar historiography has accepted that neither of these families was of Magyar origin. The Miškovecs derived their name from Miško, the Slovak diminutive of the personal name Michael. By the eleventh and twelfth centuries, the family already held properties in the County of Borsód, centred on Miskolc (a town in north-eastern Hungary; the name is derived from Miškovec). Later they also expanded into the south-eastern part of the county of Gemer. Significantly, like the Hunt–Poznans, the Miškovecs also held properties in Transdanubia, specifically in the counties of Komárno, Moson and Sopron, which were apparently granted to them by the first kings of the House of Árpád.[17]

Medieval chroniclers placed the origin of the Bogat-Radvans in Bohemia. Their oldest family properties lay in the county of Zemplín, around the town Michalovce. Like the Hunt–Poznans, the members of this family owned property in the county of Somogy, perhaps indicating that the Bogat-Radvans had helped Stephen I to liquidate Kopány's uprising.[18]

These four noble families were among the most important representatives of the social elites descended from the old Nitran aristocracy. When a significant section of Old Magyars led by Kopány rebelled against young Stephen, the representatives of these families stood by him and, with their military retinues, helped him to defeat the rebels. With this act they legitimised themselves, in spite of their non-Magyar origins, and became significant supporters of the first kings of the House of Árpád, and the Nitran rulers. Over the subsequent centuries, descendants of these families further strengthened their position across the territories of Slovakia and Bihar.

Lower nobility

The medieval nobility of the Kingdom of Hungary included not only the higher strata, but also those drawn from the lesser ranks of nobles. Their origins can be traced through the records of the lesser royal *servientes* (officials) and castle *iobagiones* (soldiers), scattered across the individual royal counties. The origins of this privileged social group were closely connected with the military affairs of the medieval Kingdom of Hungary. Originally, all free inhabitants of the kingdom apparently had to perform

---

[17] J. Karácsonyi, *A Magyar nemzetségek a XIV. század közepeig* [The Magyar clans up to the middle of the fourteenth century] (Budapest, 1901), vol. II, pp. 363–76.
[18] *Ibid.*, pp. 248–60.

military duties. However, this system was not very successful, so the first kings of Hungary, and the county sheriffs appointed by them, determined quotas of soldiers, who had to serve in the royal and county armies. The *servientes sancti regis* and *iobagiones castri* obtained land in return for their services, roughly about 60–80 hectares each. The land was assigned from the royal property within the bounds of the county castle.

Settlements of lesser nobles gradually arose on these properties. Their inhabitants enjoyed certain privileges, as codified in the Golden Bull of Andrew II in 1222.[19] During the course of the thirteenth century, the direct descendants of these royal *servientes* and castle *iobagiones* were gradually given the status of true nobles by individual royal charters, but they gained further property only in individual instances. In the majority, the kings only confirmed existing occupancy of property. However, in many cases, the descendants of these *servientes* and *iobagiones* entered the ranks of the nobility even without special royal privileges. The most important aspect of this process was whether they maintained their noble standing and performed military service for the king.

Research into the ethnicity of these lower strata of the nobility came to the conclusion, quite some time ago, that it corresponded to the ethnicity of the surrounding majority population. Therefore, the majority of the lesser nobility in the territory of present-day Slovakia were of Slovak origin in the Middle Ages. This statement is entirely true of the areas of western and northern Slovakia where the lesser nobility were most numerous, not least in the counties of Nitra, Trenčín, Liptov, Zvolen, the northern part of Tekov, Hont, Novohrad and Gemer. The Slovak element was also significant in the counties of eastern Slovakia, although not as much as it was further west.[20] It was not uncommon for members of other ethnic groups – primarily of Magyar origin – to acquire property throughout the territory of present-day Slovakia during the Middle Ages. The ethnicity of this lower nobility can be easily traced on the basis of personal names. Their frequency shows that so-called national names, those which were characteristically Slovak, persisted among the lesser nobility until well into the fourteenth century. Then they were often replaced by universal Christian names under the influence of the Catholic Church.

---

[19] B. Klein, A. Ruttkay and R. Marsina, *Vojenské dejiny Slovenska* [Military history of Slovakia], vol. I (Bratislava, 1994).

[20] B. Varsik, *Otázky vzniku a vývinu slovenského zemianstva* [Questions of the origin and evolution of Slovak lesser nobility] (Bratislava, 1988).

4 Medieval towns

Vladimír Segeš

The oldest surviving map of the Kingdom of Hungary, and therefore also the oldest map of Slovakia, dates from the period when the Middle Ages was on the cusp of turning into the early modern age. This diagram, known as Lazar's Map, after the author who was secretary to the archbishop of Esztergom, was printed in 1528 in Ingolstadt in Bavaria under the title *Tabula Hungariae*. Lazar's Map also provides evidence that the territory that today corresponds to contemporary Slovakia was one of the most urbanised regions of the Kingdom of Hungary, and that it was an important economic and cultural base.[1]

Lazar's Map identified sixteen free royal towns, twelve larger towns and eighty-three small towns, according to their political and economic importance, legal status and function. A total of 289 settlements form the residential network of Slovakia shown on the map, but this constitutes only about 8 per cent of the total number of settlements in Slovakia at the end of the Middle Ages.[2]

The origin and development of towns

By establishing a network of towns, the kings of Hungary were pursuing two main aims: an economic goal and a defensive one. The first was part of the overall European developmental trend; the second resulted from the painful experience of the devastating Tatar (Mongol) invasion of 1241–1242. As a result of this incursion, it is estimated that at least a third of the population died directly from famine and indirectly from epidemics. After the thirteenth century, especially in Upper (northern) Hungary – roughly the territory of contemporary

---

[1] The map, along with a brief commentary, was published by T. Szatmáry, *Descriptio Hungariae. Magyarország és Erdély nyomtatott térképei 1477–1600* [Printed maps of Hungary and Transylvania 1477–1600] (Budapest, 1987), pp. 70–3.

[2] J. Žudel, 'Miestne názvy na Lazarovej mape Uhorska so zretel'om na územie Slovenska' [Place names in the territory of Slovakia on Lazar's Map of Hungary], *Slovenská archivistika*, 32 (1997), 48–59.

Slovakia – agglomerations of an urban character became increasingly more important, alongside the relatively developed network of castles.

The process of transforming villagers' communes into towns was especially apparent in those regions with deposits of ore, on busy roads, in frequented faubourgs or at a crossroads. For the most advantageously situated villages, favourable conditions also existed in agricultural regions. This was especially the case when they were located in the centre of fertile countryside, near the administrative centre of a castle with favorable pre-conditions for the development of production and the formation of markets. Therefore, location and natural conditions to a large extent determined the basic character of the three types of towns that existed in Slovakia: mining towns, commercial (and artisanal-commercial) towns and centres of agricultural production.

Modern historical research has demonstrated that colonists from the West, especially from German lands, played an important, but not an exclusive, role in the origination and development of towns in the Kingdom of Hungary. Eventually all medieval towns in Slovakia and other parts of the Kingdom of Hungary followed either the Magdeburg (north German) or Nuremberg (south German or Swabian) code of town laws, or variants of them.[3] However, there is no doubt that when these immigrants – called *hospes* (immigrants) in contemporary sources – arrived, there already existed settlements with a relatively highly developed economy, including an external market system.

The legal basis on which towns were created was the appropriate grant (*donatio*), although it is necessary to emphasise that no town gained urban rights and privileges on the basis of a single charter. Usually immigrants were not granted urban privileges immediately upon their arrival, but after a delay of several years. These privileges applied not only to foreign colonists but largely also to the local indigenous population, or at least a part of it. The towns with the earliest charters included: Trnava (1238), Starý Tekov (1240), Zvolen and Krupina prior to the Tatar invasion (before 1241), Spišské Vlachy (1243), Košice (before 1248), Nitra (1248), Banská Štiavnica (before 1255), Banská Bystrica (1255), Nemecká Ľupča (1263), Komárno (1265), Kežmarok (1269), Gelnica (before 1270), Bratislava (1291) and Prešov together with Veľký Šariš and Sabinov (1299); the Saxons in Spiš were granted a collective charter in 1271.

In the fourteenth century the tempo of town development increased throughout the territory of Slovakia. About thirty towns already had

---

[3] D. Lehotská, 'Vývoj mestského práva na Slovensku' [The development of town jurisdiction in Slovakia], *Historica*, 10 (1959), 65–114.

charters, and these were joined by another sixty localities. By the end of the fourteenth century, it is therefore possible to identify about a hundred privileged towns or townships in the legal sense.[4] However, it is necessary to add that, from an economic perspective, many were little different from villages.

Bratislava serves as a useful example of the form and content of the privileges and freedoms contained in a royal charter. Bratislava developed from a faubourg into a medieval town long before King Andrew III of Hungary (1290–1301) granted it a charter (2 December 1291). It contained a list of privileges documenting Bratislava's high level of urban development. The most important of these were:

> freedom from the payment of land tax for a period of ten years from the issuing of the charter;
>
> the right to elect a judge (*iudex*, *Richter*) and twelve jurors annually;
>
> the right of Bratislava's tradesmen to trade undisturbed in the county of Bratislava, and freedom from tolls for the crossing of fords by persons, cattle or carts;
>
> freedom from customs duty for foreigners coming to Bratislava with goods for sale;
>
> the right of burghers to be tried only by the judge of Bratislava and local jurors;
>
> the right to appeal to the king against the Bratislava town court's judgements;
>
> equality of rights of Jews with other burghers;
>
> the right of immigrants to enjoy the same privileges as burghers of Bratislava;
>
> the right of the judge and burghers to expel from the town persons who refuse to respect the rights and customs observed in the town;
>
> the right of burghers not to appear before the court of the Palatine; and
>
> the right of all tradesmen from the kingdom to deposit their goods in the town and offer them for sale.[5]

---

[4] The earliest town charters were published by Ľ. Juck, *Výsady miest a mestečiek na Slovensku (1238–1350)* [The charters of boroughs and small towns in Slovakia (1238–1350)] (Bratislava, 1984).

[5] Facsimile and edited version in V. Horváth, *Bratislavské mestské privilégium. (Ondrej III.– 2 December 1291)* [Bratislava's town charters (Andrew III–2 December 1291)] (Bratislava, 1991).

The granting of a charter of privileges to a town not only conferred certain rights, but also entailed certain obligations. In particular, there was a duty to pay a regular monetary tax (*census*) to the king and the land tax (*terragium*), which applied only to owners of fixed property. The mining towns had an obligation to deliver an eighth of the extracted silver or a tenth of the extracted gold. The majority of towns had an obligation to provide hospitality for the king and the territorial lord and their retinues if they visited the town. Special charter regulations were concerned with the payment of church tithes, which belonged to the local bishop. However, it was usually the local parish priest who collected these tithes. In general, all payments were collected in money form. Payments in kind continued only in smaller towns with undeveloped self-government.[6]

Definition and concept of a town

By the beginning of the fifteenth century, and as a result of a long-term process, two categories of towns had already crystallised within the Kingdom of Hungary: a smaller group of developed urban settlements called *civitates* in Latin, and a larger group of smaller towns called *oppida*. The so-called Little Decree of King Sigismund (1387–1437) of 1405 offers perhaps the clearest distinction between the two forms. What emerges from a reading of the introduction to the decree is the intention to strengthen and surround towns with walls, and to raise some free villages or small towns up to the level of full towns.[7] The emphasis placed on the need to fortify towns has to be viewed against the background of the Turkish threat.

Provided certain conditions were fulfilled, a developing urban settlement could acquire the character and rank of a town, or more precisely recognition as a town with full rights even without fortifications. However, King Sigismund insisted that town walls were a basic criterion for full recognition as a town. In fact, the legislative basis for regarding the construction of town walls as a characteristic feature of a town had existed since 1351. It was King Louis I (1342–1382) who decreed that only fortified towns (*civitates muratae*) were freed from payment of the

---

[6] J. Karpat, 'Fiškálne hl'adisko pri vzniku miest a ich rozvoji v stredoveku' [A fiscal aspect of the origin of towns and their development in the Middle Ages], *Historické štúdie*, 19 (1974), 99–108.

[7] 'Quasdam civitates, murorum ambitu cingendas, quasdam liberas villas seu oppida, civitatis honore sublimandas': F. Döry, G. Bónis and V. Bácskai, *Decreta regni Hungariae. Gesetze und Verordnungen Ungarns 1301–1457* (Budapest, 1976), p. 191.

ninth part of the produce to their territorial lord.[8] Thus, from the middle of the fourteenth century, the town building process in the Kingdom of Hungary displayed tendencies that were later defined by Stephen Werböczy (Verböcius) in 1514 in his collection of Hungarian customary and valid aristocratic laws in three parts (called in short *Tripartitum*) that served as a legal handbook until 1848.[9]

Werböczy determined the characteristic of a town on the basis of historical experience whereby the free royal towns served as a model. He derived the Latin term *civitas* for the town from *cives* (burghers), and identified it with *civium unitas* – the community of burghers. The town was perceived in the dual or bilateral combination of the inhabitants and commune, on the basis of which he regarded the town as 'a collection of houses and streets surrounded by necessary walls and bastions, bestowing the privilege to enjoy a good and dignified life'.[10]

This definition of a town underlines that fortifications constituted an essential attribute of a commune enjoying full rights as a town. Fortifications and town walls clearly highlight the central military significance of towns. Town walls undoubtedly served as a physical source for the justified psychological self-assuredness and self-confidence of the burghers, a sentiment shared by all inhabitants of the medieval town. Fortification of a town practically and symbolically proclaimed its invulnerability. They also outwardly demonstrated the self-sufficiency, prosperity and independence of the urban community. This was also clearly reflected in town heraldry.[11] Thus it was a combination of economic and military power that provided the key

---

[8] *Corpus Juris Hungarici. Magyar Törvenytár. 1000–1526, évi törvénycikkek* [Book of Hungarian code, laws 1000–1526: annual statutes] (Budapest, 1899), p. 172; Döry et al. (eds.), *Decreta regni Hungariae*, p. 132.

[9] 'Tripartitum opus juris consuetudinarii inclyti regni Hungariae per magistrum Stephanum de Werbewcz…editum': *Corpus Juris Hungarici. Magyar Törvénytár. Werböczy István Hármaskönyve* [István Werböczy's Book of Hungarian legal code in three parts] (Budapest, 1897).

[10] 'Quia de liberis quoque civitatibus, paucis tractandum occurit, idcirco sciendum: quod civitas dicitur, quasi civium unitas, eo quod ibi populorum pluralitas sit convocata. Est autem civitas, domorum et vicorum pluralitas, moeniis, et praesidiis circumcincta necessariis, ad bene honesteque vivendum privilegiata': *Corpus Juris Hungarici. Werböczy*, pt III, p. 388.

[11] Throughout Europe, the motif of fortifications in the form of town walls, gates or towers was frequently found on medieval town seals. Fortifications were used as a symbol by the Community of the Saxons of Spiš and by seven towns and small towns in Slovakia, but only two, Bratislava and Komárno, were really fortified. See J. Novák, *Slovenské mestské a obecné erby* [Slovak town and communal coats of arms] (Bratislava, 1967); P. Kartous, J. Novák and L. Vrtel', *Erby a vlajky miest v Slovenskej republike* [Coats of arms and flags of towns in the Slovak Republic] (Bratislava, 1991).

step in the process of constituting the towns into a privileged fourth estate of medieval Hungarian society.[12]

However, without appropriate support from the ruler, the independence and freedom of these towns were only illusory. In several cases the king mortgaged royal towns, which in turn fell into long-term or permanent subjection to a secular or ecclesiastical feudal lord. In this way they sank back to the level of feudally dependent towns or townships. Then, in the end, in spite of a high level of autonomy and municipal self-government, and in spite of town fortifications, no town could really be self-sufficient in Hungary or elsewhere in Europe.[13]

Around 1500, the legal categorisation of towns in the Kingdom of Hungary was ratified by resolutions passed by the Diet. Legislative article no. 2 (1492) importantly distinguished between free towns and small towns. Accordingly all towns without walled fortifications were obliged to pay the territorial lord the ninth part of produce in kind. In the decree of King Vladislav II Jagiello (1490–1516) of 1498 (article no. 2), the ten most important towns in the Kingdom of Hungary are listed, with six located in the territory of Slovakia: Košice, Bratislava, Bardejov, Prešov, Trnava and Levoča.[14] A more detailed categorisation of towns dates from 1514.[15] From this listing we find that more than half of the royal towns and free mining towns in the Kingdom of Hungary were located in the territory of present-day Slovakia. At the end of the Middle Ages, about two hundred other localities (settlements) were considered urban from a functional point of view.

Regarding size, there were no large towns in Slovakia or in the whole of Hungary. Buda, the largest town and capital of the kingdom, had a population of up to 15,000 at the end of the fifteenth century. By the end of the Middle Ages, the largest towns in Slovakia were Košice and Bratislava. By European standards, these were middle-sized towns with 5,000 to 10,000 inhabitants. Banská Štiavnica, Levoča, Trnava, Bardejov, Banská Bystrica, Prešov, Kremnica and possibly Kežmarok were smaller middle-sized towns with populations of about 2,000 to 5,000 people. The other towns in Slovakia contained fewer than 2,000 inhabitants, with the great majority of small towns containing fewer than 1,000 people, and in many cases only 500 or so.

---

[12] In contrast to the majority of feudal states in Europe, the Kingdom of Hungary had four privileged estates: church dignitaries of high rank (*praelati*), great nobles (*magnates*, *barones*), noblemen (*nobiles*) and the free royal towns.

[13] D. Matthew, *Atlas of Medieval Europe* (Oxford, 1983), p. 131.

[14] *Corpus Juris Hungarici, 1000–1526*, pp. 614–16.   [15] *Ibid.*, p. 708.

Towards the end of the Middle Ages, few towns in the Kingdom of Hungary enjoyed free status. Legally only the free royal towns possessed this status, and they accounted for only about 5 per cent of the total population of Slovakia (about half a million people). Taking the Kingdom of Hungary as a whole, approximately 110,000 inhabitants in about thirty royal towns formed 3.8 percent of the total population. In comparison with the rest of Europe this was still a relatively low proportion, not least in comparison to the German lands where 15 per cent of the population lived in towns.

Town unions and associations

In Hungary/Slovakia, as in other parts of Europe, some towns joined together in the interest of protecting their privileges and common interests, in addition to co-ordinating policy in jurisdictional and military matters. As the Reformation gathered pace, alliances were increasingly formed on the basis of confessional interests. Those towns which were geographically close, towns of related or identical legal status, and towns with related economic interests were the most frequently associated.[16]

The oldest union originated in the Community of the Saxons of Spiš (*Communitas, Universitas* or *Provincia Saxonum de Scepus*), which was created on the basis of the collective charter of privileges granted by King Stephen V (1271). This process brought together German *hospes* settled in the Poprad and Hornád basins. At the time of the confirmation of this collective charter of privileges by King Charles I in 1317, the Community of the Saxons of Spiš included thirty larger settlements, situated across forty-three localities. But in the first half of the fourteenth century, this number was reduced to twenty-four, bringing about a formation later called the Province of twenty-four Spiš towns (*Provincia XXIV oppidorum terrae Scepusiensis*). To this day it is still not entirely clear which localities belonged to this organisation during the fourteenth century. However, we do know that they included communes inhabited by 'Slovak guests'; as a result the community of the Saxons of Spiš should not be regarded as an exclusively German ethnic or national organisation.

This region's autonomous administration was headed by the count of Spiš province (*comes provinciae*), who was elected annually. All the inhabitants of the Spiš towns used the local code of laws, called the *Zipser Willkühr*. Originally, this was based on the customs that the Saxon

---

[16] On town unions in medieval and early modern Slovakia, see O. R. Halaga, *Spoločenstva miest na Slovensku* [Associations of towns in Slovakia] (Martin, 1984), pp. 51–67.

population had brought with them from their homeland, but over time it came under the influence of Hungarian practices, so that when it was eventually codified it differed from Saxon law. In 1412, King Sigismund of Hungary mortgaged the thirteen richest Spiš towns to King Vladislav II Jagiello of Poland for 37,000 *sexgena grossorum* (perhaps 100,000 Hungarian gulden). The Polish administration was limited to supervision by a chief officer residing in Ľubovňa castle. These mortgaged towns were re-incorporated into the Kingdom of Hungary just before the so-called first partition of Poland in 1772. Those towns that were not mortgaged returned to their former legal status and formed a new autonomous entity called the Spiš province of eleven Spiš royal towns (*Communitas XI regalium civitatem terrae Scepusiensis*). But, they were unable to maintain this privileged position: in the second half of the fifteenth century they sank back to the level of feudally subject towns and villages, and became possessions of Spiš castle.[17]

Professional and regional predetermination was the basis for close co-operation and later for the formation of the union of free royal mining towns in central Slovakia, also known as the Lower Hungarian Mining Towns (*Niederungarische Bergstädte*). In the middle of the fifteenth century, it included seven towns, customarily ranked as follows: Kremnica, Banská Štiavnica, Banská Bystrica, Nová Baňa, Pukanec, Ľubietová and Banská Belá. This mining region was prominent in Europe for the extraction, smelting and production of precious metals. Around the middle of the fourteenth century, Hungary produced about 2,000–2,500 kg of gold annually, with Kremnica alone producing 400 kg, and by the end of the fifteenth century perhaps 250 kg. The greatest producers of silver were Banská Štiavnica and Banská Bystrica. During the second half of the fourteenth century, these towns produced a substantial proportion of the Kingdom of Hungary's total silver, estimated at 100 tons annually, which represented perhaps 25 per cent of Europe's total output of the metal.

The production of gold and silver had decreased by around 1500, but the output of copper increased thanks to the Thurzo-Fugger Company, founded in 1495 by the local entrepreneur Ján Thurzo and the German banker Jakub Fugger of Augsburg. This entity became the prototype of a large capitalist enterprise, active throughout Europe. It was based in Banská Bystrica – Neusohl in German – and was called the *Neusohler Kupferhandel*. Using its agents in Wrocław (Breslau), Gdańsk, Antwerp, Nuremberg and Venice, the company exported

---

[17] J. Žudel, *Stolice na Slovensku* [The counties of Slovakia] (Bratislava, 1984), pp. 111–12.

Figure 1 Mining regulations current in the Lower Hungarian Mining Towns (1703)

copper and silver worldwide (for mining regulations in the Lower Hungarian Mining Towns, see Fig. 1).[18]

In connection with the Lower Hungarian Mining Towns the queen's 'dowry' towns should also be mentioned. These were the towns and properties that the king of Hungary gave to his bride as a gift in the fifteenth and sixteenth centuries. King Sigismund started this arrangement in 1424, when he granted his wife Barbara several royal towns and royal properties, or more precisely the regular payments they transferred to the royal treasury. These dowry towns included, in addition to the mining towns in central Slovakia, the royal towns of Brezno, Krupina and Zvolen, and the castle estates of Dobrá Niva, (Slovenská) Ľupča, Šášov, Vígľaš and Zvolen. The ruler did not have the right to sell or give away the dowry properties but he could mortgage them, especially if he was unmarried. The dowry towns as an institution disappeared in 1548 when Maria, widow of Louis II Jagiello, then serving as governor of the

---

[18] On mining towns and mining, see R. Marsina (ed.), *Banské mestá na Slovensku* [Mining towns in Slovakia] (Martin, 1990).

Netherlands, returned all the dowry properties to her brother King
Ferdinand I of Hungary (1526–1564) of the House of Habsburg.

A combination of commercial and economic interests brought about
the alliance of five royal towns in eastern Slovakia known as the *Pentapolitana* or *Pentapolis*. In its final form, this union included Košice,
Levoča, Bardejov, Prešov and Sabinov. They played an important role
in the transit business, since old trade routes criss-crossed the region
from north to south and from west to east. Representatives of the towns
regularly met in Košice, which headed the group. The king, royal offices
and magnates also made use of the well-organised information service
of the *Pentapolitana* and its contacts abroad.

The Union of mining towns of eastern Slovakia (*oppida montana
Partium superiorum*), also known as the Upper Hungarian Mining Towns
(*Oberungarische Bergstädte*), was closely connected with the *Pentapolitana*. In 1487, a statutory assembly meeting in Košice (the seat of the
Royal Chamber) decided – consistent with old customs and justice – that
the mining towns had to sit and vote in the following order: Gelnica,
Smolník, Rudabánya, Jasov, Telkibánya, Rožňava, Spišská Nová Ves.
(Two of these towns – Rudabánya and Telkibánya – are today located
in Hungary.) The order of rank was determined by the age and the
extent of privileges each town enjoyed as well as by the value of the
output of the mines. Iron ore and precious metals, especially silver and
copper, had been extracted in the eastern Slovak mining region from
early times. In the first third of the fifteenth century, at Smolník alone
about 182 tons of copper were extracted annually. By the end of the
fourteenth century 'Spiš copper' dominated the markets in northern
Europe. It was transported through Cracow and Toruń to Gdańsk,
and from there by sea to Sweden, Flanders and England.

Urban society

According to the old German saying '*Stadtluft macht frei*', 'town air
liberates' – medieval towns' most important characteristic was their liberation from the yoke of feudal subject dependence or, more exactly, the
gaining of personal freedom. Yet it should be remembered that the royal
towns and their burghers, even with the full rights they enjoyed, were still
feudal subjects of the king. The burghers themselves were actually 'legal
associates', and their association had an institutional character. All burghers
or inhabitants of a town were not equal since, in principle, they were divided
into burghers with full rights and other inhabitants with significantly limited
rights. Different social, economic-property and political factors were thus
reflected in the hierarchically structured urban community.

The social structure within a town depended on several internal and external circumstances as well as on its size. It is generally true that larger towns were socially more differentiated than towns with smaller populations. Therefore, given the smaller size of towns in Slovakia, there the social divisions were not as marked as in Buda or in the large towns of Western Europe. As for wealth, the medieval towns of Slovakia were inhabited by three basic social strata: first, a small rich patriciate; second, a broad, considerably differentiated (in terms of social status and ownership of property) burgher stratum; and finally a relatively numerous lower stratum of the poor. This model of social structure applies variously to different types of urban area (royal towns, feudally dependent towns, mining towns and so on). Evidence is provided by analyses of the extant town tax registers, even though these do not use identical criteria from town to town. Social stratification differed in each town resulting from its own internal dynamics.

For example, the leadership of Bratislava in the middle of the fifteenth century was in the hands of the richest burghers, who paid tax of ten to ninety gulden and composed 7.5 per cent of the population. This patriciate included big merchants, wealthier master craftsmen and well-to-do owners of vineyards. The middle rank of burghers consisted of people who paid one to ten gulden in tax. This group made up the largest segment – 65.5 per cent – of the registered taxpayers. They included traders, craftsmen, owners of smaller vineyards, hired labourers and members of the intelligentsia, that is, officials, teachers and priests. The poorest inhabitants of Bratislava formed up to 27 per cent of registered taxpayers. They paid tax of less than one gulden. These included day-labourers, hired artisans, journeymen, apprentices, building workers, grocers and town servants. The majority of these people lived in the suburbs in their own cottages or as sub-tenants. Servants of both sexes, many journeymen and apprentices, coachmen and carters – that is, all those who did not have their own households, and for whom tax was paid by their employers – also need to be counted among the urban poor. In addition, vagrants, beggars, thieves, professional gamblers and jugglers, prostitutes, the poor in hospitals, and various other 'undesirables' lived in towns.

Any investigation of medieval urban society in Slovakia reveals that about a third of town inhabitants did not enjoy full burgher rights. Applicants for burgher status had to submit written testimony regarding their honourable origin from the places they came from or lived in; burgher status could not be acquired automatically or by inheritance. Thus even the son of a burgher had to apply for the status. Proof of ownership of property in a given town – that is, purchase of a house or land or acquisition of the same by marriage to the daughter or widow of a burgher – was a significant condition for acceptance as a burgher. Usually two burghers had to guarantee that the applicant would fulfil this condition within a year and a day. The newly accepted burgher took a ceremonial oath before the *iudex* and the town council.

The greatest privilege of a town lay in serving on its autonomous administration. Usually this consisted of a twelve-member town council headed by an *iudex* and a 24-member (later up to sixty members) outer council headed by a speaker (*tribunus, Vormund*). The *iudex* represented the town both internally and externally in relation to the king or the territorial lord. He wielded administrative and judicial authority and usually held office for one year. Another important functionary was the mayor (*magister civium, Bürgermeister*) who was in charge of the administrative and economic agenda of the town. The town captain commanded the local defence force. He was concerned with military defence of and order in the town, and safety in case of fire. Thus he also fulfilled important police and fire fighting roles. At the end of the Middle Ages, all privileged towns had a well-constructed and functional administration with many permanent employees and servants.

Towns were centres of craft production. Craftsmen of the same or similar crafts were organised in guilds, which appeared relatively late in Slovakia. The first guilds (of shoemakers) with written statutes came into being at Podolínec in Spiš in 1415. These early guilds were more concerned with promoting the interests of craftsmen than with helping to represent craftsmen on town councils.

The life of medieval towns obviously revolved around work, but also encompassed celebrations, entertainment and plays. Public executions, mostly held on market days, when the town was busy, became special occasions. The oldest municipal judicial protocol from Bratislava and other documents show that six methods of execution were commonly used in Bratislava in the last quarter-century of the Middle Ages: hanging, breaking on the wheel, decapitation, burning at the stake, drowning and quartering. The order in which these capital punishments are listed also indicates their frequency. Women (about 10 percent of those executed) were put to death by drowning or burning at the stake. In the majority of towns in Slovakia the gallows stood outside the most frequently used town gate. This was symbolic, and served as an obvious deterrent to all passers by that law and order

Figure 2 *Privilegium pro Slavis – decree by King Louis I the Great* on German–Slovak parity in the town council of Žilina (1381)

prevailed in the town, and that disturbers of communal peace and criminals would be punished.

The ethnic composition of towns

German speakers were the most numerous segment of Slovakia's town populations. But at the end of the Middle Ages, the position of ethnic Slovaks was significantly strengthened, as many had by then achieved burgher status. In accordance with this development, for example, King Louis I in 1381 issued a *privilegium pro Slavis* (see Fig. 2), granting Slovak speakers the right to hold half of the seats on Žilina town council. Antagonism between Slovak and German speakers arose in Trnava over the choice of a parish priest. This led to the intervention of King Matthias I Corvinus Hunyady (1458–1490), who decreed in 1486 that anyone inflaming ethnic disputes was to be executed. The evolving emancipation of the Slovaks found further expression in the fact that Slovak became the language employed by magistracies (town council offices), especially in smaller towns. In the Slovakisation of towns during the fifteenth century, a significant role was played by the Czech Hussite mercenary armies, especially those led by Captain Jan Jiskra of Brandýs (d. 1470). Known as the 'little brethren' (*bratríci*), their activities caused many German burghers to flee from, and Slovaks to flock to, towns.

Apart from Germans and Slovaks, a smaller number of Magyars lived in the towns of Slovakia, as did, sporadically, Jews, who were confined to a separate quarter as a compact and outwardly isolated community. The Jews in the Kingdom of Hungary were under the direct protection of the king. They had their own administrations in towns but they were still obliged to observe all royal and municipal laws and ordinances.

The distribution and proportions of the ethnic groups in the towns cannot be exactly determined today. They can be reconstructed only approximately on the basis of indirect evidence and indicators, such as language(s) employed in administration, personal records, judicial documents and church services as well as the names by which persons or things were commonly referred to.

The defence of the country and towns

The towns and the burghers did not play a key role in the military defence of the Kingdom of Hungary, but they always had an irreplaceable role in the defensive system of the country. The form of military obligations of the privileged – free royal and mining – towns as well as small towns depended on the character of military conflicts and contemporary conditions, and thus it experienced many changes.

It was typical of the urban policy of King Béla IV (1235–1270) to assign military and defensive tasks to a town when he granted it privileges. That having been said, burghers were not charged with personal military obligations, as was the custom in the case of noblemen. Initially, military obligations were assigned to towns on an individual basis, depending on several sets of circumstances and situations; this was therefore not a unified system. The oldest documented procedure involved a limited military obligation according to number of households. For example, according to the charter of 1238, Trnava had an obligation to provide 'one soldier most honourably equipped with all military necessities for every hundred households'; however, this obligation applied only when the king personally led the army.

From 1271, the Spiš Saxons had an obligation to provide fifty lancers who had to fight under the royal banner. In 1317, they were freed from this obligation but, instead, their annual financial contribution quadrupled from 300 silver marks to 1,200. In 1299, King Andrew III freed the *hospes* of Vel'ký Šariš, Prešov and Sabinov from participation in the royal army, but they were charged with an obligation to pay the king 150 silver marks annually. By 1400, military service had therefore become a relatively expensive obligation.

By the end of the Middle Ages, the military duties of towns formed a stable and functional system, based on legislation issued or approved by the king or the Diet. The military obligations of towns and their burghers lay in their involvement in the defensive system of the whole state: they paid military taxes and supplied the royal army with weapons, equipment and food, as well as providing the prescribed number of soldiers. The direct defence of a town was mainly a matter of building and maintaining town fortifications; furnishing sentries and guard services; or, in the event of a direct threat, burghers and other male inhabitants, including Jews, serving in combat roles. Urban military contingents were generally of higher quality than the most numerous permanent sections of the Hungarian armed forces – county units of noblemen, sometimes supplemented by the county portal units (*militia portalis*). The reason for the high quality of these urban detachments and field units lay in the growth in the number of mercenaries employed by towns. This development increasingly freed the burghers from the burden of performing military service as well as from participation in military campaigns away from home. Another important factor was that town mercenaries not only possessed better individual military experience than did the burgher and county levies, but they were also better armed and equipped. A town usually provided high-quality but expensive weapons and equipment, while the nobles were obliged to arm and equip themselves at their own expense. King Matthias I Corvinus often demanded and used the services of town mercenaries during his long reign, though he had a standing army of mercenaries of his own.[19]

The towns' role in the massive expansion in the provision of firearms and artillery was crucial. That is, they were the main producers and suppliers of these novel weapons, as well as of gunpowder and ammunition. Around the middle of the fifteenth century, almost all free royal towns had gun foundries and mills for making gunpowder not merely for their own requirements, but also for sale. A number

---

[19] For more detail, see V. Segeš, 'Die Städte in der Slowakei und das Militärwesen an der Wende des Mittelalters', in D. Kováč (ed.), *XXII. Kongres der internationalen Kommission für Militärgeschichte. Von Crécy bis Mohács – Kriegswesen im späten Mittelalter (1346–1526). Acta 22* (Vienna, 1997), pp. 238–47.

of craftsmen participated in producing weapons and ammunition. It is estimated that a gun foundry building larger cannons employed about thirty to forty persons. At the end of the Middle Ages, the manufacture of arms in Hungary was largely concentrated in the towns of Slovakia.[20]

[20] On the role of towns in the development of artillery and manufacture of arms, see B. Iványi, *A Magyar tüzerség fejlödésének vázlata a XV. és XVI. században* [An outline of the development of Hungarian artillery in the fifteenth and sixteenth centuries] (Debrecen, 1916).

5 Renaissance and humanist tendencies in Slovakia

Eva Frimmová

The arrival of the Renaissance across Central Europe must be examined in its wider context, including especially the economic, social, political and cultural conditions that were present in each country where its influence can be identified. The territory of present-day Slovakia, included in the multi-national Kingdom of Hungary, was a relatively developed region by 1500.[1] Hungary flourished under the rule of Matthias Corvinus. His reign led to the general stabilisation of the country and to the creation of appropriate conditions for the development of academic life, culture, and art, all of which were key features of the Renaissance.

The Kingdom of Hungary's situation changed after the Battle of Mohács in 1526, when the Turkish victory and death of the young King Louis resulted in the effective dissolution of this medieval kingdom. Thereafter, Europe faced repeated Turkish raids. The struggle with the Turks, religious disturbances and anti-Habsburg uprisings formed the background to Hungarian history for the next 150 years.

When Slovakia became part of the Habsburg monarchy its territory formed a substantial part of Habsburg Hungary; the southernmost parts of Slovakia belonged to four *sanjak*s, which represented the administration of the Ottoman Empire in the region. After the occupation of central Hungary by the Turks, the central offices of state, including the Hungarian Royal Chamber, were moved from Buda to Bratislava,[2] which also served as the coronation town of the kings of Hungary from

---

[1] Thanks to rich deposits of gold, silver and copper, Slovakia provided a quarter of the revenue of the Kingdom of Hungary in the Middle Ages. The Thurzo-Fugger copper company of Banská Bystrica was established in 1494. Its activity looms large in the history of economic development of Europe. According to the German knight Almud von Harff, who visited Egypt and neighbouring countries in 1496–1499, precious metals worth 300,000 ducats (100–110 kg of pure gold) were exported from the Kingdom of Hungary each year. See J. Vozár, 'Rudné baníctvo na Slovensku od 12. storočia do prvého použitia strelného prachu roku 1627' [Ore mining in Slovakia from the twelfth century to the first use of gunpowder in 1627], *Rudy*, 32 (1984), 5, 69.

[2] Posonium (Latin), Prešporok (Slovak), Preßburg (German), Pozsony (Magyar).

1563 to 1830. In 1543, the office of the Archbishopric of Esztergom, responsible for the ecclesiastical administration of almost the whole of Slovakia, was transferred to Trnava.[3]

However, the unfavourable political situation arising from Turkish rule had little discernible impact on the demographic development of the country in the sixteenth century. The population of Slovakia at the beginning of the century is estimated at 500,000–550,000; by the end of the century, the number of inhabitants had grown to 800,000–900,000. The royal free towns and mining towns, such as Bratislava, Trnava, Banská Bystrica, Banská Štiavnica, Kremnica, Levoča and Bardejov, contained a strong ethnic German presence in their administration, because of the notable German involvement in economic activity.[4]

Cultural and educational developments also took place, although with some delays, and in spite of the problematic political and economic situation. During the fifteenth and sixteenth centuries, two modern streams of thought began to emerge: the first showed the influence of the Italian Renaissance, and the second that of the German Reformation and its associated intellectual humanism. The initial spread of the Italian Renaissance, as well as of the *devotio moderna* religious movement, occurred during the second half of the fifteenth century, under the rule of Matthias Corvinus and the House of Jagiello. These processes unfolded over a protracted period, but their effects were limited mainly to intellectuals from the highest social circles. In contrast, the second wave, of so-called late German humanism, had already influenced burghers and the patriciate, especially in the royal free towns, throughout the sixteenth century and continuing afterwards. It was during this period that the influences of the humanism of the Dutch scholar Desiderius Erasmus and the German Protestant theologian Philip Melanchthon associated with the Reformation materialised. Some authors argue that the Reformation itself was a direct consequence of humanist influences.

The Renaissance facilitated the emergence of a new world-view and the reconsideration of man's place within it. The Renaissance and Reformation had an immense influence on every aspect of social life, including the early development of a proto-national culture, language and literature. In conjunction with increasing levels of education, more

---

[3] From 1635 to 1777, Trnava (fifty kilometres north-east of Bratislava) was the seat of an important Jesuit university. After the dissolution of this order in 1773 by the decree *Dominus ac redemptor noster* of Pope Clement XIV, the university, with its printing press and part of its library, was transferred to Buda.

[4] M. Kohútová, *Demografický a sídlištný obraz západného Slovenska* [The demographic and settlement character of western Slovakia] (Bratislava, 1990), p. 73.

schools and academic activity, literature became the most important medium for the continued transmission of humanist thinking.

The beginnings of humanist literature can be traced to the period 1500–1540, and its apogee to the period 1540–1620; its influence began to fade by 1650, a period that overlaps with the arrival of Mannerism, by which stage features of Baroque art and thinking had begun to appear. Literary historical research has identified more than 1,400 educated persons in Slovakia during this period, some of whom were invited from other countries to work there.[5] Even though a large proportion of students remained abroad after their studies, all these groups of educated persons had some relationship to Slovakia and contributed to its cultural and academic development.

The first currents of Renaissance and humanistic thought

When considering the earliest epoch of the Renaissance, it is necessary to point to Italian influences in Hungary during the Middle Ages, especially during the reign of King Charles Robert (1308–1342) of the House of Anjou. At the beginning of the fifteenth century, these influences percolated through the royal court, especially through individuals from Transylvania and Croatia,[6] but also by means of students registered at foreign universities.

These currents began to show signs of promise in the second half of the fifteenth century, during the reign of Matthias Corvinus. His court at Buda became one of the most brilliant centres of humanism in Europe, to which important scholars and artists such as Antonio Bonfini, Galeotti Marzio, Pietro Ransano and Giovanni Gatti were summoned. A famous library was established that eventually contained some 2,000–2,500 illuminated and specially produced manuscripts and printed books.

Any discussion of the Renaissance and humanism in Slovakia during this period should note the brief existence of the Istropolitana University in Bratislava (1465/7–1490).[7] It was founded according to the principles

---

[5] J. Minárik, *Renesančná a humanistická literatúra. Svetová, česká, slovenská* [Renaissance and humanist literature. World, Czech, Slovak] (Bratislava, 1985); J. Kuzmík, *Slovník autorov slovenských a so slovenskými vzťahmi za humanizmu* [Dictionary of humanist authors from Slovakia or with Slovak connections], 2 vols. (Martin, 1976).

[6] Such as John Vitéz of Sredna (+ 1472), Archbishop of Esztergom and tutor of Matthias Corvinus. Vitéz was taught by Pier Paolo Vergerio Vegesius, an Italian humanist living in Hungary.

[7] K. Rebro, 'Istropolitana a Bologna' [Istropolitana and Bologna], in Ľ. Holotík and A. Vantuch (eds.), *Humanizmus a renesancia na Slovensku v 15–16 storočí* [Humanism and the Renaissance in Slovakia during the fifteenth and sixteenth centuries] (Bratislava, 1967), pp. 15–20.

espoused by Bologna University, and was intended to address the require-
ment for domestically educated graduates to help administer the state
and to limit the spread of 'heretical' Utraquist ideas from Bohemia.[8]
The chancellor of the university and archbishop of Esztergom, John Vitéz
of Sredna, and the vice-chancellor and provost of Bratislava, George
Schomberg, were responsible for its foundation. Its faculties were organised in the humanist spirit, and modern methodology was applied to
teaching and choice of subject matter. The lay element and the new
humanist understanding of life and the Church were also applied. Important personalities from contemporary academic life were invited to lecture at
the university. These included the professor of astrology Johann Müller
Regiomontanus from Königsberg (who was critically concerned with the
geocentric system in the work *Almagest* by the ancient author Claudius
Ptolemaeus), his pupil Martin Bylica from Olkusz, Peter of Verona,
Erasmus Adlman, Matthias Gruber from Medling and Laurence Koch
from Krompachy in Slovakia. Their teachings were strongly influenced
by humanism, with interests in philology, rhetoric and natural philosophy
combined with astronomy.

Apart from King Matthias Corvinus, some reference should be made
to his second wife, the Aragonese princess Beatrix from Naples, who
had been educated along Renaissance lines.[9] Beatrix helped Corvinus
achieve his ambition of building up a splendid Renaissance court,
and she influenced court etiquette and culture in the wider sense of
the word. The royal couple frequently resided at various places in
Slovakia, including the much praised *curia* of Bratislava, Komárno
and Levoča or in the central mining towns of Banská Bystrica, Banská
Štiavnica and Kremnica, which belonged to the dowry of the queen of
Hungary.

It was in this atmosphere that *devotio moderna*, the critical religious
movement of the late Middle Ages, has had some impact, not least
through the printing press. There is reference to the activities in
Bratislava of the 'wandering printer', *typographus Confessionalis*. On the
basis of typographic analysis it has been argued that Matthias Moravus
(who had worked in the printshop of the Naples court), his factor or
another printer Johannes Bulle probably produced, between 1476 and
1480, the *Confessionale* by Antonino Florentino and three other small
items: the poster *Brief gegen Kaiser Friedrich III* in which Corvinus

[8] A. Bonfini, *Historia Pannonica sive Hungaricarum rerum decades, IV* (Cologne, 1690),
decade IV, book I, p. 391.
[9] A. de Berzeviczy, *Béatrice d'Aragon, reine de Hongrie (1457–1508)*, 2 vols. (Paris, 1911).

declared war on the emperor in 1477; the *Vita beati Hieronymi* by Laudivio Zacchio; and the letter of remission of sin (*Litterae indulgentiarum*) from canon Ján Han of Bratislava for a lady *Agnes de Posonio*. Whoever operated it, this was probably the oldest printing press in operation in Bratislava.[10]

The development of literary culture was clearly identifiable throughout the country, as posts in the state services were filled by humanists and graduates of foreign universities. A more comprehensive picture would require an account of various individuals in political, cultural and religious life, and of the activities of other institutions outside Bratislava with a rich ecclesiastical and cultural heritage, in central Slovakia (Kremnica, Banská Štiavnica and Banská Bystrica) and eastern Slovakia (Levoča, Bardejov and Košice).

From an early date, a large number of students from these regions were educated at foreign universities, mainly in Cracow, Prague and Vienna, as well as Italy.[11] The surviving documentary material from various offices, scriptoria and *loca credibilia* (trustworthy places) is valuable evidence for a relatively high level of written expression. Analysis of archive materials and of the surviving books of private and institutional libraries has brought forth a host of interesting results for historians.[12]

[10] E. Frimmová, 'Rekapitulácia poznatkov o najstaršej bratislavskej tlačiarni' [A restatement of information about the earliest printing press in Bratislava], in M. Domová (ed.), *Kniha '93–'94. Zborník o problémoch a dejinách knižnej kultúry* [Book '93–'94. Collection about the problems and history of book culture] (Martin, 1996), pp. 26–34.

[11] In the period 1400–1525, 2,105 students from Slovakia were registered at Cracow University: 'Naši študenti na Krakovskej univerzite od 1400–1525' [Our students at Cracow University from 1400–1525], *Viera a veda*, 2 (1931), 174–8; S. Osuský, 'Naši bakalári, magistri a dekani na Krakovskej univerzite od 1400–1525' [Our bachelors, masters and deans at Cracow University from 1400 to 1525], *Viera a veda*, 2 (1931), 226–33. During the second half of 1450, 19,780 students were recorded in the main register of the university. Among these 4,151 Hungarian, Czech and Polish students declared themselves to be of the *natio Hungarica*. Of these, 2,929 certainly came from the Kingdom of Hungary. By the end of the fourteenth century, Prague University was the most popular central European university for students originating from the Kingdom of Hungary. After the Hussite wars interest declined somewhat, but by the end of the fifteenth and the sixteenth century Prague was still sought after by Slovak students (their nationality was explicitly recorded as *Sclavus* or *Slavus*), mainly as a result of their closeness in nationality and language. See B. Varsik, *Slováci na pražskej univerzite do konca stredoveku* [Slovaks at Prague University until the end of the Middle Ages] (Bratislava, 1926), p. 37; Varsik, *Husiti a reformácia na Slovensku do žilinskej synody* [The Hussites and the Reformation in Slovakia up to the synod of Žilina] (Bratislava, 1932), pp. 138–47. See also K. Schrauf, *Magyarországi tanulók a bécsi egyetemen* [Hungarian students at Vienna University] (Budapest, 1892).

[12] J. Sopko, *Stredoveké latinské kódexy v slovenských knižniciach* [Medieval Latin codices in Slovak libraries] (Martin, 1981); Sopko, *Kódexy a neúplne zachované rukopisy v slovenských knižniciach* [Codices and incompletely preserved manuscripts in Slovak libraries] (Martin, 1986); Sopko, *Stredoveké latinské kódexy slovenskej proveniencie v*

Original work was also produced, such as that of the scribe of the Benedictine monastery at Štôla, who completed the work of an unknown monk called Malogranatum. It became one of the basic texts of the *devotio moderna*. A work on poetry, *Laudes artis poeticae*, from 1461, was written by Krištof Petschmessingloer from Levoča as an introduction to a copy of Juvenal's satire.[13] Thus often indirect signs indicate that a strong educational environment had been established in this period, which brought more conspicuous results later in the sixteenth century.

New currents at the beginning of the sixteenth century

Around 1500, various important individuals became active in cultural, political and religious life in Slovakia. They settled in the region, some temporarily and some permanently. The Venetian-born humanist Hieronymus Balbus served the king as an educator and ambassador. In 1515, he also became provost of the chapter of Bratislava, and some of his poems, letters and speeches clearly concern this region. In a text on the Turks (*De rebus Turcicis*), he indicated the magnitude of the Turkish threat to the whole of Christendom. In the poem *Ad Johannem Baptistam Calvum sodalem*, he ironically described the debauched life of Pannonian notables, for which he was later criticised.

Konrád Sperfogel from Switzerland became mayor of Levoča, and recorded local events in Spiš in his *Diarium* (1516–1536). The English humanist Leonhard Coxe, headmaster in Levoča and Košice, propagated humanist educational principles in his writings *Libellus de erudienda juventute* (1526) and *Methodus humaniorum studiorum* (1523). Valentin Eck from Lindau in Bavaria worked as head of the *gymnasia* at Košice and Bardejov. His numerous writings included important school textbooks on poetry and reading, especially *De arte versificandi* (1515)

Mad'arsku a v Rumunsku [Medieval Latin codices of Slovak origin in Hungary and Romania] (Martin, 1982); J. M. Olivier and M. A. Monégier du Sorbier, *Catalogue des manuscrits grecs de Tchécoslovaquie* (Paris, 1983); I. Kotvan, *Inkunábuly na Slovensku* [Incunabula in Slovakia] (Martin, 1979); Kotvan and E. Frimmová, *Inkunábuly zo slovenských knižníc v zahraničných inštitúciach* [Incunabula from Slovak libraries in foreign institutions] (Martin, 1996).

[13] J. Sopko, 'La littérature antique dans les manuscrits slovaques médiévaux', *Graecolatina et orientalia: zborník Filozofickej fakulty Univerzity Komenského*, 5 (1973), 167; J. Minárik, *Stredoveká literatúra. Svetová, česká, slovenská* [Medieval literature. World, Czech, Slovak] (Bratislava, 1977), pp. 235–7.

and *De ratione legendi auctores libellus* (1523).[14] He also wrote a unique account describing the preparations for the betrothal of the grandchildren of the Emperor Maximilian I of Habsburg, Ferdinand and Maria, to the heirs to the Hungarian throne, Louis and Anna of the House of Jagiello, in 1515 at Vienna. This dynastic wedding was preceded by a long period of complex diplomatic negotiations in Bratislava. In his work *Hodoeporicon* (1515), Riccardo Bartolini gave a lively picture of the everyday life of the royal ambassadors, courtiers and scholars, who brought an extraordinarily favourable cultivated atmosphere in the town of about 5,000 people.

Education

The Renaissance placed man at the centre of thought and action and influenced all areas of social and cultural life. These shifts in perception brought an end to the medieval world-view, although this change did not occur across all of Europe at the same time. For the majority of trans-Alpine countries, the complex of conceptual and other phenomena that unfolded under the rubric of the Renaissance merged into the wider Reformation.

In comparison with economically more developed states such as Italy, France and Germany, the situation in the Kingdoms of Hungary, Bohemia and Poland was less favourable. A strong prospering middle stratum or burgherdom, which would be the main bearer of the new views, still did not exist in the fifteenth century. Therefore, the forms of humanism closely connected with educated persons affected only the monarch, the higher nobility and the Church hierarchy.

Under these conditions, and unlike the situation elsewhere in Europe, the corrosive effect the Renaissance and humanist education had upon the medieval order, not least on its rigidity and one-dimensional thinking, was moderated. The Renaissance and humanism gained more influence only once they were linked to the Reformation, which added a religious aspect.

The writing and thinking of Slovak humanists were closely connected to the law and legal thought, but also to the formation of proto-national

---

[14] D. Škoviera, 'Das humanistische Lehrbuch De versificationis arte opusculum von Valentinus Ecchius Lindaviensis', *Graecolatina et orientalia: zborník Filozofickej fakulty Univerzity Komenského*, 17–18 (1985–6), 45–65; Škoviera, 'Antike Autoren und Autoritäten in dem versologischen Handbuch des Humanisten Valentinus Ecchius Lindaviensis', *Graecolatina et orientalia: zborník Filozofickej fakulty Univerzity Komenského*, 19–20 (1987–8), 31–51.

feelings and the development of a native language, which marked the beginnings of the modern Slovak nation.

Legal and political thought

In the sixteenth century, the problem of building a better society, together with on-going criticism of the existing situation, was not an uncommon theme. At this time, the law and legal norms were still being formed. Canon law was in decline, and Roman law was still accepted, while customary law continued to be employed, including adherence to principles based on German law. Efforts to improve society in accordance with ideal or philosophical conceptions (Aristotle, Plato, Campanella, Thomas More, Machiavelli) are well known. However, Valentín Eck, Martin Rakovský and Juraj Kopaj were responsible for embedding them in the domestic Slovak environment. Significant politico-philosophical works, which theoretically considered the administration of the state, the virtues of the ruler, and the relationship of the ruler to the law appeared at a relatively early stage. In 1520, Eck working in Bardejov produced a tract on the administration of the state (*De reipublicae administratione*), dedicated to Alexi Thurzo, the author's patron and future secretary to King Louis II.[15] For Eck, the primary question, when considering the good of the state, was the relationship between the law and the king, since 'legal norms are the nerves of the state'.

Another resident of Bardejov, Leonard Stöckel, concerned himself with the problem of public administration in his collection of the sayings of famous men: *Apophthegmata illustrium virorum* (1570). He mentions '*virtutes politicae*' as the most important qualities of the citizen in the framework of education in virtue, and among them he places '*iustitia*' first.[16] Arguably more significant were the works of Martin Rakovský (1535–1579): first, his text on the division of the population into classes and the causes of changes of government, containing 348 elegiac distichs, *Libellus de partibus reipublicae et causis mutationum regnorum imperiorumque* (1560); and, second, the text on state authorities, containing 316 elegiac distichs, *De magistratu politico* (1574).[17]

---

[15] D. Škoviera, 'Der Dialog De reipublicae administratione von dem Humanisten Valentinus Ecchius', *Graecolatina et orientalia: zborník Filozofickej fakulty Univerzity Komenského*, 23–4 (1992), 73–84.

[16] D. Škoviera, 'Ecchius – Stöckel – Rakovský', in E. Tkáčiková (ed.), *Martin Rakovský a latinská humanistická kultúra na Slovensku* [Martin Rakovský and Latin humanist culture in Slovakia] (Bratislava, 1998), pp. 26, 22–3.

[17] M. Okál, *Život a dielo Martina Rakovského* [The life and work of Martin Rakovský], vols. I and II (Martin, 1979, 1988).

This philosophical-didactic poetic composition, concerned with societal divisions, offers the reader an analysis of the state of society at that time and provides philosophical positions for its improvement. It has a critical Erasmian approach, strongly influenced by Aristotle's *Politics* and Melanchthon's commentaries, combined with a Christian point of view.[18] The composition was unique in the whole Kingdom of Hungary, and deserves the highest recognition in terms of both form and content.

As a monarchist, Rakovský listed the basic virtues of a ruler. He saw social inequality as the main cause of all disharmony. If a monarch is not capable of directing the state, the vice-regent cannot do better. He categorised citizens according to their property holdings, and considered the middle stratum in terms of property ownership as most useful to the state. He emphasised the virtues of citizens and the need for education, which should be subject to Christian sentiments and were also the route to personal happiness. He expressed sympathy for the socially over-looked and the poor, and he pleaded for improvement of their position in society: that is, he wrote about the social question. He also concerned himself with the causes of changes and disruptions within the state. In dealing with state authority, he appealed to the natural rights of man. Although he inclined to monarchy in his view on power, the ruler and the state, he went on to condemn tyrannical government. His criticism of the existing situation was moderate and lay within the accepted framework of moralist civil principles. Probably because *Libellus de partibus reipublicae* was written while he held the office of notary of the Hungarian Chamber in Bratislava, both it and *De magistratu politico* were dedicated to the Habsburg emperor, Maximilian II.

One of the sharpest criticisms of the ruling stratum and court life, *Vita aulica* (1580), was written by Juraj Kopaj and dedicated to Antonio Bruso, Archbishop of Prague. Kopaj ironically appeals to those who enjoy worldly glory and pleasures to come to court, and he gives them advice on how to succeed in this immoral environment. He expresses in verse his view that it was better to be an exile than to enslave oneself to a dishonest way of life. According to him, wealth corrupts noble morals, and lordship has no restraints upon its emptiness and passions; it does not respect the law or the commandments of God.

This admiration for ancient ideals, consideration of virtues, and time-less moralising over permanent human faults is also found in the writings of Jan Filický and Jan Bocatio. Interest in the unhappy fate of his home-land is evident in the work of Peter Fradelius, a native of Banská Štiavnica,

---

[18] P. Melanchthon, *In Aristotelis aliquot libros Politicos Commentaria* (Paris, 1536).

who became a professor at and rector of Prague University. He spent time at several foreign universities and was received at royal and aristocratic courts, where he established many contacts. An excellent poet, he recited his own verses to three monarchs: the Habsburg emperor Matthias II at Nuremberg in 1612, King Louis XIII of France at Angers in 1614 and King James I of England in London in 1616.

It is not surprising that legal issues predominate in the work of Fradelius, as he was familiar with the state of affairs in the wider region of Central Europe. In the existing uncertain situation, apart from war, the only reasonable way forward lay in observing the laws and legality. Feelings of security and stability are anchored in the legal system and in respect for it. Leaders, whether of town or country, deserve respect, as do those towns and countries which themselves observe the law, as he wrote in his collection of verses concerned with description of the bitter-sweet, *Kakokalon h.e. felleorum et melleorum descriptio* (1618), published on the occasion of a session of the Hungarian Diet in Bratislava, and dedicated to the Hungarian estates and theologians. In the dedication he writes that the sacred senate or town council represent a true image of God and guarantee legality in the homeland.

The poem in this collection dedicated to his native town, his dearest homeland, *Ad patriam charissimam in illud Lex urbis anima*, in which Fradelius acknowledges his relationship to Banská Štiavnica, is more interesting. He considers that his native town developed by observing the laws, and that, thanks to this, its representatives secure order and defend property.

Criticism of society is linked with a proposal for improvement through law and legality, culminating in the remarkable poetic and theoretical tract on the good judge, *Bonus iudex* (1620). Fradelius describes the characteristics of a good judge and the opposing qualities of a bad one. He gives good-natured, general advice on what a judge should be like to achieve the appropriate aim. The account or rather the poem is in the first person, with psychologically convincing observations, and it gives a glimpse into the problems of society. The verses also imply some degree of timelessness, including an ironic and critical subtext: the judge's fat belly swells and he has to be careful not to become part of the school of Epicurus in his idle life. The composition also expresses the ideal qualities of the judge, who had to be (at all times) of the best character.

Melanchthon and Erasmus

In their efforts to improve society, the adherents of humanism and the Renaissance soon came into contact with the Reformation. The followers of emergent Reformation had recourse to original Christianity and the Bible. They relied on authorities from the patristic period and expressed an interest also in education and in the natural sciences. Melanchthon played an especially important role here, by attempting to unite the new Church with the old scholarship in his *Loci communes theologici* (1521). His teaching, along with the school reforms of Johann Sturmius, and according to the model laid down by Pierre de la Ramée, elicited strong responses in the Czech Lands and in Slovakia. His students at Wittenberg included a high percentage of Slovaks,[19] who remained in written and personal contact with him long after completing their studies. The Reformation shared many features with humanism, and therefore significant evidence of its influences can be identified among the humanists of Slovakia.

In eastern Slovakia, a favourable environment had long existed for the reciprocal interplay of humanism and Reformation, thanks to close contact with Cracow and intensive contacts with Erasmus of Rotterdam. Erasmus maintained personal and written contact with many individuals from Slovakia, some of whom became his close friends. Ján Antoninus Cassoviensis of Košice was his personal doctor in Basel, and later a member of his inner circle in Cracow. Mikuláš Oláh, Anton Vrančič, Ján Henkel and Stanislav Thurzo all exchanged letters with Erasmus. Correspondence, of a public as well as a private character, was an important medium for transmitting aesthetic and social information, for spreading views and for influencing opinions.

Erasmus's influence on Slovakia has yet to be sufficiently researched, and there remains much work to be done in tracing the use of his works in the libraries of private persons and institutions. So far, only a small selection of published sixteenth-century printed items from Slovakia, from an estimated total of 30,000 copies, serve as an example of his influence. The most frequently found works of Erasmus are his praise of madness, *Stultitiae laus – Moriae encomium*; a collection of proverbs and quotations, *Adagiorum chiliades*; customary conversations, *Colloquiorum familiarum opus*; instructions for the Christian knight, *Enchiridion christiani militis*; and a consideration of the richness of words, *De duplici copia verborum*.

However, the Council of Trent put Erasmus's texts on the list of prohibited works due to his sympathies towards the Reformation, in spite of the fact that Erasmus had never joined Luther. Though he was

---

[19] The orientation towards the German Protestant universities has been documented, for example, by the fact that about 1,000 students from the Kingdom of Hungary, 360 of them from Slovakia, graduated from Wittenberg University during the period 1522–1600. See V. Matula and J. Vozár (eds.), *Dejiny Slovenska* [History of Slovakia], vol. II, *(1526–1848)* (Bratislava, 1987), p. 128.

not willing to examine the programme of the Czech Hussite *bratrík*s (Little Brethren) (who had influence in Slovakia), his views spread in Slovakia and prepared the ground for the eventual acceptance of the Reformation.

The Slovak language and Baroque Slavism

One of the basic features of the Renaissance was the gradual appearance of literature in the vernacular, rather than in Latin. Although Latin was the official language across the Kingdom of Hungary and was clearly dominant in humanist literature, it should be acknowledged that a shift towards national and Renaissance manifestations did occur. The translation of the Bible into local languages became quite common.

An outstanding Czech translation of the Bible – *Bible kralická šestidílná* (Bible of Kralice in six parts) – prepared by a team of eleven scholars led by Professor Ján Blaho, was first published at Kralice from 1579 to 1594. The Czech Bible was soon being used among Slovak Protestants, and its language, called Biblical Czech or Slovakised Czech, was used in the Protestant liturgy until the 1980s. It also influenced the formation of the Slovak language, since it formed the basis for extensive Protestant religious literature. The influence of Czech can also be seen in other areas, such as at Prague University, where many students from Slovakia had studied since the Middle Ages.

Slovak had been used by preachers for quite some time already. Archives and published literature contain a multitude of records of Slovak preachers – *plebanus, concinator sclavonicus* or *sclavus* – working alongside Germans and Magyars in all the more important towns from the fourteenth century.

It is generally accepted that people's views in this period were strongly influenced by preaching, and the importance and extent of medieval sermons are immense. For example, in the *incunabula* period, sermons represent the second most extensive genre. Sermons, correspondence, account books and songs in Slovak represent the oldest written expressions in the national language. The Renaissance and Reformation strengthened this orientation towards the use of the Slovak language. In the introduction to his Czech grammar, Vavrinec Benedikt, a professor of Slovak origin at Prague University,[20] rebuked his compatriots for neglecting the cultivation of their own language, and condemned the fact that, when they have to speak their native language, they must speak it 'half in Latin'.

[20] He also wrote the first work of Czech grammar, *Grammaticae Bohemicae ad leges naturalis methodi conformatae et novis numeris illustratae ac distinctae libri duo* (Prague, 1603).

Apart from helping to shape the vernacular, the Renaissance witnessed the emergence of national consciousness in Slovakia. This process was expressed in 'Baroque Slavism' by the end of the seventeenth and the beginning of the eighteenth centuries. Although the humanists had a tendency to detach themselves from the national framework and join the supra-national scholarly community, they declared their origins in various ways. The concept of nation and national solidarity on an ethnic basis expresses itself as a form of territorial patriotism. Moreover, it is also motivated by a confessional aspect, as innumerable pieces of evidence in the literature of the time demonstrate. Names indicating places of origin were used by many scholars, not only those of noble origin, such as Peter de Réva and Daniel Basilius de Deutschenberg (from Nemecká Ľupča, now Partizánska Ľupča), but also by non-nobles who designated their place or country of origin, usually in Latin. Examples include Pavol Rubigall Pannonicus (around 1500 'Pannonicus' was used mainly by scholars from Slovakia), Ján Antonius Cassoviensis (Košice), Peter Fradelius Schemnicenus or Schemnicensis (Banská Štiavnica), Ján Sambuccus Tyrnaviensis (Trnava) and Vavrinec Benedikt Nudozierinus (Nedožery). Indeed, the enthusiastic botanist Juraj Purkircher also used Pisoniensis, from Latin *pisum* – pea – instead of Posoniensis from Posonium, the Latin name for Bratislava. The work of Ján Sambuccus includes impressive verses devoted to his homeland and his hometown of Trnava – *Tirnaviae patriae meae arma* – in the collection *Emblemata* (1564). Peter Fradelius also celebrated his native Banská Štiavnica; and Valerián Mader wrote a poem about the shield of the town of Trenčín, *Prosopopaeia in arma reipublicae Trencziniensis* (1588).

Various authors progressed from local patriotism to praising, celebrating or expressing regret over the fate of their ethnic group. The sufferings of Slovaks at the hands of the Turks were a crucial and common element here. An epic-reflective poem with strong national feeling – *Gentis Slavnicae lacrumae, suspiria et vota* ['Tears, sighs and prayers of the Slovak nation'] (1642) – was written by Jakub Jakobeus in the same spirit. The personified Mother of the Slovaks laments over the miserable state of the country and the sad fate of her nation, which is perceived in ethnic terms. Jakobeus also pointed to the glorious past of the Slavs and to the tradition of Great Moravia, to defend them against the attacks of other national groups living in the territory of Slovakia, mainly Germans and later the Magyars. Similar ideas were presented earlier by Ján Filický in his mocking *Ad sphettium* (*Carminum libri duo*, 1614), in which he wrote that the Slovaks are courageous in battle and have not changed at all since the time of their ancient forefathers.

The beginnings of Slovak national consciousness took various forms. It appears to have been a continuation of the medieval tradition of celebrating heroes, who were usually exceptional personalities – such as military leaders from the ranks of the higher nobility. Rakovský's *Encomium* on Thomas de Nadasd[21] was a celebration of the Palatine of Hungary, for defending the interests of the lower nobility against the magnates. He is especially praised for his ardent struggle against the Turks. Rakovský expressed his criticism of poets from the Kingdom of Hungary who do not praise such heroes, since they did not inspire further anti-Turkish campaigns. They give more praise to the actions of profligate rich men, who control them with money and influence. Similar sentiments resound in a criticism of scholars and the lack of restraint of the lives of the propertied.

New trends in art and literature

The development of culture across the territory of Slovakia did not progress in a linear way. Over the course of almost two centuries, its expressions were very varied. It was affected by the lack of an academic centre (with the exception of the short-lived Istropolitana in Bratislava) or a royal court. Nevertheless, a number of areas arose with a mature and educated hinterland, supported throughout Slovakia by the Church, nobility, rich burghers and town associations.

The numerous royal free towns in Slovakia became centres of political, cultural and economic life, and significant evidence of rich cultural traditions can be found in them. Such evidence can be observed in the architecture of the towns – their important civic buildings and decorations – in paintings and statues, and in the multitude of artefacts demonstrating, for example, the high level of craft abilities. It is also possible to identify 'new' aspects as compared to the Middle Ages, with 'new' and 'modern' ideas appearing at various levels. Elements of proto-humanism in its traditional form – Augustinianism, *devotio moderna* and dynamic national self-consciousness; from Nominalism through to Wyclifism and Platonic realism – gradually evolved. These tendencies had echoes in developments in the Church, as well as in criticisms of and solutions to various societal problems.

Humanism and its variants – Ottonian, Carolingian, Scholastic, Christian and Utraquist – are understood as a literary-philological current directed towards reclaiming the wisdom of Antiquity. However, the idea

---

[21] M. Rakovský, *Encomium spectabilis et magnifici domini comitis Thomae de Nadasd, in his Libellus de partibus reipublicae* (Vienna, 1560).

that it was only humanists who quoted ancient authors does not give us a reliable and accurate image of this period, since the university-educated medieval scholar was certainly as concerned with classical texts as the humanist was. In addition, the reworked ancient forms often concealed conservative ideas. However, in other senses, as declared by Erasmus, classicism tended towards toward the active, creative and balanced pursuit of life.

This understanding was reshaped by Melanchthon, and his views were accepted in various places in Slovakia. In terms of literature, it was more than a matter of high aesthetic aims from the points of view of form, style, metre and content. Poetry remained the dominant form, but apart from the conventional brief, poetic compositions, inseparable from humanism, it was seeking new ways of representing contemporary concerns, both social and personal. This is especially noticeable in poetry and religious writings. It found expression in the writings by poets mentioned earlier: Martin Rakovský, Ján Sambuccus, Juraj Kopaj, Ján Filický, Ján Bocatio and Vavrinec Benedikt.

Copies of Benedikt's poetry have not survived, although he was the founder of Czech metric prosody, based on syllabic quantity, a result of his paraphrasing and translation of the psalms composed by King David, *Aliquot psalmorum Davidicorum paraphrasis rhythmometrica, lyrico carmine ad imitationem Latinorum nunc primum attentata/Zialmowé někteřj w písně cžeské na spůsob werssů latinských w nowě vwedeni a wydáni* (Some psalms in Czech in the form of Latin verse) (1606). Ján Silván, who originated Slovak hymn writing, has been referred to as a 'poet of human passions and suffering'. His verses often evoked his sinful youth and a less than virtuous life.

The natural sciences

Active interest in natural science and natural philosophy was common and widespread during the Renaissance. Humanists began to concern themselves seriously with scientific disciplines with an individualistic approach, even writing poems about them. In a tract celebrating plants, *In laudem botanices seu rei herbariae carmen heroicum* (1612), Peter Fradelius wrote about the importance and strength of medicinal plants. Further collections of his poems celebrate the cock, *Galli gallinacei encomium* (1620), and the nightingale, *Laus lusciniae ex elegantiarum poetarum flosculis* (1620), the latter collection including verses by other authors. Martin Rakovský wrote a poem about crabs, lobsters and crayfish (*rak* in Slovak), while Ján Filický concerned himself with ants. A large group of humanists were concerned with a range of natural scientific problems, and thus promoted the development of the sciences in Slovakia.

Foreigners also participated, attracted by the natural wealth of the country, including mining. Thus from the agent (factor) of the Fuggers in Banská Bystrica Johann Dernschwam gave information about Slovak mining and metal working to Georgius Agricola, who included it in his work, *De ortu et causis subterraneorum libri V* (1546), mentioning Spiš, Smolník, Banská Bystrica and Banská Štiavnica as important mining centres. The famous physician Philip Theophrastus Paracelsus, who pioneered the use of minerals in medical practice, made two journeys to Slovakia because of its mining sectors, and George Verner (Wernher) published a work on the noteworthy mineral waters and springs of Hungary.[22]

As for astronomy, Joachim Rheticus (d. 1574), a pupil of Copernicus, lived in Košice for some time. It was due to him that Copernicus's seminal work on the movements of the heavenly bodies was published posthumously (1543). There was Daniel Basilius, Professor of Astronomy at Prague University who supported heliocentrism in *D.O.M.A. Quaestiones aliquot ex utilissima materia successionum ab intestato, cum quibusdam philosophicis miscellaneis* (1614). Basilius also wrote various star annuals, minutiae and ephemerides, as well as eight extensive calendars. The oldest Slovak minutiae date from 1615, and the oldest calendar from 1618. These were the first calendars in Slovak.[23]

If we leave aside the religious question, the consequences of the Renaissance and humanist influences are most evident in the development of culture and education. It is due to such trends that printing developed and extensive religious literature in the vernacular spread in sixteenth-century Slovakia. In education, laicisation took place within the framework of various reforms, with strong influences from the Renaissance, humanism and the Reformation identifiable in both the Catholic and Protestant camps. Novel forms of teaching and pedagogy crystallised, largely enduring into the eighteenth century. A network of town and parish secondary schools grew up as well. Spiritual and cultural life was transformed, with progress comparable to that of neighbouring countries, even though it affected a relatively small section of the population. The latest literature was also increasingly available, mainly from Bohemia, Germany and Italy, thanks to close contacts that existed already during the Middle Ages. We must also take into account further

---

[22] J. Wernher, *De addmirandis Hungariae aquis hypomnemation* (Basel, 1549); Wernher, *Hypomnemation de aquis in Scepusio admirandis* (Vienna, 1551).

[23] E. Frimmová, *Daniel Basilius (1585–1628)* (Bratislava, 1997), pp. 49–53, 67–77.

socio-cultural factors, such as changes in the social position of clerics and the social prestige of scholars, in spite of there being a shortage of members of the lower clergy and intelligentsia. At the same time, the Catholic Church's power and economic position declined, while the political importance of the towns increased, a process that resulted in some minor democratisation of society. Many principles, such as the postulates of humanity – the desire for education and knowledge, the desire for harmony of the spiritual and physical realms, the effort to live peacefully and in accordance with Christian principles – were already accepted in the period of the Renaissance and humanism, and positively influenced further generations.

The Renaissance also made its impact felt in art in Slovakia. Many monuments in the Renaissance style still survive in the towns of Slovakia. The development of Renaissance architecture was primarily influenced by Italian architects, who participated in the construction of anti-Turkish fortresses. This brought about the reconstruction of the old fortress at Komárno, the building of the new fortress of Nové Zámky and the fortification of Banská Bystrica, Krupina, Pukanec, Banská Štiavnica, Zvolen and other Slovak towns, mainly in the south. Manor houses (which also had a defensive function) as well as town houses were built in the Renaissance style, which in turn affected the way urban spaces were arranged. Relics of the Renaissance spirit in architecture are still to be found in most Slovak towns.

6　The period of religious disturbances in Slovakia

Viliam Čičaj

The defeat at the Battle of Mohács by the Ottomans, in late August 1526, and the extinction of the Jagiellonian dynasty heralded the end of the medieval Hungarian state. Subsequently, Central Europe entered a new period of history, most commonly referred to as 'modern'. This period was characterised by a range of new political, economic, social and cultural phenomena, which determined developments in the following centuries. The territory of Slovakia suddenly became the centre of the Kingdom of Hungary, with all the related consequences that came with this change. The ascendant Habsburg dynasty increasingly integrated this part of Europe more firmly into the wider continent. For almost 150 years, southern Slovakia became a frontier region with the Ottoman Empire, which represented another world, culture and religion. It recognised entirely different values, unknown and often incomprehensible to Christian civilisation. The constant alternation of military conflicts with periods of peace hindered the straightforward economic and social development of this region.

The fact that the territory of the Kingdom of Hungary had also become an arena of constant armed conflict between the Hungarian nobility and the royal court, fought under religious and estate banners, was also a disturbing factor.[1] This political unrest also triggered wider social conflicts, and had cultural as well as economic effects. At much the same time, the unity of the medieval world was under assault by the triple influences of humanism, the Renaissance and especially the Reformation, which gradually undermined its cohesion. The Counter-Reformation was also an essential aspect of the growing ferment of this period. At first, its adherents attempted to renew the original medieval world-view; however, conditions did not allow them to achieve their

---

[1] V. Dangl and V. Kopčan (eds.), *Vojenské dejiny Slovenska II* [Military history of Slovakia II] (Bratislava, 1955); P. Horváth and Kopčan, *Turci na Slovensku* [The Turks in Slovakia] (Bratislava, 1971); Kopčan and K. Krajčovičová, *Slovensko v tieni polmesiaca* [Slovakia in the shadow of the crescent] (Martin, 1983); Kopčan, *Turecké nebezpečenstvo a Slovensko* [The Turkish threat and Slovakia] (Bratislava, 1986).

goal. This turbulent era, characterised by armed struggle, violence, cruelty and irreconcilable views, was only brought to an end in the eighteenth century.[2] Considering that Slovakia was at that point the only territory of the Kingdom of Hungary under Habsburg rule, these dramatic and bloody events had a considerable influence on the processes that assisted the formation of Slovak society.

The Habsburg dynasty endeavoured to create a united centralised state across its domains in Central Europe. In terms of foreign policy, the Habsburgs remained true to their dynastic and great power traditions throughout the sixteenth and seventeenth centuries. Their continued adherence to the cause of Catholic universalism was a constant source of hostility towards other confessions. The retention of the imperial title and the universalistic claims derived from it were therefore often in conflict with their efforts to create a centralised state that included the Kingdoms of Bohemia and Hungary as well as the Austrian hereditary lands.

A close connection between politics and religion was typical of this period. Apart from its own spiritual duties, the Church fulfilled many other roles, essentially performing many functions of the state. Since it was a matter of struggle for supremacy, individual Church institutions were drawn into it – directly or indirectly.

The expansion of the Reformation

In the first half of the sixteenth century, the Reformation spread to Slovakia from the German lands. As a result of the political disintegration following the defeat at Mohács, of civil war, and of the serious erosion and weakening of the Catholic ecclesiastical hierarchy (apart from the king, both Hungarian archbishops and five bishops died at the Battle of Mohács), the Reformation rapidly gained ground. The Habsburgs indirectly, and one presumes accidentally, contributed to the further spread of the Reformation. In their struggle for the throne with the Transylvanian duke John Zapolya, they attempted to gain allies by pursuing a tolerant policy towards the towns and the nobility. The concessions made to Protestants in the German lands and other regions were also the result of the continued military activities of the Ottoman Empire in Eastern Europe.

The ideas of the Reformation soon spread to the mining towns and towns of east-central Slovakia, such as Levoča and Bardejov. These towns contained numerous German-speaking burghers who maintained

---

[2] See L. Gogolák, *Beiträge zur Geschichte des slowakischen Volkes*, vol. I (Munich, 1963).

close economic and cultural contacts with the German lands. The Reformation then reached towns in west-central Slovakia, such as Trenčín and Žilina, emanating from communities in Bohemia and Moravia. The concept of religious reform was spread among feudal subjects (*poddaný*) under pressure from their territorial lords. For the Hungarian nobility, the Reformation was a political issue: when they felt that the new Church could be a useful instrument, they supported it. That having been said, religious toleration was applied only to adherents of the moderate reformers and not to the radical sects.

In 1548, the Hungarian Diet adopted strict measures against the Anabaptists and Calvinists. When royal free towns were accused in the Diet of tolerating radical preachers, the individual towns worked out their own justifications against these accusations. The *Confessio Pentapolitana*, a confession of faith by five eastern Slovak towns (Levoča, Prešov, Bardejov, Košice and Sabinov), originated in 1549. It was compiled by Leonhard Stöckel, headmaster of the school at Bardejov. This confession formed the basis of the *Confessio Heptapolitana* (of 1559), issued by seven central Slovak mining towns – Kremnica, Banská Štiavnica, Banská Bystrica, Nová Baňa, Pukanec, Banská Bela and Ľubietová – and of the *Confessio Scepusiana* (1569), adopted by the fraternity of parish priests of twenty-four towns in the county of Spiš. These confessions of faith contained provisions distancing the new Protestant religious movement from the teachings of the radical sects.[3]

During the second half of the sixteenth century, the moderate Lutheran form of the Reformation, based on the Augsburg Confession of 1530, predominated across many parts of Slovakia. The majority of the nobility, burghers and feudal subjects openly professed their allegiance to it. The doctrinal and organisational structure of the Protestant Church was eventually finalised at the Synod of Žilina in 1610. Only a small part of the Slovak population in the south and east had accepted Calvinism.

Re-Catholicisation and uprisings of the Hungarian nobility against the Habsburgs

Until the 1540s, the Catholic Church's reaction to the spread of the Reformation had been decidedly limited. The Catholic hierarchy was primarily concerned with retaining hold of Church property, and with

---

[3] V. Bruckner, 'Die oberungarischen Glaubensbekentnisse und die Confessio Augustana', in *Gedenkbuch anl. 400 jährigen Jahreswende der Confessio Augustana* (Leipzig, 1930), pp. 1–67.

strengthening its organisation and unity, which had been disrupted by Turkish expansion and occupation of a large part of the country. In spite of the support it received from the royal court, the Catholic Church maintained its position only in western Slovakia, around Bratislava and Trnava, where the central royal offices, the archbishop of Esztergom and the high clergy moved to escape the Turks. By the 1570s there were up to 900 Protestant parishes in Slovakia. When Mikuláš Oláh became archbishop in 1553, he activated the Counter-Reformation. Much was expected with the arrival of the Jesuits in Hungary, but their activities in Trnava ended in failure in 1567.[4] However, this was only the first stage of the Church's reaction to reform. The effectiveness of the Counter-Reformation was strengthened during the reign of Emperor Rudolf II (1576–1612). In this period, the resistance of Protestants to re-Catholicisation merged with the struggle of the Hungarian nobility against the Habsburg dynasty and its efforts to centralise its authority.

In January 1604, the main church of Košice was taken from the Protestants on the initiative of the Catholic hierarchy, supported by the imperial court. There were also attempts at re-Catholicisation in other towns. Understandably, the Protestant estates objected to these activities. Emperor Rudolf II rejected their demands, renewed the validity of older laws against non-Catholics and banned any discussion of religious questions in the Diet. Transylvanian exiles who had fled to territory occupied by the Turks took advantage of the growing unrest in Hungary. In 1604, they succeeded in winning over the magnate Stephen Bocskay, a former ally of the emperor. The rebels demanded restoration of the old rights of the nobility and the freedom of worship for the privileged strata in the population. Negotiations ended with signing of a peace treaty in Vienna on 23 June 1606, which confirmed the existing prerogatives of the Hungarian estates, and guaranteed religious freedom for the entitled inhabitants.

The Peace Treaty of Vienna was supposed to become valid only after the conclusion of a separate peace with the Turks, with whom the emperor had been at war for fifteen years.[5] The emperor's brother, the Archduke Matthias, used this situation for his own gain. He concluded a peace with the Turks on 11 November 1606 and formed a confederation with the Hungarian, Austrian and Moravian estates. On 24 June 1608,

---

[4] V. Bucko, *Mikuláš Oláh a jeho doba* [Mikuláš Oláh and his time] (Bratislava, 1940); Bucko, *Reformné hnutie v arcibiskupstve ostrihomskom do roku 1654* [The reform movement in the Archbishopric of Esztergom until 1654] (Bratislava, 1939).

[5] See J. Blaskovics, 'Some Notes on the History of the Turkish Occupation of Slovakia', *Acta universitatatis Carolinae – Philologica Orientalia Pragensia*, 1 (1960), 41–57.

he forced his brother Emperor Rudolf II to give up the throne of Hungary and hand it over to him.[6]

The Protestant estates used this succession struggle to strengthen their position. They secured recognition of their rights and confirmation of the Treaty of Vienna from the newly elected King Matthias II (1608–1619) of Hungary at the coronation Diet held in Bratislava in September 1608. The most important point of the treaty concerned religious freedom, which would relate not only to the free strata in the population, but also to the inhabitants of the subject villages and small towns without regard to the religious views of their territorial lord. It was also accepted that every legally recognised Church could freely select its own leadership. Finally, a resolution was passed that prevented vacant church property in the Kingdom of Hungary from being automatically granted to the Jesuits, a measure designed to limit the power of the Catholic Church.

In the political field, the Protestant nobles succeeded in restoring and gaining control of the central offices of the Kingdom of Hungary (palatine, chancellor, treasurer and others). After the death of Palatine Stephen Illésházy in 1609, conflict over appointment of his successor broke out between the Catholic minority and Protestant majority in the Diet. George Thurzo, a Protestant, was eventually elected palatine. The Protestants in Slovakia used their religious freedom, confirmed at the 1608 Diet, to build up their Church organisation. In 1610 they called a synod at Žilina, which organised the Church in central and western Slovakia by establishing three superintendencies. Three inspectors were chosen for the Magyar and German inhabitants of these regions. The Protestant Church in eastern Slovakia was organised at the Synod of Spišské Podhradie in 1614. Two superintendencies were established in this region – one included the royal towns (Košice, Prešov, Levoča, Bardejov and Sabinov) and the other the rural churches of the region. The palatine issued a charter for the county of Gemer, according to which the Protestants were permitted to organise their affairs independently.

The archbishop of Esztergom Francis Forgách protested against this new organisation of the Protestant Church. In 1611, he called a synod of Catholic priests at Trnava and developed a plan for the re-Catholicisation of the area. Yet the victorious advance of the Counter-Reformation is more often associated with Peter Pázmány, who became archbishop of Esztergom in 1616. In 1635, he founded a university at Trnava.[7] He was

---

[6] K. Benda, 'Die Haiduckenaufstand in Ungarn und das Erstarken der Stände in der Habsburgermonarchie, 1607–1608', *Nouvelles études historiques*, 1 (1965), 299–313.

[7] V. Čičaj (ed.), *Trnavská univerzita v slovenských dejinách* [Trnava University in Slovak history] (Bratislava, 1987).

particularly interested in winning over members of the higher nobility. The power and influence regained by members of the nobility who had returned to the Catholic Church allowed the Habsburgs to stop observing the conditions of the Peace Treaty of Vienna concerning questions of religious freedom.

In response to this pressure from the Catholic Church supported by the Habsburg court, the Protestant nobility led by the prince of Transylvania, Gabriel Bethlen, retaliated.[8] In 1619, Bethlen formed an alliance with the Protestant magnates and occupied Košice. On 14 October, the palatine Sigismund Forgách handed the royal crown to him in Bratislava. In 1620, religious freedom was proclaimed by the Diet in Bratislava, which also decided to expel the Jesuits from Hungary. Bethlen then opened peace negotiations with the court in Vienna, and signed a peace agreement on 6 January 1622 at Mikulov. He received the title of 'prince of the empire', and the Hungarian estates kept the rights and privileges granted to them by the Diet of 1608. As a result of these actions, the Counter-Reformation in Slovakia had been stopped in its tracks for the time being.

Re-Catholicisation was re-invigorated in 1630. The religious freedom of 1608 related only to the freedom of confession. In the question of the possession and construction of religious buildings, the principle of *cuius regio, eius religio* applied in practice. When the Protestants of Bratislava began to build a new church, disregarding earlier prohibitions, the Catholic party protested at the Diet of 1637. There were also quarrels in the Diet over churches taken from Protestants and given to Catholic clergy by formerly Protestant territorial lords who had converted to Catholicism.

Once again Protestant nobles rose in resistance. On 17 February 1644, Prince George I Rákóczi of Transylvania declared himself the protector of all non-Catholics in the Kingdom of Hungary, and began military activities. A series of military successes enabled the rebels to set conditions at the peace talks. In the resulting agreements the religious freedoms enjoyed by the Protestants of Hungary were once again confirmed, and these were equally extended to the feudal subjects.

The Hungarian Catholic hierarchy and nobility refused to ratify the peace agreement, and the Emperor Ferdinand III (1637–1657) had to enforce ratification at the Diets of 1646–1647. The Protestants recovered scarcely 90 of the 400 churches they had demanded be returned.

---

[8] N. Relkovic, 'Gabriel Bethlen, Fürst von Siebenburgen, und die königl. Kammern der niederen Bergstädte des Oberlandes', *Karpathenland*, 5 (1932), 23–6.

In the first half of the seventeenth century, these earlier conflicts were subsumed within the wider European conflagration commonly known as the Thirty Years War, set in motion by the famous defenestration in Prague (1618). The Peace of Westphalia of 1648 ended this conflict with mutually accepted compromise that included a religious dimension. The Habsburgs did not achieve their aim of securing mastery over Europe and building a worldwide empire, but they kept their existing territories and retained their position within Central Europe. However, the Hungarian nobility were determined not to submit to Habsburg demands in either the political or religious field. After 1648, the Hungarian nobility continued to resist Habsburg domination until the beginning of the eighteenth century. These clashes followed a familiar pattern: uprisings led by the nobility, who allied themselves with their enemies' arch-enemy – the Turks. In effect, the territory of Slovakia served as the main theatre for these continuing wars.

Struggles in Hungary after the Peace of Westphalia

During the second half of the seventeenth century, disputes between the royal court and the Hungarian nobility in the economic, political and religious spheres led to the emergence of a new anti-Habsburg movement, based in eastern Slovakia.[9] However, the struggle for religious freedom soon receded in importance among the rebels and was replaced by an emphasis on political and estate-constitutional demands. This included the magnates' movement led by Francis Wesselényi, but it was betrayed and the leaders of the conspiracy were executed. (Wesselényi died before the betrayal occurred.) A special court under Count John Rotthal summoned more than two hundred nobles to Bratislava from February to September 1671. Found guilty, they were sentenced to complete or partial confiscation of their property.

Although the religious question was not central to this armed uprising, the court in Vienna and Catholic clergy attempted to use the participation of Protestants to justify the renewal of re-Catholicisation measures. The emperor directed the eastern Slovak towns to return former Franciscan churches and monasteries to the order. In Košice, the army seized the main church from the Protestants, an act replicated in other localities. The Moravian Brethren exile Mikuláš Drabík was executed in Bratislava. Superintendent Joachim Kalinka, leader of the Protestants, was also imprisoned.[10]

---

[9] B. Obál, *Die Religionspolitik in Ungarn nach dem Westfälischen Frieden während der Regierung Leopold I* (Halle, 1910).
[10] J. Oberuč, *Les persécutions des Luthériens en Slovaquie au XVIIe siècle* (Strasbourg, 1927).

Feudal subjects also revolted in response to this new wave of forcible re-Catholicisation. In July 1672, the inhabitants of Turá Lúka killed the councillor of the Court Chamber, John Bársony, and injured his brother George, the bishop of Nagy-Várad (Oradea). These events led to a renewal of religious conflict.

After the Peace of Westphalia, the Habsburgs were free to strengthen their position in their Central European domains. It was at this point that they stopped compromising and turned instead to an unambiguous policy of re-Catholicisation. Thus, the Counter-Reformation was given new life during the 1670s. Attacks were launched against Protestant pastors and teachers, who were accused of supporting the anti-Habsburg resistance movements. Trials of Protestant pastors began in the autumn of 1673, when clergy and teachers from the counties of central Slovakia were summoned to Bratislava. All of them, led by Superintendent Kalinka, went into exile rather than accept conversion. In March 1674, pastors and teachers from other counties were also summoned; about 350 of the 700 summoned actually arrived in Bratislava and almost three-quarters of them converted to Catholicism in prison.[11]

The Protestant nobility did not, however, give up: they responded to the renewed imposition of the Counter-Reformation with a new uprising. The rebels were drawn from the ranks of the nobles who had fled from Rotthal's tribunal. They succeeded in establishing contacts with the French, who helped to recruit an army of 3,000 men in Poland. In 1678, the rebels invaded royal territory and won control of eastern and central Slovakia. Emerich Thököly was elected their leader at an assembly held in Hajdúszoboszló in January 1680. Under the impact of Thököly's successes, Emperor Leopold I called a Diet at Sopron in April 1681. The emperor granted an amnesty and declared religious tolerance. However, under pressure from the Catholic party, the emperor excluded the demands of the Protestants from discussion in the Diet. This provided an excuse for Thököly to continue the revolt.

The Diet finally acknowledged the right to confess religion freely, but this policy was extended only to the free population. It prohibited forcing Protestants to attend Catholic services and the removal of preachers. It also allowed the return of exiled preachers and teachers.

---

[11] J. Kvačala, *Dejiny reformácie na Slovensku, 1517–1711* [History of the Reformation in Slovakia, 1517–1711] (Liptovský Svätý Mikuláš, 1935); B. Varsik, *Husiti a reformácia na Slovensku do žilinskej synody* [The Hussites and the Reformation in Slovakia until the Synod of Žilina] (Bratislava, 1932); J. Doruľa (ed.), *Obdobie protireformácie v dejinách slovenskej kultúry z hľadiska stredoeurópskeho kontextu* [The period of the Counter-Reformation in the history of Slovak culture in Central European context] (Bratislava, 1998).

Churches built by Protestants had to be returned to them. In each county where the Protestants had no church, two places were to be identified where new wooden 'articular' churches could be built (employing only wooden joints). The Protestants could retain their existing churches in the royal towns. If a royal town did not have a Protestant church, a new one could be built, but only of wood and located in the suburbs. However, Thököly did not accept these resolutions passed by the Diet. In the autumn of 1682, he gained control of a large part of Slovakia with the help of Turkish units, expelling and murdering Catholic priests.

Thököly's position was significantly weakened when the Turks besieging Vienna were defeated in 1683. When Emperor Leopold I declared a general amnesty at the beginning of January 1684, several magnates and town representatives abandoned Thököly. The remnants of Thököly's adherents in Slovakia were tried by a judicial tribunal convened in Prešov (the so-called Butchery of Prešov) under General Antonio Caraffa. From March to September 1687, more than twenty burghers and noblemen were publicly executed, ostensibly because they were suspected of preparing for another uprising. The Diet called by Emperor Leopold I in Bratislava from October 1687 to January 1688 enacted an amnesty for the participants in the anti-Habsburg struggle and abolished the court of Prešov. The Diet accepted the Habsburgs as the legitimate hereditary rulers of the Kingdom of Hungary. The Jesuits gained the right to live in Hungary and the Catholic Church regained its leading role in religious life. The Protestants obtained only a general renewal of the resolution of the Sopron Diet of 1681.

The last anti-Habsburg uprising broke out in 1703, at the beginning of the War of the Spanish Succession. Elements of the Calvinist population of the Tisa region took advantage of the war to invite the Transylvanian prince Francis II Rákóczi to return from exile in Poland and lead a rebellion. At the beginning of the uprising, Rákóczi issued a patent, according to which feudal subjects would be freed from all obligations during the period of service in his army. At the climax of the uprising, 100,000 feudal subjects served under his flag.[12] Discontented with the prolonged nature of military operations and a worsening economic situation, many feudal subjects and nobles began deserting from Rákóczi's cause en masse. The imperial army gradually pushed the rebels back into Transylvania. On 30 April 1711, the two sides concluded a compromise settlement at Satu Mare. Yet the political and power relations were not substantially altered as a result. The balance between the

[12] A. Markó, 'Upper Hungary and Rákóczi II', *Hungarian Quarterly*, 3 (1938), 278–301.

Hungarian estates and royal absolutism remained a characteristic feature of the political scene for the next century. The nobility retained various privileges, which limited the absolutist tendencies of the monarch. The Protestants were allowed to practise their religion, but the Catholic Church, supported by the royal court, retained its ascendancy.

Protestant and Catholic schools

The ideas of the Reformation, together with the concepts of humanism, reached the Kingdom of Hungary by means of students drawn from the ranks of the lesser nobility and burgherdom. Attending Italian universities until the middle of the sixteenth century, but also the universities of Cracow and Vienna, they acquired a humanist education. The rapid expansion of the Reformation turned students away from earlier humanist centres, and towards German-language universities, especially Wittenberg. Students from burgher milieus were especially interested in philosophy and Christian humanism. In essence, graduates of German universities returned home having absorbed a theologised version of humanism, which hardly went beyond what the Church demanded or the university offered.[13]

The Reformation-era ideology that spread across Slovakia from the beginning of the sixteenth century sprang up in many various shapes, including Lutheran, Calvinist, Zwinglian and Anabaptist forms of worship.[14] In the second half of the sixteenth century, the moderate Lutheran doctrine, based on the terms of the Augsburg Confession of 1530, became dominant in Slovakia. One irrefutable achievement of the Reformation was that it 'nationalised' Latinised humanism. In an effort to achieve its aims, it directed attention to the education of the broad strata of population, leading to a change not only in the structure of education, but also in literature, music, theatre, printing and publishing, and other areas of culture. The Reformation left deep traces in the spiritual life of society and evoked changes that determined the development of culture in Slovakia until the end of the eighteenth century.

---

[13] P. Švorc and K. Schwarz (eds.), *Die Reformation und ihre Wirkungsgeschichte in der Slowakei* (Vienna, 1996); J. Borbis, *Die evangelisch-lutherische Kirche Ungarns in ihrer geschichtlichen Entwicklung* (Noerdlingen, 1861).

[14] G. Loesche, *Luther, Melanchton und Calvin in Österreich-Ungarn* (Tübingen, 1909); M. Szlávik, *Zur Geschichte des Anabaptismus in Ungarn* (Leipzig, 1897); P. Ratkoš, 'Die Anfänge des Wiedertäufertums in der Slowakei', in K. Obermann and J. Polišenský (eds.), *Aus 500 Jahren deutsch–tschechoslowakischen Geschichte* (Berlin, 1958), pp. 41–59; R. Friedmann, 'Die Habaner in der Slowakei', *Wiener Zeitschrift für Volkskunde*, 32 (1927), iii–iv, 45–54.

Humanism and the Renaissance, together with the Reformation and the Counter-Reformation, brought significant qualitative changes in the development of schooling and education in Slovakia during the sixteenth century. One issue that both sides in the religious conflict agreed upon was the importance of education. As a result, school education became subsumed under ecclesiastical or religious affairs. The schools of town parishes came under the town administration during this period. The town magistracies materially supported schools and recruited eminent teachers. School authorities were established, which, led by the town parish priests/pastors (*scholarchate*), controlled the teaching programmes, approved school regulations and dealt with disputes between teachers, pupils and parents.

Protestant education lacked a clear hierarchy or a unified organisation; the structures employed were wholly reliant on local conditions, the number of teachers available, and the education and teaching experience of the rectors (head teachers). The uniformity of the programmes of study reflected the fact that education followed contemporary educational ideas and practices. The textbooks used throughout Europe also contributed to a certain level of uniformity. The most systematic study programme was that taught at the school in Levoča from 1589, compiled by Ján Mylius. Leonhard Stöckel, a native of the town, compiled the oldest regulations of the school at Bardejov in 1540. In 1574 rector Abraham Schremmel devised a study plan for the school in Banská Bystrica. School plays and public debates also had an important role in the education process.[15]

Catholic schools of the period were fairly similar to Protestant ones. After Mikuláš Oláh became archbishop, education was actively developed by the Catholic Church. The decrees of the Council of Trent (1545–1563) proved to be an important development for Catholic schools. They increased the interest of the high clergy in education and committed members of individual religious orders to educational service. Members of the Jesuit order played a central role in the development of education in Slovakia. In the sixteenth century, they worked in schools at Trnava, Kláštor pod Znievom and Šaľa nad Váhom.[16]

---

[15] P. Vajcík, *Školstvo, študijné a školské poriadky na Slovensku v XVI. storočí* [Education, study and school regulations in sixteenth-century Slovakia] (Bratislava, 1955); V. Ružička, *Školstvo na Slovensku v období neskorého feudalizmu* [Education in Slovakia in the period of late feudalism] (Bratislava, 1974); J. Rezik and S. Matthaeides, *Gymnaziológia. Dejiny gymnázii na Slovensku* [Gymnasiology. The history of gymnasia in Slovakia] (Bratislava, 1971); J. Mátej, *Dejiny českej a slovenskej pedagogiky* [The history of Czech and Slovak education] (Bratislava, 1976).

[16] E. Krapka and V. Mikula, *Dejiny Spoločnosti Ježišovej na Slovensku* [The history of the Society of Jesus in Slovakia] (Cambridge, Ont., 1990).

The method of educating young people in the towns crystallised during the 1500s, and its significant features were retained in schools until the eighteenth century. The majority of children from burgher families participated in Church teaching of the catechism. For those who wanted to learn to read, write and count, the teaching provided by the town's Latin school was sufficient. The children of the higher social strata completed the grammar or humanities-level courses offered at the *gymnasium*. Only students preparing for the priesthood or for university study completed a course in theology. Elementary schools for girls were not uncommon in towns. Protestant noblemen began to establish schools on their estates as a consequence of the Reformation.

The Synod of Trnava of 1560 ordered that schools should be established in every rural parish. The network of village schools in Slovakia at this time was rather uneven. For example, in 1598, the areas of the Small Carpathians and Záhorie, in the county of Bratislava, had a school in almost every village, whereas in the mountainous regions of central Slovakia the density of schools was much lower. We have evidence of 132 schools operating across the territory of Slovakia during the second half of the sixteenth century. Perhaps sixteen town schools and eight schools for the nobility could be characterised as *gymnasia*. The Kingdom of Hungary had no university of its own in the sixteenth century. Until the middle of the century, students attended the universities of Cracow, Vienna and Prague. After the expansion of the Reformation, during 1522–1600, as noted previously, about 360 students from Slovakia graduated from Wittenberg University. Scholars from Slovakia found employment at European universities.[17]

The development of widespread education also stimulated the development of a book-based culture. At first, printing presses and related activities were mobile, a result of the religious disturbances of that period. Printing presses began to operate permanently from the 1570s, for example, in Košice, Banská Bystrica, Plavecký Hrad, Bratislava, Trnava and Bardejov. In 1581, Luther's catechism was published in Slovak at Bardejov. It was not uncommon for noblemen and burghers to have their own private libraries.[18] The religious struggles also had a beneficial influence on the development of literature. The Reformation resulted in a great flowering of religious song writing by adherents of both confessions, Catholic and Protestant. Religious poems were written

---

[17] J. Tibenský, *Dejiny vedy a techniky na Slovensku* [The history of science and technology in Slovakia] (Martin, 1979).
[18] V. Čičaj, *Knižná kultúra na strednom Slovensku v 16.–18. storočí* [Book culture in central Slovakia in the sixteenth to eighteen centuries] (Bratislava, 1985).

by Ondrej Sklenár-Bánovský, Ján Pruno-Fraštacký, Ondrej Cengler, Matúš Urbanovský and Eliáš Láni.[19]

The impact of the Reformation and Counter-Reformation on cultural life

The religious struggles that reached a peak in the seventeenth century also affected Slovak society's culture. Both confessions actively participated in the development of education and culture, which led to a gradual sharpening of antagonism between the two religions. Protestant education flowered in the seventeenth century: several teachers emerged in this period who were to be of more than regional importance; they contributed to the growth of Central European education. Anton Graff, rector of the school at Trenčín, wrote about the rules of poetry for the use in schools. The rector of the school at Košice, Ján Mautner from Súča, worked out tables of instruction on logic for pupils. Jakub Röser, rector of the *gymnasium* at Levoča, published new school regulations. Rector Dávid Praetorius and the well-known geographer Dávid Fröhlich worked at Kežmarok. Ján Schwartz, the rector at Bardejov, wrote a textbook on logic. The *gymnasium* at Banská Bystrica excelled in the period 1626–1637 with its rector, Ján Duchoň.

During his tenure at Banská Bystrica, from 1708 to 1714, the polymath Matej Bel (1684–1749) based himself on more recent, Pietistic views. The plan to establish a Collegium scholasticum was approved by the convent of eastern Slovak towns in 1665 at Prešov. On 18 October 1667, the collegium was ceremonially opened; thirteen teachers headed by Samuel Pomarius from Wittenberg taught at the college. The Slovak atomist Izák Caban and the logician Ján Schwartz also worked there. In 1711, the institution and its property were taken over by the Catholic Church.[20] The political events that unfolded during the final decades of the seventeenth century adversely affected the Protestant school system. From the large number of Protestant *gymnasia* established in Slovakia before 1640, only ten remained by the beginning of the eighteenth century.

The Jesuit order played an eminent role in Catholic education in the seventeenth century. The Jesuits founded *gymnasia* in Bratislava, Komárno, Trenčín and Skalica in the seventeenth century, and later at

---

[19] J. Mišianik, *Dejiny staršej Slovenskej literatúry* [History of older Slovak literature] (Bratislava, 1958).
[20] I. Sedlák (ed.), *Prešovské kolégium v slovenských dejinách* [The Prešov Collegium in Slovak history] (Košice, 1967).

Banská Bystrica, Banská Štiavnica and elsewhere. On 12 May 1635, Archbishop Peter Pázmány issued a foundation charter for a Jesuit *studium generale* at Trnava with faculties of theology and philosophy. Teaching began on 13 November 1635.[21] Teaching at the law faculty started in the academic year 1667–1668. Twenty professors taught there, and about a thousand students attended the institution. The bishop of Eger, Benedict Kisdy, from Sečany in Novohrad, established a *studium generale* in Košice on 26 February 1657. It was attended by about 400–500 students, and a university press was established here in 1674. The members of other orders also developed activities within the framework of Counter-Reformation activity. The Piarists organised schools in Podolinec, Prievidza, Nitra and elsewhere. The Benedictines, Capuchins and Minorites also devoted attention to education in schools. The Ursulines ran schools for girls in Bratislava, Trnava and Košice.

Doubtless the universities at Trnava and Košice became centres of academic life. One of the first professors of mathematics, Henrich Berzevici from Brezovička, published an arithmetic textbook. Increasing attention was devoted to astronomy, with the *Calendarium Tyrnaviense* published regularly from 1663. The most important professor of Trnava University was Martin Szentiványi from Liptovský Ján. He collected his findings in the work *Curiosa et selectiora variarum scientiarum miscellanea*. The first atlas of the Kingdom of Hungary was published at Trnava in 1689. The first topographical work about the towns of Hungary by Samuel Timon also originated here.

The Protestant collegium at Prešov became a centre for attempts to transcend Aristotelian philosophy – Izák Caban (atomism), Ján Bayer (logic). Also outside the academic world there were individuals who advanced scientific knowledge. Ján Lip(p)ai, for example, carried out botanical research in Bratislava. The Bratislava-based medic, Karol Rayger, proposed a pulmonary test for newborn babies. The Prešov physician Ján Weber published the work *Amuletum* on the treatment of the plague in 1645. Ján Peterson Hain and Izrael Hiebner founded an observatory at Prešov in 1672. The geographer Dávid Fröhlich published calendars with geographical supplements at Kežmarok for more than twenty-three years. The Croatian humanist Faustus Vrančič, working in Bratislava, published a drawing of a man with a parachute in the work *Machinae novae* (1616).[22]

---

[21] J. Šimončič (ed.), *Trnavská univerzita 1635–1777* (Trnava, 1996).

[22] J. Tibenský (ed.), *Priekopníci vedy a techniky na Slovensku I* [Pioneers of science and technology in Slovakia I] (Bratislava, 1986).

The period of the Reformation and Counter-Reformation significantly influenced the output of printed materials in seventeenth-century Slovakia. The most productive printing press was at Levoča, where more than 900 titles were published in this period. The second was at the Trnava university press, which printed about 600 titles by the end of the century. Košice, Bardejov and Bratislava were also centres of publishing. Czech exile publishers, who operated at Senica, Trenčín and Žilina after the Battle of the White Mountain west of Prague in 1620, were of great importance in the development of the Slovak publishing trade.[23]

The literature produced in seventeenth-century Slovakia faithfully reflected the social situation. Mannerism appeared in the poetry of Ján Filický, Eliáš Láni and Jakub Jakobeus. The leading representative of Mannerism was Peter Benický from Benice, who wrote poems in both Magyar and Slovak. The Baroque appeared first in religious songs and sermons. The main hymnbooks of the seventeenth century were the Protestant *Cithera Sanctorum* written by Juraj Tranovský[24] and the Catholic *Cantus Catholici* produced by Benedikt Szöllösi. Gašpar Motešický, Eliáš Mlynarovich, Ján Glosius and others also published collections of hymns. Baroque poetry included historical songs, concerning Turkish incursions, Counter-Reformation struggles and uprisings by the estates. Artistic prose, especially memoirs and travel writing, spread by the end of the seventeenth century. The memoirs of Tobiáš Masník, Ján Simonides, Juraj Láni, Daniel Krman and others deal with the period of religious persecutions of the 1670s.[25]

The theatrical arts were also involved in the struggle between Protestantism and Catholicism during the Counter-Reformation.[26] Izák Caban, Eliáš Ladiver, Ján Schwartz and Ján Rezik wrote typical school plays. Other authors of school plays include Zachariáš Kalinka at

---

[23] J. Repčák, *Prehľad dejín knihtlačiarstva na Slovensku* [A review of the history of book printing in Slovakia] (Bratislava, 1948); J. Čaplovič, *Bibliografia tlačí vydaných na Slovensku do roku 1700* [Bibliography of prints produced in Slovakia before 1700], vols. I and II (Martin, 1972); J. Valach, *Staré tlače a tlačiari na Slovensku* [Early prints and printers in Slovakia] (Martin, 1987).

[24] S. Št. Osuský (ed.), *Tranovského zborník* [Tranovský, a collection] (Liptovský Mikuláš, 1936); W. Stöckl, 'Georg Tranoscius, der grösste lutherische Liederdichter der Slowakei', in D. Alexy (ed.), *Ein Leben für Volk und Kirche. Zum 90. Geburtstag d. Prof. Roland Steinacker* (Stuttgart, 1960), pp. 54–78.

[25] J. Minárik, *Baroková literatúra svetová, česká, slovenská* [World, Czech and Slovak Baroque literature] (Bratislava, 1964).

[26] M. Cesnaková-Michalcová, 'Divadlo na Slovensku v období feudalizmu' [The theatre in Slovakia in the period of feudalism], in M. Cesnaková-Michalcová (ed.), *Kapitoly z dejín slovenského divadla I* [Chapters from the history of Slovak theatre I] (Bratislava, 1967), pp. 13–179; Cesnaková-Michalcová, *Premeny divadla* [Transformations in the theatre] (Bratislava, 1981).

Prievidza, Andrej Sartorius at Ilava, Michal Mišovic at Rožnava and Dávid Praetorius at Kežmarok. In the period 1601–1773, the Jesuits organised more than 10,000 school plays across the Kingdom of Hungary, the majority of them in Slovakia. Ján Lip(p)ai, Daniel Mitis and Pavol Alexandri were authors of Jesuit-influenced plays. Only the Jesuits at Trnava had a permanent theatre hall in the seventeenth century, which was built by the palatine Paul Esterházi in 1692.

The competition between the confessions during the Reformation and Counter-Reformation had a range of negative impacts on culture, especially when armed conflict intervened. It often led to the seizure of churches, the destruction of cultural monuments and literary works, and to the murder of priests or pastors (who were the main representatives of culture).

The Catholic Counter-Reformation, taking advantage of the international situation and supported by the ruling dynasty, skilfully employed the undoubted splendour of the Baroque style, as well as all the resources of the state and Church institutions, in order to gradually assert its dominance. Consequently, the social and cultural influences of the Reformation became subdued for many decades.

7 The Enlightenment and the beginnings of the modern Slovak nation

Eva Kowalská

Nationalism, a crucial component in the formation of the modern Slovak nation, was a process that involved the search for and definition of a national identity through which the non-dominant ethnic group could shed its linguistic, cultural, political and social inferiority.[1] In Slovak historiography, the concept of a 'national renascence or awakening' is normally used to describe this process even if, at least from the viewpoint of the theory of national movements, it is not an entirely adequate one. These terms presuppose the existence of a subject entity that, for a certain period of time, lost its identity or fundamental characteristics. It was therefore the task of at least two generations of national 'revivers' to bring this community back to life once more.[2]

At first glance, the situation in which the Slovaks found themselves in at the beginning of the modern era provided little evidence that they might possess the requisite attributes to be an ethnic group; a common language, a collective memory of a shared history or an institutionally anchored territory. The Slovak ethnic group was indistinctly defined through social membership, since they belonged to an ethnic group with an incomplete social structure divided by confessional diversity. During the eighteenth century, and well into the nineteenth, allegiance to one of two distinct and previously antagonistic confessions, the Protestant (Lutheran) and the Catholic faiths, was the decisive factor that determined the cultured form of language used,[3] the passing down of traditions and the way in which concepts of cultural orientation were

---

[1] M. Hroch, *V národním zájmu. Požadavky a cíle evropských národních hnutí devatenáctého století v komparativní perspektivě* [In the national interest. Demands and aims of the European national movements of the nineteenth century in comparative perspective] (Prague, 1996), pp. 10–11.

[2] Similar problems of terminology were also present in Czech historiography. See H. LeCaine Agnew, *Origins of the Czech National Renaissance* (Pittsburgh, 1993), pp. 3–17.

[3] J. Skladaná, 'Die Sprache der slowakischen Katholiken und Protestanten im 16.–18. Jahrhundert', in L. Kačic (ed.), *Gegenreformation und Barock in Mitteleuropa, in der Slowakei* (Bratislava, 2000) pp. 157–64.

articulated. The elements of a common consciousness, the decisive bond for the majority of developed national collectives,[4] had a different quality in the Slovak case: the Protestant intelligentsia clung to the Czech literary language in public official presentations; in writing and in their liturgy, they emphasised the traditions and myths which they held in common with the Czech ethnic group, not least the tradition of Hussite influence in Slovakia. This does not mean, however, that they doubted the existence of a single Slovak ethnic group as a distinct or specific whole. Their acceptance of a foreign language that was, to be sure, similar to the colloquial Slovak they spoke at a time when language began to be considered as a decisive attribute or symbol of a national collective might be characterised as indicative of the inability of the whole Slovak ethnic group to transform itself into a fully fledged nation.

Therefore, the processes within the national movement had a distinctly cultural as well as a social dimension. Those individuals who set about forming the national collective lacked access to an ethnically crystallised upper social stratum, that is, the burghers drawn from the most important towns and from at least the middle-ranking nobility, which limited the scope and reception of their activities as 'national revivers'.[5]

The Enlightenment as the starting point of the national movement

Even though expressions of ethnic consciousness were present during the preceding period, for the Slovaks as for other ethnic groups, the Enlightenment was the catalyst that activated the national movement process.[6] The Enlightenment in Slovakia was not expressed, however, in

---

[4] E. J. Hobsbawm, *Nationen und Nationalismus. Mythos und Realität seit 1780* (Frankfurt am Main and New York, 1991), ch. 2.

[5] On social structure in Slovakia in the eighteenth century, see P. Horváth, 'Štruktúra spoločnosti v prechodnom období' [The structure of society during the transition period], in V. Matula (ed.), *Slovensko v období prechodu od feudalizmu ku kapitalizmu (teoreticko-metodologické a sociálno-ekonomické problémy)* [Slovakia during the period of transition from feudalism to capitalism. Problems of theory, methodology and social and economic development] (Bratislava, 1989), pp. 131–51. On the problem of Slovak intellectuals and their social background, see J. Hučko, *Sociálne zloženie a pôvod slovenskej obrodenskej inteligencie* [Social composition and origins of the Slovak renascent intelligentsia] (Bratislava, 1974).

[6] For the most penetrating analysis of the role of the Enlightenment in Slovak history, see J. Tibenský, 'Príspevok k dejinám osvietenstva a jozefinizmu na Slovensku' [Contribution to the history of the Enlightenment and Josephinism in Slovakia], *Historické štúdie*, 14 (1969), 98–115; Tibenský, 'Adam František Kollár ako osvietenský mysliteľ' [A. F. Kollár as an enlightened thinker], *Literárnomúzejný letopis*, 19 (1985), 107–32; M. Vyvíjalová, 'Osvietenský program Adama Františka Kollára' [The enlightened program of A. F. Kollár], *Literárnomúzejný letopis*, 16 (1982), 55–112; Vyvíjalová, 'Anton Bernolák a

exactly the same form it had been in Western Europe, that is, by philosophical discourse, the development of scientific enquiry and the gradual emancipation of the burgher. Its content, character and results were diametrically opposed to these aspects in the countries where it had first emerged. The role of spreading the concepts of the Enlightenment was not primarily undertaken by the free flow of ideas through contemporary literature, the press and the theatre; on the one hand, these media were still being created and, on the other, they were not accessible to the lower social strata, those with the most members. The dissemination of Enlightenment concepts occurred instead through the mechanisms of complex reforms which, in themselves, contained the message of Enlightenment ideas and affected all social groups. Moreover, individual reforms during this era, especially those introduced by the Empress Maria Theresa (1717–1780), were motivated more by efforts to preserve the integrity and sustainability of the state than by an interest in enlarging the intellectual treasury of contemporary thought. These Enlightenment influences were most clearly identifiable in school reform, for these changes in education established the conditions for increased literacy, raised the educational level of the total population and assisted with the modernisation of society,[7] even if they initially penetrated only to the urban stratum of the population.

However, it was precisely this social stratum that appreciated the significance of education as an important precondition for acceptance into the urban community and participation in its self-governance or as a method of social mobility. During the course of the eighteenth century, a relatively large proportion of the urban population in Slovakia had completed the higher types of schools, or even the lower classes of a *gymnasium*.[8]

---

osvietenstvo' [A. Bernolák and the Enlightenment], *Historický časopis*, 28 (1980), 75–111; Vyvíjalová, 'Bernolákovci v kontexte európskeho osvietenstva' [The Bernolák generation within the context of the European Enlightenment], in J. Chovan and M. Majtán (eds.), *Pamätnica Antona Bernoláka* [Commemorative volume in honour of A. Bernolák] (Martin, 1992), pp. 22–42; M. Hamada, *Zrod osvietenskej kultúry na Slovensku* [Birth of Enlightened culture in Slovakia], *Slovenská literatúra*, 37 (1990), 393–427; J. Považan, *Bernolák a bernolákovci* [Bernolák and his generation] (Martin, 1990).

[7] J. Van Horn Melton, *Absolutism and the Eighteenth-Century Origins of Compulsory Schooling in Prussia and Austria* (Cambridge, 1988), pp. 13–23; M. Csáky, 'Von der Ratio educationis zur educatio nationalis. Die ungarische Bildungspolitik zur Zeit der Spätaufklärung und des Frühliberalismus', in G. Klingenstein, H. Lutz and G. Stourzh (eds.), *Bildung, Politik und Gesellschaft* (Munich, 1978), pp. 205–38.

[8] A. Špiesz, *Slobodné kráľovské mestá na Slovensku v rokoch 1680–1780* [Free royal towns in Slovakia 1680–1780] (Košice, 1983), pp. 125–34; E. Kowalská, 'Das Volksschulwesen und die Gestaltung der Bildung in den Städten der Slowakei im 18. Jahrhundert', *Studia historica slovaca*, 17 (1990), 125–51.

A significant part of their instruction was conducted in the mother tongue, a process that allowed Slovak to acquire a stable form. Since other cultural institutions did not as yet exist, schooling, especially at the primary and lower middle grades, thus shaped the foundation of the educational make-up of the Slovak population.

The modern Slovak nation was not exclusively shaped by access to elementary education in the mother tongue, but also by broadening the educational spectrum to include training in ethics and civics. Even though secondary (Latin) schools continued to be dominated by a curriculum oriented towards the classics, these subjects became the first mediator of knowledge concerned with the principles of natural law and the ordering and functioning of a civil society.[9] Moreover, through this mechanism the number of people who were able to reflect upon the organisation of society and who recognised the importance of a broad social movement increased. By the late 1780s numerous tracts and books began to be circulated in the urban regions of the Habsburg monarchy that championed the idea that the non-noble population had the right to be represented in both public and political life.[10] Even ideas that had emanated from the French Revolution found an audience.[11] It was, however, irrelevant that during this process the national message was not always communicated in Slovak: Latin,[12] German and in many cases Magyar were often used and were equally accessible and under-standable because of the multi-ethnic composition of urban population.

Textbooks proved to have an especially powerful influence on whole generations and were an equally important product of the aforemen-tioned school reforms of the eighteenth century. While textbooks did exist in the pre-Enlightenment era, a comparison of the two types reveals

---

[9] *Ratio educationis totiusque rei litterariae per Regnum Hungariae et Provincias eidem adnexas*, I (Vindobonae, 1777), § 151; the textbooks written by Charles Martini, Joseph von Sonnenfels and Gottfried Achenwall were obligatory reading in the royal academies (the highest level of the high schools), *Ratio educationis*, § 188–189; see H. Reinalter, 'About Sonnenfels and Achenwall', in H. Reinalter (ed.), *Joseph von Sonnenfels* (Vienna, 1988); G. Valera, 'Statistik, Staatengeschichte, Geschichte im 18. Jahrhundert', in H. E. Bödecker, G. G. Iggers, J. B. Knudsen and P. H. Reill (eds.), *Aufklärung und Geschichte. Studien zur deutschen Geschichtswissenschaft im 18. Jahrhundert* (Göttingen, 1986), pp. 132–8; P. Pasquino, *Politisches und historisches Interesse 'Statistik' und historische Staatslehre bei Gottfried Achenwall (1719–1772)* (Göttingen, 1986), pp. 144–68.

[10] J. Šimončič, *Ohlasy Francúzskej revolúcie na Slovensku* [Echoes of the French Revolution in Slovakia] (Košice, 1982).

[11] Ernst Wangermann, *Von Joseph II. zu den Jakobinerprozessen* (Vienna, Frankfurt am Main and Zurich, 1966), pp. 23–48.

[12] I. György Tóth, 'Latin as a Spoken Language in Hungary During the Seventeenth and Eighteenth Centuries', in E. Andor, A. Pető and I. György Tóth (eds.), *CEU History Department Yearbook, 1997–1998* (Budapest, 1999), pp. 93–111.

some fundamental changes made to later texts prepared in accordance with the prescribed curricula for individual kinds of schools.[13] This process affected elementary and secondary schools as well as other types of schools. The subject matter did not depend merely on what the staff were able to offer to their pupils and students, but on what the state recognised as valuable or necessary. At the same time, textbooks were an important commercial commodity, and were a stable and easily renewed source of profit for printers in several towns in Slovakia (such as Ján Michael Landerer in Bratislava and Košice and Ján Šteffani in Banská Bystrica).

When discussing the issue of textbooks the reader should note that their most important function was, technically speaking, to create standards. These were not solely concerned with the definition of the content and the manner of instruction, but also with creating workable standards for the transmission of language. In Protestant schools, where future pastors were being trained, the mother tongue as a subject in its own right, with its own textbooks, had surfaced by the middle of the eighteenth century.[14] The problem was that this written language differed completely from the commonly spoken language: instead, it was the Czech employed in the Bible of Kralice (1579–1588) in which the Divine Liturgy and religious literature were promoted – the so-called *bibličtina*. It was, however, only the Lutherans who were able to accept this form of language as their own, but they made up only about 20 per cent of the population. A form of language that was so closely connected with a minor, and after 1781 a marginalised, confession was simply not acceptable to the wider ethnic group.

As a result of the school reforms, *Ratio educationis* of 1777, the mother tongue was taught in all elementary schools as a specific subject and was analysed in accordance with defined criteria. In this connection, preparations were underway for a collection of textbooks of Slovak grammar, orthography and syntax for use in state schools. By the early 1780s, the first systematically prepared forms of the commonly spoken Slovak language began to appear in print, even if these essentially followed the

---

[13] At the elementary school level Johann Ignaz von Felbiger was a leading authority, and his works were adopted for use among various nations in Hungary. See D. Kosáry, *Müvelödés a XVIII. századi Magyarországon* [Culture in Hungary in the eighteenth century] (Budapest, 1980), pp. 461–2; E. Kowalská, 'Učebnice pre štátne ľudové školy na Slovensku koncom 18. storočia' [Textbooks for state elementary schools in Slovakia at the end of eighteenth century], *Kniha*, 90 (1991), 63–77.

[14] E. Jóna, 'Belove učebnice národných jazykov Uhorska' [Bel's textbooks of national languages in Hungary], in J. Tibenský (ed.), *Matej Bel. Doba, život, dielo* [Era, life and work of M. Bel] (Bratislava, 1987), pp. 133–9.

elements and structures of Czech (therefore defined as a type of Slovakised Czech). The principles of Anton Bernolák's (1762–1813) language codifications (1787) were, however, implemented step by step in these textbooks. Bernolák, who came from northern Slovakia and attended the seminary in Bratislava, adopted the cultured form of the Slovak language, as spoken in the western regions of the country, as the basis for his codification.

The use of these textbooks, which became obligatory within the state-controlled schooling system, was an important step in the creation of a coherent language being used by all the population, although at first it predominated among Catholics. Lutheran schools, established after the proclamation of the Edict of Toleration in 1781, successfully defended themselves against the state, which wanted to control their operating structures and procedures. Lutherans refused to accept the textbooks approved by the state administration or, if they did, they adjusted their use to the standards of the language they preferred. In spite of this, the process of establishing a codified language in Slovakia began as a result of the school reforms that were reflected in the linguistic works of that period.[15]

The crucial importance of elementary schools, the only level of education where instruction was given in the mother tongue, was also recognised by the adherents of the Josephinian model for the renewal of ecclesiastical life, as practised at the General Seminary in Bratislava.[16] Its curriculum accepted the demands of reformed Catholicism and emphasised those elements in the training of future parish priests who had to be prepared to act not only as servants of Church and state, but also as agents for the moral renewal of society. A parish priest had therefore to be conscious both of his mission and of his responsibility for the fate of the souls entrusted to him. In all of his activities, the principle of the purity of faith, morals and ceremonies had to

---

[15] H. Keipert, 'Anton Bernoláks Kodifikation des Slovakischen im Lichte der theresianischen Schulschrifte', in K. Gutschmidt, H. Keipert and H. Rothe (eds.), *Slavistische Studien zum XI. internationalen Slavistenkongress in Preßburg/Bratislava* (Cologne, Weimar and Vienna, 1993), pp. 233–46.

[16] There is very limited material available on the General Seminary in Slovak historiography apart from M. Vyvíjalová, 'Bratislavský generálny seminár a jeho význam pre slovenské národné hnutie' [The General Seminary in Bratislava and its importance for the Slovak national movement], in M. Petráš (ed.), *Slovenské učené tovarišstvo 1792–1992* [The Slovak Learned Society 1792–1992] (Trnava, 1993), pp. 19–40. On the character of priestly education in the Habsburg monarchy in general, see E. Winter, *Josefinismus a jeho dějiny* [Josephism and its history] (Prague, 1945; original in German, Winter, *Der Josephinismus. Die Geschichte des österreichischen Reformkatholizismus 1740–1848* (Berlin, 1962)).

predominate. Nothing in this style of life forbade a priest from devoting himself to more secular activities, preferably in sciences and arts. The cultivation of such interests was encouraged by the seminary itself: a core component of the course of study was becoming acquainted with the principles of school reform, with teaching the catechism and with the principles of modern agricultural knowledge and health care. The cultivation of the mother tongue and extra-curricular activities were also supported. As a consequence of the central focus on theological studies, over the course of almost a decade a coherent group of Catholic clerics emerged who saw meaning in their activities among, and on behalf of, the general populace. These clerics saw their work as including the promotion of the education of the public and the furtherance of cultural activities, especially through the publication of works intended for the literate populace, for example, the encyclopaedic work on agriculture produced by Juraj Fándly (1750–1811).

The language question: the dilemma of two versions of written Slovak

The first generation of representatives of the national movement, who emerged from the environment of the General Seminary (Anton Bernolák, Juraj Palkovič (1763–1835) and Juraj Fándly), established their scholarly interests in the language and in Slovakia's history as the aims of the national movement. Any investigation and codification of the language were understood, for example by Bernolák in 1787, as justifying or creating the preconditions for the development of a culture for the ethnic whole or nation, a process that was itself anchored within the broader framework of all Slavic peoples, but one that also represented an individual ethnic (national) unit. Language still was not considered to be an existential value or symbol, as would later become the case especially under the influence of Johann Gottfried von Herder and Romanticism. Rather, it was assigned the role of a sign that was equivalent to other 'identifiers' (such as tradition, religion, territory and so on). A logically ordered and codified language had to mediate to its users a number of universally valid and reasonable underlying truths. In the ensuing discussions over what form codification should take, various contemporary Enlightenment conceptions of language were in evidence, and these kindled further debates among the members of the Catholic intelligentsia.

There were two fundamental perspectives that would determine the form that the language should take or the style of its codification. The first of these was the Platonic concept concerning the existence of a logically ideal language that existing languages might try to approximate, despite mutual differences or anomalies, through the acquisition of new conventions. This starting point did not reject the adoption of elements from the spoken language, in which were preserved certain aspects of language purity. It was from this idealised perspective that Bernolák based his codification of the language that drew upon an older cultured usage employed by intellectuals, but which, at the same time, also integrated several elements from the vernacular (dialects).[17] On the other side of the debate one found the concept of language as a direct reflection of things. If language was designed to represent their form and variety, it had to develop not from customarily used forms (dialects) of speaking, but from the linguistic usage of the intellectuals who clearly best understood the logic of things. If such usage did not exist, it had to be invented, and nothing restrained the creation of a new language based on logical rules. The Catholic priest and writer Jozef Ignác Bajza (1755–1836) took this route and applied his concept of language to the extensive collection of literary works he produced. These were grammatically different from Bernolák's work, yet Bajza continued to employ his own form of language and issued several sharp polemical attacks against Bernolák.

Thus it was only after some discussion that Catholic intellectuals accepted Bernolák's codification of the Slovak language, but it was completely rejected by representatives of Slovak Lutheranism. Their linguistic consciousness was oriented towards the *bibličtina* as the bearer of theological doctrine and the liturgical language. The position of Slovak Lutherans was strengthened by the acceptance of the Edict of Toleration that had given them a certain degree of autonomy within society and had stimulated an intense interest in ecclesiastical life. The intervention of state power into traditional schooling and even liturgical autonomy[18] strengthened the Lutherans' defensive posture towards linguistic reform; it was, in addition, to a large degree expressed in the traditional form of the Czech language. The connection between Slovak Lutherans and the renewed interest in Protestant ecclesiastical structures in Bohemia and Moravia, where dozens of Slovak pastors happened to be working, became yet another factor that helped to preserve their use of the Czech language. The importance of resolving

---

[17] The language codified by Bernolák is called *bernoláčtina* or *bernolákovčina*. See I. Kotulič, 'Bernolákovčina a predbernolákovská kultúrna slovenčina' [The Bernolák language and the cultivated Slovak of the pre-Bernolák period], in Chovan and Majtán (eds.), *Pamätnica Antona Bernoláka*, pp. 79–90.

[18] E. Kowalská, 'Die Schulfrage und das Toleranzpatent: die politischen Haltungen der lutherischen Protestanten in Ungarn', *Bohemia*, 37 (1996), 23–37.

internal ecclesiastical disputes within the Kingdom of Hungary and the controversial relationship between Lutherans and Calvinists concealed, at least for a time, the urgency of accepting a codified form of the Slovak language across the whole ethnic community.

Inventing a national history

The Enlightenment's impact on Slovak intellectuals' conceptual sphere can be clearly identified in the second important factor required for the formation of a national consciousness: the establishment of a common historical consciousness. The position of the Slovak ethnic group within the Hungarian state prevented the emergence of a stabilised tradition across the whole national society. The institutions of political power were not directly bound to Slovak ethnic society, and official Hungarian 'state' historiography cultivated a tradition of belittling the significance of the non-Magyar ethnic groups that were present when the Kingdom of Hungary was created. The existence of a previous Slavic state unit, Great Moravia, was studiously ignored and tendentiously distorted by the authorities at the beginning of the eighteenth century. General awareness about the existence of a pre-Hungarian independent state began to emerge only with the development of critical historiography, and even then only within the context of a narrowly defined group of Slovak intellectuals. Therefore, historical consciousness was not based upon a genuinely popular and widely transmitted conception of the oral traditions of the Slovak people. Rather, it was artificially created, based upon an exacting and theoretically elaborated collection of views, concerning certain phenomena from the past that were deemed to have a national significance. In this context, Great Moravia was declared to have been a state unit, the creation of which had involved the Slovaks, and the mission of St Cyril and St Methodius was viewed as a source of Slavic and Slovak culture.[19]

Since the tradition of Great Moravia was not linked to an existing system of political power, to any bureaucracy or to the social privilege of its carriers, such as Matej Bel, from the first half of the eighteenth century the history of this entity began to be used to demonstrate the non-existence of the feudal type of state structure in the era prior to the

---

[19] J. Butvin, 'Cyrilometodejská a veľkomoravská tradícia v slovenskom národnom obrodení' [Role of the tradition of Saints Cyril and Methodius and of Great Moravia in the Slovak national revival], *Historické štúdie*, 16 (1971), 131–48; J. Tibenský, 'Funkcia cyrilometodskej a veľkomoravskej tradície v ideológii slovenskej národnosti' [Function of the tradition of Cyril and Methodius and Great Moravia in the ideology of Slovak ethnic identity], *Historický časopis*, 40 (1992), 575–94.

emergence of the Kingdom of Hungary. In fact, all of the above elements were retrospectively projected back on to the era of Great Moravia, a period that was presumed to contain all the rational building blocks of society, such as the principles of natural law, the social contract, civic equality, liberty, national equality and democracy.[20] Great Moravia was thus imbued with all the characteristics that many Slovaks argued were lacking in the contemporary Hungarian state. Works about Great Moravia, or ancient Hungarian history, therefore contained a further dimension: they communicated to their readers an awareness that at least their predecessors had once participated in civic (state) affairs as persons with equal rights.

This idealistic picture of Great Moravia, however, was little more than a historical reminiscence, as it did not bind real political representation to changes in the social order, especially in terms of offering burgherdom an enhanced level of participation in the administration of the state. Their presence within the territorial Diets remained symbolic, and non-nobles continued to enjoy limited access to some minor offices of state. Therefore, as direct parallels with the tradition of Great Moravia were limited, the Slovak 'Enlighteners' began to cultivate the tradition of St Stephen. However, in contrast to the traditional interpretation based upon the old Hungarian chronicles, the Enlighteners' view was infused with new content. In the works of Adam Francis Kollár (1718–1783), Andreas Plachý (1755–1810) and even Anton Bernolák himself, the old Hungarian state was regarded as a successor to the statehood of Great Moravia. The Hungarian state had developed, at least according to their views, by a process of contract with the Slavs, as well as the assumption of all of the civilised attainments of the latter. Early Hungarian society, according to this perspective, did not recognise slavery, the vestiges of which these authors identified in the institution of serfdom.

These Slovak intellectuals had therefore created their own space to justify the existence of their ethnic group, enjoying full civic rights, within the framework of the political system of Hungary. In doing so they had to return to the time of St Stephen, who had stressed the contribution that ethnic diversity could make to a state. Therefore these Slovak intellectuals were sympathetic to those political forces that would reform civic and consequently (so they hoped) national relationships along the lines of a civil society. They had an idealised vision of the state and this became the foundation for accepting a state-based form

[20] M. Vyvíjalová, 'Formovanie ideológie národnej rovnoprávnosti Slovákov v 18. storočí' [Formation of the ideology of national equality of the Slovaks in the eighteenth century], *Historický časopis*, 29 (1981), 373–403.

of patriotism, as opposed to a territorial form. Eighteenth-century Hungarian patriotism thus became an integral part of Slovak national consciousness, not only during the Enlightenment, but also in the mindset of the representatives of the national movement well into the nineteenth century.

This idealised memory of the Great Moravia tradition and the knowledge that their Slovak predecessors had taken part in the building of the state, the Christianising mission and acculturation of their own Magyar conquerors therefore became vital factors during an era when political theory was dominated by the concepts of natural law and the social contract. In everyday political life these issues were adopted only by those subjects who had at their disposal access to real political power. Therefore, basing contemporary political arguments on the legacy of the Great Moravia might be seen as having been overly nostalgic and not much use in the increasingly divisive power struggles and national conflicts of the period.

Its function of mobilising the interest of the nation remained, despite the fact that these ideas were being spread by a very small number of books. As the book market was not fully developed (for example, the most widely read newspaper, the *Preßburger Zeitung*, had a circulation of only around 2,000), the response of readers to these works was *a priori* quite limited. It is sufficient to mention here that even a popular work about Slovak history (by Juraj Fándly) was unlikely to be widely distributed. This was not least because it was written in Latin, a language understood only by a few intellectuals. Even the official school textbooks on history were silent about Great Moravia, and teachers found that their manuscript compilations (in effect, textbooks) also reached a very limited circle of readers.

Nevertheless, the Great Moravia tradition penetrated more deeply into the Slovak national consciousness with the development of higher literature, through the epics of Ján Hollý (1785–1849), written in the language codified by Bernolák. Paradoxically, Hollý's own work became the source of critical knowledge about the past because in creating his work he had strictly adhered to the contemporary state of historical research; this can be illustrated by an examination of his collections of preserved notes and drafts.

Thus, the Enlightenment found expression also in literary works, couched in a classicist style, including, idylls, moralising tales, travelogue novels, and discussions of contemporary problems in the form of dialogues. Their selection was conditioned partly by actual requirements (for example, the defence of several reforms introduced by Joseph II (1741–1790) that encroached on ecclesiastical life) and partly through a reconsideration of the previously one-sided orientation of literature towards religious themes. Poetry continued to be considered as the highest literary genre, in accordance with the framework of the enforced classical model of education. The style of Baroque poetry, however, was not really suitable for formulating new ideas and perceptions. It was replaced by natural or pastoral lyrics and idylls, a type of poetry which made possible the forging of new ideas into modern literary forms. The Italian Arcadia, whose aesthetic programme and forms of work corresponded to a great degree with the literary process in Slovakia, probably mediated or inspired this development.[21] Even literature that lacked a long tradition, as was the case with that of the Slovaks, was thus able, at least in the field of poetry, to convince the public of its vitality and gained an opportunity to be included within the stream of contemporary literature.

The social background of the national movement

Those authors who wrote in Slovak, however, still continued to have a very small readership. The recipients of the printed word were still restricted to a narrow stratum of educated urban burghers and nobles who persisted in prioritising publications in Latin and German. In Slovakia, in addition to the popular local *Preßburger Zeitung*, they subscribed to German and Latin newspapers from Vienna, Erlangen, Leipzig and other German towns. Reading rooms and booksellers offered publicly, for a short period in the 1780s, French publications and literature. As a result, the reading public was heavily oriented towards contemporary issues, especially coverage of foreign affairs, which in a broader sense represented a source of curiosities. The domestic Slovak press, printed in the vernacular, contained limited coverage of regional news reports that were insufficiently stimulating to hold readers' attention, and many Slovak newspapers did not survive for long. There were not enough Slovak readers to sustain the printing of periodicals and popular works on agricultural and economic affairs, even when such publications found subscribers in other parts of the monarchy. However, textbooks, especially those used in schools, helped to propagate and popularise specific methods of agricultural work (the regular fertilising of fields with manure, keeping cattle in sheds, cultivating fodder and abandoning the fallow field system); they helped to introduce new agricultural products (such as potatoes) and emphasised the

---

[21] P. Koprda, 'Il sensismo e le poetiche settecentesche', in P. Koprda (ed.), *18. storočie/18e siècle* (Bratislava, 1992), pp. 59–70.

importance of manufactories, crafts and commerce for the economic growth of the country and individual families.

From the 1780s, there was a limited shift in favour of printed matter produced in the vernacular. The first Slovak cultural institution designed for the promotion of publication activities in Slovak, the Slovak Learned Society (1792–1800), was established at around the same time. Despite a limited number of subscribers, a newspaper of more than local importance was printed in Slovak between 1783 and 1787: *Prešpurské noviny* (Preßburg news). An analysis of the content in this newspaper gives us some indication of the difficulties involved in establishing a market share, not least as most readers were satisfied with foreign-language newspapers. By the same token, an examination of the newspaper reveals much about the requirements of the audience and their tastes as well as their social and cultural values. *Prešpurské noviny* can be partially characterised as a 'tabloid' or populist paper in light of the frequent reports it contained on murder cases, thefts and catastrophes. However, it also offered space for discussions about the need to codify and the form of the codification of the Slovak language, calling attention to the reforming goals of government policies and agitating on their behalf.[22] The paper placed a heavy emphasis on the importance of toleration in the development of society and reported on its manifestations. These included information from correspondents about the new churches and congregations of Lutheran Protestants. The alleviation of confessional conflicts, which had reigned for more than 150 years in Slovak society, was something that journalists saw as the chief contribution and central meaning of the Enlightenment.[23]

Religious themes, however, still made up a significant proportion of literary production, whether developed under initiatives from the Slovak Learned Society[24] or as a result of the efforts of Protestant authors. The significant influence of German Pietism and later Jansenism oriented this type of literature towards a reconciliation of faith and reason, the building of a new individualised and emotional relationship to God, and emphasising the moral responsibility of Christians to shape

---

[22] F. Rutkay, *Stopami slovenského písomníctva* [On the tracks of Slovak literature], (Martin, 1991), pp. 39–51.

[23] See J. Hrdlička, 'O časech osvícených' [About Enlightened times], in *Staré noviny literního uměni 1785* [Old news of literary art 1785], pp. 293–313, republished in C. Kraus, *Kritika v slovenskom národnom obrodení (1780–1817)* [Criticism in the Slovak national revival (1780–1817)] (Bratislava, 1990), pp. 24–9.

[24] H. Radváni, *Slovenské učené tovarišstvo. Organizácia a členstvo 1792–1796* [The Slovak Learned Society. Its organisation and membership 1792–1796] (Trnava, 1992), pp. 18–21. This type of literature has yet to be properly analysed.

the conditions of life for themselves and their close relatives and friends. Religiousness conceived in this manner already reflected national needs. This included verse sermons about 'national' saints in the collection of sermons by Fándly, and reflections about the form of the language in an introduction to a book on meditation by Michal Institoris (Mossóczy/Mošovský). At the same time, it was possible to treat issues such as the practical improvement of the situation of those believers who were from the lower social strata as a part of the wider process of spiritual renewal. The publication in Slovak of a popular multi-volume encyclopaedia on agriculture, or of treatises dealing with basic physical phenomena written by priests, was intended for exactly this type of audience.[25]

More intensive forms of mass communication did not develop solely as part of national revival activities. The first professional and regional associations (made up of teachers, regional learned societies and library societies) were also being established at this time. The impact of their work was often weak and short-lived, but they contributed to the growing realisation of the need to broaden the process of cultural communication. The members of these associations discussed not only the requirements of the national movement, but also more general possibilities for spreading Enlightenment values, such as education, to a broad spectrum of the population. The Slovaks' incomplete social structure and their position as a non-dominant ethnic group bereft of full rights meant that these concerns would remain relevant for some time to come. These same issues were acknowledged by generations of actors in the national movement well into the nineteenth century. In this sense, the Enlightenment was not only an inspirational process, but one that remained an integral part of the national movement.

---

[25] J. Fándly, *Pilný domajší a poľný hospodár I–IV* [An industrious farmer at home and in the fields, I–IV] (Trnava, 1792–1800); Fándly, *Zelinkár* [Herbalist] (Trnava, 1793); P. Michalko, *Rozmlouváni učitele s několik sedlákmi o škodlivosti pověry při obecném lidu velmi panující* [Discussion between a teacher and some peasants about the harmfulness of superstition widespread among the common people] (Bratislava, 1802; reprinted 1977).

8   Slovak Slavism and Panslavism

(+)Ľudovít Haraksim

There is a widely held view that the Slovak people have long associated themselves with a generalised Slavic identity and that they presented themselves to the outside world simply as Slavs. It was only much later, so this argument goes, that they began to identify themselves as a separate Slavic nation.[1] It has also been argued that the words *slovanský* (Slavic) and *slovenský* (Slovak) were rarely differentiated; the Slovaks sometimes referred to themselves as *Slovania* (Slavs), and sometimes as 'Slovaks'. Further, it has been contended that the author of this idea of Slavic reciprocity was the Slovak poet, Ján Kollár (1793–1852), who composed the epic poem *Daughter of Sláva*,[2] and *On the Literary Reciprocity Between the Slavic Tribes and Dialects*, which was also published in German.[3]

---

[1]   There is an extensive body of literature that covers the relationship between the Slovaks and other Slavic nations. These questions were considered at a conference on the idea of Slavic reciprocity held in 1959. The materials from this conference were published in *Historický časopis*, 2–3 (1960). The work *Slovanství v národním životě Čechů a Slováků* [Slavdom in the national life of the Czechs and Slovaks] (Prague, 1968) also considers these questions in the chapters written by O. R. Halaga, J. Tibenský, Ľ. Haraksim and V. Borodovčák. The following older works also deserve attention: F. Wollman, 'Slovanská myšlienka od Dobrovského a Kollára k Masarykovi' [The Slavic idea from Dobrovský and Kollár to Masaryk], in *Co dali naši země Evropě a lidstvu* [What our countries have done for Europe and the human race] (Prague, 1939), pp. 124–47; W. Bobek, *Slovensko a Slovanstvo* [Slovakia and Slavdom] (Bratislava, 1936); J. G. Lochner, *Het pan-Slavisme bij de Tsjechen en Slovaken* [Czech and Slovak Panslavism] (Groningen, 1933); V. Clementis, *Slováci a Slovanstvo* [The Slovaks and Slavdom] (London, 1944). On Slavism and Panslavism in general, see M. Weingart, *Slovanská vzájemnost* [Slavic reciprocity] (Bratislava, 1926); J. Macůrek, *Slovanská idea a dnešní skutečnost* [The Slavic idea and present-day reality] (Brno, 1947); Clementis, *Slovanstvo kedysi a teraz* (Prague, 1946) (in English, *Panslavism Past and Present* (London, 1943)); A. Fischel, *Der Panslavismus bis zum Weltkrieg* (Stuttgart, 1919); H. Kohn, *Panslavism. Its History and Ideology* (Notre Dame, IN, 1953); J. Kolejka, *Slavjanskije programmy i ideja slavianskoj vzaimnosti v 19. i 20. vekach* [Slavic programmes and the idea of Slavic reciprocity in the nineteenth and twentieth centuries] (Prague, 1964).
[2]   J. Kollár, *Slávy dcera we třech zpěwich* [The daughter of Sláva in three parts] (2nd edn., Buda, 1824).
[3]   J. Kollár, *O literarnej wzájemnosti mezy kmeny a nářečimi slawskými* [On the literary reciprocity between the Slavic tribes and dialects], *Hronka*, 1 (1836), 39–53 (in

101

Another influential Slovak author from this period was Pavol Jozef Šafárik (1795–1861), who wrote pioneering Slavic works such as *Slavic Antiquities* and *Slavic Ethnography*.[4] Other Slovak scholars also developed the terms 'Slavic reciprocity' (*slovanská vzájomnost'*) and 'Panslavism', which are still in use in specialist texts today. Those who are interested in the history of the Slavic nations may also recall that the author of one particularly influential Panslavic programme was Ľudovít Štúr (1815–1856),[5] who was an important figure in the gradual development of a Slovak national identity.

While this brief description is largely accurate, it is necessary to be far more precise about the concept of a Slovak identity. The expressions of Slovak Slavism mentioned above cannot be understood without examining how it developed. It is therefore important to evaluate the changes this process passed through, how its representatives shaped the idea of a Slavic reciprocity, and why it finally led to a Panslavic programme that remained unknown in Slovakia and in effect had no substantial influence on Slovak thinking.

Slovaks as 'Slavs' within the Kingdom of Hungary

During any investigation into the roots of Slovak Slavism, one is surprised to discover that the sources demonstrating a Slovak awareness of the common origin of all the Slavic nations, their relatedness and the relatedness of their languages emerged relatively late. This does not mean, however, that the Slovaks were unaware of the relatedness of the Slavic nations, but rather that the sources confirming these links are hard to find. The Slovak experience of having Czechs (Moravians), Poles and Russians (Ruthenians) as neighbours, surrounding them on three sides, meant that the Slovaks realised they were related peoples. These experiences included: visits by Slovaks to these nations for trade and later for education at the universities of Prague or Cracow; visits to Slovakia by Czechs and Poles and contacts with the Russians (Ruthenians) who settled in the east and north of Slovakia. This relatedness was evident not only in their languages, which they understood, but also in

German *Über die literarische Wechselseitigkeit zwischen den verschiedenen Stämmen und Mundarten der slawischen Nation* (Pest, 1837)).

[4] P. J. Šafárik, *Geschichte der slawischen Sprache und Literatur nach allen Mundarten* (Budapest, 1826); Šafárik, *Slovanské starožitnosti* [Slavic antiquities] (Prague, 1837); Šafárik, *Slovanský národopis* [Slavic ethnography] (Prague, 1847).

[5] Ľ. Štúr, *Das Slawentum und die Welt der Zukunft* (Bratislava, 1931). It was first published in Russian, 'Slavianstvo i mir budushchego', in the Moscow journal *Chteniya v Obshchestve istorii i drevnostei rossiiskikh* (Moscow, 1867).

some shared customs that remained from the era before the Slavs were differentiated into separate nations. These experiences obviously could not be replicated with the Slovaks' other neighbours – the Magyars and Germans, whom the fortunes of history brought to the territory of Slovakia.

As known, the Slovaks found themselves part of the Kingdom of Hungary after the disintegration of the Great Moravian Empire around AD 905. Within Hungary, they were designated as being *Slavi* in official documents (charters, laws), and in medieval chronicles such as that penned by an anonymous notary of King Béla III at the beginning of the thirteenth century. Another significant document was the *Privilegium pro Slavis*, issued by King Louis I in 1381 (Fig. 2).[6] The *Slavi* granted this privilege were the Slovak burghers of the town of Žilina, who therefore enjoyed the same rights as the German patriciate. Other Slavs were not referred to as *Slavi*. The Czechs were called *Bohemi*, Poles were *Poloni*, the Croats were *Croati* and so on. These names were derived from the Latin names of the regions they inhabited, or the states they had created: Bohemia, Poland or Croatia.

As the Slovaks had not established their own state they continued to be known as *Slavi*, a term that was the Latin equivalent of the Old Slavic *Slavieni*. Therefore, the fact that the Slovaks were still referred to as *Slavi* (sometimes also as *Sclavi*) was not an expression of any especially strong Slavic identification among the Slovaks during this period. Rather, it indicated their different historical fortunes compared to the other Slavic nations.

The Slovaks were known as *Slavi* not only during the Middle Ages, but also later up to the middle of the nineteenth century, when the ethnonym 'Slovak' began to be used to designate their identity, while *Slovan* was used to differentiate members of other Slavic nations. From the middle of the fifteenth century, after a period with Latin derivations of this word, such as *Slavinia, Sclavonia, Slavonia* (and its other Slavic forms, e.g., *Slovinia, Slovenia, Slováky, Slovenská zem*) were used, finally *Slovensko* also began to designate the territory inhabited by the Slovaks, that is, the territory of Slovakia, distinguished from the other parts of the Kingdom of Hungary inhabited by people of a different ethnic origin.[7]

[6] On the *Privilegium pro Slavis*, see R. Marsina (ed.), *Dejiny Slovenska* [History of Slovakia], vol. I (Bratislava, 1986), pp. 344–5.
[7] O. R. Halaga, 'Slovanství na Slovensku v 15.–16. století' [Slavdom in Slovakia in the fifteenth and sixteenth centuries], in V. Šťastný (ed.), *Slovanství v národním životě Čechů a Slováků* [Slavdom in the national life of the Czechs and Slovaks] (Prague, 1968), pp. 57–8.

The Slavic world and Slavdom as represented in Slovak literary texts from the sixteenth to the eighteenth centuries

One of the oldest sources in which Slovak ideas on Slavdom and the 'Slavic world' are identifiable is a work concerning the Kingdom of Hungary written by Peter de Rewa (Révay) (1568–1622).[8] This important local dignitary, who originated from Turiec, a county in central Slovakia, highlighted the wide distribution of the *lingua slavica seu ilyrica* (Slavic or Illyrian language), which he considered to be comparable in glory to the Latin language. Rewa also wrote about the origins of the Slavs. As was common at the time, he regarded the Slavs as descendants of Japheth, one of the sons of Noah. Allegedly, Alexander the Great had rewarded the Slavs for their services by allowing them to settle in an extensive region between the Adriatic and Baltic seas.

It is also possible to extract from Rewa's works how the scholarly world of the time viewed the Slavs more generally. Rewa regarded the Slovaks as part of a larger Slavdom, and he clearly attributed to them all the characteristics regularly attributed to the Slavs. The information Rewa utilised about the Slavs in his work was essentially the same as could be found in contemporary works by scholars from other Slavic nations. This fact illustrates that Slovak scholars disseminated similar information about Slavdom as did scholarly circles in other Slavic nations. This repetition continued well into the seventeenth century; nearly all works about the Slavs by Slovak authors utilised very similar information about the greatness and numbers of the Slavs, the extent of their area of settlement, their common origin, relatedness and (occasional) feeling of solidarity.

There were some authors, however, who did not limit themselves to replicating these views. One of them was Daniel Synapius-Horčička (1640–1688). In the introduction to his collection of proverbs and sayings, he noted that the 'Slavic language' had been made a liturgical language (868), and that Emperor Charles IV (1316–1378) had advised the German princes to learn this language.[9] He also recalled the virtues of the Slavs, such as their talents, warm hospitality and capacity for hard work. Another Slovak writer, Ján Fischer-Piscatoris (1672–1720), wrote

---

[8] *De monarchia et sacra corona Hungariae* (Frankfurt am Main, 1659), p. 147; R. Brtáň, *Barokový slavizmus* [Baroque Slavism] (Liptovský Mikuláš, 1999), pp. 67–72; J. Tibenský, 'Predstavy o Slovanstve na Slovensku v 17. a 18. storočí' [Ideas about Slavdom in Slovakia in the seventeenth and eighteenth centuries], *Historický časopis*, 8 (1960), 206–19.

[9] *Neoforum latino-slavonicum* (Leszno, 1679).

about the origins and usefulness of the 'Slavic language';[10] he made references to its wide geographical distribution and its practical usefulness in maintaining commercial contacts with Russia. A number of other Slovak scholars from this period also wrote about the Slavs in a similar vein.

However, it is typical of the Slovak Slavism of this period that none of these Slovak scholars reached any firm conclusions on the matter of Slavdom, in direct contrast to the Croatian Catholic priest Juraj Križanič (c. 1618–1683), whose views anticipated those of Jan Kollár.[11] Almost two centuries before Kollár, Križanič pointed out the importance of Russia for the Slavic nations. He expected Russia, as the only independent Slavic state, to work for the greater Slavic good. Interestingly, this concept was not apparent in Slovak Slavism from this period, which also lacked an active Slavic feeling, in spite of the fact that the works of Slovak scholars constantly referred to the common origins and greatness of the Slavs as a whole.

Surprisingly, nor did these ideas appear in the works of Daniel Krman (1663–1740), one of the most productive Slovak writers of the age, who was well known as the author of several Slavic works that evoked a significant response among his contemporaries. Thus he followed the army of King Charles XII of Sweden campaigning through Russia, Poland, Belarus and Ukraine. He came into contact with the Slavic populations in these countries, but he showed no sign of sympathy towards them. His travel diary, regarded as one of the best works of this genre in the history of Slovak literature, testifies to this fact. Krman did not have a good word to say even about the Hetman of Ukraine, Ivan Mazepa, in spite of spending a number of days in close contact with him and being in receipt of a safe conduct from him. Krman included the document in his book, but only in order to make it clear that the Ukrainian and Slovak languages were similar to each other.[12]

By examining the writings of Slovak authors from the seventeenth century and the beginning of the eighteenth, one can conclude that they were very impressed by the extent and size of Slavic habitats, not least because their eastern settlements extended up to the borders of China. However, it is characteristic that Slovak scholars never mentioned that

---

[10] *De origine, jure ac utilitate linguae slavonicae* (Wittenberg, 1697); Tibenský, 'Predstavy', 209; A. A. Baník, *Novšie údaje na poznanie J. B. Magina, jeho dielo i doby* [New information about J. B. Magin, his work and times] (Trnava, 1937), pp. 104–10.

[11] See Brtáň, *Barokový slavizmus*, pp. 218–22.

[12] D. Krman, *Itinerarium/Cestovný denník z rokov 1708–1709* [Itinerary/travel diary from 1708 to 1709] (Bratislava, 1969). The Latin text of the diary is published on pp. 305–509; the safe conduct from Mazepa is on p. 449.

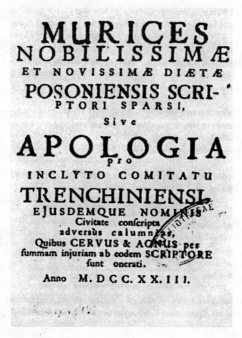

Figure 3 Title page of J. B. Magin's *Apologia* (1723)

the 'Slavic nation', as they called the Slavs, was neither politically nor otherwise united. Neither did they comment that its subjects lived in different states and belonged to different confessions, and that disagreements often led to conflicts. Clearly, this did not accord with the idealised image of Slavdom, or the concept of a 'Slavic nation', which they wished to have and promote.

A similar picture of Slavdom can be identified through the authors of the 'defences of the Slovaks' that began to appear during the early decades of the eighteenth century. These 'apologies' were texts in which Slovak scholars defended the autochthonous character and the equal rights of the Slovaks in the Kingdom of Hungary. These texts could be labelled as being broadly Slavic and contained many of the points mentioned above. This was certainly the case of the defence written by Ján Baltazár Magin (1681–1735) (Fig. 3).[13]

---

[13] J. Baltazar Magin, *Murices nobilissime et novissimae diaetae posoniensis scriptori sparsi, sive apologia pro inclyto comitatu Trenchiniensi* (1728); A. A. Baník, *Ján Baltazár Magin a jeho politická, národná a kultúrna obrana Slovákov roku 1728* [Ján Baltazár Magin and his political, national and cultural defence of the Slovaks in 1728] (Trnava, 1936).

In this period, however, ideas about the nature of a 'Slavic nation' began to change. Some writers did not yet recognise it as a homogeneous ethnic mass, but rather as a conglomerate of tribes, that is Czechs, Poles, Russians, Croats and of course the Slovaks. At this stage the Slovaks were regarded as another tribe, or as a component of the Czechoslovak tribe.[14] This tribal interpretation of the 'Slavic nation' can be found in the works of Matej Bel (1684–1749) and in the introduction to the Slavic grammar produced by Pavol Doležal (1700–1788).[15]

In response to this tribal conception of the 'Slavic nation', the Slovaks entered a new phase of their national development, subsequently known as the 'national renascence/awakening'. A new understanding of the term 'Slavic nation' was emerging, combined with older ideas about the 'Slavic world', which did not always correspond to reality.

The written output from the beginnings of this nation-forming process was extensive – works with scholarly ambitions and diverse articles and poems by Slovak authors. They clearly illustrate that the Slovaks regarded themselves as either part of the 'Slavic nation' or as one of its numerous tribes. One major difference in these interpretations was that Catholic scholars regarded the Slovaks as a separate tribe with its own language (dialect), while the Slovak Protestants considered themselves as part of a 'Czechoslovak tribe', that is, a common tribe of both Czechs and Slovaks, with Czech as their common written language.

This division of views about the identity of the Slovaks was finally overcome in the 1840s. But this issue did not prevent the members of the two camps from jointly celebrating 'dear Slavia', declaring their allegiance to Slavdom by writing of its greatness, as Slovak scholars had done previously. This Slavic element appeared in the poetry of Bohuslav Tablic (1738–1802) and Ján Hollý, and was strongly represented in the historical work of Juraj Papánek (1738–1802) and the linguistic works of Anton Bernolák, including his *Gramatica slavica*, which codified Slovak as a written language.[16]

Consequently, the Slovaks were by this stage in the cultural development conscious of being Slavs, but they lacked any active pan-Slavic feelings. This factor was especially apparent in their attitude to the

---

[14] Tibenský, 'Predstavy', 211, 217–18.

[15] Pavol Doležal, *Grammatica slavo-bohemica* (Bratislava, 1746).

[16] See B. Tablic, *Poezye, díl druhý* [Poetry, part two] (Vacov, 1806), pp. 119–20, and Tablic, *Poezye, díl čtvrtý* [Poetry, part four] (Vacov, 1812), pp. 13–26; Jan Hollý, *Básně Jana Hollého* [Poems of Jan Hollý] (Buda, 1841), 'Žalospewi' [Elegies], pp. 111–38, and 'Pohľed na Slowakow' [A look at the Slovaks], pp. 191–7; J. Papánek, *Historia gentis Slavae. De regno regibusque Slavorum, Quinque Ecclesiae* (Pécs, 1780); A. Bernolák, *Gramatica slavica* (Posonium [Bratislava], 1790).

various partitions of Poland in 1772, 1791 and 1794, events in which Slavic Russia was a significant protagonist. Although Slovak intellectuals were well aware of these developments, they ignored them.

Slavic reciprocity according to Kollár and Šafárik

A new phase in the development of Slovak Slavism began soon after the Napoleonic Wars, when an unprecedented rise in Slavic consciousness was clearly observable. The successes of Russia in the wars against Napoleon, the influence of the ideas of Herder on the glorious future of the Slavs and the teaching of Hegel on the developmental stages of history had an electrifying effect in Slovakia. The views of Šafárik and Kollár were to a large extent shaped by this environment, one that was saturated with Slavic emotions. These two authors became the leading ideologists of Slavic reciprocity. Their conceptions of a Slavic feeling intensified during their studies at Jena University (Šafárik in 1815 and Kollár in 1817), where they learned about contemporary German nationalism and German efforts to achieve national unity. They adopted the idea of national unity and, after returning home, applied it to the Slavic situation. A crucial part of this process was the rejection of the additional fragmentation of the 'Slavic nation' into tribes, an issue that directly concerned the Slovaks.

In spite of his Slovak origins, the rigorous Kollár was not willing to recognise Slovaks as a separate tribe, although Bernolák's group of Catholic Slovak intellectuals had already done so at the end of the eighteenth century. Preserving the unity of the Slavs or the 'Slavic nation' was nevertheless a central concern for some Slovak scholars, as demonstrated by the attempts by Ján Herkel' (1786–after 1842) to produce a universal Slavic grammar.[17] Today this grammar is of interest to scholars because it contains the first reference by Herkel' to the expression 'Panslavism'. He understood the term to mean 'concerning all the Slavs', which was quite different to the meaning attached to it at a later date.

It is now quite clear that the most important expression of Slovak Slavism in the period of the Slovak national revival was the idea of Slavic reciprocity, worked out by Kollár in his treatise *On the Literary Reciprocity Between the Slavic Tribes and Dialects* (1836). According to Kollár, this work was designed as a programme for co-operation between the Slavic nations; it also contained the ideas of Šafárik, who thus may be

---

[17] Ján Herkel', *Elementa universalis linguae slavicae* (Buda, 1826).

regarded as its co-author. Šafárik also contributed to the birth of the idea of Slavic reciprocity with his work *Dejiny slovanských jazykov a literatúry všetkých nárečí* (The history of Slavic languages and literature of all the dialects) (1826), in which he revealed the spiritual richness of the Slavic world – little known even to the Slavs. These two Slovaks – deemed to have originally developed the concept of Slavic reciprocity – also propagated it zealously.

As soon as the idea of a literary Slavic reciprocity had become established, it was immediately labelled as being 'Panslavic' even though Kollár had clearly stated in the introduction to *On the Literary Reciprocity* that he had no political agenda. He went on to state that the idea of Slavic reciprocity 'does not involve the political union of all the Slavs', but rather the 'participation of all the national branches in the spiritual formation of their nation', that is, the participation of all the Slavic tribes in the spiritual formation of the Slavic nation, 'by the reciprocal buying and reading in all the Slavic dialects published texts and books'. Kollár explained that 'every dialect has to draw new strength from the others, so that it rejuvenates, enriches and educates itself without encroaching on the other and being encroached, [it has] to maintain its own free sphere among others'. 'In this reciprocity', continued Kollár, 'all tribes and dialects remain unshaken in their old places, but foster through cross-fertilisation and emulation the flowering of a common national literature.' There was no political subtext in this programme for a literary and Slavic reciprocity. The ways to achieve this aim, as Kollár sets out in the separate chapter 'Ways and means of this reciprocity', were entirely peaceful.

It was somewhat surprising that outside the borders of the 'Slavic world', this programme was seen as a serious threat that could bring Europe to the brink of destruction, a threat not seen since the Mongol invasions. This assertion was even more surprising in view of the fact that, a year after its publication in Czech, Kollár's treatise appeared in German. Thus it became accessible to non-Slavic peoples with an interest in the subject. Certain sonnets from Kollár's *Slávy dcera* (Fig. 4) condemned 'envious Teutonia' and challenged the Slavs to awake from their lethargy or to turn to Russia, the 'mighty oak' that doggedly resisted bad times; these were known in the non-Slavic environment and sounded disturbing to non-Slavic ears. On the other hand, they failed to notice that in the same sonnets Kollár pointed out that when 'you call out Slav', the word 'human being' should be the echo, and that 'a person worthy of his own freedom values the freedom of all', while 'a person who holds slaves is himself a slave'. In this sense, the ideas contained in Kollár's sonnets were commensurate with the

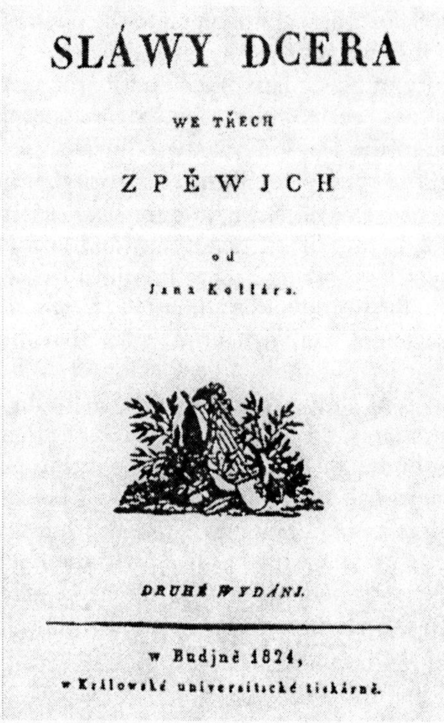

SLÁWY DCERA

WE TŘECH

Z P Ě W J C H

od

Jana Kollára.

DRUHÉ WYDÁNÍ.

w Budjně 1824,
w Králowské universitické tiskárně.

Figure 4 Title page of J. Kollár's *Sláwy dcera* (Sláva's daughter) (1824)

humanitarian thinking of the era. It is clear that these ideas equally belong to the conceptual arsenal of Slovak Slavism and must be taken into account.

The programme of Slavic reciprocity demanded co-operation between the Slavic nations, that is, the development of literary and cultural co-operation. This eventually happened, but to a much lesser extent than Kollár generally expected. There were good contacts between Slovaks and Croats and Serbs who lived in the Kingdom of Hungary. These relationships were enhanced by the fact that many southern Slavs studied at the Protestant Lyceum in Bratislava (Preßburg, Prešporok), an institution that contained predominantly Slovak students. There were also close relations with the Czechs, whose language was used by Protestant Slovaks in both literature and liturgy.

It is rather surprising that contacts with Russia, the 'mighty oak' shielding the Slavic nations according to Kollár, were rare until the end of the 1830s, even though many Slovaks retained pro-Russian sentiments from the Napoleonic period. Russia's prestige among Slovaks was seriously damaged, however, by the harsh suppression of the Polish uprising of 1831–1832.

The 'fratricidal conflict', as this conflict between the Poles and Russians was known, also affected the creators of the idea of a Slavic reciprocity, Kollár and Šafárik. In particular, Šafárik strongly condemned the Russian intervention against the Poles, and even questioned whether the Russians could really be regarded as Slavs.[18] Young Slovaks studying at the Lyceum in Bratislava also reacted sharply to events in Poland. They turned away from Russia to befriend the Poles, and this situation continued until the end of the 1830s. Russian intervention against the Poles triggered a minor crisis in Slovak Slavism, which was overcome only at the beginning of the 1840s, when a new generation of Slovak writers and thinkers emerged. This grouping came to be known as the 'generation of Štúr' after its most important representative, Ľudovít Štúr (1815–1856).

Štúr's notion of Slavdom

The generation of thinkers entering Slovak intellectual life at the end of the 1830s viewed Slavdom and Slavic reciprocity differently from Kollár and Šafárik. The members of this new generation already possessed a highly developed Slavic consciousness, but they held the view that they should not subordinate the interests of their own 'tribe', i.e. nation, to the interests of the Slavs in general, as Kollár had demanded. They also argued that there would be greater gains for Slavdom and Slavic reciprocity if all Slavs acted in the interests of their own tribe, i.e. nation. This was also the view of the young writer Jozef Miloslav Hurban (1817–1888), a point confirmed by an entry in his notebook from 1838, stating that the Slovaks must preserve their tribal identity. They should first and foremost regard themselves as Slovaks, he argued, as only on this basis could the Slovaks regard themselves as Slavs.[19] Clearly this argument could also be applied to the other Slavic tribes and nations.

[18] V. Žáček, Z revolučných a politických poľsko-slovenských stykov v dobe predmarcovej [From the revolutionary and political Polish–Slovak contacts in the pre-March period] (Bratislava, 1965), p. 45; Ľ. Haraksim, 'Slovanská idea v obrozenské ideologii Slováků' [The Slavic idea in the revivalist ideology of the Slovaks], in V. Šesták (ed.), Slovanství v národním životě Čechů a Slováků [Slavdom in the national life of Czechs and Slovaks] (Prague, 1968), p. 140.

[19] Ľ. Haraksim, 'Od Kollárova slovanství k slovenství (1835–1848)' [From Kollár's Slavdom to Slovakdom (1835–1848)], in Šesták (ed.), Slovanství, pp. 159–61.

This generation of Slovaks also viewed differently the inherent possibilities of the wider world of Slavdom, and, in contrast to Kollár, they did not exclude the prospect of a closer union of all the Slavic tribes, not just a 'spiritual union'. Equally important was the issue of the 'sovereignty' of one Slavic nation over other Slavs, from which it was only a short step to the recognition of the 'sovereignty' of tsarist Russia over all Slavs.

Štúr shared this perspective. His views were influenced not only by the works of Herder and Hegel about the Slavs, which intensively occupied his mind, but also by Slavophile literature more generally, which he had studied.[20] Obviously, the roots of his pro-Russian and Panslavic views, as expressed at the beginning of the 1850s in a pamphlet written in German, *Das Slawenthum und die Welt der Zukunft* (Slavdom and the world of the future), reached back to this earlier period. However, it is necessary to note that even before Štúr expressed these views, he had criticised the oppression of Slavic nations under Russian domination.

In this period, when his position in Slovak national life was already recognised, that is, in the 1840s, Štúr criticised tsarist autocracy. However, this did not prevent him from being a Russophile and from cultivating sympathy towards the Russians and Russia, from which he, like Kollár, expected much in return. Russian scholars and Slavists who visited Slovakia from the end of the 1830s also influenced Štúr's Russophile feelings. Some of these Russian specialists stayed in Slovakia for protracted lengths of time, learnt about the aspirations of Slovak national life, and lent moral support to the emancipation efforts of the Slovaks. They aroused the vague hope that Russia might one day help the Slovaks. In fact, Russia had no intention of giving official support to the emancipation efforts of the Western Slavs, although the Slovaks had no way of knowing this. The tsar's minister of education at that time issued a directive that expressly forbade the spreading of sympathy for the Western Slavs, on the grounds that the latter were said to be a 'world apart', as much as Russia was a 'world apart' from them.

Pro-Russian sentiments were undoubtedly in evidence in Slovak society in the 1840s, but some members of Štúr's group rejected the idea of the 'sovereignty' of one Slavic nation over all others, as well as the Russophile views of their colleagues. These members of Štúr's

[20] J. V. Ormis, *Súčasníci o L'udovítovi Štúrovi* [Contemporaries on L'udovít Štúr] (Bratislava, 1955), p. 319; V. Matula, 'Štúr a Slovanstvo' [Štúr and Slavdom], in V. Matula (ed.), *L'udovít Štúr. Život a dielo 1815–1856* [L'udovít Štúr. Life and work 1815–1856] (Bratislava, 1956), pp. 374, 377; Haraksim, 'Od Kollárova slovanství k slovenství', pp. 163–4.

generation considered it superfluous to highlight the size and strength of the 'Slavic world' since they noted that this aroused concern among non-Slavic nations. According to these Slovaks, the future of the Slavs was dependent not merely on their strength and power, but also on their developing a spirit of freedom and social justice. Janko Král' (1822–1876), one of the most revolutionary poets of Štúr's generation, was an exponent of these opinions.[21] These views were largely unknown outside Slovakia but, if they had penetrated the non-Slavic world, they would have done little to reduce anxieties about 'Slovak Panslavism'. Within the Kingdom of Hungary, under whose rule the Slovaks lived, these fears simply could not be ignored. This is why Štúr attempted to alleviate these concerns in a series of articles entitled *Panslavismus a naša krajina* (Panslavism and our country), but without much success.[22] In one of these pieces he wrote:

Suddenly an outcry about Panslavism has swept through Europe; this word has produced an echo and has been uttered with alarm among nearly all European nations, hundreds and hundreds of periodicals have discussed it. It has been the prevailing topic of conversation, and fiery speeches denouncing it have actually been delivered in several parliaments ... It might perhaps be supposed that beneath the slogan and pretext of Panslavism some kind of crusade is to be waged against all the nations of Europe ... If the cry of Panslavism was raised anywhere, then it was assuredly in our country, and nowhere so much as there. Newspapers and periodicals were full of it, everyday life was full of it. Every undertaking, on however small a scale, to promote enlightenment or well-being, to prevent the rights of the Slav nations from being forgotten, was decried as Panslavism ... A cry against the Slavs has passed through Europe; it was raised by the Germans, and the Magyars have associated themselves with it.[23]

This quotation from Štúr's large article on Panslavism in the Kingdom of Hungary demonstrates that in this country not only political efforts, but even the most harmless cultural movements or expressions of national identity by the Slovaks (or other Slavic nations within its frontiers) were regarded by the authorities as indicative of Panslavism.

Slovak representatives other than Štúr failed to refute these widespread suspicions about Panslavism. They did, however, produce works defending their ideas against unjust accusations, which were included in

[21] V. Matula, 'Snahy o prehĺbenie demokratickej línie *Slovenských národných novín* a formovanie revolučného programu slovenského národného hnutia' [Efforts to deepen the democratic line of *Slovenskje národňje novini* and the formation of the revolutionary programme of the Slovak national movement], *Historický časopis*, 4 (1958), 202–3.

[22] *Slovenskje národňje novini*, 3, 7, 10 and 14 September 1847.

[23] Cited by Clementis, *Panslavism*, p. 24.

brochures in German containing information about the various language disputes within the Kingdom of Hungary and on Slavism in Hungary.[24] However, these efforts had no effect, and their opponents continued to stress alleged Slovak Panslavism, although before the revolutionary events of 1848–1849 nobody contemplated political independence for Slovakia, or believed any sort of political union with Russia was a serious possibility. True, some ideas were floated about the possibility of one Slavic nation extending its 'sovereignty' over others and of the union of all the Slavs within one whole. It was to be a spiritual union, but it was a distant prospect.

Before the outbreak of the revolutions of 1848–1849, Štúr, while undoubtedly pro-Russian, couched his understanding of Russia in literary and cultural terms: that is, in terms of cultivating a literary and cultural reciprocity as Kollár had demanded. Prior to 1848, Slovak Slavism was still not synonymous with Panslavism, and the Slovaks were not advocating Panslavic aims, although they were frequently accused of doing so. Here it is necessary to point out that although Štúr frequently used the term 'Panslavism', he employed it exclusively in terms of the cultural reciprocity of the Slavic nations.

As the revolutions of 1848 began to unfold, Slovak leaders headed by Štúr attempted to secure national rights for the Slovaks within the framework of the Kingdom of Hungary, but they met with total opposition from the Magyar political representatives, who decisively influenced the political direction of the country. It was only after they had failed to have their demands recognised that the Slovaks began to look towards other Slavic peoples within the Habsburg lands to help them achieve their ambitions.

Following the fall of the oppressive regime of Prince Klemens Metternich (March 1848), many Slovak leaders saw an opportunity not only to gain national rights for Slovaks themselves, but also to renegotiate the status of the Slavic nations within the Habsburg Empire, where they formed the majority of the population. This aim underlined the proposed creation of a 'Pan-Slavic Union', which was to be a federal formation of all the Slavic nations. It was followed somewhat later by the proposal for a 'Union of independent Slavic communes', that is, a union of Slavic communities and regions of the Habsburg monarchy. The proposal was submitted to the Slavic Congress held in Prague on 2–12 June 1848. Štúr's idea of a 'Pan-Slavic Union' that included Russia

[24] S. Tomášik (Világosváry), *Der Sprachenkampf in Ungarn* (Zagreb, 1841); S. Hojč, *Apologie des ungarischen Slawismus* (Leipzig, 1843); J. Čaplovič, *Slawismus und Pseudomagyarismus* (Leipzig, 1842); anon., *Panslavismus in Ungarn* (Pest, 1848).

was not an expression of Slovak Panslavism, nor an attempt to place the 'Slavic world' under Russian domination. Such intentions were entirely foreign to Slovak leaders at this juncture.

Ľudovít Štúr, despite his pro-Russian inclinations, sharply criticised tsarist Russia, going so far as to describe it as an enemy of 'Slavic nationality', comparable to the Magyars and Germans.[25] The Russians, who laboured under autocratic conditions, were not regarded as a free nation by the Slovaks, as was demonstrated by an appeal from Slovakia 'to help the Russians achieve freedom'. Leading Slovaks, including Štúr, Jozef Miloslav Hurban and the Protestant cleric Michal Miloslav Hodža (1811–1870) called on all Slavs to join hands 'before the world', and to declare that they regarded themselves as one. This 'public and active' demonstration of unity was necessary to acquaint the world with their objectives. Accordingly, only if they were united could the Slavic nations defend themselves and achieve their goals. Such appeals were expressions of Slovak Slavism, demanding Slavic reciprocity from the Slavic nations. Conceptually, these views remained indicative of Slovak Slavism up to the summer of 1848, when significant changes occurred, that is, when Štúr's attitude towards Russia changed.

Štúr set out his revised view of Russia in the treatise *Pohľad na európske udalosti roku 1848* (A view of the European events of 1848), published as a series of articles in the magazine *Slovenski jug* in August 1848.[26] These pieces contained views on the Russians and Russia similar to those he had expressed in his *Slavdom and the World of the Future*. We do not know for sure what caused this change in Štúr's thinking, but we can hypothesise that it resulted from the Slavic nations' failure to realise their political objectives in 1848–1849 and the repercussions that followed. These included the breaking up of the Slavic Congress in Prague, the arrest of its delegates and the harsh suppression of revolutionary activities in the city, events in which Štúr had participated. Štúr argued that it was due to tsarist Russia that the world retained a respect for Slavdom (which was not able to win its own freedom). The publication of

---

[25] D. Rapant, *Dejiny slovenského povstania r. 1848–1849* [History of the Slovak uprising of 1848–1849] (Martin, 1937), I, pp. 324, 333; V. Matula, *Štúr a Slovanstvo* [Štúr and Slavdom] (Bratislava, 1956), p. 380; Ľ. Haraksim, 'Slovanské plány Slovákov v rokoch 1848–1849' [The Slavic plans of the Slovaks in 1848–1849], in Šesták (ed.), *Slovanství*, pp. 198–9, 201.

[26] The whole text was published by F. Bokes, *Dokumenty k slovenskému národnému hnutiu v rokoch 1848–1914* [Documents concerning the Slovak national movement from 1848 to 1914] (Bratislava, 1962), pp. 27–39.

these views during the revolutionary storms, when even Slavs felt little sympathy for tsarist Russia, was quite surprising.

After the revolutionary event of 1848 had died away, it became clear that the Slavic nations could expect nothing from Vienna, because the Viennese government was not prepared to fulfil any of the promises its representatives had made during the revolutionary period. This experience led Štúr to curtail any thoughts that Slovak national aspirations might be met by Vienna, and consequently he began turning his attention to Russia as the text *Slavdom and the World of the Future*, written after the revolutionary period, clearly demonstrates.

It is necessary to point out that not all Štúr's colleagues agreed with his views. For example, we know that Hurban's views 'varied between old Panslavism, Czechoslovakism and Austroslavism', while another close colleague, Michal Miloslav Hodža, 'faithfully maintained his Austroslavism'.[27] He was not alone: Kollár also argued in favour of Austroslavism. After the revolutionary tumults, Kollár began to engage more intensively in Slovak political life. He believed that Vienna would eventually correct its mistakes and introduce 'national equality' into the monarchy.

Štúr's *Slavdom and the World of the Future* was largely an apotheosis of Russia saturated with the views he had absorbed from Russian Slavophiles. The text began with an extensive account of the past of the Slavic nations, an overview of their social relations and daily life, character traits, religious affiliations and so on, all contrasted to the realities of the Western world, which to him appeared decadent in every way. Compared to the West, everything Slavic (especially anything Russian, which he considered to be typically Slavic) appeared to be incomparably superior to its Western counterparts. Even autocracy – the absolutist government of tsarist Russia – was held in greater regard than 'constitutionalism', and credited for having protected Russia from the shocks that afflicted the West.

According to Štúr, the tsar was no despot, as the enemies of Russia claimed. This is shown by the devotion of the Russian people to the tsar and the complete trust existing between the tsar and his subjects.[28] These comments clearly illustrate that Štúr's view of Russia was, to put it mildly, highly idealised and bore little relationship to reality. He

<hr>

[27] D. Rapant, 'Štúrovci a Slovanstvo' [Štúr's group and Slavdom], *Slovanský zborník* *I* (1947).

[28] Štúr devoted the second part of the work *Das Slawenthum und die Welt der Zukunft* (pp. 50–162) to a comparison of West and East. On the rejection of constitutionalism and federalism and on the idealisation of autocracy, see pp. 145, 149, 169–70, 205, 194, 196, 200, 204–5. On the union of all the Slavs with Russia, see pp. 208, 210 and others.

expected that this idealised Russia would become more closely engaged in the affairs of other Slavic nations, help them to achieve national freedom and unite them under its leadership, which meant adding them to Russia's territory. Since he thought that the Slavs would not organise themselves into federal states, a Slavic federation, or 'under Austria', there was no other possibility. Štúr saw the union of the Slavs with Russia as the only alternative for the future. From Štúr's perspective, the Slovaks had little choice but to embrace the concept of a future union with Russia, but this view was not necessarily shared by the majority of Slovaks.

Russian 'messianism' before the First World War

Although Štúr wrote *Slavdom and the World of the Future* in German around 1853, it did not become well known until after 1867, eleven years after his death, when Vladimír I. Lamanskij (1833–1914), a leading Russian Slavist with Slavophile views, published a Russian translation in St Petersburg. It is possible that very few people in Slovakia knew of Štúr's treatise until it appeared in Russian, since it was not originally intended for public consumption. *Slavdom and the World of the Future* was designed as a memorandum for Grand Duke Constantine of Russia. Štúr had hoped to stimulate interest within Russian government circles about those Slavic nations living beyond the frontiers of Russia, and to encourage them to adopt an active Slavic policy.

When news of this work finally reached Slovakia, the situation there had altered since Štúr had originally written his text. Although the nationality situation in the country had worsened, few Slovaks now wished for a union with Russia. Russia's brutal suppression of the Polish uprising of 1863 evoked strong emotions among nationally conscious Slovaks, and this event affected Slovak attitudes towards it.

Even before this happened, Slovaks had begun to re-evaluate the idea of Slavic reciprocity, as formulated by Ján Kollár, as well as Štúr's ideas for the unification of all the Slavs under Russian leadership, which was originally drafted in the wake of the conflicts of 1848–1849.

This shift in views was most apparent in the work of the writer and Roman Catholic priest Ján Palárik (1822–1870), especially in his treatise *O vzájomnosti slovanskej* (On Slavic reciprocity) published in 1862 and 1864, in which he expounded the views he had already developed in the 1850s.[29] Palárik belonged to a group of Slovak intellectuals (including

---

[29] The text is published in *Ján Palárik. Za reč a práva l'udu* [Ján Palárik. For the language and the rights of the people], vols. I and II (Bratislava, 1956), pp. 173–92.

several Roman Catholic priests) who rejected Slavophile views of Russia and critically assessed the domestic situation in Russia. In spite of their critical attitude towards Russia, several members of this group maintained contacts with Russian cultural figures. Their conception of the Slavic question was based on the idea that all the Slavic nations were 'equal' in terms of rights, and that this equality had to be maintained mutually. They rejected the concept of one Slavic nation exercising 'sovereignty' over other Slavs, in opposition to what Štúr saw as a possibility in *Slavdom and the World of the Future*.

Clearly then, Panslavism was neither the pre-eminent nor the sole component of Slovak Slavism even after Štúr had adopted its ideology. Other currents of Panslavism also existed, and these took a different view of the relationships and co-operation between the Slavic nations, based on the principle of equality. It is therefore impossible to say that Slovak Slavism, which was a permanent part of Slovak consciousness, led directly to Panslavism, although there were always individual Slovak figures who were sympathetic to this concept. Ján Palárik described those Slovaks and other Slavs who held such views as people who 'harmed' the Slavs, and who spread across Europe the 'erroneous view of political Panslavism that the efforts of the Slavs were really oriented towards Russian centralisation'. According to Palárik, this was 'an erroneous conception of Slavic reciprocity'.

Conclusion

The pro-Russian form of Slavic ideology enjoyed a revival in Slovak political life during the period of the Dual Monarchy. Experiences of political struggles showed that the Slovaks were unable to raise the question of Slovak political autonomy, since both the ruling Magyars in the Kingdom of Hungary and the Viennese court rejected this concept. After the Austro-Hungarian Compromise of 1867, the Magyars took advantage of the favourable situation and began rigorously to enforce their conception of a one-nation Hungarian state. In principle, this was a political idea, and the Magyars did not hesitate to introduce harsh Magyarisation measures in order to achieve their goal. As a result, the Slovaks not only lost any hope of realising their political demands, but were also deprived of their last cultural institutions, including schools with Slovak as the language of education. This tendency was further strengthened after the conclusion of the Dual Alliance between Germany and Austria-Hungary.

The stronger ally – Germany – unequivocally supported centralisation and the Kingdom of Hungary's policies of Magyarisation. Faced with this situation, the Slovaks closed ranks around their only political party – the Slovak National Party – while acknowledging that only a change in the prevailing international situation would alter their position. Many Slovaks came to view the national liberation struggle being waged by the Southern Slavs against Turkish suzerainty, in which Russia played an important role, as an example for themselves and their organ the *Národné noviny* (National newspaper). These struggles were seen as a potential method for solving the Slovak question. These ideas survived in the Slovak environment until the outbreak of the First World War in 1914.

9 The Slovak political programme: from Hungarian patriotism to the Czecho-Slovak state

Dušan Kováč

The ideology of nationalism exerted a powerful influence on the social thought, politics, culture and economics of Europe from the end of the eighteenth century through the nineteenth century; these factors also affected the Slovaks.

European nationalism rooted itself in the fertile soil produced by the rapid social changes that were occurring all over Europe during this period, but always in specific historic forms. Industrialisation, urbanisation and the modernisation that was associated with them combined with the rapid expansion of the socio-economic influence of the industrial and financial bourgeoisie, weakened the old social relationships that had been based on feudal principles and on the ancient privileges of the nobility. The advocates of the Enlightenment and incipient liberalism were soon engaged in a struggle against the old monarchic, dynastic and feudal principles that continued to dominate the continent, and they directed their attention not to traditional groups, but rather to what they defined as natural human communities.

Across a large swathe of Europe, the new cultural phenomenon of Romanticism became obsessed with ethnic manifestations – folk languages, folk literature and folklore. The comparative studies of Miroslav Hroch have shown that many ethnic groups, even those without their own ethnic or national states, all followed much the same line of development. The typical national movement began with a scholarly phase, in which an intellectual elite took an intense interest in the language, literature and history of its nation. Eventually, this scholarly interest led to a phase of political agitation. This process would appear to present a common path towards the formation of a modern nation,[1] which the

[1] M. Hroch, *Social Preconditions of National Revival in Europe: A Comparative Analysis of the Social Composition of Patriotic Groups Among the Smaller European Nations* (Cambridge, 1985).

small 'non-political' nations, that is, those without their own nation-states, experienced. The great nations also passed through this phase of development, although its specific form was always modified by the local historical context.

The culmination of these currents of European nationalism was the concept of the nation-state. Where an appropriate state framework already existed, it was only a matter for the state to transform itself into a 'nation-state', with new social classes taking control of the levers of power. In the cases of Germany and Italy, however, where ethnic communities were fragmented into various small states, the liberal bourgeoisie first had to stimulate a process of national unification. Where various ethnic groups lived within the framework of a single state or empire, there was a political struggle to control the state, as was the case with the Habsburg monarchy.

This Europe-wide process of nation-state formation also affected the Slovaks. In the second half of the eighteenth century, an educated Slovak elite began an intensive study of the language, history and literature of the Slovak people.[2] In 1787, Anton Bernolák completed the first codification of Slovak as a literary language.[3] A gradual transition from the scholarly to the political phase also occurred, and the first Slovak political programme was formulated by the middle of the nineteenth century.

Proto-political phase of Slovak nationalism

As a consequence of the fact that in the tenth century the Slovaks had been absorbed into the Kingdom of Hungary, which was a multi-ethnic state, a proto-political phase of national development occurred prior to the formation of an actual political programme. Its characteristic feature was ethnically defined disputes about the state as well as about member-ship of the historically more developed *natio Hungarica*. The first such dispute arose in 1721, in connection with the assembly of the first Hungarian Diet after the end of the Turkish wars. Mihály Bencsik, a professor of law at Trnava University, argued that the burghers of Trenčín did not have a right to participate in this parliament, because they were descended from those Slavs conquered by the Magyars. He called them 'Svätopluk's people', on the basis of the hypothesis that the

---

[2] See J. Papánek, *De regno, regibusque Slavorum atque cum prisci civilis et ecclesiastici, tum hujus aevi status gentis anno Chr. 1780* (Pécs, 1780); M. Bel, *Adparatus ad historiam Hungariae*, I–II (Posonium [Bratislava], 1735–46); Bel, *Notitia Hungariae novae historico geographico divisa in partes quatuor, I–IV* (Vienna, 1735–42).

[3] A. Bernolák, *Dissertatio philologico-critica de literis slavorum* (Posonium [Bratislava], 1787).

Great Moravian Empire had been subjugated by the Magyars. A priest, Ján Baltazár Magin, wrote a polemical response to this tract that affected all ethnic Slovaks, not just the burghers of Trenčín; it is known today as the first published *apologia* of the Slovaks (see Fig. 3).[4]

This dispute centred on the question of whether ethnic Slovaks could be regarded as equal citizens within the Kingdom of Hungary. The educated priest Magin argued on the basis of Roman law that the Slovaks should enjoy equal rights with the ethnic Magyars. Similar disputes and defences of the Slovaks, applying various historical arguments, were written by Slovak patriots up to the nineteenth century.[5] These disputes, provoked by early Magyar proto-nationalism, had an unambiguously political character. It was a matter of securing equal rights for the Slovaks within the Kingdom of Hungary, and the Slovaks unambiguously expressed themselves in these disputes as Hungarian patriots.

The second phase of proto-political nationalism arose at the beginning of the nineteenth century in response to the Napoleonic Wars and the emerging ideas of Slavic reciprocity. Napoleon's armies crossed Slovak territory on several occasions, passing through the territory twice – first during the campaign against Austria, and again during Napoleon's inglorious retreat from Moscow in 1812. These events profoundly influenced Slovak intellectuals, especially those who studied ethnic expressions of Slovak identity.

The most significant scholars of this period were the poet Ján Kollár and the literary scholar, linguist and historian Pavol Jozef Šafárik. Kollár and Šafárik became the most influential propagators of the idea of Slavic reciprocity. Kollár formulated an idea of a great Slavic nation, in the sense of all the Slavs forming one great nation. In the past it had been united, he argued, but it was later divided into smaller language groups. Within this Slavic nation, Kollár identified four 'branches': Russian, Polish, Czecho-Slovak and Illyrian (Yugoslav, i.e. Southern Slavs). Kollár's ideas were supported by Šafárik through his studies of Slavic history and language.[6]

During this period, the primary arguments for Slavic unity were cultural in nature, i.e., that a great nation could promote itself more

[4] J. Baltazar Magin, *Murices nobilissimae et norissime diaetae posoniensis scriptori sparsi, sive apologia pro inclyto comitatu trenchiniensi...* (no location, written in 1723, but first published in 1728).
[5] See J. Tibenský, *Chvály a obrany Slovákov* [In praise and defence of the Slovaks] (Bratislava, 1965).
[6] Kollár disseminated this idea in his poem *Slávy dcéra* [Sláva's daughter] (Pest, 1825); Šafárik in his historical work *Slovanské starožitnosti* [Slavic antiquities] (Prague, 1837).

effectively in the cultural field than could a smaller nation. It was no accident, therefore, that the representatives of one of the lesser Slavic nations – the Slovaks – became the most important and recognised representatives of the idea of Slavic reciprocity. Although it had yet to be clearly stated, it is possible at this stage to identify the emergence of a political idea, which is that a great nation weathers political storms and wars, such as those in Europe after the French Revolution, more effectively than a fragmented one. While no overt political programme had yet been proposed, the conditions for its emergence were gradually maturing.

Catholics and Protestants

The Slovaks entered the period of emergent nationalism as a small nation, but not as a united one. A clear dividing line existed, drawn along the lines of religion. The majority of Slovaks were Catholics, but the Protestant minority were very active in the cultural field, especially after the Edict of Toleration issued by Joseph II (1741–1790) in 1781. This division was the result of both the Reformation and the Counter-Reformation, as well as of the political struggles of the seventeenth century.

This confessional division also exhibited a linguistic aspect. The Slovak Protestants, mostly Lutherans of the Augsburg Confession, utilised Czech as their liturgical language. It was the Czech in which the Bible of Kralice was written (1579–1588). It codified literary Czech which became the literary as well as the liturgical language for Slovak Protestants. Catholics, however, still used Latin as their liturgical language, and various Slovak dialects for preaching. Slovak Catholics used Czech only in minor literary works, which were often strongly Slovakised, and sometimes only referencing the Czech orthographic system. Important literary works were still written in Latin. Therefore, it was no accident that a Slovak literary language was codified for the first time by a Catholic priest – Anton Bernolák. However, Bernolák's codification was accepted only by Catholic intellectuals, who were primarily concentrated around the two cultural centres of Bratislava and Trnava. Meanwhile, Slovak Protestants continued to write in Czech.

This linguistic division also had a wider significance: Protestants were often supporters not only of linguistic but also of cultural unity between the Slovaks and the Czechs. Thus, they represented a linguistic and cultural form of nineteenth-century Czechoslovakism. By way of a contrast, Catholics tended to see Slovaks as a separate Slavic nation. However, since these differences were still only an expression of existing differentiations in linguistic and cultural spheres, Protestants and Catholics co-operated without major conflict, and there were repeated efforts to unite the two currents organisationally.

The first political programme

The development of a coherent Slovak political programme is most closely associated with the ideas of Ľudovít Štúr and his colleagues. The members of this new generation, sometimes also called the 'Young Slovaks', were predominantly drawn from the Protestant faith and had been educated at the Protestant Lyceum in Bratislava. They were sympathetic to the ideas of Ján Kollár, from which they drew heavily, and as Protestants they used Czech as their literary language. However, the transition from Kollár's ideas to a Slovak political programme occurred quickly – over the course of a single decade.

In 1836, Štúr and his friends met in the ruins of Devín castle at the confluence of the Danube and Morava rivers, a symbol of the glorious Slavic past, and connected with the history of the Great Moravian Empire of the ninth century. In line with the spirit of contemporary Romanticism, the young students took a 'national oath', declaring their intent to work for the good of and the improvement of their nation. Furthermore, they decided that during their school vacations they would travel through Slovakia and 'awaken' the dormant Slovak nation to national consciousness. This was a classic example of an activity we would now call 'national agitation'.

National agitation and its associated demands to introduce education conducted in the mother tongue drew a sharp reaction from the representatives of Magyar nationalism. When the Slovak Protestant intelligentsia presented its linguistic demands to King (and Emperor) Ferdinand V (1835–1884) in Vienna in 1842,[7] the Magyar cultural and political elite began a determined campaign to resist these Slovak demands, as a result of which Štúr had to leave his teaching post at the Protestant Lyceum in Bratislava.

This was not Štúr's first encounter with Magyar nationalism, but its intensity and effectiveness seem to have caught him by surprise. It was a clear signal that Magyar nationalism had already entered the political stage and was firmly committed to the idea of a one-nation Hungarian state. This was basically a political idea that paralleled the model of the West European political nation, but it also contained cultural, linguistic

---

[7] The memorandum was entitled *Slovenský prestolný prosbopis* [Slovak petition to the throne]; see D. Rapant, *Slovenský prestolný prosbopis z roku 1842* [Slovak petition to the throne of 1842] (Liptovský Svätý Mikuláš, 1943).

and ethnic dimensions. The Hungarian nation had to be unambiguously Magyar, which meant that it had to be united by use of the Magyar language in all administration, literature and education. These demands were obviously unacceptable to the Slovaks, for whom Magyar was an entirely foreign language.

Štúr understood that the most difficult phase of his struggle for the Slovak nation would occur within the Kingdom of Hungary, that is, in direct conflict with Magyar nationalism. He further realised that historic destiny and existing political development distinguished the Slovaks from the Czechs, who were also part of the Habsburg monarchy, ruled by the Austrian administration. If the Slovaks wanted to assert themselves in their historic homeland – the Kingdom of Hungary – they would have to act independently. Thus, Štúr, a Protestant who wrote in Czech, decided to codify Slovak as a literary language. In his view, Bernolák's codification was not acceptable because it was based on the western Slovak dialect, and, according to Štúr, it was the central Slovakian dialect that had the ability to integrate all the Slovak regions. In 1843, Štúr codified the written Slovak language for a second time.[8] As he had hoped, this led to the gradual linguistic unification of all Slovaks. Given the historical context in which this codification occurred, it would be reasonable to conclude that this was not merely a linguistic issue, but also a highly political statement.

In 1845, soon after the codification of the written language, Štúr established a Slovak-language newspaper,[9] in which he published a series of articles designed to help formulate a political programme for the Slovaks. The leadership of the Slovak national movement was therefore well prepared for the revolutions of 1848. In spring of that year, mass meetings were held in various regions of Slovakia to organise their revolutionary demands. The revolution in Hungary had two primary aims: the social and the national. In the social field, the main demand was the abolition of feudal subjection, which not only maintained high levels of rural poverty, but also restricted the agricultural development of the country. The nationality question was complicated and often contradictory. On the one hand, the ethnic Magyar revolutionaries demanded Hungarian independence from Austria and the establishment of a one-nation Hungarian state. On the other hand, the Slovaks and other

---

[8] For his main work on codification, see Ľ. Štúr, *Nárečja slovenskuo alebo potreba písaňja v tomto nárečí* [The Slovak language and the need to write in it] (Prešporok [Bratislava], 1846); this work was written by Štúr in the newly codified Slovak language, in contrast to Bernolák, who wrote in Latin.

[9] *Slovenskje národňje noviní* (Slovak national newspaper) was published from 1845 to 1848.

non-Magyar nationalities demanded linguistic and cultural equality, and autonomy for their 'national territories', without stating precisely their extent. The Magyar national programme and the programme put forward by non-Magyars soon came into conflict with one another.

The main demand of the Slovak political programme was the recognition of the Slovaks as a separate nation and autonomy for the territory inhabited by the Slovaks. Apart from Štúr's newspaper and the regional meetings, Slovak representatives formulated their demands at a large meeting held at Liptovský Svätý Mikuláš on 11 May 1848. The document was entitled *The Demands of the Slovak Nation (Žiadosti slovenského národa)*. This political programme contained fourteen points. Apart from the central demand – autonomy for the Slovaks – it called for the Kingdom of Hungary to be transformed into a country of nations with equal rights and own Diets. Slovak was to become the official language in Slovak counties. The programme also demanded the abolition of feudal subjection, reform of the political system and the introduction of universal and equal suffrage.[10] Thus the revolution accelerated the formulation of the first Slovak political programme, which was founded on the Hungarian patriotism of the Slovaks, pressing for the reform of the country based on decentralisation along ethnic principles.

The failure of the leaders of the Magyar Revolution to make any concessions to Slovak demands eventually brought the two groups into armed conflict with each other. On 16 September 1848 in Vienna, a political and military body constituted itself to represent Slovak interests – the Slovak National Council. Three days later in Myjava, it openly declared its disobedience towards the Hungarian government, and contemplated that Slovakia would remain within the framework of the Habsburg monarchy as a separate Crown land. However, this idea was never implemented. Vienna eventually crushed the Magyar Revolution and, at the same time, rejected the Slovak political demands.[11]

The problem with the realisation of the first Slovak political programme was that insufficient time had elapsed between the beginnings of national agitation (1836) and the outbreak of the revolution (1848). During this period, Štúr and his colleagues had managed to elicit support for their national programme only in certain regions (mainly in western Slovakia), not across the whole country. While national agitation

[10] F. Bokes, *Dokumenty k slovenskému národnému hnutiu v rokoch 1848–1914* [Documents concerning the Slovak national movement 1848–1914], I (Bratislava, 1962).
[11] See the monumental work of D. Rapant, *Slovenské povstanie roku 1848–1849. Dejiny a dokumenty* [The Slovak uprising of 1848–1849. History and documents], I–V (Bratislava, 1937–72).

continued after the outbreak of the revolution, Slovak peasants were primarily concerned with the abolition of feudal subjection and not the wider political agenda. Where this issue connected with the national idea, many Slovak peasants were persuaded to join the ranks of the Slovak rebels. In regions where Magyar revolutionaries had begun to agitate first, Slovak peasants joined them, and fought in the ranks of the Magyar national guards. At this stage, national agitation among the Slovaks was only in its infancy and did not achieve any meaningful successes during the Revolution of 1848–1849.

The *Memorandum of the Slovak Nation*

Slovak leaders recognised that their actions in the 1848–1849 Revolution had failed in their primary objective of achieving their political programme and its realisation. Nevertheless although the Viennese court remained in full control of the situation across the whole country after the Revolution, and granted the Slovaks linguistic and educational rights (which they did not enjoy until after the Austro-Hungarian Compromise of 1867), Slovak began to be used as the language of instruction in Slovak areas and also as the official language in contacts with the local population. But Vienna was determined to resist any moves towards decentralisation of the country, and rejected outright the romantic idea of the Slovaks: federalisation along ethnic lines. The maxim of legitimacy applied by Vienna might lead to federalisation, but only within historical boundaries, which meant that the Slovaks would remain within the Kingdom of Hungary. Thus the Croats and Transylvania – and not Slovaks – could achieve autonomy on the basis of historic rights.[12]

The political failures of 1848–1849 disappointed and depressed many Slovak leaders. It was a situation that encouraged Štúr to write his work *Slavdom and the World of the Future*, in which he returned to the idea of Slavic unity inspired by Herder and propagated by Ján Kollár. He also outlined a clear political definition: all the Slavs should unite under Russian leadership. The Slovaks had to renounce their adherence to the Kingdom of Hungary. It is also interesting to note that the Lutheran Štúr went so far as to encourage Slovaks to convert to Russian Orthodoxy. Štúr wrote this work in 1853, just as the Crimean War between Russia and Turkey had begun. His early death in 1856 meant that

---

[12] On 28 November 1850 the pro-Viennese *Slovenské noviny* [Slovak newspaper] in the article, 'O centralisme a federácii' [On centralism and federalism], wrote 'The more federalism, the more Slovak slavery.'

this work proved to be his last. For a long time it remained unknown in Slovakia because Štúr had written it in German, and the Slovak intelligentsia became aware of it only after the text was published in Russian.[13]

The transformation of the Habsburg monarchy after its defeat in the Franco-Austrian war of 1859 and the collapse of Bach's absolutism (named after the hated minister of the interior Alexander Bach, a former liberal) also stimulated renewal of political activity within Slovakia. Numerous assemblies, at which Slovaks submitted new demands, were held. The newspaper *Pešt'budínske vedomosti* (Pest-Buda intelligence), which began to appear in March 1861, attempted to reformulate the Slovak political programme. It was published by a younger member of Štúr's group, a rebel commander from 1848–1849, Ján Francisci (1822–1905). Among the new ideologues in the national movement, Štefan Marko Daxner (1822–1892) stood out. He too had been one of the younger supporters of Ľudovít Štúr.

Following an announcement in *Pešt'budínske vedomosti*, all leading figures in Slovak politics met at Turčiansky Svätý Martin on 6 and 7 June 1861. A new Slovak political programme, referred to as the *Memorandum of the Slovak Nation*, was set before an assembly of perhaps five thousand people.[14] Like Štúr's previous programme, which was most clearly formulated in *The Demands of the Slovak Nation* (1848), the 1861 programme restated the basic idea that the Slovaks were a separate nation. The recognition of the Slovaks as a separate political nation led to demands for Slovak autonomy in the territory they inhabited. Here, Slovak was to be the official language of administration and education. All further linguistic and cultural demands stemmed from this fundamental idea. The Slovak leaders first sent the *Memorandum* to the Hungarian Diet, which rejected it. Then it was sent, in a revised form (the demands for autonomy being more clearly set out), to Emperor Francis Joseph I (1830–1916) in Vienna.

The *Memorandum* of 1861 can therefore be regarded as the Slovak response to the growing popularity of the concept of the nation-state. However, the Slovaks were not demanding an independent national state, but rather statehood in a limited form – territorial autonomy along national and ethnic principles. After the revolutionary interlude of 1848, there had been a return to the idea of 'Hungarian patriotism', because the Slovaks had redeclared their allegiance to the historic Hungarian state.

---

[13] The work was first published in Russian in Moscow in 1867, the original German manuscript was published in 1931 in Bratislava, and a Slovak translation eventually became available in 1993. See n. 5 in L'. Haraksim's essay in this volume.

[14] See Bokes, *Dokumenty*.

Figure 5 Title page of Statutes of Matica slovenská in Slovak (Cyrillic and Latin alphabets) (1863)

The *Memorandum* failed to achieve its stated objectives. The Magyars strictly rejected it, while Francis Joseph responded with vague promises. It was clear that he did not intend to accept the programme. These setbacks did not prevent further Slovak national activity. In subsequent years, Slovaks used their own resources to establish a national cultural institution, the Matica slovenská (1863) (Fig. 5) and three Slovak *gymnasia* that used Slovak as the language of instruction. However, Austria's defeat in its war with Prussia (1866) and the resulting Austro-Hungarian Compromise (1867) brought even these limited reforms to an end.

A gradual estrangement from the Hungarian state

The Viennese court sought to solve the deep internal crisis caused by the crushing defeat in the war with Prussia by sacrificing the loyal nations and reaching a settlement with the nation that had been most rebellious – the Magyars. The Habsburg monarchy was divided into two parts; the Austrian and Hungarian. In the Kingdom of Hungary, all legislative power was transferred to the Hungarian Diet, while the Hungarian government held exclusive executive power. As a result any monarch crowned in Budapest as the king of Hungary gave up a large part of his powers to his opponents, because the Diet and government of Hungary were entirely in the hands of ethnic Magyars.

This new state system, known as Dualism, placed the Slovaks in an awkward position.[15] Somewhat predictably, the Magyars utilised the new situation to their advantage, and began to transform the Kingdom of Hungary into a one-nation state. This was the very situation that the Slovaks had long feared. The signing of the Dual Alliance between Austria-Hungary and Germany (1879) further reinforced Magyar centralisation in Hungary. Germany, as the stronger partner in the alliance, actively supported Magyar centralism because it saw it as a way to strengthen the internally unstable Dual Monarchy. Consequently, Hungary's uncompromising policy of Magyarisation was carried out with German support.

The change to Dualism caused a crisis within the Slovak national movement. It became clear that the political programme set out in the *Memorandum* of 1861 could not be implemented under such conditions. Some Slovak political leaders chose to abandon the demands of the *Memorandum* and formed the so-called New Slovak School represented by the priest Ján Palárik, the writer Ján Mallý-Dusarov, and the Pest businessman Ján Bobula.[16] The members of this New School began with the assumption that policies had to be realistic and should set out achievable aims. In return for abandoning the *Memorandum*, they demanded linguistic and educational rights from the Magyars. On this basis, they first wanted to buttress Slovak culture as well as the economic infrastructure. Only at an appropriate time, once the national community had been strengthened, would it submit political demands.

Such a programme contained some substance. The problem was that the Magyars were in no mood to make concessions. Instead, they gradually liquidated the Matica slovenská, suppressed the three existing Slovak *gymnasia*, and eradicated all the linguistic and educational gains achieved by the Slovaks following the Revolution of 1848–1849. Consequently, the New School lost its *raison d'être* and ceased to operate.

---

[15] See L. Holotík (ed.), *Der österreichisch–ungarische Ausgleich 1867* (Bratislava, 1971).
[16] See B. Kostický, *Nová škola slovenská* [The new Slovak school] (Bratislava, 1959); T. Pichler, *Národovci a občania. O slovenskom politickom myslení v 19. storočí* [Patriots and citizens. On Slovak political thought in the nineteenth century] (Bratislava, 1998).

The *Memorandum* of 1861 thus remained the only official Slovak political programme, despite the fact that its basic demands were essentially unachievable given the political realities of the day. This situation exerted a marked influence on Slovak political and cultural life throughout the period of the Dual Monarchy. Up to the end of the First World War, practically the only Slovak political party – the Slovak National Party – continued to base its agenda on the *Memorandum*. It had its headquarters in the small town of Turčiansky Svätý Martin, where it printed its own newspaper, the *Národné noviny*. Over time, the *Memorandum* programme became a declarative programme expressing defiance. In reality, the newspaper and the Slovak National Party had to maintain a stubborn struggle simply to preserve the essence of Slovak national life – its literary language, literature and culture. Thus, the programme of national agitation receded into the background.

In this difficult situation the *Národné noviny* devoted ever more space to the question of international relations. This change in editorial policy was caused by the Slovaks' increasing reliance on changes in the international situation to bring about a change in their domestic position as well as a solution to their national and political demands. This belief in foreign salvation, a form of political messianism, was strongly reinforced by events in the Balkans during the last third of the nineteenth century, when Russia and the other great powers played a major role in liberating several Balkan nations from Turkish rule. It was no accident that the leading ideologue of the Slovak national movement at the turn of the century – the poet Svetozár Hurban Vajanský (1847–1916) – titled a collection of his poems *Tatry a more* (The Tatras and the Sea). The reference to the Tatra mountains was designed to be a symbol of the Slovaks, and the sea was a reference to the Southern Slavs (Yugoslavs). Vajanský's symbolism suggested that, at least in his mind, there was more than just a simple linguistic and[17] ethnic relationship between these two parts of the Slavic world.

Whether desired or not, messianic ideology and reliance on outside intervention led to an increasing level of passivity within the national movement. The new generation that entered national life at the end of the nineteenth century was not satisfied with this situation, as it stifled any kind of meaningful activity. Therefore, its representatives sought to bring new ideas into Slovak political life. The effort to shake off the demoralising pressures of the Hungarian regime (which had succeeded in completely suppressing the Slovak language in education by the

---

[17] The process of Magyarisation culminated in 1907 with the Apponyi laws, which forced all primary school children to read, write and count in Magyar for the first four years of their education. From 1909, religion also had to be taught in Magyar.

beginning of the twentieth century) led to attempts to form co-operative links with kindred national forces within and outside Hungary. These attempts at co-operation with other non-Magyar nations of the Kingdom of Hungary culminated in the nationalities congress of 1895. Moreover, close links were forged with Czech political and cultural life, which had been developing under more favourable conditions. This new generation of Slovak nationalists demanded more activity, including more national agitation and greater efforts to reconstruct the national infrastructure.

The group of young Slovak intellectuals eager for close Slovak and Czech co-operation gathered around the magazine *Hlas* (The voice). The Hlasists were greatly influenced by the ideas of Tomáš (Thomas) Garrigue Masaryk (1850–1937), a professor of philosophy at Prague University, giving high status to small-scale educational, intellectual and political activities. The Slovak Social Democrats adopted similar proposals, although from a different ideological standpoint,[18] as did the emerging Catholic people's movement that had been stimulated by the Papal encyclical *Rerum novarum* (1891). In addition to the magazine *Hlas* (followed from 1909 by a new magazine *Prúdy* (Currents)), *Slovenský týždenník* (Slovak weekly), the newspaper produced by the young politician and founder of the Slovak agrarian movement, Milan Hodža (1879–1944) (Fig. 10), was also very popular. From 1905, the Social Democrats published the *Robotnícke noviny* (Workers' newspaper).

New political programmes emerged from the activities of these resurgent movements. The most important of these was the demand for universal suffrage, supported by all Slovak political organisations, regardless of political orientation. The government opposed universal suffrage because it feared that the non-Magyar majority would put to rest the idea of a Magyar nation-state, and install a federal system in which the Magyars would lose their dominant position. The struggle for universal suffrage reached its apogee in the years 1905–1907 when it was introduced in the Austrian part of the monarchy but was prevented from reaching the Kingdom of Hungary.[19]

Co-operation between Milan Hodža and the Belvedere Group, a circle of influential figures close to the heir to the Austro-Hungarian throne, Archduke Francis Ferdinand (1863–1914), represented another novel

---

[18] S. Sikora, V. S. Hotár and I. Laluha (eds.), *Kapitoly z dejín sociálnej demokracie na Slovensku* [Chapters from the history of social democracy in Slovakia] (Bratislava, 1996).

[19] See M. Podrimavský and D. Kováč (eds.), *Slovensko na začiatku 20. storočia (Spoločnosť, štát a národ v súradniciach doby)* [Slovakia at the beginning of the twentieth century: society, state and nation] (Bratislava, 1999).

departure. Francis Ferdinand was a firm opponent of Dualism, and he was prepared to end it and introduce a federal system, which he believed would strengthen the position of Vienna as arbiter within the empire. He expected that this policy would meet with strong opposition from the Magyars, so he mobilised support from all those who demanded change in the monarchy's political system. The non-Magyar nations of the Kingdom of Hungary were expected to support these reforms. It is difficult to assess whether Francis Ferdinand seriously intended to implement such a radical change, but these rumours encouraged many Slovaks to believe that their position might be about to change. For this reason, Hodža actively co-operated in making the project happen.[20]

All these new developments disturbed the previously peaceful waters of Slovak political life. The programme of the *Memorandum* of 1861 remained technically valid and was in the end recognised in principle by the younger generation. The authority of the Slovak National Party also continued. The pro-Russian messianism was gradually replaced by an orientation towards the Entente bloc, and the conservatism of the leadership of the Slovak National Party was complemented by the democratic orientation of the younger generation. The continued lack of any meaningful concessions by the Hungarian governments to Slovak national demands as well as to the question of universal suffrage led to the gradual estrangement of the Slovak cultural and political elite from the Hungarian state. As a result of increased national agitation, the feeling of estrangement gradually spread through the wider Slovak population.

The new programme: the Czecho-Slovak state

The outbreak of the First World War in 1914 radically altered the prevailing international situation, although the consequences of this change were slow to reveal themselves. The Slovaks, who were preparing for just such a change, understood immediately that the war would decide their national destiny for many years to come. In the first years of the war, however, when repression and censorship in the Austro-Hungarian regime intensified, Slovaks were rather passive and inclined to wait. Where there were large communities, such as in the United States and Russia, Slovaks living abroad were active. Theoretically there

---

[20] D. Kováč, 'Milan Hodža. Vom Belvederekreis zum Föderationsgedenken im Zweiten Weltkrieg', in R. G. Plaschka, H. Haselsteiner, A. Suppan, A. M. Drabek and B. Zar (eds.), *Mitteleuropa-Konzeptionen in der ersten Hälfte des 20. Jahrhunderts* (Vienna, 1995), pp. 165–70.

were a number of ways the Slovak question could be raised again and a Slovak political programme formulated, including Slovak autonomy within Hungary on the basis of the *Memorandum*. Other options were also possible, such as a union with Russia,[21] or the creation of a Polish–Czech–Slovak federation. Gradually, however, both at home and abroad, the idea of a common state with the Czechs gained ground.

T. G. Masaryk, who was not only an academic but also a politician and whose father was a Slovak, championed the idea of a Czecho-Slovak state in the Entente countries from as early as the autumn of 1914. In a memorandum entitled *Independent Bohemia* (1915), Masaryk presented a comprehensive plan for a Czecho-Slovak state. It was worked out after meeting the Scottish writer and journalist R. W. Seton-Watson who was in contact with the British government.[22] In addition, the Czech and Slovak communities in the USA[23] and in Russia[24] gradually came to support this programme. The Conseil national des pays tchèques was created as the central authority of the Czecho-Slovak resistance movement. One of Masaryk's closest colleagues was a French citizen of Slovak origin, the astronomer and airman, Milan Rastislav Štefánik (1880–1919).[25]

The Czech and Slovak politicians at home also gradually came to support the programme for a Czecho-Slovak state. Every piece of information gleaned from abroad was important for Slovak political and cultural representatives. They gradually became convinced that activities abroad would ultimately be successful. A secret organisation, Maffia, played an important role in providing information.[26] Masaryk was also keen that domestic politicians supported his activities, not least as he realised that unity of action would greatly increase the chances of the resistance movement abroad achieving its objectives.

[21] The programme of uniting Slovakia with Russia was worked out by Ján Kvačala, a Slovak academic at the University of Tartu (Juriev), who was an expert on Comenius.

[22] R. W. Seton-Watson, memorandum for the Foreign Office, based on his conversations with T. G. Masaryk at Rotterdam, 24–25 October 1914, records of the Foreign Office, FO 371/1900, pp. 115–24, and T. G. Masaryk, memorandum for the Foreign Office, 'Independent Bohemia', April 1915, FO 371/2241, pp. 98–103, both at the National Archives, Kew, London.

[23] The Cleveland Agreement between the Czech and Slovak communities in the United States was signed in October 1915. A further agreement (the Pittsburgh Agreement) was concluded in May 1918.

[24] The agreement of the Slovak community in Russia for a Czecho-Slovak state was obtained by Milan Rastislav Štefánik in August 1916 (the so-called Kiev Minutes) in spite of opposition from pro-Russian circles.

[25] There is a large quantity of literature on the Czecho-Slovak resistance movement, especially with regard to the question of the Czecho-Slovak legions in Russia. For publications in English, see G. J. Kovtun, *Czech and Slovak History. An American Bibliography* (Washington, DC, 1996), chap. 9.

[26] See E. V. Voska and W. H. Irwin, *Spy and Counterspy* (New York, 1940).

Figure 6 *Declaration of the Slovak Nation* made in Turčiansky Sv. Martin (30 October 1918), published in *Národnie noviny*

Slovak domestic politicians came to support the formation of a Czecho-Slovak state in the final year of the war. The decisive date proved to be a secret meeting of Slovak representatives held on 25 May 1918, at Turčiansky Svätý Martin, where the Catholic priest Andrej Hlinka (1864–1938) (Fig. 9) unequivocally stated: 'Let us not evade the question. Let us say clearly that we support the Czecho-Slovak orientation. The thousand-year marriage with the Magyars has failed. We must divorce.'[27]

Thus the definitive separation of Slovakia from the Hungarian state was clearly and unambiguously formulated. The creation of the Czecho-Slovak state was widely accepted as the new Slovak political programme. The transition to this programme had been a gradual one. Some circles had already held this view before the First World War,[28] but such plans became a realistic possibility only once they gained international accept-ance. Slovaks publicly confirmed their adherence to this new programme on 30 October 1918, at a public assembly, when a new representative body of the Slovaks – the Slovak National Council – adopted the *Declar-ation of the Slovak Nation* (Fig. 6).[29] By then, the first Czechoslovak Republic had already been proclaimed. This act was undertaken by the National Committee in Prague on 28 October 1918. The new Slovak programme had been realised so quickly that a large proportion of the Slovak public did not even notice that a new phase in their national development had dawned.

Finally, the concept of the 'nation-state' that appeared in this pro-gramme took a quite specific form. The Slovaks had relinquished the earlier concept of independent statehood or political autonomy. Instead, they had supported the idea of building a common state with the Czechs, accepting the principle of a 'nation-state of the Czechoslovak nation'. Thus the idea of Czechoslovakism played an eminent role in the history of the Slovaks, although it soon came into conflict with the realities of Slovak national consciousness.

[27] M. Hronský, *Slovensko pri vzniku Československu* [Slovakia at the time of the formation of Czechoslovakia] (Bratislava, 1988).

[28] Views on the possible political union of the Slovaks and Czechs appeared in an article in the magazine *Prúdy* in 1914. It was not published until 1919 because of the war.

[29] See D. Kováč et al. (eds.), *Muži deklarácie* [Men of the Declaration] (Martin, 1991, 2nd edn, Bratislava, 2000).

10   Slovakia in Czechoslovakia, 1918–1938

Natália Krajčovičová

The First World War provided a dramatic prologue to the formation of the Czechoslovak Republic in October 1918. As the end of the war approached, developments on the domestic political scene accelerated, although they did not proceed evenly across both halves of the Austro-Hungarian monarchy. In Austria, a certain amount of political relaxation had already occurred by 1917, while in Hungary government repression continued. A re-organised National Committee was active in the Czech Lands from as early as July 1918. In Slovakia, preparations to establish a Slovak National Council developed more slowly. The historic moment came on 30 October, when an assembly of representatives from the whole of Slovakia met at Turčiansky Svätý Martin, and elected a Slovak National Council that adopted the *Declaration of the Slovak Nation*. The council declared that only it, and not the Hungarian government or any other authority, was authorised to speak and act in the name of the Slovak branch of the Czechoslovak nation living within the Kingdom of Hungary. It also announced its support for future participation in all activities of the Czech nation.

On 28 October 1918, the National Committee in Prague declared the creation of an independent state of the Czechoslovak people, of which it formed the government. It also issued the First Act of the Czechoslovak State, decreeing the legal continuity of the new situation and subordinating all existing state and representative administrative authorities to it. The medically trained Hlasist Vavro Šrobár (1867–1950) (Fig. 8), who became minister for the administration of Slovakia, signed both documents on behalf of Slovakia. These state-forming acts – in Prague and in Martin – testified to the joint will of the political elites of the two nations to apply their right to self-determination within a common state.

Later consideration of these events has sometimes cast doubt on their importance. Such interpretations have commonly been formed on the basis of pre-existing ideological or political biases, rather than on the basis of serious academic research, and should be evaluated with some caution. Nevertheless, the state that was formed by these two acts was

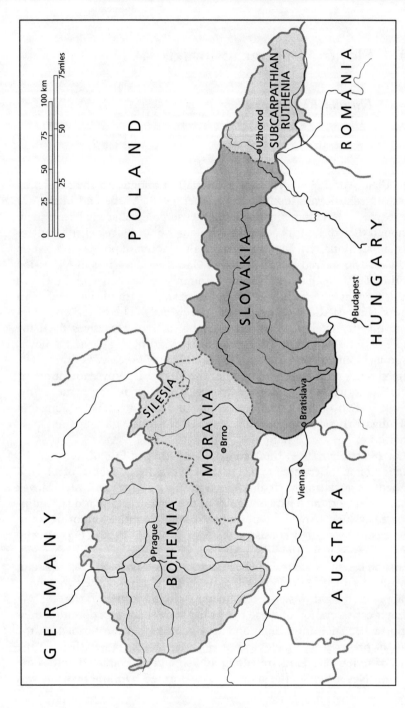

Map 4 The First Czechoslovak Republic 1918–1938

Figure 7 Milan Rastislav Štefánik

endowed from the beginning with democratic and humanistic values passed on by their creators – the future president of the republic Tomáš Garrigue Masaryk, General Milan Rastislav Štefánik (Fig. 7) and the last president of the First Czechoslovak Republic, Edvard Beneš (1884–1948). They also opened up a space for the realisation of the vital interests of the Slovak and Czech nations.[1] Consequently, these events are among the most important in modern Slovak history. That having been said, the prominent Slovak historian Ľubomír Lipták noted

[1] See R. W. Seton-Watson, *The New Slovakia* (Prague, 1924).

shrewdly that 'the Czechs and Slovaks experienced historic events together, but occasionally rather differently'.[2] This statement conveniently applies to the period of their mutual coexistence during the interwar period. Managing this common state proved to be a demanding task for Slovakia and the Czech Lands, not least because of their different historical experiences.[3]

The incorporation of Slovakia into the Czechoslovak state

The method of incorporating Slovakia into the political system proved important, as this process determined the direction as well as limiting the ultimate success of the whole project.[4] The Czechoslovak Republic was based on the principles of democracy – that is, the recognition of the equality of all citizens, their natural rights and freedoms, parliamentary institutions, democratic elections and the division of powers between the legislative, executive and judicial branches. These postulates were laid out in the Constitutional Charter of the Czechoslovak Republic, adopted on 29 February 1920, almost a year and a half after the establishment of the state. During this difficult initial period, the new state was built and slowly consolidated. Its sovereignty was established across the whole territory of the republic and recognised in the international arena. In the Czech Lands (Moravia-Silesia), this process was complicated by strong opposition from the German-speaking minority and by a dispute with Poland over the Těšín district. The situation in Slovakia was even more complex. Hungarian military units occupied a large part of its territory from November 1918 to July 1919, and after an intervention by the Entente powers, the Hungarian Red Army withdrew from Slovakia. Problems with defining the Slovak–Hungarian frontier persisted until 6 June 1920, when the peace treaty with Hungary was signed at Trianon. However, concerns about Magyar revisionist and irredentist efforts continued and permanently marked the Slovak political scene.

---

[2] Ľ. Lipták, 'Slovenská historiografia o medzivojnovom Československu 1918–1938' [Slovak historiography on inter-war Czechoslovakia 1918–1938], in J. Valenta, E. Voráček and J. Harna (eds.), *Osudy demokracie ve střední Evropě I* [The fates of democracy in Central Europe I] (Prague, 1999), p. 49.

[3] See C. Skalnik Leff, *National Conflict in Czechoslovakia. The Making and Remaking of a State, 1918–1987* (Princeton, 1988).

[4] On the history of the First Czechoslovak Republic, see E. Diekroegger, *The Political History of Czechoslovakia. October 1918–May 1938. A Bibliography of References in English* (Madison, 1938); G. J. Kovtun, *Czech and Slovak History. An American Bibliography* (Washington, DC, 1996).

As a result of the Treaty of Trianon, for the first time in history, the administrative borders of Slovakia were confirmed. Within these frontiers, Slovaks represented a majority of the citizenry, but the state also contained Magyars in the south, Ruthenians in the east and Poles in the north; Czechs, Jews, Roma and other small nationalities in the whole country represented nearly 20 per cent of the population.

Parliamentary democracy, anchored in the constitution and the electoral system, based on the right to universal, secret, direct and equal voting, also created favourable conditions for the formation of political parties in Slovakia.[5] However, the intervention of the Hungarian Red Army caused an extraordinary situation in Slovakia, and the development of political life was stopped until August 1919. Local council elections had already been held in the Czech Lands in June 1919, but it was not possible to hold similar ballots in Slovakia. This delay was also confirmed by the Club of Slovak Deputies, which collectively represented the Slovak political parties in the Provisional National Assembly in Prague. They not only wanted to hold elections for the local councils, but also proposed a postponement of the approaching parliamentary elections and a tightening of the election laws in Slovakia.[6]

As a result of these difficulties, an authoritarian form of government emerged in Slovakia from December 1918, overseen by the Ministry with Full Power to Administer Slovakia, headed by Vavro Šrobár (Fig. 8). The minister appointed (temporarily) by the government received extensive legal powers. At first, the ability to issue decrees, as well as executive powers, was concentrated in his office. To begin with, his position was temporary, and the government could limit his activity at any time. The Prague ministries had already done this in autumn 1919. They began to disband the departments of the ministry, gradually establishing branches of the central ministries and introducing centralised control. In an attempt to avoid weakening Czechoslovak statehood, the Club of Slovak Deputies did not protest against this centralist method of administration, and did not assert its objections to the fiction of a unitary Czechoslovak nation, anchored in the preamble of the Constitutional Charter and in the Language Act. Paragraph I of this act stated: 'The Czechoslovak language is the state, official language of

[5] Z. A. B. Zeman, 'Czechoslovakia Between the Wars; Democracy on Trial', in J. Morison (ed.), *The Czech and Slovak Experience. Selected Papers from the Fourth World Congress for Soviet and East European Studies* (Harrogate, 1990, and New York, 1992), pp. 163–6.

[6] 'Žiadosti slovenského klubu formulované na porade 19 júna 1919' [Requests of the Slovak Club formulated at a meeting on 19 June 1919], Rotnáglova pozostalosť', 6406, Archív literatúry a umenia, Martin [Archives of literature and arts, Martin] (ALU Martin).

Figure 8 Vavro Šrobár

the Republic.'[7] At first, the Slovak members of parliament proposed that the term 'Czechoslovak language' be replaced by the formulation 'Czech and Slovak language'. When their view was not accepted by the Constitutional Committee, they satisfied themselves with the fact that the act admitted the possibility of official activity in the Czech Lands 'usually in Czech, in Slovakia usually in Slovak.' Since the Czechoslovak language did not in fact exist, bilingualism prevailed in practice. However, it was sometimes necessary officially to remind Czech employees in Slovakia to use Slovak. The language problem, as well as recognition of the separate identity of the Slovak nation, gradually acquired a political dimension.

The principal reason behind the systematic imposition of the fiction of a unitary Czechoslovak nation during the First World War was the effort to gain the Allies' agreement for the creation of a 'Czechoslovak nation-state'. The transformation of this fiction into the political doctrine of the new state, and its inclusion in the constitution, proved less successful in terms of creating a unified Czechoslovak political nation. The Slovaks in particular had reservations about this policy because it mirrored the Magyar idea of a unitary Hungarian nation. As the historian Roman Holec has noted, under its cover a brutal linguistic and

---

[7] Act no. 122/1920, 1920, *Sbírka zákonů a nařízení státu československého* [Collection of acts and decrees of the Czechoslovak state].

ethnic assimilation was carried out. A further, no less serious reason for rejecting the idea of a unitary Czechoslovak nation was the fact that, for it to succeed, the two sides would gradually have to come closer together. However, this was possible only on the assumption that the unitary political nation was created by two equal parts.[8]

The essence of this dispute also lay in the fact that the fiction of a unitary Czechoslovak nation, upon which a unitary Czechoslovak statehood was based, was supplemented by the fiction of a Czechoslovak language that directly affected the ethnic identity of the Slovak nation. In October 1918, most of the Slovak political elite accepted this rationale for tactical reasons; the unity of the Czech and Slovak nation would assist in the separation of Slovakia from Hungary, followed by union with the Czech nation in a common state, according to the *Declaration of the Slovak Nation*. The acceptance of the constitution and the retreat from national and autonomist positions prior to the April 1920 parliamentary elections were also undertaken in the same spirit.

Political differentiation

In the first elections, Slovaks predominantly voted for parties on the left of the political spectrum, which reflected the harsh living conditions experienced by a large part of the population after the war. The Social Democrats – both Czech and Slovak, together with Magyar- and German-speaking Social Democrats – gained 47 per cent of the votes. However, parties loyal to the state – the Slovak National and Peasant-Farmers' Party (Agrarians), the Czechoslovak National Socialist Party, the Czechoslovak People's Party (as part of which the Slovak People's Party participated in the election) and the Czechoslovak Social Democrats – gained a total of about 80 per cent of the votes. In spite of the varying orientations of these parties, this result was extraordinarily important, since their common priority was the building and strengthening of Czechoslovak statehood. After these elections, and the signing of the Treaty of Trianon, the situation relaxed. The axioms that the existence of the Czechoslovak Republic was entirely dependent on maintaining Czechoslovak unity and that any acceptance of a separate Slovak identity would lead directly to the disintegration of the state were no longer accepted by the Slovak public as a whole.

Political differentiation continued in Slovakia. The dilemma of 'one nation or two', and the associated demand for enhanced legislative

---

[8] D. Kováč, *Slováci a Česi. Dejiny* [The Slovaks and Czechs. A history] (Bratislava, 1997), p. 123.

autonomy, became a polarising factor in relations with the Czechs; this was in addition to class, social and religious differences. The Slovak National Party, which separated from the Slovak Agrarians, intended to keep the question of Slovak autonomy alive. The Agrarians gave priority to the corporatist principle. In the summer of 1922, they merged with the Czech Agrarians under the name of the Republican Party of Agricultural and Small Peasant-Farming People. The Slovak People's Party then took up the call for legislative autonomy. After the elections, it radicalised its nationalist and populist rhetoric and aimed at winning autonomy for Slovakia via the parliamentary route.[9] In January 1922, the Slovak People's Party submitted the first official proposal for the legislative self-government of Slovakia. The proposal was legally flawed and was therefore not discussed on the floor of the Chamber of Deputies.[10]

The Slovak political scene was becoming increasingly fragmented. Throughout the inter-war period, the tone was set by two parties: Hlinka's Slovak People's Party (the new name of the Slovak People's Party from 1925, espousing the Führer principle, embodied at the time by the charismatic Catholic priest Andrej Hlinka (Fig. 9)), and the Republican Party (whose members were known as 'Agrarians'), organised throughout Czechoslovakia. The Republicans had a dominant position in the state, holding some of the most important levers of executive power. This enabled Slovak Agrarians also to participate in the central executive in Prague; a prime example was the leading representative of the Agrarian movement in Slovakia, deputy chairman of the Republican Party, head of various ministries and the last prime minister of pre-war Czechoslovakia – Milan Hodža (Fig. 10).

Hodža was able to adapt his policies flexibly to suit specific situations, altering and clarifying his position, and from an initial rejection of legislative autonomy, he gradually progressed to regionalism, in the framework of which Slovakia should have had limited autonomy. From the beginning of his political career, he constantly emphasised that the special needs of Slovakia and its economic and cultural interests required a supreme organ of administrative self-government. This was to result from administrative reforms; the final aim of these was the removal of

---

[9] See Dorothea H. El Mallakh, *The Slovak Autonomy Movement 1935–1939. A Story in Unrelenting Nationalism* (Boulder, 1979).

[10] The parliament (National Assembly) was composed of the more powerful Chamber of Deputies and the second chamber, the Senate. On the attitude of the political parties, see K. Hoch, *Political Parties in Czechoslovakia* (Prague, 1936); L'. Lipták (ed.), *Politické strany na Slovensku 1860–1989* [Political parties in Slovakia 1860–1989] (Bratislava, 1992).

Figure 9 Andrej Hlinka

Figure 10 Milan Hodža

the dualism of public and state administration in the Czech Lands and Slovakia. The first attempt at unification of the administration by means of the County Act (1920) did not succeed, because it was implemented only in Slovakia and only in a significantly altered form.

A new administrative reform programme emerged after the 1925 parliamentary elections. The victorious parties – Hlinka's Slovak People's Party, commonly known as the Ľudáks, and the Agrarians – actively participated in preparing this legislation, and they repeatedly concentrated on the question of executive power. The Social Democrats and the National Socialists opposed any introduction of a land constitutional system (*krajinské zriadenie*), which was the aim of these reforms. As opponents of autonomy and supporters of a unitary Czechoslovak state and the oneness of the Czech and Slovak nation, they were basically against the Ľudáks gaining the upper hand in social and political developments in Slovakia. Therefore, their leading representatives – the Social Democrat Ivan Dérer and the National Socialist Igor Hrušovský – energetically opposed the adoption of the law on the provincial constitutional system. After it was passed by parliament in 1927, they endeavoured to ensure that the majority in the provincial assembly, known as the Slovak Land Representation (*zastupiteľstvo*), would be formed according to the 'Czechoslovak' principle, and not according to the majority of the Agrarian–Ľudák coalition in parliament. It was composed of the more powerful Chamber of Deputies and the Senate. They also failed to achieve this goal. The Agrarians agreed on the division of ministerial posts with the Ľudáks, while the Slovak National Socialists condemned the compromises with the Ľudáks as a fatal mistake. However, the fatal mistake precisely proved to be the removal of the Ľudáks from positions of power and responsibility. This gave them the opportunity to launch a campaign of populist criticism and to present themselves as the only defenders of Slovak political interests.

In due course, the balance of forces in the Land Representation, which was composed of both elected and appointed members, was reordered in favour of the 'Czechoslovak' parties. The Agrarian Party had eight elected and eight appointed members after the regional elections of 1928; the autonomist Ľudáks had nine elected and only five appointed members; the Social Democrats had only three elected and one appointed members; the Magyar parties had six elected and no appointed members; the Czechoslovak National Socialists had one elected and one appointed member, as did the Czechoslovak People's Party and the National Democrats. The small autonomist Slovak National Party had one elected member, but no appointed members. The Communist Party of Czechoslovakia also did badly. It had five elected members, but no appointed members in the land assembly.[11]

The Slovak political scene became ever more fragmented after the 1929 parliamentary elections, when there was an increase in mutual accusations instead of co-operation in the interest of Slovakia. The Ľudáks, who joined the government in January 1928, were caught off guard by the 'Tuka affair'. Vojtech Tuka (1880–1946) was a former university professor of constitutional law who became, in the 1920s, a leading figure in Rodobrana (Home Defence) – an illegal paramilitary movement, sympathetic to Italian fascism. As editor-in-chief of the daily *Slovák*, the main organ of Hlinka's Slovak People's Party, he authored a piece for the 1928 New Year's issue that caused intense political excitement. By referring to a 'secret' but really non-existent appendix to the Martin *Declaration*, the article asserted that the Slovaks agreed to be part of Czechoslovakia for a 'probationary period' of ten years. In the absence of a constitutional re-arrangement of the Czech–Slovak relationship, by 30 October 1928, Slovakia would effectively cease to be part of Czechoslovakia – in view of the ensuing *vacuum juris*.

Tuka was tried for high treason and spying for Hungary, and sent to prison for fifteen years on 5 October 1928. Three days later – well before parliamentary elections in 1929 – the Ľudáks left the government. While this development suited them at the time, their strongest political opponent, Milan Hodža, became an embarrassment to his governmental allies due to charges of corruption, and retired temporarily from politics for 'health reasons'.

Attempts to decentralise power further continued throughout the 1930s. In May 1930, the Ľudáks submitted a second official proposal for Slovak legislative autonomy, but again it was not discussed on the floor of the Chamber of Deputies. However, the immediate aim of the Slovak political elite remained the enhancement of the powers of the Land Representation and the improvement of its financial situation, so that it could more effectively participate in finding solutions to some of the more serious economic and social problems in the country.

The economic situation

Slovakia's proximity to the more developed Czech economy had an unfavourable effect on economic life and undermined its competitiveness.

---

[11] Ľ. Lipscher, *K vývinu politickej správy na Slovensku v rokoch 1918–1938* [On the development of political administration in Slovakia from 1918 to 1938] (Bratislava, 1966), p. 227.

Although the citizenry of Czechoslovakia existed in a shared environment, conditions in Slovakia were more difficult, and important economic reforms caused serious problems. The less developed economy inherited from the former Kingdom of Hungary, in addition to low levels of education and awareness of legal principles, also had an effect. The Slovak economy was slow to recover from the war and from the damage caused by the Hungarian invasion of the country at the end of 1918 and in the summer of 1919. There were a range of serious difficulties, not least with the provision of ordinary everyday needs, steady inflation and growing unemployment, all of which caused growing social tension. These problems undermined the authority of the new administration, which lacked independent funds and was wholly dependent on the Prague ministries.[12] In the first few years of the Czechoslovak Republic, these social tensions led to conflicts and forcible interventions against the discontented inhabitants of some towns and in some rural areas. Martial law in Slovakia was finally lifted only in 1922.

Industry had to deal with supply difficulties too. Factories and works suffered from a shortage of raw materials and energy resources and a lack of direct investment, and they failed to use the growth in demand after the war to renew productive capacities. The post-war economic crisis hindered renewal and the essential restructuring of the economy. The question of how to formalise the coexistence of the Slovak and Czech economies became an urgent one. The currency separation introduced by the minister of finance, Alois Rašín, aimed to create an independent Czechoslovak currency by putting special stamps on old banknotes from the monarchy, and by keeping 50 per cent of the existing money supply as a compulsory state loan with 1 per cent interest. This reform was swiftly introduced without many hitches in the Czech Lands.[13] In Slovakia, however, these reforms were complicated by the invasion of the Hungarian Red Army. The stamping of these old notes proved to be a slow process, and many citizens kept hold of their cash rather than have the state take 50 per cent as an enforced loan. 'White money' printed by the Hungarian Bolshevik regime was also in circulation. Czechoslovak officials refused to stamp this currency, so people in some parts of Slovakia had no stamped money. This situation was resolved only in October 1920, when the minister of finance ordered the stamping of all previously unstamped banknotes.[14]

---

[12] See E. Bloss, *Labour Legislation in Czechoslovakia* (New York and London, 1938).

[13] V. Lacina, *Alois Rašín* (Prague, 1992), p. 22.

[14] R. Holec, 'Hospodársky vývoj Slovenska bezprostredne po vzniku ČSR v kontexte česko-slovenských *vzťahov*' [The economic development of Slovakia immediately after

The economic differences between Slovakia and the Czech Lands were further exacerbated during the post-war financial crisis. The iron foundries at Krompachy were closed, as were the metal working facilities at Zvolen, while engineering, chemical, shoe and paper industrial production shrank; some textile enterprises moved to Hungary after the war. The result was high unemployment, emigration and social discontent. Not unsurprisingly the opposition parties – the Communist Party of Czechoslovakia, the Magyar minority parties and increasingly also the Ľudáks – made use of this discontent, pointing to the inability of the centralist state to provide healthy economic and social development across the entire country. This situation led to a rising tide of anti-Czech sentiment in Slovakia. Relations between the Czechs and Slovaks worsened, and anti-Czechoslovak propaganda, promulgated by the domestic and foreign opponents of the state, increased.

Measures designed to resolve these economic discrepancies had to originate with the state; they included the unification of the transport system, railway expansion, the reduction of the tax burden, the removal of inequalities in social legislation and other legal norms inherited from the pre-1918 situation. Critical reports about this economic dualism soon began to appear in the press and in parliament through petitions and memoranda addressed to the government, to political parties (both government and opposition) and to various societies and economic organisations. These economic and social problems had a direct influence on the political situation and gradually developed into what became known as the 'Slovak question'.

Slovakia's position within the Czechoslovak economy was also of concern to economists. Their view was that Slovakia, where about 60 per cent of the population worked in the agriculture sector, compared to 39 per cent in the Czech Lands, should be able to supply the whole Czechoslovak market with its agricultural needs. However, it soon became clear that the state of Slovak agriculture – low agricultural productivity, unfavourable soil conditions and an uneven division of land ownership – meant that it was simply unable to meet these objectives.

Some type of land reform was therefore necessary, and the Land Confiscation Act of 1919 was enacted as a result. The act empowered the state to take over tracts of land that exceeded 150 hectares of cultivated land and 100 hectares of forest. For the public good, an owner could retain 500 hectares of land in exceptional cases, according to article 11 of the act. This process was not designed to liquidate the large

the formation of the Czecho-Slovak Republic in the context of Czech–Slovak relations], in Valenta *et al.* (eds.), *Československo*, p. 274.

estates, as was claimed by the former owners of latifundia, who organised protests against the reforms, including complaints to the League of Nations. The aims of the land reform process, which had political and social as well as economic dimensions, were to strengthen the position of middle-sized farms and to liberalise the trade in land, a large part of which was owned by German or Magyar noblemen.

However, government assistance for middle-sized land-owners was only partly successful in Slovakia. While farms of 20–50 hectares of land represented 5.1 per cent of all enterprises in Bohemia by the mid 1930s and 3.1 per cent in Moravia and Silesia, in Slovakia they accounted for only 2.4 per cent. Very small-scale agriculture also expanded to some extent: owners gained an average of 1.21 hectare of land. However, these results were undermined by the economic crisis at the beginning of the 1930s, which hindered the repayments of loans for buying land. When debtors defaulted on these loans they were threatened with the lawful seizure of property, and another problem appeared in Slovakia. In 1932, there were 83,000 lawful seizures of property, 70 per cent of them from peasant-farmers; as well as land, the Slovak courts confiscated livestock, machinery, agricultural equipment and feed, unlike in the Czech Lands. This anomaly arose because of differences in legislative and judicial practice in the two regions; in Slovakia, 'belongings' was interpreted more widely, so peasant-farmers there suffered more penalties. Various legislative adjustments empowered the government to moderate the impact of bankruptcy proceedings during this crisis. However, the repayment of debts was delayed only for a short time, and indebted farmers were not able to gain credit, but, at least in some cases, financial ruin was avoided.[15] Nevertheless the demand for land redistribution persisted; those people who could not support themselves by working in either agriculture or industry during the Great Depression swelled the ranks of the unemployed.

In 1931–1932, there were almost 200,000 unemployed persons in Slovakia, more than 50 per cent of the number of employed persons; almost three-quarters of these were agricultural workers. According to contemporary experts, the problem of the excess population of Slovakia (those who were unable to emigrate during the crisis because of the anti-immigration policies of destination countries) had now to be solved

---

[15] N. Krajčovičová, 'Predpoklady realizácie pozemkovej reformy na Slovensku v medzivojnovom období' [Preconditions for the realisation of the land reform in Slovakia in the inter-war period], in I. Frolec (ed.), *Československá pozemková reforma 1919–1935 a její mezinárodní souvislosti* [The Czechoslovak land reform 1919–1935 and its international contexts] (Uherské Hradiště, 1994), pp. 13–20.

by rapid industrialisation. This concept also had supporters among economists and entrepreneurs, who were convinced that the government had to support industrialisation in those parts of the republic where agriculture could not provide an adequate living for the population. Another group of experts, mostly Czech, did not accept the necessity of state intervention. They argued that industry had to be left to develop 'naturally'. However, Slovak industry and Czech industry were not equal partners, and this economic dualism persisted. Only the looming threat of military conflict and the need to defend the republic in the second half of the 1930s stimulated the decentralisation of production to Slovakia. An important centre of industry began to be built up along the Váh river valley region, and the state concerned itself with improvement of the taxation, transport, tariff and supply policies. Slovakia thus began to develop beyond the level it had previously reached within the framework of the Kingdom of Hungary.[16]

Educational and cultural progress

Education, culture and art proved to be areas where progress was made more swiftly and successfully than in the industrial sector.[17] The achievement of state sovereignty was accompanied by the reform of education and by the creation of favourable conditions for the development of Slovak culture. By the mid 1920s, the former Hungarian school system had been totally reformed, the Slovak language had been introduced in schools, and compulsory school attendance had been reinforced by the terms of the Little Education Act of 1922. During a period when Slovak secondary and vocational schools were being developed (they did not exist prior to 1918), assistance from Czech teaching personnel proved vital. It was essential for the establishment of Comenius University in Bratislava (1919).

Although there were some Czech professors, whose presence promoted the idea of the ethnic unity of the Czech and Slovak nation, the university's importance lay in the quality of the professional training of university-educated Slovak intelligentsia. This previously very narrow stratum of Slovak society became active in the Slovak national emancipation process. It is also necessary to mention the crucial help given to

---

[16] M. Fabricius, 'Vývoj názorov na postavenie Slovensku v hospodárstve Československa (1918–1968)' [The development of views on the place of Slovakia within the economy of Czechoslovakia (1918–1968)], in Valenta et al. (eds.), Československo, pp. 279–88.

[17] I. Kamenec, 'The Development and Orientation of Slovak Culture in the Years 1918–1938', Studia historica slovaca, 12 (1982), 33–61.

Slovakia by Czech officials, technicians, engineers, railwaymen, communications workers and military personnel. All of these professionals sacrificed time and energy to assist with the introduction not only of the state administration, but also of transport and communications infrastructure, industrial production, building work, and agriculture and forestry in Slovakia after 1918. These individuals made up for the shortage of Slovak professionals, and especially for the absence of many Magyar professionals who had refused to take an oath of allegiance to the new state or who had left the republic.

The revived Matica slovenská played a central role in helping to cultivate and develop Slovak culture and academic life. The output of its academic departments – historical, ethnographic, linguistic and literary – was based on the recognition of a separate Slovak identity and nation. Matica slovenská applied this principle to all its work throughout the inter-war period, in spite of some attempts to change its orientation. Unfortunately, this endeavour was not confined to intellectual arguments, but sometimes spilled out into the political sphere. Science, art and culture were also institutionally anchored in various societies, which organised and supported these activities. The Šafárik Learned Society, part of Comenius University, was an important example. It produced the bilingual (Czech and Slovak) periodical *Bratislava*, which published the scientific findings of its members.

The arts in general, but also individual forms, underwent a renaissance in Slovakia during the First Czechoslovak Republic. The first professional theatre in the land, the Slovak National Theatre, was established; initially it had a Czech and world repertoire. A Slovak section of the Slovak National Theatre was established only after a sufficient number of Slovak actors had been trained. The theatre went on to make a significant contribution to the advancement of Slovak dramatic arts, and promoted the cultivated use of the Slovak language. Slovak fine art was also very successful. Slovak artists proved themselves within the context of world modernism, and many of them presented their work abroad, as well as at numerous exhibitions at home. An Academy of Music and Drama was opened, which, in conjunction with musical education in schools, became the basis for the education of musicians in Slovakia. The works of Slovak composers of the period were in harmony with modern European musical development, but also drew on rich domestic musical resources.

The Czechoslovak state attached great importance to general public education, so much so that an act designed to encourage the organisation of free educational courses for adults was adopted in 1919. The Public Education Union for Slovakia organised public educational activities, fostering co-operation between various public educational institutions, cultural and sports societies. They were carried on by Matica slovenská, Živena (a women's organisation), the Czechoslovak Red Cross, the Slovak League, the non-denominational Sokol and the Catholic Orol gymnastic societies. In addition there were workers' educational bodies concerned with gymnastic as well as professional and religious activities. These organisations formed the basis for the development of civic initiatives and education alongside the running of public affairs. Slovak radio began broadcasting from Bratislava in 1926, from Košice in 1927 and from Banská Bystrica in 1936. These stations were also involved in spreading general education and information. Radio also helped to form the Slovak national identity and a sense of civic solidarity within the framework of Slovakia and the whole state. By connecting the whole of Slovakia, radio acted as an integrating factor for its individual regions, which had formerly been isolated from each other and unevenly developed.

Bratislava became the recognised cultural centre of Slovakia. Thanks to its important administrative and economic position, the city's population grew rapidly, and its national structure changed in favour of its Slovak and Czech inhabitants. The regional administrative and commercial centres – Košice and Prešov in eastern Slovakia, Žilina and Zvolen in central Slovakia, and Trnava and Nitra in western Slovakia – did not lose their importance. That having been said, the development of towns across the country was uneven. The County Act of 1920 abolished ten of sixteen historic counties (*župy, stolice*), which led to the decline of the towns serving as their administrative and commercial centres. Whole industrial areas and their urban centres were also affected. They paid for the post-war economic crisis and for the economic crisis at the beginning of the 1930s.

Political crisis in the second half of the 1930s

During the mid to late 1930s, the worldwide economic crisis and the tense social situation led to the strengthening of central government, a move that triggered radicalism and extra-parliamentary activities by Slovakia's opposition parties. Hlinka's Slovak People's Party formed an Autonomist Bloc with the Slovak National Party in 1932. The parties jointly adopted the so-called Zvolen Manifesto, in which they emphasised a united and energetic effort to achieve the legislative autonomy of Slovakia on the basis of recognition of the separate identity of the Slovak nation. However, these two parties did not submit a joint proposal for Slovak autonomy to parliament. Instead, they launched their joint manifesto at public rallies such as in Nitra in 1933. The occasion was the official celebration of the consecration of Pribina's church 1,100 years earlier; the autonomists hijacked this event and proclaimed their manifesto.[18] They participated in the 1935 parliamentary election as a united force and gained 30.1 per cent of the vote. In spite of these electoral successes, the Autonomist Bloc disintegrated soon after.

The elections led to a surprising result in the Czech Lands, where Konrad Henlein's Sudeten German Party won 15 per cent of the vote and became the strongest parliamentary party. The success of the Sudeten German Party in the Czech Lands and of the electoral coalition of Magyar parties in Slovakia, which secured the 14.2 per cent of the vote, reflected the growing pressure for a solution to the nationality question in the Czechoslovak Republic. At the same time, the government in Prague had to take into account the new international situation after the Nazis' rise to power in Germany, and their determination to recover that country's status as a great power.

The Nazis soon rejected the Versailles system and aimed to exert control over foreign territories inhabited by German-speaking minorities. Therefore, Czechoslovak foreign policy actively participated in talks regarding the system of collective security. The only result of these negotiations was the conclusion of a Franco-Soviet and Czechoslovak–Soviet treaty of alliance in May 1935, with the restriction that the Soviet Union would help Czechoslovakia only if France provided assistance as well. But the European great powers persisted with their policies of appeasement, which did not provide much hope for the future. It was only a question of time until a re-armed Germany was in a position to re-assert its position in Europe, which included attacking Czechoslovakia.

Although Czechoslovakia, as a small state, gave priority to diplomatic and political instruments to help secure its existence in this increasingly tense international environment, this did not mean that it neglected defence through legislative, economic, political and military means. An Act for the Defence of the State was passed in 1936, which included measures designed to prevent any threat to state sovereignty, independence, integrity, constitutional unity or democratic-republican forms, and to avert the danger of direct attack on the Czechoslovak Republic. The construction of an interlinked series of fortifications around its borders and provision of modern equipment for the army also continued. Units of the State Defence Guard were organised to defend the state frontiers and maintain public order. A Defence Training

[18] I. Dérer, *Slovenský vývoj a ľudácka zrada* [Slovak development and the Ľudák treason] (Prague, 1946), p. 222.

Act was adopted, according to which all persons aged six to thirty were to receive some form of military training.[19]

The government's measures to consolidate the internal political situation were no less important. These were initiated by the first Slovak to become prime minister, the Agrarian Milan Hodža. He realised that the need to settle the position of the national minorities was linked to finding a solution to the Czech–Slovak question. This issue dominated political debates during the second half of the 1930s. Hlinka's Slovak People's Party appointed itself the only political representative of the Slovak nation, and expressed its attitude to pluralist democracy in the slogan 'One nation, one party, one leader'. Its deputy chairman, Jozef Tiso (1887–1947), who later replaced the ailing Andrej Hlinka as leader, claimed that the party supported the Czechoslovak Republic and its integrity, but his rhetoric hardened as the Czechoslovak and European political crisis worsened.[20]

To mark the republic's twentieth anniversary, various solutions designed to settle the nationality problem were proposed, but a comprehensive programme for settling Czech–Slovak relations remained elusive. One such solution for the nationality questions in the Czechoslovak Republic was prepared by the government, headed by Prime Minister Hodža, and with the active participation of President Edvard Beneš. A Nationality Statute divided the republic into four autonomous Lands: Bohemia, Moravia, Slovakia and Subcarpathian Ruthenia. Each Land was to be a legal entity from the point of view of public and private law, and was to be responsible for the health, social, economic and cultural spheres of the state's administration, as long as issues of state were not at stake. Land Diets with curias representing every nationality were envisaged, and the creation of Land governments and widening of the competencies given to the lower representative bodies was also contemplated.

The instigators of this project were primarily concerned with the solution of the Sudeten German question, which posed a serious threat to the stability of the internal political situation in Czechoslovakia – rapidly escalating into an international crisis. However, the Sudeten German Party categorically rejected these proposals, and Hlinka's Slovak People's Party did not agree with these suggestions either. Instead, the latter prepared its own proposals for Slovakia autonomy

[19] M. Hronský, A. Krivá and M. Čaplovič (eds.), *Vojenské dejiny Slovenska (1914–1939)* [Military history of Slovakia (1914–1939)], vol. IV (Bratislava, 1996), p. 184.
[20] L. Kamenec, *Tragédia politika, kňaza a človeka (Dr Jozef Tiso 1887–1947)* [The tragedy of a politician, priest and human being (Dr Jozef Tiso 1887–1947)] (Bratislava, 1998), p. 58.

that were published in the daily *Slovák* on 5 June 1938. It demanded the creation of a separate Slovak Diet and government, along with the introduction of Slovak as the official and teaching language on the basis of recognition of the separate identity of the Slovak nation.

President Beneš held talks with Hlinka's Slovak People's Party and submitted a counter-proposal to Tiso on 22 September 1938. Beneš promised to help with the economic equalisation of Slovakia with the Czech Lands by means of state subsidies, personnel changes in the central organs in favour of the Slovaks and, finally, a Slovak Diet. He also retreated from the position of a unitary Czechoslovak nation by distinguishing between Czechs, Slovaks and Czechoslovaks. Tiso demanded that all changes should be clearly formulated, and some of them guaranteed constitutionally, including the recognition of the separate identity of the Slovak nation, the official status of the Slovak language and the establishment of a Ministry for the Administration of Slovakia as the representative organ of executive power. Although these talks were not ultimately successful, the situation changed after the Munich Agreement of 1938, when the central government accepted Tiso's demands. Henceforth, Hlinka's Slovak People's Party left nothing to chance and pushed for the full implementation of its autonomy project. The position of the post-Munich government facilitated this situation – all the other proposals to solve the Slovak question came too late. Neither Hodža's modified nationality statute nor the Social Democratic proposal to widen the powers of local government bodies and rationalise the decentralisation of the state administration stood any chance of success. Nor did the proposal for the creation of a Diet and the adoption of a language act put forward by the prominent Slovak social democratic politician Ivan Dérer (1884–1973), who did not recognise the separate identity of the Slovak nation.

Hlinka's Slovak People's Party utilised the political uncertainties in Slovakia, a direct result of the internal political crisis and international tension after the Munich Agreement, to force through its proposal for settling the Czech–Slovak constitutional relationship. By signing the Žilina Agreement of 6 October 1938, the Slovak political parties (excluding the Communists and the Social Democrats) submitted to Hlinka's Slovak People's Party. Thus it embarked decisively on the road to an authoritarian regime and a totalitarian Slovak state after twenty years of activity within a pluralist democracy.

11 Slovakia from the Munich Conference to the declaration of independence

Valerián Bystrický

How Slovakia became the focus of Germany's Central European policy

The Munich Agreement was signed on 29 September 1938, by the British and French premiers, N. Chamberlain (1869–1940) and É. Daladier (1884–1970), the German Führer A. Hitler (1889–1945) and the Italian duce B. Mussolini (1883–1945). It significantly altered the balance of power among the great powers in the Danubian region, and led to Nazi Germany acquiring a dominant position in Central Europe. These events signalled the end of Czechoslovakia's role as a regional force. The republic ceased to be a subject of international politics and retained only a nominal level of formal independence.

However, the agreement between the four great powers did not lead to the successful culmination of the aggressive aims of Nazi foreign policy, as the goals set by Hitler in November 1937, and later made more specific in May 1938 (*Fall Grün*), were only partially achieved. One of the preconditions for the success of Nazi aggression in Europe was the elimination of Czechoslovakia as a political and military factor in the region, its removal as a threat to the Reich's flanks in case of conflict, and the acquisition of additional economic resources for waging war. Hitler's original directive from 30 May 1938, 'I have taken an unchangeable decision to destroy Czecho-Slovakia by military action in the near future',[1] gained a renewed impetus after Munich. As a result of the way in which Czechoslovakia had been undermined, it no longer represented a significant obstacle to Nazi aggression.[2] Nevertheless, in the event of a military confrontation, Germany required a continuous eastern frontier. For these reasons Hitler made clear his 'unshakable decision' to destroy Czechoslovakia completely by the beginning of October.

---

[1] *Akten zur deutschen auswärtigen Politik 1918–1945* [henceforth *ADAP*], Series D (1937–1945) (Baden-Baden, 1952), vol. II, Doc. 221, p. 282.

[2] G. L. Weinberg, *The Foreign Policy of Hitler's Germany. Starting World War II* (Chicago and London, 1966), p. 467.

Under these conditions German policy would take the form of what was euphemistically called a 'pacification action'; Berlin's aim was to carry out a lightning occupation of Bohemia and Moravia and to isolate Slovakia.[3]

At the beginning of 1939, Hitler gradually informed his immediate political circle and the secret services of his decision to begin direct preparations to carry out this plan. It would be achieved by the declaration of an independent Slovak state, Hungary's occupation of Subcarpathian Ruthenia, and finally by the German occupation of Bohemia and Moravia. The liquidation of Czechoslovakia had to be publicly presented as the internal disintegration of the state. Various inflammatory and terrorist actions, provocations by the German minority, for example, would accompany the whole process, while German units would guarantee the security of the Slovak–Czech frontier against any intervention by the Czechoslovak (Czech) army.[4]

After the resolution of the Czechoslovak crisis at Munich, Germany modified its attitude towards Slovakia. Berlin understood the geopolitical importance of Slovakia in this new situation and its practical value with regard to the plans to liquidate Czechoslovakia. For a while, Bratislava became a crucial component of the Reich's Central European policy.[5] Prior to this development, it had been assumed that in the event of military confrontation Hungary would occupy Slovakia, but after 29 September 1938 the situation changed. With the signing of the Munich Agreement, E. Woermann, an assistant secretary of state in the German Foreign Office, wrote a memorandum on a possible solution to the Slovak question. Hitler approved this alternative on 8 October 1938. In line with the terms of the Munich Agreement, but also in the interest of concealing Berlin's real aims, the memo approved supporting the 'autonomy of Slovakia by placing pressure on Prague'. It also raised the possibility that they might want 'to one day lead the Slovaks from autonomy to state independence'.[6] Until late 1938, German representatives, journalists and agents talked to Slovak politicians, from both the radical and moderate wings of Hlinka's Slovak People's Party (whose

[3] J. Goebbels's diary entry, 3 October 1938, in D. Irving, *Goebbels. Pán myšlenek třetí říše* [Goebbels: mastermind of the Third Reich] (Brno, 1988), p. 371; E. Kordt, *Wahn und Wirklichkeit. Die Aussenpolitik des Dritten Reiches* (Stuttgart, 1948), p. 137.

[4] J. K. Hoensch, *Die Slowakei und Hitlers Ostpolitik. Hlinkas Slowakische Volkspartei zwischen Autonomie und Separation 1938 bis 1939* (Cologne and Graz, 1965), p. 100.

[5] L. Deák, *Hra o Slovensko* [The game for Slovakia] (Bratislava, 1991), p. 149f.; D. Kováč, *Nemecko a nemecká menšina na Slovensku (1871–1945)* [Germany and the German minority in Slovakia (1871–1945)] (Bratislava 1991), p. 130.

[6] *ADAP*, D, vol. IV, Docs. 50 and 69, pp. 51, 76–7.

members were known as Ľudáks), and assured them that Berlin supported the autonomous position of Slovakia within the framework of Czechoslovakia. But, by the beginning of 1939, official and unofficial circles gradually began to inform the radicals from the ranks of the Ľudáks about their real intentions. Essentially, they gradually applied pressure on these contacts to encourage them to declare Slovak independence, and they offered assistance to help achieve this goal.

Slovak autonomy

The central issue in Czechoslovak politics during the 1930s was the exact nature of Czech–Slovak relations, the place of Slovakia and the Slovaks within the republic and related questions of political, economic and cultural life, and the attitude to the separate identity of the Slovak nation. This debate was reflected in three decisive projects that had a substantial influence on the solution of the Slovak question in 1938. The first proposal was put forward by Hlinka's Slovak People's Party on 5 June 1938. They proposed the formation of a federation in which the separate identity of the Slovak nation would be explicitly recognised. The second was a nationality statute presented by Prime Minister Milan Hodža in the summer of 1938, as a comprehensive method of solving the nationality problems of the republic. Obliquely, Hodža proposed a solution to the question of the separate identity and autonomous position of Slovakia. The third proposal, made by President Edvard Beneš on 22 September 1938, on the 'Settlement of the Relationship Between the Czechs and Slovaks in the Republic', attempted to solve this question via a compromise. This was the first attempt at a more comprehensive government-led effort to solve the Slovak question, including the problems of executive power and the economy.[7] In spite of the facts that this proposal was overshadowed by the influence of internal and foreign political pressure, that it was not straightforward and that it came too late, it became the stimulus for renewed discussions.

The Ľudáks used these changes in the internal political situation to their own advantage. After the conclusion of the Munich Agreement, the Ľudáks ceased all talks with other political groups in Slovakia and stubbornly insisted on the implementation of their own federation project, first announced on 5 June 1938. This problem was addressed in

---

[7] V. Bystrický, 'Slovensko v roku 1938 (východiská a perspektívy)' [Slovakia in 1938 (starting points and perspectives)], in J. Valenta, E. Horáček and J. Harna (eds.), *Československo 1918–1938. Osudy demokracie ve střední Evropě. I* [Czechoslovakia, 1918–38. The fate of democracy in Central Europe I] (Prague, 1999), p. 201.

talks held between the Slovak political parties, primarily the Ľudáks and the Agrarians at Žilina on 5 and 6 October 1938. The various Slovak parties, with the exception of the Communists and the Social Democrats, signed the Žilina Agreement, which included the statement: 'The constitutional position of Slovakia will be definitively solved by the constitutional acceptance of this proposal.' They also agreed to issue a constitutional act on the autonomy of Slovakia based on Hlinka's Slovak People's Party proposal from June 1938.

The next day, after talks in Prague, Jozef Tiso, the leader of the Ľudáks, was appointed head of an autonomous government. Matúš Černák, Ferdinand Ďurčanský and the Agrarians Ján Lichner and Pavol Teplanský were also made ministers. The leaders of the Czech political parties, the chairman of the Chamber of Deputies, Jan Malypetr, and the chairman of the Senate, František Soukup, acknowledged the Žilina Agreement on 6 October 1938. After further talks in Prague, held two days later, the representatives of the Czech political parties and of Hlinka's Slovak People's Party and the new members of the autonomous government met in parliament and issued a declaration, in which they adopted a proposal to issue a constitutional act proclaiming the autonomy of Slovakia. By this action, the Czech and Slovak political representatives demonstrated that they agreed to the new constitutional arrangements that were supposed to be definitive. The Constitutional Act on the Autonomy of Slovakia was passed on 22 November 1938.[8]

Thus the republic became an asymmetrical federal state, with the central government and National Assembly in Prague and an autonomous government and a Diet of the Slovak Land (Snem Slovenskej krajiny) in Bratislava. The National Assembly held legislative power for the whole territory of the republic concerning questions of the constitution, foreign policy, national defence, citizenship, currency, customs, transport and so on. The state was renamed the Czecho-Slovak Republic, a hyphen being inserted to indicate the Slovaks' newly established status. The conclusion of the Žilina Agreement and passing of the Constitutional Act of 22 November 1938 completed the struggle over the implementation of the principles of the Pittsburgh Agreement and the general position of Slovakia within the state. This opened a period when Slovak statehood within the framework of the Czecho-Slovak Republic was enhanced. At his trial in 1947, Jozef Tiso stated that he considered '6 October 1938 to be the climax of our political aims'.

[8] *Dokumenty slovenskej národnej identity a štátnosti* [Documents on Slovak national identity and statehood] (Bratislava, 1999), vol. II, pp. 188–95.

However, there were currents in Hlinka's Slovak People's Party that had a different view on these questions.

The emergence of an authoritarian regime

The conclusion of the Žilina Agreement led to the regrouping of political forces. The Ľudák–Agrarian bloc became the decisive power in Slovakia, and Hlinka's Slovak People's Party came to dominate politics. Right-of-centre tendencies were greatly strengthened, while the influence and importance of the democratic parties and currents declined. As a result, the conditions for the gradual construction of an authoritarian regime were created.

The first aim of the Ľudáks after coming to power was to build a monopoly position in the political, economic and cultural life of Slovakia by destroying the existing political structure. The internal political changes in Slovakia in autumn 1938 led to the disintegration of political parties, a process the Ľudáks accelerated with administrative measures. On 9 October 1938, they banned the Communist Party of Czechoslovakia in Slovakia and on 16 November 1938 the Social Democratic Party; gradually other parties were likewise banned. The 'voluntary simplification' of political life culminated on 8 November 1938, when the Agrarian, National Unity, National Socialist and Fascist Parties all merged with Hlinka's Slovak People's Party.

This political grouping retained the name Hlinka's Slovak People's Party and supplemented it with the subtitle the Party of Slovak National Unity. It was typical that the representatives of the amalgamaled political entities did not receive any positions and their reward was a few seats in the subsequently elected Diet of the Slovak Land. The autonomous government also used orders and bans to disband the majority of social organisations and societies, trade union organisations, and cultural and gymnastic organisations. At the same time, new organisations were 'put on the right track' by Hlinka's Slovak People's Party, the paramilitary Hlinka Guard or appropriate state institutions. The process of building an anti-democratic authoritarian system contained all the usual features, characteristics, methods and procedures of similar developments in other authoritarian and fascist countries, with some nationally specific features.

The creation of a paramilitary organisation was an important part of the process of strengthening the position of Hlinka's Slovak People's Party in political life. The Hlinka Guard had been formed in June 1938 and grew rapidly after the power-political changes at the beginning of October, but its formation, existence and activity were not defined by legislation. The Hlinka Guard provided political and military support for the new regime. It assisted in the achievement of a power monopoly in Slovakia, but it was not armed. Its representatives – such as Karol Sidor (1901–1953), editor-in-chief of *Slovák*, who was the first commander of the Hlinka Guard – actively participated in political life; they promoted themselves within state power structures and attempted to develop the Guard according to the example of the Nazi Party's Sturmabteilung (SA). The Hlinka Guard became the standard bearer of Slovak nationalism, due to the separatist forces concentrated in its ranks, but it also contained working-class elements and naturally careerists. Its 'elite' unit Rodobrana (Home Defence), the activities of which were revived by Vojtech Tuka after his release from prison in October 1938, was expected to play a decisive role in helping to achieve the party's political and separatist ambitions.

Influencing and directly guiding public opinion via control of the mass media were important methods of strengthening the 'new' regime. Hlinka's Slovak People's Party gradually strengthened its monopoly over the provision of information. Through the creation of the Office of Propaganda, headed by Alexander Mach (1902–1980), one of its most extreme radicals, the party placed government officials (commissars) in the individual daily newspapers. Yet it was the gradual elimination of the periodical and non-periodical press, and of political dailies with the exception of the historic *Národné noviny*, that proved to be the decisive factor. Thus, the new regime gradually prevented conceptual or ideological political opposition, excluded or limited plurality of views, and eradicated most of the press of the former political parties by the end of 1938.

As the polity increasingly indulged in a kind of racist scapegoating (of Czechs and Jews) and other types of intolerance, policies in Slovakia following the seizure of power by Hlinka's Slovak People's Party were oriented towards defining or identifying the 'enemy'. This process led to the ratcheting up of nationalist sentiments, increasingly in a negative direction. The specific character of developments in Slovakia during autumn 1938 arose from the fact that anti-democratic measures were more or less tolerated or accepted by the population, because the achievement of a 'united front' and the calming of the political scene were regarded as priorities. The idea of building a 'new' Slovakia gained currency and was widely propagated. This policy justified most of the anti-democratic measures imposed by the new regime, from the 'simplification' of political life to the solution of the so-called bread-and-butter questions, all accompanied by slogans such as 'we ourselves will rule', 'we will be masters in Slovakia' and so on. Hlinka's Slovak People's

Party unambiguously presented itself as the decisive force building the 'new' Slovakia. These activities, as well as the preceding struggle for autonomy, justified the party's right to rule in Slovakia.[9]

This effort to achieve comprehensive control over Slovakia's political and social life also saw the creation of a unified trade union movement. The trade unions were disbanded after 6 October 1938, and the only new trade unions allowed were Christian-based. At the same time, a campaign of typical social demagoguery, coloured with anti-capitalist and nationalist slogans and associated with anti-Jewish and anti-Czech feelings, was launched.

The government and power apparatus led and directed by Hlinka's Slovak People's Party dealt with the economy and with reconstruction of the bureaucratic apparatus in much the same way that it dealt with the political field. Appointed administrators were placed in organisations such as the Chamber of Commerce, the Chamber of Industry and the Agricultural Council, that is, in all the important organisations concerned with different areas of the economy. On the other hand, because they had too few potential substitutes, the Ľudáks had to leave experts in their posts, without regard for their political orientation, including so-called Czechoslovakists.

Anti-Jewish and anti-Czech measures

During the process of taking over and consolidating its power, the Hlinka's Slovak People's Party had already endeavoured to limit the economic role and overall social influence of the Jewish and Czech inhabitants of Slovakia. This political activity often led to the deliberate provocation of anti-Jewish and anti-Czech sentiments, which they justified by efforts to gain places in the state apparatus or local government for the faithful supporters of the new regime. These tendencies first appeared in the period after the signing of the Vienna Arbitration (to which I will return), when, on the basis of a decree from the prime minister of the autonomous government, Jozef Tiso, poor Jews from Slovakia were deported to the territories acquired by Hungary.[10]

The process of 'Slovakising' society included demanding the repatriation of Czechs employed in Slovakia. This issue was a long-term and

---

[9] F. Lukeš, *Podivný mír* [Strange peace] (Prague, 1969), p. 186.
[10] I. Kamenec, *Po stopách tragédie* [Following the tracks of tragedy] (Bratislava, 1991), p. 25; E. Nižňanský, *Židovská komunita na Slovensku medzi československou parlamentnou demokraciou a slovenským štátom v stredoeurópskom kontexte* [The Jewish community in Slovakia between Czechoslovak parliamentary democracy and the Slovak state in the Central European context] (Prešov, 1999), p. 36.

controversial problem. In the years immediately after the First World War, help from Czech intellectuals, teachers and various experts not only was necessary, but also was regarded as a positive benefit to all. However, the emergence of a Slovak intelligentsia, to which these Czech teachers had greatly contributed, led to a situation in which this new generation could not find work in state service, partly because many places were occupied by Czechs. As a result of the changes after October 1938, this issue was re-opened. In an effort to strengthen its position, the new regime endeavoured to secure control of the state administration, security apparatus and army, thus taking over the levers of power of the central government. Apart from personnel changes, the removal of Czech state employees from Slovakia was viewed as a way to solve this problem. For example, the force of 4,300 gendarmes in Slovakia was made up of 1,500 Slovaks and 2,800 Czechs. The new regime deliberately built up a power structure loyal to itself, and endeavoured to create conditions for enforcing political influence on the educational process by dismissing teachers and professors from Bohemia and Moravia. The party also had to reward impatient supporters and provide appropriate positions for them.

For these reasons, the removal of Czech employees was vigorously pursued. The action was based on an agreement between the autonomous and central governments in December 1938, leading to the departure of 9,000 Czech employees from Slovakia. The implementation of the 'provision of Czech employees of the central government' corresponded with the existing political system and was in conflict with the democratic solution of similar questions.[11]

In autumn 1938, the ruling party also made personnel changes in the most important state posts. The eradication of political parties was followed by the dissolution of local government bodies and the exclusion from others of opponents of the Ľudáks. The appointment of politically acceptable deputies in the local government strengthened the position of the regime in the first stages of its rule. However, this takeover, carried out 'with smiling faces', was not accompanied by mass or individual repression against representatives of the former regime in the form of imprisonment or the persecution of opponents, but mainly by means of depriving people of positions and influence. These policies are characteristic of an authoritarian regime; as a result, the democratic system was effectively dismantled. The new system had not yet been fully

[11] J. Rychlík, *Češi a Slováci ve 20. století. Česko-slovenské vztahy 1914–1945* [The Czechs and Slovaks in the twentieth century. Czecho-Slovak relations 1914–1945] (Bratislava, 1997), p. 154.

established at this stage, but the process of transition from a democratic to an authoritarian system had already developed so far that citizens had no chance of freely expressing their views about the political and social situation. This process was also influenced by international factors, not least by fears for Slovakia's territorial integrity.

Territorial changes

The decisions reached by the four great powers at Munich also led to territorial changes in Slovakia. On the basis of the Munich Agreement, the territory of Petržalka, that is, the part of Bratislava located on the right bank of the Danube, was ceded to the German Reich. Later, Germany took control of ancient Devín castle and its immediate surroundings for strategic reasons.

The Supplementary Declaration of the four great powers signed at Munich agreed to solve the question of the Magyar and Polish minorities in Slovakia by means of further alteration to the existing state boundaries. These actions weakened the republic more and raised the possibility of its ultimate dismantlement. It was an opportunity, especially for the Magyar political elite, to demand additional changes to the territorial settlement in Central Europe, in accordance with its traditional plans and ambitions. Hungary's most ambitious goal for Slovakia was for it to return to its pre-1918 status. However, the Hungarian political elite lacked the strength to achieve this aim. A decisive factor was that the ambitions of the regime in Budapest not only lacked the support of Nazi Germany, but were also in direct conflict with its plans for the Danube basin after the Munich Conference.

Hungary justified its claims in many ways: using historical arguments; proposing to enable Slovaks to work towards self-determination; demanding that territories with an ethnic Magyar population of more than 50 per cent (according to the distorted census figures of 1910) be ceded to it; deploying economic arguments; and so on. Budapest persisted with the self-created political illusion that the Slovak nation longed for, or had an interest in returning to, its 'former homeland'. What was ignored was that in democratic Slovakia national consciousness and self-confidence had strengthened and that they had definitely achieved the status of a political nation.

The signatory powers of Munich had formally left the solution of the question of the Magyar minority in Czechoslovakia in the hands of the interested governments. As a result of the changes of 6 October 1938, Hlinka's Slovak People's Party claimed the right to conduct the negotiations. The head of the Slovak autonomous government, Jozef Tiso, who

Figure 11 The Vienna Arbitration (1938). Italian foreign minister
Count Galeazzo Ciano (seated left) and German foreign minister
Joachim von Ribbentrop (standing and reading). Facing away from
the camera: Jozef Tiso

participated in inter-state negotiations for the first time, became chairman of the Czecho-Slovak delegation.

Talks with the Hungarian delegation, led by Foreign Minister Kálmán
Kanya, were held at Komárno from 9 to 13 October 1938, although
given the conditions and considering the existence of completely different proposals they were unlikely to succeed. After complex diplomatic
talks and an unsuccessful exchange of views, the two governments
decided to ask Germany and Italy to arbitrate, and agreed in advance
to accept their decision. On the basis of the Vienna Arbitration, concluded on 2 November 1938 (see Fig. 11), Czecho-Slovakia was obliged
to cede 11,833 km^2 of territory and 972,000 inhabitants to Hungary, of
which Slovakia lost 10,390 km^2 and 854,000 persons. More than
270,000 of them were of Slovak nationality; a few were Czechs.[12] This
dramatic forfeit of territory seriously disrupted the state's railway and
communications network and the wider economy; important centres
such as Košice, Nové Zámky, Levice and Lučenec were lost.

An anti-democratic regime was established across these occupied
territories, Magyar chauvinist attitudes increased and there was systematic imposition of denationalisation and repression. As a result of this
policy, the Slovak residents in these occupied territories soon came into

[12] Deák, *Hra*, p. 169.

conflict with Hungarian authorities and there were bloody incidents at Šurany, Komjatice and Čechy.

Poland also exploited the complicated situation left by the Munich Agreement. In mid-October it made further territorial demands, this time in Slovakia. The extent to which the territorial demands made by Warsaw were to be implemented also depended on how willing Bratislava was to adapt to Polish power ambitions in the Danube region. After intense diplomatic pressure, the central government accepted Poland's demands at the beginning of November, and smaller areas of territory in the north of Kysúce and Orava regions and the High Tatra Mountains were transferred. When the territorial changes were implemented, violence and political incidents occurred: the local population resisted, and demonstrations and protests were organised against the decisions of the autonomous and central governments to accept the ultimatum from Poland. The total loss of territory amounted to 226 km^2 inhabited by 4,280 persons.

The weakness of the opposition parties

The Vienna Arbitration and the surrender of territory to Poland were serious foreign policy failures of the autonomous government. They cast doubt on its ability to maintain the territorial integrity of Slovakia. This fact, as well as the growth of separatist tendencies and the creation of an authoritarian regime, led to an opposition movement gradually forming within the framework of the former political parties.

One important feature of the transfer of power in Slovakia at the beginning of October 1938 was that it happened at a time when a direct threat to the territorial integrity of the country had emerged. The moderation shown by the opponents of Hlinka's Slovak People's Party, that is, the representatives of the centralist parties (the Agrarians, Social Democrats and others), was strongly influenced by efforts not to complicate the internal political situation, to achieve consolidation as soon as possible and to appear united before the international community. The former centralist parties also had an interest in collaborating with Ľudáks in government because they did not want to take responsibility for the unavoidable amputation of parts of Slovak territory. The delusion also spread in these parties that the policies of Hlinka's Slovak People's Party were necessary as a result of economic failures.

The participation of two Agrarians, Ján Lichner until November 1938 and Pavol Teplanský until 11 March 1939, as ministers in the autonomous government at least indicated that their party supported or participated in these political changes. The merging of the Agrarians and other parties with Hlinka's Slovak People's Party on 8 November 1938 also disoriented party members and helped to create the illusion that a 'simplification' of political life and national unification had occurred in the interest of building a 'new' Slovakia. As noted, the Communist Party of Czechoslovakia was banned on 9 October 1938, and the Social Democratic Party on 16 October. After the Munich Conference, disillusioned and disappointed adherents and supporters of bourgeois democracy were losing faith in its ideas, as it were.

The overall international and domestic situation in late 1938 meant that the regrouping of political power and the destruction of the democratic system in Slovakia took place with little opposition at that time. The disintegration of political groups led to a tendency among opponents of the regime, especially the small autonomist-oriented Slovak National Party, to absorb the membership of other parties and operate as a kind of legally functioning opposition. The Slovak National Party announced that it wished 'faithfully and loyally to co-operate with Hlinka's Slovak People's Party in building a new Slovakia',[13] but it also wanted to try to create a strong political group around itself. It had ambitions to alternate with or replace the Ľudáks in government, in a manner similar to parliamentary customs in Western Europe. Their ideas flowed from certain illusions: they underestimated the potential and abilities of Hlinka's Slovak People's Party to rule, to solve economic problems, to install an authoritarian regime and generally to keep itself in power.

A legally functioning opposition party was not created, in part because the Land Office (Krajinský úrad) banned the activity of the Slovak National Party, later permitting it to renew its activity for a few days so that it could 'merge' with Hlinka's Slovak People's Party. Moreover, the political representatives opposed to building a 'new' Slovakia failed to find common ground. Passivity, indecisiveness, hesitation and pessimism characterised this group of politicians and their adherents. For all that, a gradual change in outlook was taking place as anti-democratic tendencies markedly intensified, campaigns against the Jewish and Czech inhabitants increased, and above all calls for a separate state were being voiced more often in public. An illegal opposition began to form and organise on the basis of the former party structures. Apart from some Communist leaflets, public activity was limited, although at the beginning of 1939 there were attempts to find a common approach and turn to the public with an appeal against separatist plans. However, the course of events conspired to disrupt these political intentions.

[13] *Národné noviny*, 3 November 1938.

Institutionalisation of the authoritarian regime

The leaders of Hlinka's Slovak People's Party spent much of the autumn of 1938 and the beginning of 1939 building the foundations of Slovak statehood and securing economic stability. From the point of view of these priorities, the constitution of the Diet of the Slovak Land was considered a primary task. The Ľudáks organised elections to this parliament solely on the basis of a single list of candidates, which ensured that nobody other than the selected political representatives could be put forward.

The election held on 18 December 1938 took place in the form of a plebiscite, with only one question, 'Do you want a new free Slovakia?', and two possible answers, 'yes' or 'no'. Sixty-three members of parliament were elected, forty-seven from Hlinka's Slovak People's Party, four from the former Agrarian Party, two from the Deutsche Partei representing the German minority, one from the Magyar minority and individuals from other former political parties who were already members of the 'united' political party. The united list of candidates gained 97.5 per cent of the votes.

Immediately after the first ceremonial session of the Diet of the Slovak Land, held on 18 January 1939, the government was again reshuffled and some radicals, such as Matúš Černák, were excluded. The election of Martin Sokol (1901–1957) as chairman of the Diet was intended to indicate that the moderate wing, which supported the preservation of the common state, would prevail in political life. However, the government programme submitted by Tiso to a session of the Diet on 21 February 1939 was more controversial. It emphasised, 'Here on the floor of our Diet, we are building our state, our new state, our Slovak state'.[14] It did not mention Czecho-Slovakia, but neither did it mention independence. This ambiguity indicated worsening relations between the central and autonomous governments.

Although the adoption of the Act on the Autonomy of the Slovak Land directly defined the powers of the central and autonomous governments, it did not lead to any significant improvement in relations between the two institutions or between Czechs and Slovaks in general. This declaration was misunderstood by a large part of Czech society, not least because it was seen as further undermining the state during a period of renewed threat from Nazi Germany. After Beneš resigned as president (5 October 1938), the Czech and Slovak sides agreed on the election

---

[14] *Dokumenty slovenskej národnej identity a štátnosti*, vol. II, p. 196.

of the conservative Catholic lawyer Emil Hácha (1871–1945) (30 November 1938). On the adoption of an 'enabling act' (*zmocňovací zákon*) limiting the activity of democratic institutions, and on the conclusion of the agreement on the departure of 9,000 Czech employees from Slovakia, Hácha's unofficial Christmas visit to the High Tatras was genuinely positively received. On the other hand, there remained lingering disputes over the financing of the Slovak budget and the widening of the powers of the autonomous government.

The constitutional issue: two approaches

At the talks held in Žilina on 5 and 6 October 1938, and after the conclusion of the agreement on the autonomy of the Slovak Land, within the Ľudák Party two basic tendencies crystallised with regard to the constitutional issue. The moderate wing of the movement represented by Tiso and Martin Sokol, and gradually also by Karol Sidor, argued for the establishment of Slovak statehood within the framework of Czecho-Slovakia, and – at some ill-defined point in the future – independence was to be achieved via an evolutionary route. There was, however, a clear tendency within these circles to strengthen the powers of the government in Bratislava. They wanted to move beyond federalism towards a sort of dual state system. Although foreign policy was not officially part of its powers, the autonomous government was gradually appropriating the right to decide its own line; this was eroding the importance of the common state and of Czechoslovak statehood. The general issue of state security as a whole was marginalised; however, by the beginning of March 1939, the moderate wing of Hlinka's Slovak People's Party was also pursuing the independent existence of Slovakia, and its territorial integrity, through direct talks with Poland, bypassing the central government in Prague.

The radical wing of the Ľudák Party, represented by Ferdinand Ďurčanský (1906–1974), Alexander Mach (1902–1980), Matúš Černák and, after his release from prison, Vojtech Tuka, did not feel bound by previously adopted resolutions, and they had already discussed the alternative of an independent Slovak state by the time of the Žilina talks. This group openly discussed their ambitions and plans with various representatives of Nazi Germany, including Hitler's paladin Hermann Göring and Foreign Minister Joachim von Ribbentrop. Tuka and Mach continually promoted these goals in the press, at public assemblies and in published polemics with the aim of influencing the Slovak public. Until late 1938, they did not receive direct support from Nazi Germany for their plans, but this situation radically changed at the beginning of 1939.

Pressure from Germany

In correspondence with Hitler's plans for the ultimate dissolution of Czecho-Slovakia, various Nazi emissaries began to inform Slovaks that if they did not want Slovakia to become part of Hungary, then they had to declare independence. Most importantly, Tuka received direct confirmation of these intentions from Hitler on 12 February 1939. The fact that Tuka was the first leading radical Ľudák to be received by the Führer was not as important as the content of the conversation. Tuka unambiguously stated that the further coexistence of the Czechs and the Slovaks within a common state was now impossible. Hitler indicated that Czecho-Slovakia would soon be no more, and expressed willingness to guarantee the existence of an independent Slovak state if and when one was declared.

As the date for the destruction of Czecho-Slovakia approached, Berlin's position became clearer and direct pressure was applied to both the radicals and the moderates to declare independence in accord with the Third Reich's plans. During talks with a Slovak delegation at the end of February and beginning of March 1939, Göring bluntly stated that Slovak independence was a precondition for future economic co-operation with the Reich.[15] This message was repeated by the governor (*Reichsstatthalter*) of Austria, Arthur Seyss-Inquart, in talks with Tiso and Karol Sidor on 7 March 1939.

The representatives of the moderate wing of Hlinka's Slovak People's Party did not agree with this radical solution and wanted to ensure that any declaration of independence was legally proclaimed by the Diet of the Slovak Land, and was not merely the result of German pressure. A resolution signed by the top leadership of Hlinka's Slovak People's Party and leading figures in the Diet, proposed by Tiso, and adopted on 6 March 1939, gave their aim as 'To continue the building of the Slovak state by the evolutionary route and not to declare independence immediately'. However, this resolution meant that the Ľudák leadership had no intention of respecting the obligations accepted five months earlier in Žilina. The legalistic approach to any declaration of independence was based on the idea that it would be undertaken by the Diet, 'when the Slovak members of parliament will find it appropriate as the rightful legal representatives of the Slovak nation'.[16] From this perspective, the

[15] *ADAP*, D, vol. IV, Doc. 168, p. 185.
[16] K. Sidor, 'Ako došlo k vyhláseniu Slovenskej republiky' [How the declaration of the Slovak Republic came about], in M. Šprinc (ed.), *Slovenská republika 1939–1949* [The Slovak Republic 1939–1949] (Scranton, 1949), p. 46.

further preservation of Czecho-Slovakia merely served to establish the infrastructure for an independent Slovak state.

Information about the separatist ambitions of the radicals soon reached Prague, where the growing Ľudák centrifugal tendencies had been regarded with some alarm since the adoption of the Žilina Agreement. By way of a response, plans were proposed to paralyse the activity of the radical wing and partially limit the powers of the autonomous government. General Alois Eliáš (1890–1942), the former commander of the Fifth Army Corps at Trenčín (1935–1938), and minister of transport in Rudolf Beran's (1887–1957) central government, took the lead role in trying to suppress these separatist tendencies. At a secret meeting of some of the ministers in this government at Unhošt in the Nouzov woods, held on 12 February 1939, he presented a plan for a military intervention in Slovakia, with the aim of preventing the breakup of Czecho-Slovakia. He thought that if Berlin's plans could be frustrated, it would be easier to restore a common state in the future. There was no intention to limit Slovakia's autonomous status as such.[17]

At first, the central government, especially Prime Minister Beran and President Hácha, had reservations about such a radical solution. When the relations between the central and autonomous governments worsened at the beginning of March, as a result of information received about contacts between Slovak radicals and Nazi Germany, the central government decided on military intervention in Slovakia during the night of 9/10 March 1939. President Hácha dismissed Tiso as head of the autonomous government. Gendarme units from the Czech Lands and army units stationed in Slovakia, under the command of General Bedřich Homola (1887–1943), occupied important strategic places, crossroads and buildings and arrested some officials of the Hlinka Guard and Hlinka's Slovak People's Party, numbering perhaps 250 persons in all.

Military intervention provoked further anti-Czech hostility, and ultimately failed due to opposition organised by the Hlinka Guard and inadequate political backing. The military measures were revoked on the morning of 11 March 1939; however, unrest continued in Bratislava, organised by the indigenous Deutsche Partei and German agents sent to Slovakia. The situation partially stabilised after the appointment of Karol Sidor as head of the autonomous government that same evening. Nazi Germany then used 'Homola's putsch', as the military intervention in Slovakia was called, to implement its own plans.

---

[17] L. K. Feierabend, *Ve vládách druhé republiky* [In the governments of the Second Republic] (New York, 1961), pp. 139, 147.

The final liquidation of Czecho-Slovakia

Nazi pressure on the Slovaks intensified as the date for their planned German invasion of Czecho-Slovakia approached. However, there was no political group in Bratislava willing to declare an independent state in conjunction with Nazi plans, apart from the radicals in Hlinka's Slovak People's Party. The 'Viennese lords' – Governor Seyss-Inquart, Gauleiter Otto Bürckel and their colleagues – who were directly involved in the preparation of the declaration of independence did not control the situation. The whole problem had to be solved by the secretary of state in the Foreign Ministry Wilhelm Keppler, sent to Vienna by Hitler. Keppler, accompanied by the 'Viennese lords', visited the newly appointed head of the autonomous government Sidor in the early hours of 12 March 1939. They asked Sidor to declare an independent Slovak state, which he refused to do. All of a sudden in Bratislava there was no responsible politician willing to fulfil the Nazis' requests. In this situation, the choice fell to Tiso, who had withdrawn to his parish at Bánovce nad Bebravou after the military intervention.

The plan to organise Tiso's visit to Berlin and secure a meeting with Hitler had already been completed by the beginning of March by Seyss-Inquart and Bürckel. Given the new circumstances, it appeared to be the solution to this complicated situation. The former deputy premier Ferdinand Ďurčanský, who had already fled to the Austrian side of the Danube, vehemently supported this move. After complicated preparations, Tiso received an invitation and the assurance that Hitler would see him on 13 March. He then flew to Berlin with a retinue. After a welcome with the honours appropriate to a head of state, he learnt from his talks with Hitler that Slovakia faced two alternatives: they could declare an independent state or the Führer would take no further interest in its fate.[18] In this situation, as Tiso understood it, the country would be divided between its neighbours, with the greatest threat being posed by Hungary.

Tiso, ever faithful to the legalistic procedure, refused to declare independence in Berlin. In a telephone call with President Hácha, he demanded that the Diet of the Slovak Land be convened the next day, but he refused to submit the independence proposal himself. During the course of the Berlin talks, a compromise was reached. The Nazis gave up the 'revolutionary' solution and accepted the legal procedure of a declaration of independence by the Diet of the Slovak Land, if this was done

[18] A. Kuhn, *Hitlers aussenpolitisches Program. Entstehung und Entwicklung 1919–1939* (Stuttgart, 1970), p. 237.

blitzschnell (with lighting speed) and Slovakia accepted a 'defensive treaty' (*Schutzvertrag*), which would make it into a satellite of the Third Reich. It was signed on 13 March 1939. Basically, there was a harmonisation of the policies of the two states, which Joseph Goebbels stated with relief in his diary, 'No revolution, everything must be done constitutionally and with all the cards on the table'.[19]

The legalistic procedure used to abolish Czecho-Slovakia was more advantageous to Nazi Germany than the revolutionary method, because it permitted more effective justification and camouflaged aggressive intentions. It also enabled Slovak politicians to give reasons for the creation of an independent state. For Nazi Germany, it created the preconditions for explaining the events of 14 March 1939 as the internal break-up of the Czecho-Slovak Republic and the subsequent occupation of Bohemia and Moravia on 15 March 1939 as a peace-keeping action in Central Europe.

After Tiso's return from Berlin and his report to the Diet of the Slovak Land on 14 March 1939, its members agreed to declare an independent state. A group of First World War legionaries – the writers Janko Jesenský and Jozef Gregor Tajovský, General Rudolf Viest and others circulated a statement in the Diet denouncing the declaration.

The origin of the Slovak state, named in its constitution the 'Slovak Republic' (21 July 1939), was inseparably connected with the international situation, and especially with Berlin's aggressive plans for the region. The new state could not have originated or survived in the existing power-political situation in Central Europe without the direct support and approval of the Third Reich. The Slovak state and its leading representatives had to collaborate with Nazi Germany, to accept its demands and support its policies. In this way, the new state not only defined its place within the 'new Europe', but also its future direction and duration.

[19] Irving, *Goebbels*, p. 404.

Ivan Kamenec

The regime

The establishment of the Slovak state was announced in Bratislava on 14 March 1939, and was the result of a deep political and moral crisis in Europe, German aggression and the break-up of pre-Munich Czechoslovakia. This series of events determined not only the foreign and internal policy of the new state, but also the duration of its existence. In terms of its area and population Slovakia was one of the world's smallest countries. It had an area of 38,000 km² and a population of 2.6 million, 85% of whom declared Slovak nationality (as of the census of 31 December 1938). The remaining 15% included Germans (4.8%), Czechs (2.9%), Ruthenians (2.6%), Magyars (2.1%), Jews (1.1%), Gypsies (sic, 0.9%), Poles (0.1%), and others (0.1%). More than half the population was employed in the agricultural sector.[1]

The state was administratively divided into six counties and sixty-one districts. The capital city was Bratislava, which contained some 120,000 inhabitants. According to the constitution, the Slovak state had a republican system, and its official name was the Slovak Republic.[2] The government was led by a president; from October 1939, this was the Catholic priest Jozef Tiso, who had previously been the prime minister, and was at the time the leader of the ruling Hlinka's Slovak People's Party. The supreme legislative body of the state was the Diet (Snem) of the Slovak Republic, elected in December 1938 as the parliament of an autonomous Slovakia within the framework of the Czecho-Slovak state, and not as the parliament of an independent state. The parliamentary elections planned for 1943 were never held. The legislative body was supplemented by members appointed by the

---

[1] *Encyclopédia Slovenska* [Encyclopaedia of Slovakia], vol. V (Bratislava, 1981), p. 330.
[2] *Slovenský zákonník 1939* [Slovak statute-book 1939], Act 185/1939.

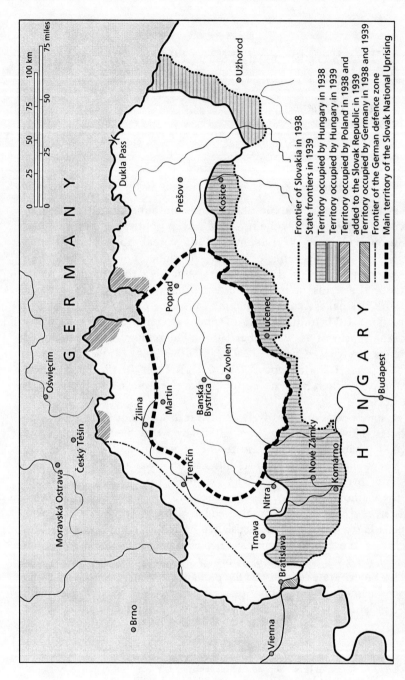

Map 5 Slovakia during the Second World War

Legend:
Frontier of Slovakia in 1938
State frontiers in 1939
Territory occupied by Hungary in 1938
Territory occupied by Hungary in 1939
Territory occupied by Poland in 1938 and added to the Slovak Republic in 1939
Territory occupied by Germany in 1938 and 1939
Frontier of the German defence zone
Main territory of the Slovak National Uprising

Map locations: Užhorod, Prešov, Košice, Lučenec, Poprad, Zvolen, Banská Bystrica, Martin, Žilina, Oświęcim, Český Těšín, Moravská Ostrava, Trenčín, Nitra, Trnava, Nové Zámky, Komárno, Bratislava, Budapest, Brno, Vienna, Dukla Pass

GERMANY

HUNGARY

Scale: 0   25   50   75   100 km
0   25   50   75 miles

president. However, the Diet gradually lost its influence and degenerated. Under pressure from domestic radical fascist forces, it was gradually stripped of its powers. These actions helped to create a totalitarian political system, of which the parliament became a part, and in the end a victim. That is, the majority of legal norms were not acts passed by parliament, but decrees issued by the government, which concentrated ever more legislative power in its own hands. Even the most important decisions of the state were often taken away from the floor of the Diet, such as entering the war on the side of the Axis powers. The role of the State Council, intended to have the function of a sort of upper chamber of parliament with the highest supervisory powers, was degraded in a similar way.

Real power in the state was held by the ruling Hlinka's Slovak People's Party, above all by the most influential members of the cabinet. The most important constitutional and party functions were concentrated in the hands of the highest representatives of the state. The first prime minister was Jozef Tiso. After he was elected president in October 1939, Vojtech Tuka took over as prime minister. Tiso was also chairman of Hlinka's Slovak People's Party, and in 1942 he gained the official title of *vodca* (Leader). Changes in the cabinet were usually initiated or directly dictated by the Nazis, often after they learnt that a government figure was deemed to be disloyal to the Third Reich, or was showing signs of pursuing a more independent Slovak policy. In summer 1940, after a Slovak–German summit in Salzburg, Berlin imposed personnel changes in key Slovak ministerial posts, promoting those who were considered most reliable. Prime Minister Tuka became foreign minister, and Alexander Mach became minister of the interior. The latter was also the chief commander of the Hlinka Guard, the paramilitary units of Hlinka's Slovak People's Party. There was another extensive reshuffle of the government in autumn 1944 after the occupation of Slovakia by German military units. Thereafter Slovak government institutions became mere transmission levers for the fulfilment of the orders of the occupying power. The increasingly unwell Tuka was then replaced as prime minister by Štefan Tiso, who also held the functions of foreign minister and minister of justice.

In 1939, the new regime took over the administrative, judicial and power apparatus of the Czechoslovak Republic, simply because it did not have enough of its own qualified and politically reliable personnel to replace them all. This action had a variety of effects in later years when the Slovak state entered a deep crisis and its administrative and power elements were infiltrated by people with opposition or resistance tendencies.[3] However, the Slovak Republic also created some new, non-standard institutions that became effective instruments in helping to build a totalitarian system: the Office of Propaganda, the Centre for State Security (the political police), the Central Economic Office (for the 'solution' of the Jewish question) and a network of concentration camps (but not extermination camps), in which real or fictional opponents of the regime were imprisoned.

The only legal Slovak political party was Hlinka's Slovak People's Party, which had its leading position in the state confirmed in the constitution and other legislation.[4] Only its members could actively participate in state power, as the chairman of the party and president Jozef Tiso put it, 'any intervention in the state administration outside the party is illegal. The party must be the organiser of the whole of public life and it must hold this function for ever. The party gives the state a parliament and government in the name of the nation. The party is the nation and the nation is the party. The nation speaks through the party. The party thinks in place of the nation'.[5] The number of party members increased steadily, and by 1943 reached almost 300,000. Being a member of the ruling party was the key to gaining not only political privileges, but also economic and social advantages. Its strict centralist character and the absence of critical reflection visibly weakened the ability of the one-party state to act, and after 1942 this situation left the country mired in passivity and crisis. It was wholly characteristic of this situation that, during the period of unlimited rule, the Hlinka's Slovak People's Party did not work out or proclaim any longer-term programme. Instead, the party relied on topical populist slogans, political manifestoes and opportunist official statements from its leading representatives. The main, and finally the sole, aim was to preserve the Slovak state, but this was possible only in close collaboration with the Third Reich.

Hlinka's Slovak People's Party attempted to control completely the whole of public life, because it declared itself to be the only political representative of the whole Slovak nation. On the pretext of 'unification', all social organisations and societies (apart from religious ones) were dissolved, and the state party replaced them with its own monopoly institutions. The Hlinka Guard and Hlinka Youth were among the most important; both were modelled on fascist organisations abroad. They

[3] J. Korček, *Slovenská republika 1943–1945* [Slovak Republic 1943–1945] (Bratislava, 1999).

[4] *Slovenský zákonník 1939*, Act 245/1939; *Slovenský zákonník 1942*, Act 215/1942; *Slovenský zákonník 1943*, Act 170/1943.

[5] *Organizačné zvesti Hlinkovej slovenskej ľudovej strany*, 1941, no. 3; *Organizačné zvesti Hlinkovej slovenskej ľudovej strany*, 1943, no. 8.

carried out educational activities in the spirit of the state ideology and occasionally participated in the repression of the civil population. The Hlinka Guard also had its own power-political ambitions, occasionally threatening the leading role of the party, of which it was an essential component. This led to permanent tensions within the government camp and internal disputes.

Members of two national minorities (German and Magyar) also had their legal political representatives. The Magyar political party, led by the member of the Diet János Esterházy, performed reciprocal functions in relation to a similar party made up of Slovak inhabitants in Hungary. The Slovak national minority in Hungary numbered around 300,000, and Magyars in Slovakia were actually collective hostages of the governments in the two countries between which existed a permanent state of tension and hostility.

The Deutsche Partei, led by Franz Karmasin, had far greater ambitions and influence. In organisation and ideology it was based on the National Socialist German Workers' Party (Nationalsozialistische Deutsche Arbeiterpartei, NSDAP). The German political party had more representation in the Diet and the State Council than did the Magyar party. Apart from this, the Slovak government also had a State Secretariat for German Minority Affairs that not only attempted to secure a privileged position for the German minority, but also tried to influence the internal policies of the state. The Deutsche Partei and Hlinka Guard were the largest pressure groups used by the Third Reich to promote its interests. Their ambitions faced not only opposition from Slovak institutions, but also irritation in Berlin, which disapproved of disputes between nationalities in its satellite states. Members of the Ukrainian-Ruthenian minority did not have their own political party, but each had one deputy in the Diet. The Jews and Romanies were entirely excluded from political life. Those members of the Czech minority who did not leave for the occupied Czech Lands (the Protectorate of Bohemia and Moravia) either voluntarily or under pressure after 14 March 1939 also had no political representatives in the Slovak state.

The Christian churches in Slovakia had a specific and somewhat contradictory role in the internal system of the state, which proclaimed its allegiance to Christian ideology. The Roman Catholic Church held a dominant position among them, with more than two million inhabitants declaring Catholicism as their religion. The Catholic Church had close ideological and personal connections with the new state and its regime. The prime minister was a Catholic priest, and dozens of other Catholic Church dignitaries and laymen held positions in the Diet of the Slovak Republic, State Council, structures of the ruling state party, Hlinka

Guard, Hlinka Youth and so on. The official representatives of the Protestant Christian churches were in the position of a sort of loyal opposition to the regime, which often transformed into a kind of resistance.

The German satellite

After 14 March 1939, Slovakia became a participant in international politics for the first time, although clearly as a German satellite. On 23 March 1939, the Third Reich imposed a so-called Treaty of Protection, which decreed that the new state must carry on its foreign, military and economic policy 'in close agreement with the German government'.[6] In return, Germany guaranteed the country's new frontiers. For Berlin, however, this was merely a non-binding formality, since at the time of the preparation of the treaty, the Slovak state was attacked by the Hungarian army. In fact, for several months after the formation of the Slovak state, Germany still had no clear ideas about its continuance, regarding it as a political commodity in negotiations with Hungary and especially with Poland. The position of the new state was strengthened only after the definitive failure of these talks in May 1939. At this juncture, the Slovak state not only became strategically significant, as one of the routes for a military attack on Poland, but it also became the only country that joined the German aggression and participated in the Second World War from the very beginning by attacking Poland.[7]

By the summer of 1939, Berlin regarded the Slovak Republic as a 'model state', and used it as an example to other countries and nations in Central and South-Eastern Europe that were considering coming into the orbit of the Third Reich. From this curious position, the Slovak state gained some temporary political and socio-economic advantages. For a large part of Slovak society, this controlled situation justified and substantially fed the illusion of the necessity and productiveness of the 'policy of the lesser evil'. However, Berlin's approach to its Slovak satellite was always a very pragmatic one. According to the German Embassy in Bratislava, the Treaty of Protection and the continued existence of the state had a 'time limit according to wider European developments'.[8] Put simply, Hitler's Germany did not allow for the

[6] *Slovenský zákonník 1940*, Act 226/1940.
[7] 'Správa ministra národnej obrany F. Čatloša na zasadnutí Štátnej rady v marci 1942' [Report of the Minister of National Defence, F. Čatloš, to a session of the State Council in March 1942], File Slovensko, S-104-1, Slovak National Archives (SNA), Bratislava.
[8] *Akten zur deutschen auswärtigen Politik 1918–1945*, ed. by Archiv des Auswärtigen Amtes (Frankfurt am Main, Baden-Baden, Bonn and Göttingen, 1950–79), series D, vol. X, doc. 17, p. 16, 'Report of the German ambassador in Bratislava H. Bernard, June 1940'.

existence of the Slovak state, or even of the Slovak nation, after the war, when it was supposed that the Slovak population would be either Germanised or 'moved to the East'.[9]

The Slovak Republic gradually gained recognition from twenty-seven states, although these diplomatic contacts were often only formal and limited in duration – according to the course of military and world political developments. Slovakia was primarily recognised by countries allied to Germany and by some neutral states. The Soviet Union had an important and neutral diplomatic mission in Bratislava until the summer of 1941. Berlin determined Slovakia's international political position, not only through a system of bilateral treaties, but partly also through the Deutsche Partei in Slovakia and through a network of German advisors. They were active in all domestic political, economic and above all military institutions. The complete subordination of Slovakia's foreign and military policy to the Third Reich drew the state into a fatal series of conflicts and alliances, which were supposedly designed to secure its existence: 'Our alliance with Germany is logical because it guarantees our state sovereignty. We are also participants in this war. Together with other struggling European nations, we entered it determined to triumph and to ensure our state independence'.[10]

In November 1940, the Slovak Republic joined the Axis powers (Nazi Germany, fascist Italy and imperial Japan), which led to the declaration of war on the Soviet Union in June 1941, and on Great Britain and the USA in December 1941. While the declaration of war against the Western powers was only a formality, an army of 60,000 men was sent to the eastern front to fight the Soviets. After serious material and human losses, this force was partially withdrawn from the front and reduced to 17,000 men. About 4,000 members of the Slovak army died or were wounded on the eastern front.[11] The Slovak army suffered further losses through desertions, motivated mainly by the idea of Slavic solidarity. At first only individuals deserted, but later up to 3,000 men were crossing the lines at a time. These men, together with Slovak prisoners of war, were gradually reincorporated into Czechoslovak military units organised in the Soviet Union. In the autumn of 1943, all Slovak units were withdrawn from the eastern front; some of these were then immediately transferred to Italy as technical or non-combatant divisions.[12]

---

[9] V. Prečan (ed.), *Slovenské národné povstanie. Nemci a Slovensko. Dokumenty* [The Slovak National Uprising. The Germans and Slovakia. Documents] (Bratislava, 1965), document no. 3, p. 48.

[10] *Slovák*, 4 April 1944, 22 April 1944 and 1 June 1944.

[11] File Slovensko, no. 99–3, SNA.

[12] V. Štefanský, *Slovenski vojaci v Taliansku* [Slovak soldiers in Italy] (Bratislava, 2000).

Thus Slovakia's support for Nazi Germany resulted in ever greater international isolation, and reduced its chances of a possible post-war existence, especially when in 1941 the Allies accepted the restoration of Czechoslovakia as one of their war aims.

Slovak–Hungarian relations, which were permanently strained or hostile, although both states were German satellites, were an important concern of Bratislava's foreign policy. Slovakia intensively but unsuccessfully endeavoured to achieve a revision of the Vienna Arbitration, that is, to regain its southern territories. Hungary, however, wanted further territorial gains at the expense of Slovakia. There were frequent incidents and mutual provocations on the Slovak–Hungarian border. Both satellite states sought support in Berlin, where each accused the other of insufficient loyalty towards their protector. The Nazis promised a positive resolution of their demands to both sides, but only after 'victory in the war'. The two satellites were expected to set aside their differences and make the greatest possible effort to struggle for the creation of a 'new order in Europe' under German political and military leadership.

The Slovak Republic's relations with other German satellites, occupied countries and neutral states were limited to economic or cultural co-operation. However, from 1944, certain neutral countries began to break off diplomatic relations with the Slovak Republic. Vatican–Slovak relations, in which the Slovak government placed great faith, had been burdened since 1939 by several diplomatic conflicts, and especially by the 'solution' of the Jewish question in Slovakia. Attempts by parts of the ruling establishment to detach themselves from the ever more disadvantageous alliance with the Third Reich began to appear sporadically in 1943. After the fall of Mussolini's regime in Italy, they stayed put and the situation ended in a complete fiasco. Moreover, the German intelligence service and diplomats monitored such activities and concluded that 'today Slovak politicians cannot separate from us, so they pretend that they do not want to'.[13]

Internal politics

The development of Slovakia's internal political system passed through several stages: from an authoritarian regime to totalitarianism with significant fascist elements, but also with several specifically Slovak

[13] Prečan (ed.), *Slovenské národné povstanie*, doc. no. 21 a, p. 71, 'Report by H. Gmelin, of the German Embassy in Bratislava'.

features. The formation of the political system was influenced not only by German pressure or other foreign examples, but also by domestic political forces, which were convinced that the 'values of democracy were discredited, the authoritarian principle now shows the way. If we sincerely want to build a totalitarian party, which would be the bearer of political power and representative of a united nation, we must follow where Germany has gone, but without the intention to imitate it'.[14]

Originally the regime was based on three ideological pillars: a Christian world-view, Slovak nationalism and corporate solidarity. But in political practice only the national idea prevailed. In the end, national-ism also became – much to the surprise and incomprehension of the ruling elite – the stimulus and focus for domestic anti-fascist, anti-German resistance. The Christian world-view, relying theoretically and legalistically on several preceding papal encyclicals, clashed with the national socialist ideology imported from Nazi Germany. Moreover, it conflicted with the inhuman measures employed by the regime. The attempt to establish a corporatist system within a framework where soci-ety was to be divided into six 'estates' also collapsed. It was opposed both by the leaders of the Deutsche Partei (who feared that the corporatist arrangements would erode their privileged status in the existing order) and by the domestic supporters of the idea of 'Slovak national socialism'.

In the formation of the internal regime there were in play a number of ideological or political conceptions influenced by several foreign examples and especially by international developments. These first included the outbreak of war and Slovakia's participation as Germany's ally, repeated Nazi interventions into the state's internal policies, and later the fall of fascism in Italy, the catastrophic defeats of the Axis powers and so on. Of course, Slovakia did not have the luxury of time in which to develop its political system. The state existed for only six years, during a hectic period of war, uncertainty and constant tension, which did not allow the establishment of a 'pure' model of a totalitarian state, as was the case with Hitler's Germany or Mussolini's Italy.

In the first period of the state (up to about the summer of 1940) there had been some attempts to preserve the remnants of an independent policy and more liberal methods of rule. However, the Nazis eliminated these tendencies by forcible diplomatic intervention by the middle of 1940. The totalitarian-fascist character of the regime manifested itself most openly and drastically in the period 1941–1943, with all the

---

[14] *Ústava Slovenskej republiky a jej zásadné smernice* [The Constitution of the Slovak Republic and its basic provisions] (Bratislava, 1939); general secretary of Hlinka's Slovak People's Party Jozef Kirschbaum, writing in *Slovák*, 20 September 1939.

associated political and moral consequences, expressed in increased collaboration with the Third Reich, active participation in the war, and the deportation of the majority of Jewish inhabitants to Nazi extermination camps. After these events, the Slovak state and its regime fell into a deep internal crisis and international isolation, from which its leaders could find no way out. They were irredeemably compromised by their co-operation with the Nazis, involving activities that had already been described as crimes against humanity by the Allies, and increasingly also by several neutral states. After the occupation of Slovakia by German units in autumn 1944, the executive bodies of the state were merely active in assisting the occupying forces in the suppression of armed resistance, in cruel repressive measures against the civil population and in the implementation of German orders. Attempts at intervening to moderate these actions met with little success. In any case, they were merely undertaken to establish resistance credentials.

From the beginning of the existence of the Slovak Republic, a power struggle within the ruling elite shaped the political system of the state. In 1939, there were two wings with opposing views, a conservative-clerical group headed by President Jozef Tiso, and a radical fascist one led by Prime Minister Vojtech Tuka and the minister of the interior and commander in chief of the Hlinka Guard, Alexander Mach. The conservatives relied on the functionaries of the ruling party and the administrative apparatus of the state, and they received substantial support from the Church hierarchy. The radicals with their demands for the 'completion of the Slovak revolution' sought support from the Hlinka Guard and elements of the lumpenproletariat. Above all they relied on support from the Nazis. That is, they were openly promoting the need to introduce national socialist ideas and methods of government into the Slovak state. However, both groups fully agreed on the necessity to build a totalitarian system, on the closest collaboration with Germany and on the need to 'solve' the Jewish question. They differed only in their views on the speed of implementation of these ideas and on the methods required.[15]

However, ideological and political differences played only a subordinate role in the struggle within the government camp. Paramount were the power interests and ambitions of the protagonists. Thus, Vojtech Tuka was clearly after the position of president or party chairman, that is, leadership of the state. When he failed, he wanted to subordinate the party apparatus completely to the government administration, which he headed. In 1941, he even planned a Mussolini-style 'march on Bratislava' with the help of selected units of the Hlinka Guard, with the aim of installing a national socialist regime. However, the radicals, with their nationalism and social demagogy, failed to generate much support among the Slovak population, and their reliance on decisive help from Berlin proved unsuccessful. Berlin evaluated the situation pragmatically and decided that the conservative group headed by President Tiso, because of his significant authority in Slovak society, had proved far more able to maintain an effective collaborationist policy in Slovakia. This decision flowed not so much from Tiso's own political qualities as from his priestly dignity, which was traditionally understood in Slovak society as a moral guarantee of honesty and rectitude. Apart from this, the president managed to defeat his opponents in the radical camp by using their own weapons: deepening collaboration with Germany, verbal acceptance of the idea of national socialism into which he endeavoured to insert 'Slovak Christian characteristics', declarations of war against the Allies, the introduction of the Führer principle, and the authorisation and public approval of a radical 'solution' to the Jewish question. A large part of the population understood that the power struggle within the ruling camp was a necessity, and the result was a policy of the lesser evil preventing the radicals from gaining hold of the most powerful positions within the state.

In 1942, the internal power struggle ended with the unambiguous defeat of the radicals. The ailing Prime Minister Tuka was removed from the top leadership of Hlinka's Slovak People's Party and lost his decisive influence in the government. His supporters were either pushed on to the defensive or went over to the side of the victors, in this case the minister of the interior and commander of the Hlinka Guard, Mach. The radical fascist tendencies in the ruling camp persisted, but only at a lower level in the official hierarchy and at a reduced level of political influence. They became more prominent only in the autumn of 1944, when German units occupied Slovakia. The Nazis supported the Slovak radicals, primarily as a potential means of putting pressure on the conservative wing. Until the state collapsed, the German government regarded President Tiso as an irreplaceable person who guaranteed the effective collaboration of the Slovak Republic, in spite of denunciations and insinuations from the Reich Security Service. The Germans valued his consolidating and pacifying role in crisis situations (see Fig. 12).[16]

---

[16] See V. Bystrický and Š. Fano (eds.), *Pokus o politický a osobný profil Jozefa Tisu* [Attempt at a political and personal profile of Jozef Tiso] (Bratislava, 1992).

Figure 12 Jozef Tiso (right) meeting Adolf Hitler (1941)

The economy

Economic and social developments in the war-time Slovak Republic
were influenced both by its status as a satellite of the Third Reich and
by its role as a 'model state'. Berlin exploited Slovakia's economic
potential by administrative political and natural economic means.
Slovakia was placed within the Nazis' planned 'greater European economic space' and had a precisely defined position and role. Slovak
industry had to orient itself towards German requirements: the Reich
was the destination for 70 per cent of all exports, especially military
materials. The Third Reich also exploited Slovakia's raw materials, and
it was able to take any amount of agricultural products. As the military
conflict and especially the bombing of German territory intensified, an
increasing amount of military production was moved to Slovak territory,
which was at that time not directly affected by military events.

Chemical, textile, wood processing and engineering companies, as
well as actual armaments production, were physically moved to Slovakia.
This process led not only to the militarisation of the Slovak economy
with all the associated negative results, but also to a war-time economic
revival manifested in the growth of investment in many areas of

industrial production, energy resources and the construction, or reconstruction, of all kinds of communications. This war-time economic
boom meant the elimination of one of the traditional social problems
in Slovak society – unemployment. The annual migration of 40,000
Slovaks to undertake permanent or seasonal work in Germany also
contributed to this situation. The reduction in unemployment, the
war-time economic boom associated with inward investment, tax relief
and the growth of industrial and agricultural production that was sold on
the domestic and foreign markets all influenced the growth of real wages
and the purchasing power of the population.[17]

The subservient relationship of the Slovak Republic to Germany was
also shown in the imposition of a fixed exchange rate between the Slovak
crown and the Reichsmark, to the disadvantage of Slovakia. The real
exchange rate between the Slovak crown and the Reichsmark was one to
five but in practice a rate of one to eleven was deployed. Cashless or
clearing accounting for mutual commercial transactions between the
two states was also applied. Since nearly three-quarters of all Slovak
exports went to Germany, which could not pay for these products with
its own exports, the debts were added to the clearing account. This debt
gradually increased to some eight billion crowns, a figure that would
never be repaid.[18] After the occupation of Slovak territory in the autumn
of 1944, the subsequent pillaging by Germans of raw materials, finished
products, food and entire productive facilities occurred under the pretext of taking possession of the spoils of war. The German clearing debt
towards the Slovak state grew by a further three billion crowns during
the final months of the war.[19]

Agricultural production brought relatively good results for the economy during the war, both in terms of self-sufficiency and from the point
of view of exports, especially to Germany. However, Slovak peasant-
farmers waited in vain for a new phase of land reform, which when it
finally occurred only involved the distribution of Jewish-owned land.

---

[17] P. Heumos, 'Slovensko vo vojnovom hospodárstve Tretej ríše' [Slovakia in the war-time
economy of the Third Reich], in V. Bystrický (ed.), *Slovensko v rokoch druhej svetovej
vojny* [Slovakia during the years of the Second World War] (Bratislava, 1991), pp. 70–2;
M. Fabricius, 'Hospodársky stav Slovenska na konci druhej svetovej vojny' [The
economic state of Slovakia at the end of the Second World War], in Bystrický and
Š. Fano (ed.) *Slovensko na konci druhej svetovej vojny (stav, východiska, perspektívy)*
[Slovakia at the end of the Second World War (situation, starting points,
perspectives)] (Bratislava, 1994), pp. 49–55.

[18] Fabricius, 'Hospodársky stav', pp. 49–55.

[19] J. Faltus and V. Průcha, *Prehľad hospodárskeho vývoja na Slovensku v rokoch 1918–1945*
[An outline of economic development in Slovakia from 1918 to 1945] (Bratislava,
1968).

This was part of the so-called Aryanisation process that forcibly transferred Jewish property into the possession of 'Aryans' according to the
German example. By these means, the regime not only excluded Jewish
citizens from the economic life of the state, but also created a new group
of owners who would be its political and social supporters. The Aryanisation process affected 12,000 businesses and shops, 100,000 hectares of
land, thousands of houses and finally all movable property, even the
personal possessions of Jewish citizens.[20] However, Aryanisation very
quickly degenerated into the systematic theft of Jewish property, bringing not only economic losses for the state, but also unprecedented
corruption and destruction of morale. Members of the ruling party, state
officials and others associated with the regime were most intimately
involved in this process, but its practical and moral consequences penetrated all parts of society.

The Jewish question

The Aryanisation process was part of the so-called solution of the
Jewish question in Slovakia, which began immediately after the establishment of the state and was the most revisited problem in its internal
policy. The Slovak form of the Holocaust developed under the influence of Nazi Germany. The Slovak government utilised the strained
status of Slovak–Jewish relations in the economic, national and religious fields, which had existed since the middle of the nineteenth
century, as an excuse to develop a systematic anti-Semitic policy as
part of its official programme. A civil war of extermination was
launched against nearly three and a half per cent of the population.
The 89,000 Jews of Slovakia were declared the enemies of the Slovak
state and nation. The Jews, who were originally defined according to
religion and from 1941 according to racial criteria, were gradually
excluded from economic and public life. In the end they also lost their
basic civil and human rights. In 1941, the government issued a Jewish
Code, one of the cruellest anti-Semitic laws in the modern history of
Europe.[21] Jews could be employed in state and private services only
with the consent of the appropriate offices; they were excluded from all
secondary schools and institutions of higher education; they had no
access to public social, cultural and sporting events; they had a morning and an evening curfew; they were forbidden to assemble or to

[20] L. Lipscher, *Židia v slovenskom štáte 1939–1945* [The Jews in the Slovak state 1939–
1945] (Bratislava, 1991).
[21] *Slovenský zákonník 1941*, Act no.198/1941.

Figure 13 Jewish people in Trstená boarding transport to death camps
in the East (possibly 1942)

travel; they had to wear a symbol (a six-sided yellow Star of David);
they could not marry non-Jews; they were interned in labour camps
and centres; their complete segregation into ghettos was planned; and
so on.

These developments gradually made the Jewish population into a
mass of tens of thousands of people with no rights, who finally
became an unwanted and unsolvable social burden. It was with some
relief that the Slovak government eventually accepted a Nazi offer that
the 'unnecessary' Slovak Jews could be deported 'to the East', where
the Germans had allegedly set aside a special territory for European
Jews. In spite of the fact that the highest representatives of the state
received warnings from several domestic and foreign sources that the
movement of the Jews 'to work in new homes' would mean their
physical liquidation, their deportation to Nazi extermination camps
began in March 1942. During the following six months, almost
58,000 people, that is, two-thirds of the Slovak Jewish community,
were forcibly deported from Slovakia and subsequently killed.[22] At
this time, the Slovak Republic was the only state not directly occupied

---

[22] For more details, see I. Kamenec, *Po stopách tragédie* [Following the tracks of a tragedy]
(Bratislava, 1991).

by Germany in which Jews were deported by the state's own administrative and security forces (see Fig. 13).

The remaining Jews of Slovakia avoided deportation in various ways:
by fleeing to Hungary, by going into hiding underground and especially
by gaining exemption because of work, mainly in the cases of doctors,
pharmacists, veterinarians, engineers and agricultural or other experts,
for whom the state did not have enough qualified replacements. About
4,000 Jews lived in labour camps and centres. After German units
occupied Slovakia in the autumn of 1944, a second stage of deportation
of Jews to extermination camps began, this time organised and carried
out by occupying forces. A further 13,000 people died as a result of this
process. Einsatzkommando (stand-by group) squads killed about a
thousand Jews directly in Slovakia.[23]

This brutal and murderous 'solution' to the Jewish question formed a
sort of prism through which the foreign public and diplomats perceived
the character of the war-time Slovak Republic. This question, in fact,
also traumatised Slovak society. Some people regarded the Slovak state
as the definitive solution of the Slovak question; others perceived it as a
temporary necessity (as the lesser evil) at a time when Hitler's Germany
dominated Central Europe. The Slovak state was a reality, which its
inhabitants gradually accepted as part of their everyday lives. Having
their own state also evoked feelings of national pride and self-
confidence. A large part of Slovak society identified with the concept
of an independent state, but this did not mean that they accepted its
humiliating subordination to Germany or supported its anti-democratic
totalitarian regime.

In spite of the permanent supply problems resulting from the war,
the economic and social situation in the Slovak Republic was relatively
good, and, at least up until 1943, the population enjoyed a far higher
standard of living than did people in other occupied or satellite
countries and in the Third Reich itself. By banning strike activities,
the government brought to an end any influence the already 'unified'
trade unions may have exerted but, as in the totalitarian regimes in
Germany and Italy, it also introduced some popular social measures:
child benefits, subsidies and pension payments, index-linked wages,
annual collections of money and clothes (so-called Winter Aid) for the
poor and so on.[24]

---

[23] Prečan (ed.), *Slovenské národné povstanie*, doc. no. 226, p. 457.
[24] M. Tkáč, 'Slovenské hospodárstvo v rokoch 1939–1945' [The Slovak economy, 1939–
1945], in J. Bobák (ed.), *Slovenská republika (1939–1945)* [The Slovak Republic]
(Martin, 2000), pp. 114–24.

Demise

The creation of an independent Slovak state, the departure of thousands of Czechs and especially the exclusion of Jews from public and private services provided opportunities for professionals and the social advancement of others. There were some positive developments in certain areas of cultural life, but these were limited by military events and especially by the effort of the totalitarian regime to dominate everyday life, as well as by its overall isolation as a satellite state in war-time Europe. New institutions of higher education, secondary schools, theatres and a central academic institution – the Slovak Academy of Sciences and Arts – were established. Artistic and literary life developed vigorously. This trend connected with general cultural developments, including electrification, more radio broadcasting and cinemas. At the same time, the cultural sphere became one of the centres of activity by oppositional anti-regime forces, which had begun to form as early as 1939, immediately after the establishment of the state.

Resistance activities in Slovakia were an integral part of the pan-European anti-fascist struggle, but the movement also had some specific features. During the first five years of its existence, the Slovak Republic was not directly occupied by German forces and, on the whole, it successfully played the role of a model satellite state. Primarily, resistance was directed against the totalitarian fascist regime and against the subordinate position of the state in relation to the Third Reich. It was only later that efforts to restore the Czechoslovak Republic, but one with a qualitatively new, equal position for Slovakia, became an ever more significant and integrating aim of the domestic resistance forces, in harmony with Czechoslovak resistance abroad. A new constitutional position for Slovakia was the basic precondition for the mobilisation and success of the resistance forces, although the Czechoslovak government-in-exile in London, led by President Edvard Beneš, was not willing to accept this suggestion at first.

The domestic anti-fascist struggle was divided into two main factions. One was on the left of the political spectrum, dominated by the Communists who temporarily considered the idea of the Sovietisation of Slovakia, that is, its inclusion within the Soviet Union as an autonomous republic. This group carried out intensive propaganda activity. From 1941, it began to turn towards sabotage against the regime. The democratic civil opposition was oriented primarily towards intelligence activity in support of the Czechoslovak government-in-exile, and in defence of politically persecuted persons, who were helped to travel through Slovakia to countries where they could actively participate in armed struggle. Increasing numbers of members of the ruling establishment joined the ranks of the resistance, either from political conviction or to provide themselves with democratic credentials after the war. For the most part, those who turned against the regime were officers in the Slovak army and gendarmerie, but there were also important figures in the economic, judicial and administrative apparatus. By the end of 1943, both main resistance currents united in the illegal Slovak National Council which, together with a significant portion of the officer corps of the Slovak army, began to prepare an armed uprising.[25]

The Slovak Republic gradually began to collapse during the autumn of 1944, when Czechoslovak statehood was re-established across the territory by Soviet and Czechoslovak forces (raised and organised in the Soviet Union) and under the control of the Slovak National Council. This process continued with the liberation of Slovak territory from October 1944 to April 1945. By the beginning of 1945, about 13,500 partisans were operating to the German rear. The viability of the Slovak state was inseparably connected with the existence of Nazi Germany. Therefore, the highest representatives of the satellite state headed by the president left Slovakia together with the retreating German army at the beginning of April 1945.

[25] J. Jablonický, *Z ilegality do povstania (kapitoly z občianskeho odboja)* [From illegality to the uprising (chapters from the civil resistance)] (Bratislava, 1969).

13 The Slovak question and the resistance movement during the Second World War

Jan Rychlík

International aspects of the Slovak question

The declaration of Slovak independence, on 14 March 1939, was the result of Adolf Hitler's policies in Central Europe, and culminated in the collapse of Czechoslovakia. The new Slovak state was soon recognised by all three of its neighbours – Germany, Hungary and Poland. Slovakia – known as the Slovak Republic according to the constitution of 21 July 1939 – was then gradually recognised by Germany's allies and satellites, such as Italy, Romania, Bulgaria, Japan and Finland, as well as by several neutral states. The Slovak government was also very keen to be recognised by the probable future enemies of Germany, such as Britain, France, the United States and the Soviet Union, because such acknowledgement might mean some sort of obligation to accept Slovakia as independent state even in the case of Germany's defeat. The Slovak foreign minister, Ferdinand Ďurčanský, was particularly interested in some sort of recognition for another reason: Dr Edvard Beneš, who was in the United States on 14 March 1939, sent a letter of protest regarding the German occupation of Bohemia and Moravia to the League of Nations and other Western governments; he had also begun to create a movement in exile to re-establish Czechoslovakia.[1]

In March 1939, the main Allied states (Britain, France, the United States of America and the Soviet Union) had refused to accept the annihilation of the Second Czecho-Slovak Republic and continued to recognise its diplomatic missions and diplomats. Poland had recognised the Slovak state both *de facto* and *de jure* and yet continued to tolerate Czechoslovak ambassadors in Warsaw as well as consular representation in other cities. Given this situation, it was significant that the

---

[1] E. Beneš, *Šest let exilu a druhé světové války. Řeči, projevy a dokumenty z let 1938–1945* [Six years of exile and of the Second World War. Speeches, addresses and documents from 1938–1945] (Prague, 1946), docs. 1, 2, pp. 39–60; see also Czechoslovak Ministry for Foreign Affairs, *Bojující Československo* [Fighting Czechoslovakia] (Prague and Košice, 1945), pp. 15–17.

Czechoslovak ministers in Poland, France and the United States were all Slovaks (Juraj Slávik in Warsaw, Štefan Osuský in Paris and Vladimír Hurban in Washington, DC). All three refused to submit to the new German authorities in occupied Prague, which had ordered them to hand their missions over to the local German embassies. Slávik and Hurban also refused to co-operate with the new Slovak regime in Bratislava. Only Osuský agreed to establish informal contacts with Bratislava, but even these were soon cut off.[2] This was a signal that the new regime had not been accepted by all Slovaks, and that at least some of them would prefer to see the resurrection of Czechoslovakia.

After two months, however, the attitude of some of the great powers towards Slovakia began to change. Britain asked for a new *exequatur* for its consul, Peter Pares, and on 4 May 1939 recognised Slovakia *de facto*. Milan Harminc was sent to London as the Slovak consul general. France followed the British example with *de facto* recognition on 14 July 1939, and obtained an *exequatur* for its consul, Milon de Peilion. Meanwhile, in Paris the seat for the Slovak consul remained vacant due to procedural problems. The Soviet commissar for foreign affairs, Maxim Litvinov, wrote to Iosif Stalin on 23 March 1939 that, while the Soviet Union had in fact already accepted the new situation in Central Europe, it would be wise to delay official recognition. He gave a similar response to the Latvian minister to Moscow who had asked him about the attitude of the Soviet Union towards the new border changes.[3] Slovakia, however, was not successful in obtaining *de facto* recognition from the United States.[4] The United States government did not change its view even later: in April 1940, the Slovak ambassador to Romania Ivan Milecz contacted the American envoy in Bucharest regarding the possibility of recognition, but the US Department of State's answer was negative.[5]

---

[2] J. Staško, 'Štefan Osuský's Attempts to Establish Contacts with Slovakia in 1939: A Personal Memoir', *Slovakia*, 32 (1985–6), 9–33.

[3] *Dokumenty vneshnoi politiki SSSR* [Documents on the foreign policy of the Soviet Union], vol. XXII/1, (Moscow, 1992), doc. 168, pp. 220–1, doc. 181, p. 232.

[4] Vladimír Hurban (Washington) to Karel Lisický (London), 25 March 1939, 'Karel Lisický papers', collection, box 10, School of Slavonic and East European Studies Archives, University of London; see also M. Evangela Lubek, *An Inquiry into United States–Czechoslovak Relations Between 1918 and 1948* (Cleveland and Rome, 1971), pp. 107–13.

[5] Similar attempts were made by the Slovak ambassador in Moscow, Fraňo Tiso, in March 1940, who contacted the American ambassador Lawrence Steinhardt: Lawrence Steinhardt to Department of State, 19 March 1940, microfilms 1218, roll 29, National Archives of the United States (NAUS), Washington, DC.; For Milecz's attempt, see Milecz to Ministry of Foreign Affairs, 29 May 1940, collection, MZV, box 505a, number 1901/1940, Pol. spr. 100/40, Slovak National Archives (SNA), Bratislava.

The outbreak of the Second World War changed the situation again because Slovakia, alongside Germany, took part in the invasion of Poland on 1 September 1939. As a reward, Germany returned to Slovakia the small areas of territory in northern Slovakia that had been lost to Poland in 1938. Slovakia's participation in the war against Poland, an ally of Britain and France, had, however, a negative impact on the relations between Bratislava, Paris and London. Both states recalled their consuls from Bratislava and began to consider Slovakia as a territory controlled by an enemy. Understandably, Poland also changed its attitude towards Slovakia. On 3 September 1939, the Polish government allowed Czech and Slovak émigrés on its territory to organise a legion to fight against Germany.[6]

Two further events should be noted: the Slovak consul general in London, Milan Harminc, and the Slovak ambassador to Warsaw, Ladislav Szatmáry, protested against Slovak participation in the war against Poland; they refused to obey orders from Bratislava and subordinated themselves to Edvard Beneš, the former president of Czechoslovakia, who had emigrated and by now had settled in London.[7] These events reinforced signals that the regime in Bratislava was not acceptable to all Slovaks. On 2 October 1939, Štefan Osuský signed a treaty with France, in the name of an as yet non-existent Czechoslovak Provisional Government, regarding the organisation of a Czechoslovak army on French soil.[8] A Czechoslovak National Committee was then established in Paris, which was recognised as a 'representative of Czechoslovaks abroad' by the French government on 17 November 1939 and by the British on 20 December.[9]

Official relations between the Western powers and Slovakia had been interrupted, but on the other hand Slovakia's position in the east had improved. As a result of the Nazi–Soviet Pact, signed on 23 August 1939, and in advance of the Soviet invasion to Poland (on 17 September) Moscow recognised Slovakia both *de facto* and *de jure* on

---

[6] Decree of the President of the Polish Republic, 3 September 1939, published in Czechoslovak Ministry for Foreign Affairs, *Bojujíci Československo*, p. 35.

[7] M. Harminc to J. Zvrškovec, collection no. 40 (Szatmáry), box 16, fasc. IV/28/13, Archiv ústavu T. G. Masaryka (AÚTGM) [T. G. Masaryk Institute Archives], Prague; report Szatmáry, box 16, fasc. IV/28/2, *ibid.*. See also E. Orlof, *Dyplomacja polska wobec sprawy słowackiej 1938–1939* [The attitude of Polish diplomacy towards the Slovak question] (Cracow, 1980), doc. 2, pp. 198–9.

[8] Czechoslovak Ministry for Foreign Affairs, *Bojujíci Československo*, pp. 39–42; see also F. Vnuk, *Slovenská otázka na Západe v rokoch 1939–1940* [The Slovak question in the West, 1939–1940] (Cleveland, 1974), pp. 141–3.

[9] Czechoslovak Ministry for Foreign Affairs, *Bojujíci Československo*, pp. 43, 45–6.

16 September 1939.[10] By the end of the year, the Soviet government had revoked the diplomatic status of the Czechoslovak minister to Moscow, Zdeněk Fierlinger, who left for Paris and then London. The Slovak government decided to send Fraňo Tiso, a relative of President Jozef Tiso, to Moscow as the diplomatic envoy. The Soviets then opened a huge diplomatic mission in Bratislava led by a skilled diplomat, Grigori Pushkin. Relations between Slovakia and the Soviet Union progressed smoothly.[11]

Despite London's and Paris's negative attitude towards the regime in Bratislava, neither government recognised the Beneš émigré group as the Czechoslovak government-in-exile. Nor were they convinced of the desirability of the Czechoslovak state returning to its former status. There were plans to recreate the Czech state, and to incorporate it with Slovakia within some form of Central European federation or confederation. The French government also argued that Beneš had little support in Slovakia. On 27 December 1939, the British government made it clear that they had not withdrawn their recognition of Emil Hácha and the government in Prague, nor had they rescinded the *de facto* recognition of Slovakia.[12]

The Slovak question was one of the most difficult political problems for the Czechoslovak émigrés. Like many Czechs, Beneš wanted to restore the pre-Munich republic as a single state, combined with some limited political devolution to the regions. Among the Slovak émigrés a small group supported Beneš, but the majority did not want to return to the unitary pre-Munich Czechoslovak Republic and wished the autonomy of 6 October 1938 to be retained. Štefan Osuský in Paris also adopted this policy, which led to conflict with Beneš. Osuský claimed that Beneš had resigned in October 1938 and subsequently was merely a private individual while he, Osuský, remained an official representative of Czechoslovakia through its diplomatic missions that legally continued to exist. Soon, another opponent to Beneš emerged: Milan Hodža, the leader of the Slovak Agrarians and the former Czechoslovak prime minister, who had arrived in Paris and asked to join the Czechoslovak National Committee. Hodža, like Osuský, rejected Beneš's programme and instead advocated a Czecho-Slovak Federation.[13]

---

[10] *Dokumenty*, vol. XXII/2, doc. 585, p. 82.

[11] V. V. Maryina, 'Brána na Balkán Slovensko v geopolitických plánech SSSR' [The gate to the Balkans, Slovakia, in the geopolitical plans of the Soviet Union], *Soudobé dějiny*, 6 (1996), 827–46.

[12] L. Otáhalová and M. Červinková (eds.), *Dokumenty z historie československé politiky 1939–1943* [Documents from the history of Czechoslovak politics 1939–1945] (Prague, 1966), vol. I, doc. 38, p. 66.

[13] 'Milan Hodža papers', microfilms, no. 172, Slovak National Museum Archives, Bratislava.

When Beneš refused to accept Hodža as a member of the Czechoslovak National Committee, Hodža decided to organise his own group – the Slovak National Council. On 22 November 1939, the Slovak National Council was founded in Paris with Hodža as its chairman. Its secretary was Peter Prídavok, who was in contact with Karol Sidor, the Slovak ambassador to the Vatican and through him also with moderate Ľudáks in Slovakia. Two other members of the Slovak National Council – Ján Futák and Vojtech Klein – represented the moderate anti-German Ľudák wing.[14] Hodža's Slovak National Council soon contacted a group of Czech anti-Beneš émigrés in Paris known as the Czech National Council; these organisations merged and, on 28 January 1940, the Czecho-Slovak National Council was established under Hodža's leadership.[15] The Czecho-Slovak National Council also advocated the establishment of a Czechoslovak Federation.

In the spring and summer of 1940, the international situation changed once again. After the fall of France in June, Britain stood alone and remained the only state fighting against Germany; its only allies on the continent were the populations of the occupied nations. In this situation the British government changed its attitude towards the Czecho-Slovak National Council; it announced that it was ready to recognise a provisional Czechoslovak government-in-exile on the condition that there only be one such organisation and that Hodža be included in it.[16] Because the anti-Beneš opposition was dependent on support from the French government, the fall of France strengthened Beneš's position. He offered Hodža the post of vice-chairman of the State Council, the provisional parliament-in-exile. On 21 July 1940, Britain recognised the Czechoslovak provisional government-in-exile in which Osuský was given the post of a minister without portfolio. Beneš was recognised as the president.[17] By this time, both Osuský and Hodža had lost what political influence they once held. In 1942, Osuský resigned as minister and Hodža departed for the USA, where he died in 1944.

At the same time, the Slovak minister for foreign affairs, Ferdinand Ďurčanský, made an attempt to establish contacts with the Western allies and to preserve Slovakia's independence after the war. Ďurčanský gave

[14] J. Jablonický, *Z ilegality do povstania (kapitoly z občianskeho odboja)* [From illegality to the uprising (chapters from the civil resistance)] (Bratislava, 1969), pp. 20, 34.
[15] Collection 40, box 16, fasc. IV/28/16, AÚTGM, Prague.
[16] E. Ivaničková, 'Britská politika a Slovensko v rokoch 1939–1945' [British policy and Slovakia in 1939–1945], in V. Bystrický and Š. Fano (eds.), *Slovensko na konci druhej svetovej vojny (stav, východiska, perspektívy)* [Slovakia at the end of the Second World War (situation, starting points, perspectives)] (Bratislava, 1994), p. 127.
[17] Otáhalová and Červinková (eds.), *Dokumenty*, vol. I, doc. 203, pp. 247–8.

secret instructions to the new Slovak diplomatic envoy to the Holy See, Jozef Zvrškovec, to contact British diplomats in Italy, which was still neutral. Zvrškovec also tried to contact the British government by sending the message to Milan Harminc in London, but both attempts failed. Harminc passed the message on not to the relevant British authorities but to Beneš.[18] Nor was there any response from the British authorities to Ďurčanský's initiative; instead the Italian secret service revealed the existence of contacts between Zvrškovec and British diplomats in Rome to the Germans.[19] On 28 July 1940, Hitler summoned President Tiso to Salzburg and forced him to drop Ďurčanský from the cabinet. He was replaced by Prime Minister Vojtech Tuka, who was pro-German and who aligned his policy with Nazi Germany without any reservations.[20]

Tuka believed that Bratislava had to show Berlin that the Slovaks were better allies than the Hungarians. This policy had a dual objective because it was only with German support that Slovakia could preserve its independence and reclaim the territories annexed by Hungary in 1938 and 1939. However, this policy had fatal consequences. On 24 November 1940, Slovakia joined the Tripartite Pact. On 22 June 1941, Germany attacked the Soviet Union, and the next day Slovakia sent two divisions to the eastern front. These actions altered Soviet policy towards Bratislava. On 23 June, diplomatic relations between Slovakia and the Soviet Union were terminated.[21] On 4 July, the Soviet ambassador to London, Ivan Maisky, asked President Beneš for a meeting that took place on 8 July. Maisky informed Beneš that the Soviet Union supported the restoration of Czechoslovakia.[22] On 18 July, the Soviet Union recognised Czechoslovakia within the pre-Munich borders and

---

[18] Collection 40, box 15, fasc. IV/28/2, pp. 34, 38–40, AÚTGM, Prague.

[19] The contact was maintained through Jozef A. Mikuš, the secretary of the Slovak diplomatic mission. See J. A. Mikuš, *Pamäti slovenského diplomata* [The memoirs of a Slovak diplomat] (Martin, 1998), p. 50.

[20] Ľ. Lipták, 'Príprava a priebeh salzburských rokovaní v roku 1940 medzi predstaviteľmi Nemecka a slovenského štátu' [The preparations for and the course of the 1940 Salzburg talks between representatives of Germany and the Slovak state], *Historický časopis*, 13 (1965), 329–65.

[21] *Dokumenty a materiály k dějinám československo-sovětských vztahů* [Documents and materials relating to the history of Czechoslovak–Soviet relations], vol. IV/1 (Prague, 1980), doc. 70, p. 127.

[22] *Ibid.*, doc. 76, p. 136. According to Beneš's memoirs, Maisky had asked for an audience on 5 July. See E. Beneš, *Paměti. Od Mnichova k nové válce a novému vítězství* [Memoirs. From Munich to new war and new victory] (Prague, 1947), p. 241. (The book is also available in an English translation, E. Beneš (trans. G. Lias), *The Memoirs of Dr Eduard Beneš: From Munich to New War and New Victory* (London, 1954). The references here are from the Czech original.)

simultaneously also gave full recognition to the government-in-exile.[23] The British government did the same soon after.

There was no formal US recognition of the provisional Czechoslovak government-in-exile in 1940. On the other hand, Vladimír Hurban, the last Czechoslovak ambassador to Washington, DC, remained in the USA as an official envoy. On 31 July 1941, the American ambassador to Britain, John G. Winant, informed the Czechoslovak minister for foreign affairs, Jan Masaryk (1886–1948), that the USA wished to restore diplomatic relations with the Czechoslovak government-in-exile and to appoint a representative.[24] A decision regarding full recognition was, however, postponed. On 13 December 1941, Slovakia declared war on Britain and the USA.[25] Because the USA had not recognised Slovakia, recognition of the Czechoslovak government-in-exile that took place on 26 October 1942 occurred swiftly.[26] In addition, in the summer of 1942 the British government announced that it was no longer bound by the territorial commitments of the Munich Agreement. On 29 September 1942, General Charles de Gaulle recognised Czechoslovakia within its pre-Munich borders in the name of the French Committee of National Liberation.[27]

By the end of 1942 and during 1943, the German army was defeated by British forces in North Africa and by the Soviets at Stalingrad and Kursk. In 1943, British and American forces landed in Sicily, and Italy capitulated. It had become clear that Germany would eventually be defeated and that the Slovak state would not outlive the end of the war. The Allies had no reason to accept changes in Europe that had occurred as a result of German machinations. It also became clear that the former territory of Czechoslovakia would be liberated by the Soviet army and would subsequently come under Soviet influence. Some Slovak Communists favoured Slovakia's becoming either a Soviet

[23] Otáhalová and Červinková (eds.), *Dokumenty*, vol. I, doc. 204, pp. 248–9. According to Beneš (*Paměti*, pp. 242–4), diplomatic relations were re-established on 16 July 1941, and the validity of the Czechoslovak–Soviet treaty from 1935 was renewed on 18 July. See also Charles Winant to US Department of State, 17 July 1941, microfilm 1218, roll 30, NAUS, Washington, DC.

[24] J. G. Winant to J. Masaryk, 31 July 1941, microfilm 1218, roll 30, NAUS, Washington, DC. See also Beneš, *Paměti*, pp. 266–7.

[25] *Slovenská politika*, 13 December 1941. There were no direct military clashes between Slovakia and the United States. American citizens in Slovakia were, however, prevented from leaving the country and had to remain in their places of residence. See Myjava collection, no. 42/42 prez., no. 72/42 prez. (ŠOKA Myjava), Štátny okresný archív [State District Archive], Okresný úrad [District Office], Skalica.

[26] Beneš, *Paměti*, pp. 269–70.

[27] *Ibid.* pp. 344–8; Czechoslovak Ministry for Foreign Affairs, *Bojující Československo*, pp. 115–16.

republic or a separate communist state. The Soviet Union, however, had already abandoned the idea of an independent Slovakia in any form, because Stalin saw no advantage in such a solution.[28] On 5 January 1943, the Executive of the Communist International adopted a resolution calling for a new Czechoslovakia where the relations between the Czechs and Slovaks would be put on a new (federative) basis.[29]

In December 1943, Beneš visited Moscow, where a new Soviet–Czechoslovak treaty was signed on 12 December.[30] Further evidence of Soviet support for Beneš's plans was apparent in the Soviet–Czechoslovak agreement regarding the administration of the liberated Czechoslovak territories, signed on 8 May 1944.[31] According to this treaty the Soviet military authorities agreed to hand over civil administration to the Czechoslovak government. Moscow also rejected a secret offer from General Ferdinand Čatloš, the minister for defence, in which he offered to open the Slovak borders to the advancing Soviet army in return for guarantees for a plebiscite about the future status of Slovakia.[32]

Even as late as the spring of 1944, the Slovak government still retained numerous illusions about the possibility of preserving Slovak independence after the war. However, the treaty of 8 May 1944 demonstrated that no one was interested in such a solution. This fact was confirmed by Jozef M. Kirschbaum, the Slovak chargé d'affaires in Switzerland, who visited President Tiso on 4 August to inform him that the Western allies regarded Slovakia's position as an internal Czechoslovak problem.[33]

The resistance movement during the Second World War

From the outset, the Ľudák regime faced relatively strong opposition to its rule. Many adherents of Hlinka's Slovak People's Party considered the new state to be more or less the embodiment of their long-lasting struggle for national emancipation. On the other hand, however, there

---

[28] Collection 495, op. 18, number 1340, Rossiiskii tsentr khraneniya i izucheniya dokumentov po noveishoi istorii (RTsKhIDNI) [Russian Centre for the Preservation and Study of Documents of Recent History], Moscow.
[29] Collection 495, op. 18, number 1340, p. 15, RTsKhIDNI, Moscow; see also V. Prečan (ed.), *Slovenské národné povstanie. Dokumenty* [Slovak National Uprising. Documents] (Bratislava, 1965), vol. I, doc. 1, pp. 42–3.
[30] Beneš, *Paměti*, pp. 383–5.
[31] Prečan (ed.), *Slovenské národné povstanie*, vol. I, doc. 59, pp. 192–4.
[32] Sig. 115 AC 19a, Archiv literatúry a umenia Matice slovenskej (ALU MS), [Archive of the literature and arts of Matica slovenská], Martin.
[33] J. M. Kirschbaum, 'My Last Diplomatic Report to the President of Slovakia', in the annual *Jednota*, vol. XI (1972), published by the First Catholic Slovak Union, Cleveland, Ohio.

were many who were not satisfied with this new situation. First of all, the Slovak state came into existence unexpectedly. Many people in Slovakia, even many autonomists, were closely attached to the idea of Czechoslovakia, which they – like the Czechs – considered to be their country. The conditions under which Slovakia obtained independence condemned it to absolute dependence on Nazi Germany; thus the state and its regime were not popular among the majority of the Slovak population. In addition, the new state was not democratic but totalitarian, and one-party rule was even codified in the constitution. Political rights and freedoms were abolished, including freedom of speech and freedom of the press, while political opponents were persecuted. Therefore – for one reason or another – there were many in Slovakia who were dissatisfied with the Ľudák regime and were ready to fight against it. Even within the Hlinka's Slovak People's Party there were opponents of the regime; Martin Sokol, the chairman of the Slovak Diet, who opposed the pro-German orientation of the government, led one such group. This group wanted an independent Slovakia, but was also ready to accept Slovakia's existence within a broader federation or confederation with the Czech Lands.[34]

From the moment independent Slovakia came into existence in March 1939, officers and politicians remaining loyal to the Republic of Czechoslovakia and to Beneš formed groups such as Demec, Justícia, Flóra and the Slovak wing of the all-Czechoslovak Obrana národa (Defence of the Nation) movement. These groups identified with Beneš's activities in London and were involved in collecting military and political intelligence and helping officers and resistance fighters from the Protectorate of Bohemia and Moravia to escape through Slovakia to the Balkans and then to the West.[35] All of these groups were opposed to the idea of an independent Slovakia and advocated the restoration of Czechoslovakia. However, even they realised that a simple return to the situation before Munich would not be possible. The existence of the Slovak state validated Slovaks as a separate political nation, destroying T. G. Masaryk's and Beneš's idea of 'Czechoslovakism'. Even the veteran Slovak politician Vavro Šrobár, a long-standing supporter of Czechoslovakism realised that the situation had changed. This emerges clearly from the memorandum he sent to London in 1943.[36]

---

[34] The spiritual leader of this group was Karol Sidor, the Slovak ambassador to the Holy See and accordingly the group was called 'Sidor's opposition'.

[35] See Jablonický, Z ilegality.

[36] Prečan (ed.), Slovenské národné povstanie, vol. I, doc. 19, p. 90; Jablonický, Z ilegality, p. 185.

To begin with, the most radical illegal resistance group was the Communists. The illegal Communist Party of Slovakia, now separated from the Communist Party of Czechoslovakia, opposed the Ľudák government and was probably the most persecuted political group in war-time Slovakia. The Communist Party of Slovakia's attitude towards Slovak independence and Czechoslovakia changed several times, as its policies were dependent on the official line from Moscow. Until the recognition of Slovakia by the Soviet Union, on 16 September 1939, the Communist Party of Slovakia supported the restoration of Czechoslovakia. After this date, it adopted an anti-Beneš line and accepted the idea of an independent Slovakia. After the events in the Baltic states in the summer of 1940, even the Slovak Communists began to call for a Soviet Slovakia. When the Soviet Union recognised Beneš's government-in-exile in 1941, the Communist Party of Slovakia gradually accepted the restoration of Czechoslovakia but wished it to be organised along federal lines.[37]

The Communist Party of Slovakia's calls for Slovakia to become a Soviet republic and their lack of a clear position with regard to the future existence of Czechoslovakia meant that other resistance groups regarded the Slovak Communists with suspicion in the final phase of the war. Most significant among these were the former Agrarians, who were mainly Lutherans and felt discriminated against by the predominantly Catholic Ľudák regime. The Slovak Agrarians maintained political contacts with Milan Hodža in Paris. In 1940, Ján Lichner, one of the active Agrarian resistance leaders, escaped to the West and joined Beneš's émigré group in London.[38] However, relations between Slovak Agrarians and Beneš were complex because of the government-in-exile's insistence on the idea of a unitary Czechoslovak nation, a position Lichner found unacceptable.[39]

There was little active resistance in Slovakia in 1941 or 1942. However, Slovakia's participation in the war against the Soviet Union and (from a technical standpoint) against the USA and Britain changed the situation. The alliance with Nazi Germany in general and the war against the Soviet Union in particular were not popular among most Slovaks, who considered Russians and Ukrainians as Slavic kinspeople.

---

[37] See F. Beer (ed.), *Dejinná križovatka. Slovenské národé povstanie – predpoklady a výsledky* [The historical crossroads. The Slovak National Uprising – presuppositions and results] (Bratislava, 1964), pp. 84–5, 116–18; S. Falt'an, *Slovenská otázka v Československu* [The Slovak question in Czechoslovakia] (Bratislava, 1968), p. 116f.

[38] J. Rychlík, 'Zápisky Jána Lichnera z väzenia' [The notes of Jan Lichner from prison], *Historický časopis*, 46 (1998), 101f.

[39] Otáhalová and Červinková (eds.), *Dokumenty*, vol. I, doc. 139, p. 190.

Slovakia had no reason to go to war, and the government failed to generate sufficiently robust arguments to convince the majority of the population that the war was necessary. Equally, on the eastern front Slovak soldiers began to cross over Soviet lines to join the Red Army. Following the German defeat at Stalingrad, Slovak desertions continued *en masse*. Most of these soldiers were sent to the Czechoslovak army in the Soviet Union, which was being formed in Buzuluk. Some smaller military units led by Slovak officers even joined up with Russian and Ukrainian partisans and fought with them against the Germans.[40]

It was well known in Slovakia that the Allies would not recognise a Slovak state after the war. Thus, the question was not whether Slovakia would again be part of Czechoslovakia but under what conditions. In 1943, the young generation of Communists, led by Gustáv Husák, and the Young Agrarians, led by Ján Ursíny, began to negotiate a joint programme. Both groups were essentially autonomists. They did not reject the idea of a Slovak state in principle, but they understood that the international situation made such an option unlikely. At the same time they did not totally refute the idea of a new Czechoslovakia. The result was a new slogan, Czechoslovakia as a state of two nations – Czechs and Slovaks – who would live as equal partners (*rovný s rovným*, or *'like with like'*). That is, Czechoslovakia was to be re-established as the federation of two national states that would later delegate some jurisdiction to the federal authorities.

The Communists and the Agrarians were in full agreement as far as Czech–Slovak relations were concerned. Instead, more time was devoted to developing a social programme and reaching a compromise between the Communist desire for socialist revolution and the Agrarian idea of a democratic capitalist society. This was eventually achieved when (for tactical reasons) the Communists abandoned the idea of large-scale nationalisation and agreed to a vague formulation that stated 'political democracy should be extended to economic life'. The complex programme, approved by 'the Socialist bloc' (representing the Communists and a small group of Social Democrats) and the 'Civic bloc', consisting mainly of the Agrarians, was adopted in December 1943 and became known as 'the Christmas Agreement'.[41] Three Communists – Gustáv Husák, Ladislav Novomeský and Karol Šmidke – and three non-communists – Ján Ursíny, Jozef Lettrich and

---

[40] The best-known example is Captain Ján Nálepka; before the war he was a teacher and member of the Young Agrarians. Nálepka died in the war fighting alongside Soviet forces.

[41] Prečan (ed.), *Slovenské národné povstanie*, vol. I, doc. 32, pp. 125–6.

Matej Josko – then formed the supreme illegal central resistance body, subsequently known as the Slovak National Council.[42] Its aim was to establish contact with anti-fascist officers in the army, to depose Tiso's regime, to restore the Czechoslovak Republic and to instigate open resistance against Germany.

The text of the Christmas Agreement was transmitted to Beneš via Switzerland; he received it on 4 March 1944. He made no comments about the programme. The president was, however, not informed that they did not represent political forces around his ally Vavro Šrobár.[43] Šrobár himself was by then organising his own network of national committees. These were to seize political power at the appropriate moment. But Beneš was ignorant of the fact that the Slovak National Council was in fact quite separate from Šrobár's Central National Committee (Ústredný národný výbor). When the time came, the Slovak National Council proved to be the stronger of the two groupings, because it had managed to contact the pro-democratic group of officers in the Slovak army called the Military Centre (Vojenské ústredie). The Military Centre, led by Lieutenant-Colonel Ján Golian, in the end subordinated itself to the Slovak National Council, which proved to be a crucial point when an uprising later began in Slovakia.[44]

The partisan movement was another important part of the resistance movement. In 1944, there were quite large numbers of people hiding in the forests and mountains of central and eastern Slovakia for various reasons. There were Slovak soldiers who had deserted from the Slovak army; people who had to hide from the police because of illegal activities; Jews who had escaped the transports to death camps; foreign prisoners who had escaped from camps in occupied Poland and Hungary; persecuted Czechs who had crossed the border from the Protectorate; and so on.

Soviet partisan units began to operate in eastern Slovakia during the spring and summer of 1944, and they used these 'forest people' as a reserve fighting force. The partisans could also count on some support from the local population. In August, the partisan movement extended its area of operations to central Slovakia, and the government in

[42] G. Husák, *Svedectvo o Slovenskom národnom povstaní* [Testimony about the Slovak National Uprising] (Bratislava, 1964), pp. 66–72; J. Ursíny, *Spomienky na Slovenské národné povstanie* [Reminiscences on the Slovak National Uprising] (Liptovský Mikuláš, 1994), pp. 48–59.
[43] J. Jablonický, *Slovensko na prelome* [Slovakia at the turning point] (Bratislava, 1965), pp. 30–1.
[44] J. Jablonický, *Povstanie bez legiend* [The uprising without legends] (Bratislava, 1990), p. 11f.

Bratislava soon lost control of this region. The government had no way to deal with the partisans because both the gendarmerie and the army were heavily infiltrated by resistance activities and would not fight against them. On 10 August, the Slovak government decided to declare martial law, which was enforced from 12 August.[45] But these measures had no effect, and in many cases army officers were already obeying the orders from the Military Centre working in co-operation with the partisans, and ignoring those issued by the government.

Relations between the partisans and the Slovak National Council were less than ideal. Despite repeated warnings from the Slovak National Council and the Military Centre that the Slovak army was preparing for a major uprising and required all communication routes to be fully functional, the partisans, led by Soviet officers parachuted in from the Soviet Union or by local Slovak Communists, continued to destroy roads, railways and bridges, in line with orders issued from Soviet partisans. They also attacked the local Germans living in Slovakia and Ľudáks and those active in the state and party apparatus, paying no attention to Slovak National Council warnings that such actions might provoke the German occupation of Slovakia and lead to the premature outbreak of the uprising.

This indeed is exactly what happened at the end of August 1944. Hans Eluard Ludin, the German minister in Bratislava, came to the conclusion that the Tiso government was unable to stop the partisans and he proposed, on 24 August, to send several German divisions to Slovakia.[46] Four days later, Hitler ordered the German army to occupy Slovakia, for which Ludin obtained the consent of President Tiso. The Military Centre then sent out secret instructions to its supporters to resist the German invasion by force.[47] The occupation started next day, on 29 August 1944. Officers belonging to the Military Centre then took over the headquarters of the Slovak army in Banská Bystrica; partisans entered the city the same day.[48] The Slovak National Uprising had begun.

[45] J. Korček, *Slovenská republika 1943–1945* [The Slovak Republic 1943–1945] (Bratislava, 1999), p. 98; on the development of the partisan movement, see Jablonický, *Povstanie bez legiend*, p. 77f.
[46] V. Prečan (ed.), *Slovenké národné povstanie. Dokumenty* [The Slovak National Uprising. Documents] (Bratislava, 1970), vol. II, doc. 67, p. 157, doc. 72, p. 164.
[47] *Ibid.*, doc. 166, p. 344.   [48] Jablonický, *Z ilegality*, pp. 405–9.

14   The Slovak National Uprising: the most dramatic moment in the nation's history

Vilém Prečan

Less than five and half years after the declaration of independence, and before Allied forces entered its territory the Slovak state had become the scene of an armed rising against both Nazi Germany and the local regime connected with it. The signal to begin fighting was given on 29 August 1944, the moment when units of the German army entered the region of Žilina to restore order, which had been disrupted by partisan operations. Out of the uprising emerged the military defence of a contiguous territory, led by units of the regular Slovak armed forces who declared themselves part of the Czechoslovak armed forces; they were subordinated to the high command of the military arm of the Czechoslovak government-in-exile.

In the early days of the uprising, the insurgent territory included more than 20,000 km^2 (over half the area of the Slovak state) with a population of 1.7 million (64 per cent of the total population of war-time Slovakia). The defence of the free area, which gradually decreased in size (by early October it had shrunk to only 6,800 km^2 with a population of 340,000), lasted sixty days.[1] At first, 18,000 soldiers and several thousand partisans, and later as many as 60,000 soldiers and 12,000 partisans, conducted a 'small-scale war' in the midst of the wider war, until the moment when, under the pressure of the enemy's military superiority and after the exhaustion of its own reserves, the defence of the independent free territory collapsed. Eventually, the whole country, with the exception of the wooded mountain areas of central Slovakia, found itself back under the control of the Germans and the Slovak government in Bratislava.

---

[1] I. Kamenec, 'Civilný sektor a každodenný občiansky život na povstaleckom Slovensku' [The civilian sector and everyday civilian life in insurgent Slovakia], in D. Tóth and K. Kováčiková (eds.), *SNP 1944 – vstup Slovenska do demokratickej Európy* [The Slovak National Uprising 1944 – Slovakia's entry into democratic Europe] (Banská Bystrica, 1999), pp. 129–44, esp. p. 130.

The uprising was also a democratic political coup d'état, whereby the regime of the Slovak state was *de facto* and *de jure* overthrown in the insurgent territory. The result was the emergence of a new revolutionary Slovak statehood as part of a sovereign Czechoslovakia, organised on the basis of an anti-fascist coalition and represented by the Slovak National Council (Slovenská národná rada). The illegal Slovak National Council presented itself to the public on 1 September 1944, and declared itself to be the only representative of the Slovak nation, with the exclusive right to exercise legislative and executive power in Slovakia. The Slovak National Council called upon Slovaks to join the fight against Germany and the Hlinka Slovak People's Party regime on the Allies' side, and to defend Slovakia, for which it took responsibility. The council also declared itself in favour of the idea of coexistence with the Czech nation in a common state – the Czechoslovak Republic – and it recognised President Edvard Beneš and the government-in-exile as the representatives of the Czechoslovak Republic abroad.

Considered in the widest possible context, what took place in Slovakia in summer and autumn 1944 primarily concerned the following issues: the status of Slovak society in post-war Europe; who would speak in the name of Slovakia and Slovaks; what principles would guide the formation of the Slovak political and social system immediately after the war; and what principles would guide the relationship between Czechs and Slovaks in the restored Czechoslovak Republic.

The events in Slovakia in late summer 1944 were the consequence of the actions of a whole series of individuals, who all sought to leave their mark. The German military, diplomatic and police machinery sought to pacify Slovakia quickly and to ensure that it remained a safe area for German troops to the rear, who were being pressed by the Soviets from the south, east and north. Most of the leading politicians of the Slovak state were determined to support Nazi Germany to the bitter end. Beneš and the Czechoslovak government-in-exile in London tried as hard as possible to ensure foreign assistance for the rising from all the Allies. At the same time they sought to assert their authority over the resistance at home and then over the agencies of power in the hands of the uprising. The external leadership of the Communist Party of Czechoslovakia in Moscow completely subordinated itself to Soviet policy.

An important factor in the rising was the domestic resistance to the Slovak fascist regime, a plurality of resistance forces, groups and individuals, unknown as well as influential, civilians as well as soldiers. All had their own links to various strata of the population; some even held positions that enabled them to take advantage of key financial and economic positions, government offices and the military command or police units of the Slovak state to the benefit of the resistance.

The uprising and Allied military-political strategy

Czechoslovakia did not occupy a key position in Western Allied military strategy. A memorandum from the British foreign secretary of 9 August 1944, which was presented to the cabinet, set out British interests regarding Czechoslovakia as follows: (1) it was entirely unnecessary and undesirable for Britain to accept any obligations towards Czechoslovakia which would be similar to those in the Czechoslovak–Soviet Agreement of December 1943; (2) Czechoslovakia should be independent and strong, protected from a repetition of German aggression by Soviet military assistance; (3) politically, socially, and economically the restored Czechoslovakia, which would probably remain a petty-bourgeois state as it had been before the war, should be a stable factor in Central Europe; and (4) Britain would have close relations with a Czechoslovakia of that description, and by means of economic and cultural exchanges would expand its influence in this country and therefore throughout Central Europe.[2]

In memoranda prepared by study groups in the US State Department one finds similar formulations about American interest in a restored Czechoslovakia. They thought that such a state would contribute to peace and stability in Central Europe, and emphasised the desirability of Czechoslovakia's being an independent, sovereign state sharing in the building of future international organisations and a general security system.

Though the British Foreign Office and the US State Department, in accord with their high commands, understood and accepted that a Soviet–Czechoslovak agreement on the administration of the liberated territory of Czechoslovakia had been signed on 8 May 1944, in view of the geographic factors and the presumed improbability that American and British units would enter Czechoslovak territory, they refused 'for the moment' to consider the matter.[3]

---

[2] Anthony Eden, 'Memorandum by the Secretary of State for Foreign Affairs on Soviet Policy in Europe', 9 August 1944, Cabinet Office Papers, CAB 66/53, WP (44) 436. Annex III, Central Europe, National Archives (NA), London.

[3] For example, P. Nichols to F. Roberts, 27 May 1944, Foreign Office papers, FO 371, 38922, NA, London; Schoenfeld to Secretary of State, No. 3, 17 March 1944, Secretary of State to Schoenfeld, No. 3524, 2 May 1944, RG 59, 869F.01, National Archives and Records Administration (NARA), Washington, DC.

Soviet interest in Czechoslovakia was, on the other hand, clear. From the internal memoranda of the Soviet foreign minister, it is also obvious that the December 1943 Agreement of Alliance with Czechoslovakia was meant to play a positive role in uniting the Slavic nations around the Soviet Union, to demonstrate friendly Soviet relations with the small nations and the advantages of entering into collaboration in the post-war period. The Soviets wanted once and for all to lay to rest the idea of a Czechoslovak–Polish confederation, to preclude the repetition of any *cordon sanitaire* on its western borders and, with an accommodating attitude to the Czechoslovak side, to contribute to the isolation of the Polish government-in-exile in London.

Slovakia had no special significance in overall Allied strategy. It was considered to be part of an Allied state, the restored Czechoslovakia of the future. The constitutional arrangement of the country (possibly the decentralisation of the administration, as was discussed in some American internal memoranda) was considered to be an internal Czechoslovak affair. All talks about possible Allied military assistance to armed operations on home territory came under the jurisdiction of elements subordinate to the Czechoslovak Ministry of Defence in London.

In late February and early March 1944 talks took place in Moscow between the representatives of Soviet military and security units and Czechoslovak military spokesmen. The matters under discussion included possible forms of Soviet assistance to a Slovak military operation in the event of a German attempt to occupy Slovakia. The Czechoslovak side had information to suggest that, in such an eventuality, Slovak units would make a stand with the aim of maintaining a coherent defence of the largest possible territory in Slovakia, and, if this occurred, demands would be made for Soviet support.

By order of Politburo member and People's Commissar for External Affairs V. M. Molotov, in the two-day break between the talks, People's Commissar for Security G. K. Zhukov met with Deputy-Chief of the General Staff A. I. Antonov, to assess the information available and these demands. Antonov, whose analysis and proposals were presented directly to Stalin, felt that the Slovak operation should be considered as only a possible way of creating a staging area in Slovakia for an active partisan activity that would tie up a certain number of German troops in the event of a Soviet offensive. He admitted the possibility of committing to drop two parachute brigades, one Czechoslovak, the other Soviet, and the already promised complete outfitting of arms and equipment for 50,000 soldiers. He suggested that the Czechoslovak side be recommended to abandon its ideas of a stationary defence of all Slovakia

Figure 14   Digging of an anti-tank ditch during the Slovak National
Uprising

against the Germans during the initial phase of operations; this would
enable them to take advantage of two Slovak brigades (which then came
under discussion), who might serve as the basis for further partisan
activity, mobilising and arming the local population (see Fig. 14).[4]

The insurgency takes shape on the ground

Two factors were of the utmost importance in the preparation of the
rising and its military and political features. A group of senior officers
formed around Lieutenant-Colonel Ján Golian, chief of staff of the army
command in Banská Bystrica. They thought in terms of Czechoslovakia
as a whole and established contacts with the military command of the
Czechoslovak government-in-exile in London. The other important

[4] 'Zapiska komissara gosudarstvennoy bezopasnosti G. Zhukova I. Stalinu' [Note of the
state security commissioner G. Zhukov to J. Stalin], 1 March 1944; 'Zapiska F. Golikova
i G. Zhukova I. Stalinu i V. M. Molotovu', 3 March 1944, box 1, inv. nos. 3 and 4, in
record group SDRA, National Archives, Prague (photocopies of documents held in the
Archive of the President of the Russian Federation, Moscow); see also V. V. Maryina,
'Sovetskii soyuz i slovatskoe natsionalnoe vosstanie 1944' [The Soviet Union and the
Slovak National Uprising 1944], *Novaya i noveishaya istoriya*, 5 (1996), 111–16.

factor was the creation of an illegal Slovak National Council. This 'united political centre', as it was anonymously presented to President Beneš, was not representative of all resistance groups. Resistance groups that continued to adhere to the unitary principle, of a single Czechoslovak nation, and considered Beneš and the Czechoslovak government in London the sole authority, stood aside. The illegal Slovak National Council, in fact, expressed attitudes agreed on by the leading figures of the communist underground, that is, the Communist Party of Slovakia and a section of the Social Democrats, on the one hand, and a small group of functionaries of the former Agrarian Party on the other. Golian, the head of the insurgent Military Centre, accepted authorisation from two sides: from the Czechoslovak government-in-exile in London[5] as well as from the illegal Slovak National Council.

The plan for military insurgency took definitive shape in spring 1944, when the Slovak armed forces underwent an important reorganisation. At the initiative of Minister of Defence Ferdinand Čatloš, and with the agreement of the Slovak government, two new infantry divisions comprising about 25,000 men were formed in April and May 1944. These were the best-armed units with artillery and their own small air force (of forty-two aircraft). The two divisions, distinguished as a 'field army' (*polné vojsko*), were deployed in eastern Slovakia, and their command was based in Prešov. Čatloš pursued his own plans, mainly to ensure that no Hungarian troops were sent to Slovakia as the front line approached. The creation of this field army was intended to buttress the arguments in favour of redeploying Slovak troops from Italy and Romania back to Slovakia.[6] Later, in a secret memorandum produced at the end of July, in which he offered to collaborate with the Soviets, Čatloš proposed that these forces would help the Red Army from the north 'to move smoothly across Slovakia' and to control Hungary. That is why he was trying to ensure that Slovak units were entrusted with defending the important north-east section of the Slovak border.[7] 'Malár's Army', as the two east Slovak divisions were called (after their commander General Rudolf Malár), was in August 1944 incorporated into the German

---

[5] V. Prečan (ed.), *Slovenské národné povstanie. Dokumenty* [The Slovak National Uprising. Documents] (Bratislava, 1965), vol. I, doc. 61, note 1, radiograms from London, 14 May 1944.

[6] For more on this subject, see V. Prečan, 'Nacistická politika a Tisův režim v předvečer povstání' [Nazi policy and the Tiso regime on the eve of the uprising], *Historie a vojenství*, 39 (1990), 10–14.

[7] For the text of the 'Čatloš memorandum', see Maryina, 'Sovetskii soyuz', 126–7; for a version in Slovak, see Prečan (ed.), *Slovenské národné povstanie*, vol. I, doc. 113.

Army Group North (Ukraine) (Heeresgruppe Nord-Ukraine), which was operating to the north-east of Slovakia.

Thus Malár's Army became the most important military factor in the plan for the rising, as worked out by Golian and his colleagues and approved in late June 1944 by the illegal Slovak National Council. These two divisions were given the main task in the planned military operation against the Germans, which was supposed to take place in co-ordination with an operation of the Red Army. This plan was the 'big variant of the rising', which envisaged that Slovak divisions, under Soviet direction, would attack the Germans from the rear and thus enable Soviet troops to cross the Carpathian mountain passes easily, and occupy all of Slovakia 'with lightning speed'.[8] The units of the so-called rearguard (*západná armáda*) concentrated in central Slovakia in peace-time garrisons (numbering about 14,000 soldiers) were supposed to provide support for the coup d'état. Once further mobilisation had increased their numbers, the units were to join the field army and, together with the Soviets, purge Slovakia of Germans.

A second, 'defensive' variant of the insurgency plan was prepared in the event that the Germans attempted, for any reason, to occupy all Slovakia before the Slovak military operation took place in tandem with the Soviet offensive. If this happened, it was decided to prevent the occupation of Slovakia by all means available to the insurgents, and if necessary to withdraw all armed forces to central Slovakia and fight a partisan war until the arrival of the Red Army.

These insurgency plans were reported to the Czechoslovak government-in-exile by Golian (who by then had a reliable secret radio connection with London) in the second half of June and early July 1944.[9] The Czechoslovak authorities informed the Soviets of these plans via a communiqué of 10 July, addressed to the Soviet military attaché in London, and on 14 July by the Czechoslovak military mission in Moscow.[10]

The Soviet attitude to the insurgency plans

The main question that loomed over these proposals was how to co-ordinate the organisers of the rising with the Soviet military. When it was discussing the plan in late June, the illegal Slovak National Council decided not to rely solely on mediation from London, but instead to enter

---

[8] Prečan (ed.), *Slovenské národné povstanie*, vol. I, doc. 83, radiograms from Golian to London, 31 July, 3 and 4 August 1944; also doc. 136 (Píka to Ingr, 16 August 1944).
[9] *Ibid.*, vol. I, docs. 83, 136.   [10] *Ibid.*, vol. I, doc. 92.

into direct contact with the Soviet military. To that end, the council decided to send a delegation to the Soviet Union in secret. That, however, did not take place until early August. The first delegation – a group of soldiers – was sent on 2 August. Among them was Lieutenant Ján Korecký, who had Golian's official authorisation and who took a great deal of military documentation with him.[11] The aircraft landed in Ukraine two days later, carrying Karol Šmidke, who was a Communist and member of the illegal Slovak National Council, and Lieutenant-Colonel Mikuláš Ferjenčík, whom Golian had appointed to accompany Šmidke upon agreement with the non-communist representatives of the Slovak National Council. Both men were flown to Moscow on 6 August.[12]

On 10 August, Deputy-Chief of the General Staff Antonov presented Stalin with a long report on information received from Šmidke and Ferjenčík. The debriefing of the Slovak emissaries confirmed reports about plans for an anti-German operation by the Slovak army. According to Šmidke's information, the Slovak underground was capable of raising an army of 100,000 to 120,000 men, and could assure free passage through Slovakia to Soviet troops during their southward operation. The report also mentioned that Slovakia would not accept a plenipotentiary of the Czechoslovak government-in-exile in London, as foreseen in the Czechoslovak–Soviet agreement about the administration of the territory liberated by the Red Army, because for this task, according to Šmidke's information, a Slovak National Council had been formed (in the report called the 'National Committee').[13]

As yet, no documents have been unearthed that explain how the Soviet General Staff, or Stalin himself, saw the prospects of co-operating with the Slovak underground and how they judged the plans and proposals presented by the emissaries from Slovakia. Only from later memoirs of senior officers of the Soviet General Staff during the war do we know that the Slovak military plan was considered unrealistic.[14]

[11] *Ibid.*, vol. I, docs. 118, 124, 127–8.
[12] Most recently, see J. Jablonický, 'Neúspešná misia v Moskve' [Unsuccessful mission in Moscow], in Jablonický, *Samizdat o odboji. Štúdie a články* [Samizdat about the resistance. Studies and essays] (Bratislava, 2004), pp. 129–31, 139.
[13] 'Zapiska generala armii A. Antonova I. Stalinu s prilozheniem doneseniya Slavina o besede s Shmitke' [Notes of Army General A. Antonov for J. Stalin with Slavin's report based on conversation with Šmidke], 10 August 1944, SDRA record group, box 1, inv. nos. 6–7, NA, Prague; Maryina, 'Sovetskii soyuz', 117–27.
[14] A. A. Grechko, *Cherez Karpaty* [Through the Carpathian mountains] (Moscow, 1970); S. S. Shtemenko, *Generalnyi shtab v gody voiny* [General Staff during the years of the war] (Moscow, 1973), vol. II.

After their successful offensive in Romania, the Soviets counted on being able to advance northwards through Hungary, and therefore halted preparations for a possible attack via the Carpathian mountains in the north.

The Soviet side remained silent about these Slovak proposals. No mention was made of Šmidke and Ferjenčík's visit to Moscow, despite repeated inquiries by General Heliodor Píka, the head of the Czechoslovak military mission there, whom London had informed about their departure from Slovakia. No information was communicated even in the last days of August 1944, when General Píka repeatedly informed the Soviet authorities about the anticipated occupation of Slovakia by the Germans, and about the planned military operation being prepared by the illegal Slovak military command if such an event occurred.[15] It proved impossible for Píka to get any statement or information from the Soviet side.[16]

The Soviets were continuously fanning the flames of the partisan movement in Slovakia, which was run from the partisan headquarters in Kiev, and their approval for the escalation of this operation turned out to be fatal. Soviet partisan organisers, who were parachuted into Slovakia in late July and early August 1944, formed relatively large units with Slovak volunteers. These units carried out ever more audacious acts of sabotage and were increasingly involved in fighting after 20 August, without the Soviet commanders having been informed by the Slovak National Council or the Military Centre about the plans for the rising. Counter-measures enacted by the authorities in Bratislava, including the declaration of martial law on 12 August and the despatch of Slovak police units to fight the partisans, proved utterly ineffective.

The commanders of the largest partisan units in Turiec region and the Low Tatras called upon Slovak troops to defect. After 25 August, the partisans decided to proceed with the occupation of towns and villages and, with the help of local resistance fighters drawn mainly from the ranks of the illegal Communist Party of Slovakia, to establish a revolutionary government. Thus, on 27 August the partisans occupied

---

[15] See the report of Major General Davydov to Stalin about the conversation with General Píka, 27 August 1944, record group SDRA, box 1, inv. no. 9, National Archives, Prague; Maryina, 'Sovetskii soyuz', 129–30.

[16] Later, in September and October, the Soviet diplomats' stubborn refusal to answer British questions made any effective assistance from the West difficult. For more on this point, see a short article based mostly on British sources, V. Prečan, 'The 1944 Slovak Rising', in W. Deakin, E. Barker and J. Chadwick (eds.), *British Political and Military Strategy in Central, Eastern and Southern Europe in 1944* (London, 1988), pp. 223–34.

Figure 15 Slovak National Uprising armed fighters

Ružomberok, where a district national committee was established. It is not without interest that the founder of the ruling party, Andrej Hlinka, had served here as parish priest for thirty-three years. In Turčiansky Svätý Martin (today's Martin) on the morning of 27 August, on orders from partisan commander P. A. Velichko, a unit of Slovak soldiers shot dead more than twenty members of a German military mission returning from Romania. In Brezno (a small town about twenty kilometres east of Banská Bystrica) a deputy of the Slovak Diet was killed in an exchange of fire with partisans. Thus effectively began the spontaneous political coup d'état in one region of the country.[17]

The German representatives in Slovakia informed the authorities in Berlin about these events, and suggested military intervention. Reports regarding partisan operations (in which units of the Slovak army participated; see Fig. 15), particularly about the threat to important arms factories supplying the Wehrmacht, also ultimately alarmed the German Supreme Command.

---

[17] See J. Jablonický, 'Partizáni v auguste 1944' [Partisans in August 1944] (originally written in 1983), in Jablonický, *Samizdat*, pp. 353–440.

German military intervention and the response of the Slovak resistance

On 28 August 1944, it was decided to send German military units to Slovakia immediately. This decision had probably been made at a regular meeting in Hitler's headquarters, as is clear from the stenographic records of telephone calls between the Supreme Command of the German Armed Forces and the Foreign Office.[18] The German envoy to Slovakia, Hans Elard Ludin, reported back on the afternoon of that same day that President Jozef Tiso had given his agreement for the intervention.[19]

Orders were issued and the most important preliminary measures for the pacification of Slovakia were taken by the Germans on 29 and 30 August. Responsibility 'for the occupation of Slovakia' was entrusted to Reich leader of the SS (Schutzstaffel) Heinrich Himmler, who was in charge of weaponry and commander of the reserve troops. Slovakia became a 'special theatre of war outside the zone of operations'. Under an order issued on 31 August, Himmler sent Gottlob Berger, head of the SS main office, to Slovakia, with the task of disarming Slovak troops and restoring order. At the same time, Himmler despatched Einsatzgruppe H, security police and security service, to Slovakia. He summoned SS officer Josef Witiska from Lwów (Lemberg, now Ľviv in Ukraine), who was thoroughly knowledgeable about the situation in the protectorate, to take command of the group. The German Supreme Command estimated that the operation would take roughly a week. In his first situation report, sent to Himmler from Bratislava on 2 September, Berger expressed the hope that the matter would 'be resolved within four days'.[20]

The Germans' greatest initial success was the swift disarmament of arguably the best-armed and best-trained men in the Slovak army, Malár's Army, deployed in a 'zone of operations' in eastern Slovakia. Since the overthrow of General Ion Victor Antonescu and Romania's defection to the Allies, the command of Army Group North (Ukraine) had doubts about the reliability of Slovak units. From 27 August, therefore, top secret measures were put in place to disarm Malár's men if necessary. In the original plan for the uprising, Golian and the Slovak

---

[18] V. Prečan (ed.), *Slovenské národné povstanie: Nemci a Slovensko 1944. Dokumenty* [The Slovak National Uprising: Germans and Slovaks 1944. Documents] (Bratislava, 1971), vol. II, doc. 82 and facsimile.

[19] *Ibid.*, vol. II, doc. 84, Ludin to Ribbentrop, 28 August 1944 (PA AA Berlin, Handakten Ritter, B. 39, Slowakei, E399780).

[20] *Ibid.*, vol. II, doc. 101

National Council had assigned these forces a primary role. None the less, it turned out that Malár, who was favourably disposed to an agreement with the Soviets, considered the call to begin the uprising, issued by radio in Banská Bystrica on 30 August, to be premature. On the evening of 30 August, Malár gave an ambivalent speech on Bratislava radio, which confused many because it sounded anti-insurgent. Malár believed he might be able to redeploy his troops to central Slovakia, and with this intention he flew from Bratislava to Prešov. On the evening of 31 August, however, he was arrested by the Germans and interned. He was later sent to prison in Berlin.[21] On the morning of 31 August his deputy went over to the Soviet side, taking the whole air force with him, in order to arrange for Soviet help, without issuing necessary instructions to other commanding staff.

The order to disarm both divisions was not issued by the Command of the Army Group North (Ukraine) until 31 August. The operation was completed in two days. About half of the total number of 25,000 soldiers were disarmed and interned. Some escaped and fled to their families; others joined partisan units. Only about 2,000 soldiers reached the insurgency in central Slovakia.[22] Significant stocks of weapons and military equipment, including artillery, fell into German hands. The loss of these materials proved to be a serious blow as the shortfall was not replenished by supplies flown in from abroad, and during the final ten days of fighting the insurgents lacked rifles for several thousand mobilised soldiers.

A firm barrier between insurgent territory and the Soviet–German front was thus formed in the north and east of the country. The Soviet offensive, the Dukla Operation, was launched on 8 September 1944, and soon tied up the whole of Army Group North (Ukraine). This was so effective that it was impossible for the Germans to spare a single soldier to fight against the uprising itself. It was left to the German occupying forces to attack from the north-west and south-west. None the less, they promptly established a defensive line along the summit of the Beskydy mountains, which successfully resisted the Soviet offensive. Indeed, the German defence was so effective that it prevented direct Soviet assistance to the uprising; supplies had to be flown in by means of an air bridge of a mere 150 kilometres

---

[21] See J. Jablonický, 'Generál Malár: legionár a dôstojník [General Malár: legionary and officer]', in Jablonický, *Samizdat*, pp. 464–82.

[22] J. Jablonický, 'Zlyhanie Malárovej armády v Karpatoch' [The debacle of Malár's Army in the Carpathians], in Jablonický, *Samizdat*, pp. 347–443.

in length, which was threatened by German positions in the Carpathians and by the changeable mountain weather.

The Germans also won a second early victory because Bratislava, the Slovak capital and the most important region of western Slovakia, did not get involved in the insurgency. In a short radio speech, broadcast on 29 August, Čatloš announced – in the name of the president, the government and himself – that German units were coming to Slovakia to help to protect the country from the treacherous enemy – the partisans. He called upon all Slovaks – soldiers and civilians alike – to regard German troops as friends and welcome them as allies. (Tiso did not speak on the wireless until the next day.) In addition, Čatloš assisted in the peaceful disarmament of the garrison in Bratislava, and then, on the evening of 1 September, he secretly left town.[23]

In western Slovakia, only the military garrison in Trnava, fifty kilometres north-east of Bratislava, joined the rising. The garrison held the town for twenty hours and shortly before German tanks and armoured vehicles arrived, the whole unit, numbering some 3,000 men, left with their weapons for Hlohovec. Then, upon agreement with the command in Banská Bystrica, they moved on to Žarnovice in central Slovakia.

Bratislava and the surrounding area, together with Nitra (the other administrative centre, eighty-five kilometres east of Bratislava), became a convenient staging area for German and Slovak military and police units to begin to secure occupied territory and gradually to retake other areas held by the insurgents. Military, industrial and agricultural production throughout the area (almost untouched by the insurgency) continued to serve the German war effort. The political aspects of this state of affairs were significant. Slovakia's state machinery – the president, the government, the Slovak parliament, the ministries, the bureaucracy, the police and courts, radio, the press and other instruments of the regime – was preserved and could be used against the uprising and persevered in supporting Germany.

By this stage in the war, Slovakia had acquired a strategic importance. Paradoxically, the region's significance had increased after the uprising had begun. This is evident from one of the assessments produced at the time. Written by a senior Nazi official based in Vienna, it noted: 'The

---

[23] Čatloš reached the centre of the uprising, Banská Bystrica, late on the morning of 2 September. After talking to Golian he was taken into custody; on 13 September, the Soviets took him by plane to Moscow. As noted earlier, Čatloš had written a memorandum, in which he counted on the Slovak army to go over to the Allies; this was known by the Allied side as well as by the Czechoslovak government-in-exile in London. But, as a high office holder in the Slovak state, he was unacceptable both to the Czechoslovak government in London and to the Slovak National Council.

more Slovak territory we are able to hold, the more secure the northern part of the eastern front towards the south, and the smaller the danger that the rising will spill over into the Protectorate, and also the easier it will be to form a defensive front in the peripheral areas of Hungary and the alpine regions in southern Slovakia and then to secure them.'[24]

The stabilisation of the insurgent front

The Germans had achieved two major successes, with a minimum of effort, in the first ten days of fighting, developments that revealed the strengths and weaknesses of the insurgency preparations. By 7 September, the occupiers held all of western Slovakia, the north of the country, the High Tatras and the Spiš region, part of the Liptov basin, including Liptovský Svätý Mikuláš and Ružomberok, a mere fifty kilometres from Banská Bystrica. The insurgents had by then recaptured Telgárt, which had been taken only shortly before by a special unit of the Army Group North (Ukraine), and thereby ensured the defence of the eastern frontier of the insurgent territory for the next seven weeks. Also, the German attack from north of Ružomberok was halted, and the insurgent defence there was kept up for six weeks.[25]

During the night of 4 September, and the early morning of 5 September, the first external assistance arrived in the form of anti-tank weapons delivered by the Soviet Union. Himmler had few reserve troops to redeploy in Slovakia. The idea that the uprising would be suppressed by a police operation lasting several days, which had been how both the Supreme Command and Berger had imagined the response, went up in smoke. On 20 September, Berger was relieved as German commandant in Slovakia by another high-ranking SS officer, Hermann Höfle. But Höfle too had to settle for gradually retaking chunks of territory, depending on the arrival of reinforcements (in mid-October an SS-division of 15,000 men arrived, the Dirlewanger brigade, which had recently proved itself in putting down the Warsaw Uprising). Also, partisan units were still fighting on territory re-occupied by the Germans. By the second half

---

[24] Prečan (ed.), *Slovenské národné povstanie*, vol. II, doc. 174, Rafelsberger to Kaltenbrunner, 11 October 1944.

[25] A more detailed picture of the deployment of German units against the rising, using German military sources, is provided in K. Schönherr, 'Potlačenie SNP Nemeckou rίšou na jeseň 1944' [The suppression of the Slovak National Uprising by the German Reich in the autumn of 1944], in Tóth and Kováčiková (eds.), *SNP 1944*, pp. 191–202; for a detailed description of the fighting as seen from the Slovak side, see P. Bosák, *Z bojových operácii na fronte SNP* [Actions fought in the Slovak National Uprising front] (Bratislava, 1979).

of September, after the No. 1 Independent Czechoslovak Squadron, with twenty-one aircraft, was transferred to Slovakia from the Soviet Union, the Germans no longer retained absolute air superiority.

One of the most serious crises of the insurgency occurred in early October, when German troops approached Zvolen (a mere twenty kilometres from Banská Bystrica) only to be driven back by units of a parachute brigade, flown into Slovakia by the Soviets beginning in late September. The Soviets had been shaken by heavy losses incurred in the first phase of the Carpathian–Dukla pass operation. At the same time, General Rudolf Viest (who had been sent from London) was flown to Slovakia to take command of the insurgent army. On his arrival, Golian became his second-in-command. For a while the situation seemed hopeful. When Golian sent a report to London on 9 October, describing the successful counter-attack, he stated that the Germans had been forced to retreat, and added: 'Our overall situation is no longer hopeless. We shall be able to defend ourselves.'[26] It was only after the toppling of the Hungarian ruler Admiral Miklós Horthy in Hungary that the Germans could afford to release the trained 18th SS tank division to launch a general offensive from the south. The division executed a concentrated attack against the insurgents from all sides; it managed to shatter their lines of defence over a ten-day period between 18 and 27 October.

Insurgent Slovakia

For sixty days Banská Bystrica was the seat of the insurgent army command and also the centre of the political life and administration of free Slovakia. The revolutionary Slovak National Council, with thirteen members, was fully established by 5 September, after Šmidke returned from Moscow. Together with Vavro Šrobár, the representative of the 'civic-democratic bloc' and patriarch of Slovak democratic politics, Šmidke became one of the two chairmen of the Slovak National Council. The council and its organs had on principle the same number of members from the socialist bloc as from the civic-democratic bloc. The administration of the Slovak National Council comprised twelve 'commissionerships', each run by two commissioners, representing the various political blocs.

The plenum of the Slovak National Council (comprising forty-one members from 5 September, and fifty members from October) issued decrees that had the force of law. With the first, the Slovak National

---

[26] Prečan (ed.), *Slovenské národné povstanie*, vol. I, doc. 404.

Council assumed legislative, governmental and executive powers in Slovakia, and repealed laws and decrees that ran counter to the 'republican-democratic spirit' (including all anti-Jewish laws). In addition, the Slovak, German and Magyar political parties and organisations, which formed the political structure of the Slovak state, were outlawed.

From the very first day of freedom the Communists proved to be highly active, emerging from illegality as a well-organised, tightly knit body. Their participation in the resistance, energised by the harsh persecution they suffered at the hands of the Hlinka Slovak People's Party, legitimised them as a component of the Slovak political spectrum. The authority of the Soviet Union considerably increased the esteem and reputation of the Communist Party of Slovakia. As early as 2 September, it published a declaration stating as chief aims the defeat of Hitler's Germany and the uprooting of fascism in all its forms, 'so that the working people could freely determine the ways of life they wanted'. On 10 September, the Communist daily *Pravda* (Truth), which had begun publishing the day before, printed a call for a congress of the Communists and Social Democrats. When the Communist Party merged with the Social Democratic Party at the 'unification congress' held in Banská Bystrica, on 17 September 1944, this enabled it to claim to represent all socialist forces in Slovakia.

The Democratic Party (Demokratická strana) began to organise later and more slowly. Their daily, *Čas* (Time), first appeared on 17 September, and in early October it published a relatively long programme in instalments, in which the Democratic Party presented itself as a supporter of a 'just, democratic state under the rule of law', making explicit reference to the ideals of the first Czechoslovak president, Tomáš Garrigue Masaryk. The restored Czechoslovak Republic was to be a state of three equal Slavic nations – Czechs, Slovaks and the Subcarpathian Ruthenes. The priority in foreign policy – as with the Communists – was collaboration with Slavic states, particularly the Soviet Union. The status of Slovakia was meant to guarantee conditions for its all-round development, without threatening the unity of the Czechoslovak state. The civil service, school system, courts and state-owned enterprises were to be in Slovak hands, and Slovak was to be proclaimed as the official language in Slovakia and on par with Czech as the official language throughout Czechoslovakia. The central pillars in the Democratic Party's economic policy were the principles of private ownership and free competition and the rejection of 'outdated liberalism' as well as socialism, along with a positive attitude towards the nationalisation of certain types of enterprises and some banks, and a 'just social policy'. The principles of its programme also emphasised the demand for a thorough nationalisation of the school system and the prevention of the misuse of the churches for political purposes.

Conditions were not suitable for real political competition in Banská Bystrica, nor was there time to ensure it. All energy had to be devoted to the needs of the insurgency and the maintenance of normal, everyday life for hundreds of thousands of people.[27] It was vitally important to ensure supplies for troops and the civilian population, postal and telephone communications, rail and road transport, the harvest, the threshing of corn and the milling of flour, health care and the operation of hospitals (in which the number of wounded soldiers and partisans was growing), housing for refugees from occupied territory, particularly Jews (who were fleeing labour camps and the threat of deportation), pay for civil servants, soldiers, and officers, pensions and annuities, the changing of production plans of factories and workshops to meet the needs of the army, and work on fortifications.

All of this was achieved and maintained thanks to the determined efforts of a great number of men and women as well as the commissioners of the Slovak National Council. Plans for the decentralisation of stocks and supplies, on the pretext of preventing their loss to Allied bombers had been secretly drawn up by the resistance together with co-operating senior bankers and economists; these preparations turned out to be highly beneficial. In the summer, a reserve of banknotes worth three billion crowns had been transferred to Banská Bystrica. This was more than enough to cover all expenditures in the public and private spheres. Large amounts of various raw materials, cement, fuels, material for uniforms, medical supplies, sugar and other goods were also sent there. Wood was available from local sources, as was paper for periodicals, a remarkable variety and number of which were soon being published. (The paper mills in Harmanec were still operating on 25 October.) The radio transmitter, badly damaged by German bombardment, was soon repaired. A cinema showed films, and the Banská Bystrica theatre organised special performances for soldiers.

The Slovak National Council and the Czechoslovak government-in-exile in London

Among the representatives of the Czechoslovak state in London and the political leadership of the insurgency there were many reasons for mutual distrust prior to the uprising. Recall, for example, the

---

[27] For a remarkable discussion on this subject, see Kamenec, 'Civilný sektor'.

unfavourable response to the message of the London-based government, sent on 30 June 1943, in which the principle of a unitary Czechoslovak nation was proclaimed, or the piqued reaction of the Slovak National Council in August 1944 to the appointment of a government delegation for the liberated territory without consulting the 'homeland', including their demand for a 'clear and unambiguous' position on the question of Slovakia as a separate ethnic entity.[28] By way of a contrast, one should remember the panic in London over the Čatloš memorandum of August 1944, and the dissatisfaction of Beneš and those around him with the fact that pro-Czechoslovak resistance groups had found themselves outside the political centre of the resistance, which they considered to be composed of Agrarians, Communists and collaborators who had become resistance fighters at the last minute in order to be on the right side at the end of the conflict.[29] In early September 1944, while the reasons for such tension did not decrease, its nature changed.

The Czechoslovak government-in-exile in London was outraged that the Slovak National Council had unilaterally promoted Golian to the rank of general (5 September), as only Beneš as supreme commander of the Czechoslovak Armed Forces was authorised to make such appointments. It was satisfied when the Slovak National Council proclaimed on 1 September its allegiance to the Czechoslovak Republic. But the government-in-exile could not accept the Slovak National Council's seizure of power on the ground. The Slovak National Council did not like the fact that Minister Sergej Ingr, later the commander in chief of the Czechoslovak Armed Forces, was far away in London giving orders to the command of the insurgent army. Further, the government-in-exile was presenting itself to the world as being in charge, yet was paying scant attention to securing foreign assistance to the uprising, and was – as seen from Banská Bystrica – leaving it in the lurch.[30]

The presidium of the Slovak National Council (which was not yet debating these matters in its plenary sessions) considered it petty that London demanded all decisions to be taken in conjunction with the government in-exile.[31] The national council was also dissatisfied with the fact that it had learnt of changes in the composition of the

---

[28] Prečan (ed.), *Slovenské národné povstanie*, vol. I, doc. 139, despatch from codename 'Anna' (the Slovak National Council) to the Czechoslovak government in London, 18 and 26 August 1944.

[29] *Ibid.*, vol. I, doc. 172, note 2, Drtina to Beneš, Moscow, 29 August 1944.

[30] *Ibid.*, vol. I, doc. 275, radiogram from the Slovak National Council, 12 September 1944, and doc. 322, Šrobár and Šmidke to Beneš, 20 September 1944.

[31] *Ibid.*, vol. I, doc. 258, Beneš to the Slovak National Council, 6 September 1944.

Czechoslovak government-in-exile only from wireless broadcasts.[32] These tense relations were further worsened when the government raised the question of whether it understood correctly that the Slovak National Council regarded itself as the Slovak Land (*Zemský* in Czech; *Krajinský* in Slovak) National Committee, and requested that the Slovak National Council henceforth adopt the name 'National Committee'.[33]

The proverbial last straw came with a long telegram received in Banská Bystrica on 24 September, in which the government-in-exile laid out its ideas about the land national committees (*zemské národní výbory*), putting the Slovak National Council on the same level as the three other planned land national committees,[34] stating that 'we agree that the Slovak National Council as the Slovak National Committee should establish everything necessary in the spirit of the valid Czechoslovak constitution and in the spirit of the government declaration on the national committees'. London was concerned with the subordinate nature of the national committees to the government, the continued validity of the Czechoslovak system from the period before 29 September 1938 and thus the pre-war constitution; a number of other questions were also sensitive for the Slovak National Council. On the matter of the status of 'Slovakia as an ethnic entity' (that is, recognition of the Slovak nation) the government again took the position that 'the relationship of Slovaks and Czechs will be solved later after liberation on the basis of equality and fraternal understanding'. The government went to great lengths to explain why it was necessary to create the institution of a government delegate for the liberated territory. On the Slovak side, this move aroused great displeasure and the fear of a humiliation of being subject to the government in London. However, it agreed that the delegate, Minister František Němec, was to visit Slovakia with political advisors solely as a member of the government and intermediary between the resistance groups at home and abroad.[35]

The Presidium of the Slovak National Council decided to respond with its own position on all these questions and to send a delegation back to London to discuss mutual relations between the resistance at home

---

[32] *Ibid.*, vol. I, doc. 333.

[33] *Ibid.*, vol. I, doc. 317, Šrámek and Ripka to Šrobár, 20 September 1944.

[34] All the proposals debated and prepared in London were based on the project of the four provincial national committees – of Bohemia, Moravia-Silesia, Slovakia, and Subcarpathian Ukraine. This was the idea President Beneš presented to the Slovak National Council delegation as late as 5 November 1944.

[35] Prečan (ed.), *Slovenské národné povstanie*, vol. I, doc. 349, Czechoslovak government to the Slovak National Council, 24 September 1944.

and abroad with the president and the government. The statement was approved on 29 September, in an *in camera* session of the plenum of the Slovak National Council. Its six concise paragraphs set forth the principles on which the Slovak National Council had emerged and the insurgent Slovak National Council had been established. They are worth summarising:

(1) the Slovak National Council is the supreme revolutionary organ of the resistance at home, and it leads this resistance legislatively, governmentally and executively. The president, the government-in-exile and the State Council in London retain command of the resistance abroad and everything that is connected with the representation of the state with regard to the Allies and other foreign countries.

(2) This applies until the legitimate representatives of the people are democratically elected.

(3) The Slovak National Council supports the Czechoslovak Republic as the common state of three Slavic nations – Czechs, Slovaks and Subcarpathian Ukrainians – on the principle of equality. Definitive constitutional arrangement will be made by the legitimate representatives of these nations.

(4) With regard to ensuring the international standing of Czechoslovakia, the Slovak National Council adopts the principle of the constitutional continuity of the republic, although in consequence of the developments of the last six years and the needs of the resistance at home and abroad the constitution is in many respects outdated and cannot, as a whole, be the basis for the internal arrangement of the state.

(5) The Slovak National Council considers the closest collaboration between the representatives of the resistance at home and abroad and the mutual exchange of information about essential measures to be absolutely necessary.

(6) The Slovak National Council considers the position of the Czechoslovak government on the matter of the government delegate to have been made obsolete by the uprising and the current situation. The government's position on the absolute superiority of the government delegate over the people's organs at home contravenes democratic principles and devalues the resistance at home. In the interest of co-operation, however, the Slovak National Council welcomes the presence of a member of the Czechoslovak government on its 'own', that is, insurgent, territory.[36]

[36] *Ibid.*, vol. I, doc. 372, addendum to the minutes of the secret session of the Slovak National Council, 29 September 1944.

To clarify this position, the Slovak National Council delegation flew to London from Banská Bystrica in an aircraft sent for that purpose from the US air base in Bari (Italy) on 7 October 1944. Talks with President Beneš did not begin until mid October.[37] In the meantime, a government delegation from the Soviet Union led by Minister Němec arrived at Banská Bystrica, and was given an opportunity to introduce itself and give speeches at a special session of the Slovak National Council on 10 October. After ten days of discussions, the Presidium of the Slovak National Council passed a resolution on its position with regard to the Czechoslovak government delegate, which was then conveyed to the president and the government as well as to the Slovak National Council delegation in London and to Němec.[38] The document refers to the resolution of the Slovak National Council secret plenum of 29 September, and reinforces the council's claim to its authority with the following formulation: 'The Slovak National Council will exercise all legislative power in Slovakia within the borders as they existed before the Munich Agreement, regardless of whether the individual parts of Slovakia are liberated by its own forces or by the Allied armies.' In this sense, the resolution assigned the government delegate the role of an intermediary between the Slovak National Council, the president and the government in London, on the one hand, and the Slovak National Council and the Red Army command on the other. The resolution emphasised the council's interest in working with the government delegate and his advisors. The government delegate was offered an office attached to the Presidium of the Slovak National Council and regular participation in the sessions of the Presidium and the Board of Commissioners, and the political advisors were offered an opportunity to take part in the plenary sessions of the Slovak National Council.

On 23 October, when the uprising began to falter, the plenum of the Slovak National Council passed an order, whereby all legislative, governmental and executive power was transferred to the eight-member Presidium of the Slovak National Council.[39] This measure formed the basis for the forming of the institutions of the Slovak National Council in Košice in early February 1945, as well as shaping the relationship

---

[37] For the history of the delegation, see the large collection of new documents compiled by Vilém Prečan: V. Prečan, 'Delegace Slovenské národní rady v Londýně (říjen–listopad 1944). Nové dokumenty' [Delegation of the Slovak National Council in London (October–November 1944. New documents], *Česko-slovenská historická ročenka* [Czech and Slovak historical year book] (Brno 1999), pp. 159–271.

[38] *Ibid.*, p. 211; also Prečan (ed.), *Slovenské národné povstanie*, vol. I, doc. 446.

[39] Prečan (ed.), *Slovenské národné povstanie*, vol. I, p. 1169, decree no. 40 of the Slovak National Council.

between the Slovak National Council and the government delegate on territory that the Red Army had liberated and handed over to Czechoslovak administration.[40]

The *de facto* occupation of Slovakia

The organised defence of contiguous insurgent territory ended on 27 October, when Banská Bystrica was occupied by the Germans without a fight. The last order given by the insurgency's commander, General Viest, authorised the switch to partisan-style warfare in the individual regions, but was not conveyed to most units. A chaotic, poorly organised retreat into the mountains was made more difficult by bombardment. Many soldiers managed to escape to their families, but many of them were then taken prisoner and sent to prisoner-of-war camps in the Reich.

In occupied Banská Bystrica, President Tiso led a mass of thanksgiving on 30 October 1944, in the presence of Slovak and German functionaries. After the mass, a ceremonial inspection of the victorious troops was made, and the president gave a long speech in which he declared honour and glory to the protector Adolf Hitler and his army, units of the SS, General Höfle and the present German commanders for having defended the Slovak state.

After internal discussions in the highest Nazi circles, it was concluded that nothing would change in reference to the state of relations between the Slovak state and the Greater German Reich, and that all external attributes of the independent Slovak state would be retained. However, the temporary military intervention, of course, changed the situation and soon turned into lasting occupation. The German commander in Slovakia, subordinated to Himmler, remained there. The security police and security service were also established on a permanent basis. Einsatzgruppe H had five divisions of 500 men each, and their network was spread throughout Slovakia from the beginning of November 1944. In mid November, Witiska was appointed overall commander. His subordinates acted as if they were in an occupied country. A report sent to Berlin on 9 December 1944, said that 'while securing Slovak space' almost 13,000 people were arrested, of whom almost 10,000 were Jews, most of whom were transferred to German concentration camps; 2,237

---

[40] The question of the constitutional status of Slovakia in the restored Czechoslovakia, which the Slovak National Council raised in its documents after the war, was not definitively resolved even by the Košice Government Programme, the policy document of the first post-war Czechoslovak government of the 'National Front'. The resolution of this problem became part of the political struggles after 1945. For more on this, see the chapter by Michal Barnovský in the present volume.

people were given 'special treatment' (*Sonderbehandlung*), that is, they were murdered or put to death without trial.[41]

The worst Slovak offenders in the final phase of the Second World War were the recently formed stand-by squads and Special Divisions of the Hlinka Guard and the Hlinka Youth. Formed by 7 September 1944, they performed police and security tasks and, working in close co-operation with the German military and police, they were involved in operations against partisans and civilians. Particularly after the fall of Banská Bystrica, they took part in mass murders and executions without trial, went on punitive expeditions, razing villages to the ground that had collaborated with partisans, and persecuting Jews.[42]

The government of the Slovak state was re-organised in early September 1944, when Štefan Tiso became prime minister (replacing the infirm Vojtěch Tuka), and it remained linked with Hitler's Germany until the end of the war. Fronted by the president, together with the heads of German institutions, the government abandoned Bratislava in late March 1945 and was evacuated to Austrian territory. After its members were taken into custody by the US Army, they were extradited to Czechoslovakia for prosecution.

It took six months for the Soviet–German front to move across Slovakia. Two large towns in the east of the country, Prešov and Košice (the latter had been a part of Hungary as a consequence of the Vienna Arbitration in 1938), were liberated on 19 January 1945, followed by Banská Bystrica on 25 March. With an attack from the south the Soviets occupied southern Slovakia in late March and early April, followed by Bratislava on 4 April and Žilina on 30 April. While the retreating German troops inflicted deep wounds on Slovakia, the uprising and its consequences remain of fundamental significance to what are now the Slovak Republic and the Czech Republic.

[41] Prečan (ed.), *Slovenské národné povstanie*, vol. I, doc. 559.   [42] *Ibid.*, vol. I.

(+)*Michal Barnovský*

The Czechoslovak political system in the period 1945–1948

If we want to comprehend Slovakia's position within the restored Czechoslovak Republic, and the development of Czech–Slovak relations during the period 1945–1948, we must first clarify the character of the political regime at that time. The political system formed in Czechoslovakia immediately after the end of the Second World War was not a parliamentary democracy, but neither was it a totalitarian regime. It contained heterogeneous elements. The political actors themselves gave the system various labels. The Communists called it a 'people's democracy' because they wanted to emphasise its difference to the pre-war form of parliamentary democracy, which they called formal (bourgeois) democracy. They regarded people's democracy as a temporary stage on the road to a Soviet-style system. Edvard Beneš, President of the Czechoslovak Republic, spoke of a socialising democracy. Other adjectives or descriptions were also used. Today, the majority of Slovak and Czech historians describe the people's democratic regime of this period as a limited and regulated democracy with closed plurality.

Although the non-communist parties emphasised the legal continuity of the Czechoslovak Republic after 1945, and the validity of the 1920 constitution, in reality the post-war political system was significantly different from the political system of the First Czechoslovak Republic of 1918–1938. Before the establishment of the Temporary National Assembly in October 1945, the constitutional powers of the president had been significantly increased. Beneš produced legislation by means of decrees, based on proposals from the government. The National Assembly (parliament) had one chamber. The Senate, which was the second chamber before the war, was not revived, nor was the Constitutional Court. Parliament had the right to control the government and to express lack of confidence in it but, in reality, the formation of the National Front and the absence of a realistic political opposition meant that its role declined while that of the government increased. The government not only decided on the matters assigned to it in the constitution, but also intervened in ministerial affairs if the decision was politically important. The extensive nationalisation measures of 1945 and other state interventions in the economy further extended the government's control.

The Slovak national bodies – the Slovenská národná rada (Slovak National Council or Slovak parliament) and Zbor povereníkov (Board of Commissioners or Slovak government) – and the local and district national committees (*národné výbory*) were new elements in the political system. They took over the activities of the former offices of the state administration and local government. Among other changes, it is necessary to mention the formation of a new police organisation, the National Security Force, and lowering the age for voting and extending it to members of the armed forces. The people's democratic system respected the majority of democratic rights and freedoms as defined in the constitution but, based on the principle of collective guilt, members of the German and Magyar nationalities were deprived of their civil rights, except for acknowledged anti-fascists, who were able to apply for Czechoslovak citizenship.

The political parties were part of this system and participated in shaping it. Their number had been reduced in comparison with the inter-war period. There were four parties in the Czech Lands: the Czechoslovak National Socialist Party (ČSNS), the Czechoslovak People's Party (ČSL), the Communist Party of Czechoslovakia (KSČ) and Czechoslovak Social Democracy (ČSSD). In 1945, Slovakia only had two parties, the Democratic Party (DS) and the Communist Party of Slovakia (KSS). In 1946, two further marginal parties were added: the Freedom Party (Strana slobody) and the Labour Party (Strana práce).[1] The ability to create new political groups was distinctly limited. No new political party could be formed without the agreement of the existing parties, and recognition of any party depended on its agreement with the statutory (Košice) government programme. The spectrum of political parties also changed. The classic right-wing parties were excluded from political life. The left and centre remained, but the non-communist parties shifted their policies to the left of the political spectrum.

---

[1] In contrast to the Czech Lands, the political parties in Slovakia were new political groups. The Democratic Party originated from the bourgeois resistance groups. The Communist Party of Slovakia separated from the Communist Party of Czechoslovakia in 1939, and existed as an independent party until September 1948. The Freedom Party and the Labour Party were formed at the beginning of 1946.

There were no parties that operated throughout the whole state or parties based on national minorities. All the parties operated only in the territory of one national region, that is, in Slovakia or in the Czech Lands, although the Czech parties carried the adjective 'Czechoslovak' in their names.

The main element in this power-political system was the National Front – the people's democratic coalition and supreme political body – which brought the political parties together. Its mission was to overcome the disputes between the parties and harmonise their interests. The parties sent their representatives to meetings of the National Front. All resolutions were taken unanimously, without voting, and its decisions were binding. In reality, the National Front had a monopoly on power.

The people's democratic regime did not allow parties to operate outside the National Front – in effect, as opposition parties – even though this was a characteristic feature of parliamentary democracy, which is why I use the term 'closed plurality'. However, while democracy and civil society existed, opposition to the government could not be wholly prevented, although its expression was limited. Anti-government opinions occasionally appeared in the press, in special interest organisations and in political parties. The system of limited democracy was a direct result of the weaknesses of inter-war parliamentary democracy, and the product of war-time anti-fascism and of the Soviet and Communist influence. It was not only the work of the Communists; other parties also contributed to its formation. It was in these conditions that the on-going struggle to resolve the Slovak question was taking place.

The international aspect of the Slovak question

The emergence and continued existence of small states were unthinkable without the agreement of and guarantees from the great powers. After having been destroyed in March 1939, the Czechoslovak Republic was restored in 1945 with the support of Allied powers. The Slovak state came into being and existed because of Hitler's Germany, and disappeared after its defeat. The hopes of the ruling circles of the Slovak Republic (1939–1945) – that some miracle could save it – were totally unrealistic. None of the victorious powers had any interest in its preservation. The Slovak Republic had come into being suddenly and did not last long, nor was it firmly embedded in the consciousness of the nation. A large part of the population simply did not identify with the war-time Slovak state because of its totalitarian regime and the persecutions it inflicted. Even if Slovakia had retained its independence, it would have been treated by the Allies as a defeated state, which was not an attractive option. Finally, there were fears that an independent Slovakia would sooner or later fall victim to the territorial demands of one of its neighbours. Therefore, the restoration of the Czechoslovak Republic appeared to be the only realistic alternative, and the great majority of the population of Slovakia accepted this solution either from conviction or as an unavoidable alternative.

The Czech–Slovak relationship in the restored state

In 1945, the Slovaks and Czechs were joining up in a common state together for the second time in the twentieth century, enriched with experience from twenty years of coexistence and six years of separation, from which they were drawing their own lessons. They were two linguistically and culturally very close nations, but they differed because of history, economy and social structure, and to some extent also due to mentality. The abyss that opened between them after the break-up of the Czecho-Slovak Republic, in March 1939, was bridged by the Slovak National Uprising of 1944, which rejected the totalitarian Ľudák regime and its policies and ideology, and declared its support for the restoration of the Czechoslovak Republic. However, the different views of the Slovaks and Czechs on constitutional arrangements within that entity had yet to be resolved. Czech society retained the idea of a unitary Czechoslovak nation and associated the extinction of the Czecho-Slovak Republic in March 1939 with a 'Slovak betrayal' and the failure of autonomous institutions. This view led to distrust of the Slovak national bodies that had been established during the uprising. The Czech ideal was a unitary state. But what guaranteed the strength of the republic for the Czechs was its Achilles heel for the Slovaks. In their view, an autonomous status for Slovakia and wide jurisdictional powers for the Slovak national bodies did not threaten the Czechoslovak Republic, but strengthened it. The national consciousness of the Slovaks was greatly enhanced during the period 1918–1945. It was clear that they were not going to be satisfied with their situation in the First Czechoslovak Republic of 1918–1938. Gustáv Husák, then deputy chairman of the Communist Party of Slovakia, expressed this entirely unambiguously with the question, 'What do you think the people were fighting for? To go back to 1938?'[2]

---

[2] M. Klimeš, P. Lesjuk, L. Malá and V. Prečan (eds.), *Cesta ke květnu. Vznik lidové demokracie v Československu* [The road to May. The origin of the people's democracy in Czechoslovakia] (Prague, 1965), vol. I, p. 435.

Thus, regarding Czech–Slovak relations, two different conceptions of the building of the Czechoslovak state had already emerged during the Slovak National Uprising of 1944: the conception of Beneš and his supporters in the National Socialist, People's and Social Democratic Parties, and the conception of the Slovak National Council. The first was mainly a matter of returning to the pre-Munich status quo. It was based on the premise of the lawful continuity of the Czechoslovak Republic and the continued validity of the 1920 constitution until it changed. Beneš expressed his personal view on the future structure of the state in October 1944 with the words, 'In my view, our system of state administration should not be what is usually called dualism or federalism'.[3] He favoured a unitary state with a 'Land system'.

Conversely, the Slovak National Council had its own ideas about the constitutional settlement of Czech–Slovak relations. Its members talked of a new and common Czechoslovak Republic. It recognised the continuity of the Czechoslovak Republic only from the point of view of the international position of the state, and claimed that the 1920 constitution could not be a basis for future internal political relations. It declared itself to be the only representative of the Slovak nation and appropriated all legislative, governmental and executive power across the territory of Slovakia. During the uprising, the Slovak National Council defined the future constitutional status of Slovakia within the framework of the Czechoslovak Republic in general terms, based on the application of the principle 'like with like', which could be interpreted in various ways. The Slovak National Council approved the principles of the status of the position of Slovakia in the liberated republic only on 2 March 1945. The resolution detailed the departments which were to be the exclusive responsibility of the central government (foreign affairs, foreign trade, national defence), which were to fall within the competency of the commissioners, and which were common responsibility. The Slovak National Council demanded from the new government the proclamation of the complete equality of the two nations within the framework of a united (*jednotný*) and indivisible Czechoslovak Republic; the recognition of the Slovak National Council as the only representative of the will of the Slovak nation; and the confirmation of its status in the role as the 'Slovak government and Slovak parliament'. The project of the Slovak National Council aimed at a federal constitutional structure even though the word 'federation' was not explicitly used.

---

[3] V. Prečan (ed.), *Slovenské národné povstanie. Dokumenty* [The Slovak National Uprising. Documents] (Bratislava, 1965), p. 809.

The Moscow talks of March 1945 and the Košice Government Programme

From 22 to 29 March 1945, talks were held in Moscow between representatives of the Czech political parties and a delegation from the Slovak National Council. They discussed the government's programme and the formation of the first government of the National Front of the Czechoslovak Republic. The government programme also had to find a solution to the Slovak question. The representatives of the Czech non-communist parties, who travelled from London with President Beneš, did not submit their own proposed programme or offer a solution to the constitutional relations between the Czechs and Slovaks. Instead, a proposal put forward by the Moscow leadership of the Communist Party of Czechoslovakia became the basis for the talks. The delegation of the Slovak National Council presented its own proposed solution of the Slovak question of 2 March 1945. The representatives of the Czech non-communist parties described it as a 'dualist' suggestion and did not accept it. The proposal of the Moscow leadership of the Communist Party of Czechoslovakia, which formed a separate chapter in the draft government programme, was discussed. It had various points in common with the proposal of the Slovak National Council, but it differed by not defining – even in general terms – the respective powers of the central and Slovak bodies. In spite of this, the talks about this section proved to be the longest and most complex. They were also sometimes quite dramatic, especially when the National Socialists resisted Slovak demands. In the end a compromise agreement was reached.

The government programme negotiated in Moscow was proclaimed in Košice on 5 April 1945 and is therefore known as the Košice Government Programme. This agreement determined the basic contours of the people's democratic regime, including the solution of the Slovak question in terms of constitutional relations. It acknowledged the separate identity of the Slovak nation and the equality of the Slovak and Czech nations. Thus, it rejected the idea of a unitary Czechoslovak nation anchored in the 1920 constitution. The Slovak National Council was recognised as the bearer of national sovereignty and state power in Slovakia. Slovak military units were to be formed in the territory of Slovakia within the framework of the Czechoslovak armed forces. The Košice Government Programme laid out the general principles of Czech–Slovak relations, but it did not concretely address questions of specific responsibilities and competencies. It was not explicitly a federal form of constitutional arrangement, since it contained no mention of Czech national bodies, but nor was federalism excluded.

On 4 April 1945, the president appointed the first Czechoslovak government, led by the Social Democrat Zdeněk Fierlinger (1891–1976). Slovaks held nine posts in the 25-member government. Four Czech and two Slovak political parties were represented on the basis of parity, while five other ministers were included in the government as experts or important personalities.[4] The Slovak National Council appointed the Slovak members of the government.

The knotty problem of areas of responsibility surfaced immediately when the government began its work. Under the terms of the Košice Government Programme, the Slovak National Council limited its legislative powers by Decree no. 30, issued on 21 April 1945. Until the formation of the legislative body (parliament), legislative power was executed by the president on the recommendation of the national government and in agreement with the Slovak National council. This meant that the council was the legislative organ in Slovakia and, consequently, participated in the creation of state laws (decrees). However, at this stage it was still not clear which matters belonged in the category of 'Czechoslovak state affairs', and which were exclusively a Slovak responsibility. Agreement between the Czechoslovak government and the Presidium of the Slovak National Council was therefore necessary for the enactment of state laws. Executive power in Slovakia was still concentrated in the Board of Commissioners. For some time the government had nowhere to govern, because the Czech Lands were still occupied by German forces, while the Slovak National Council governed Slovakia. After the liberation of the whole territory of the republic on 10 May 1945, the government moved to Prague, yet effectively ruled only over the Czech Lands.

If the republic was to be reunited, and this question was not a controversial one, the situation just outlined could not be allowed to persist. The Slovaks sought a solution in a permanent settlement of Czech–Slovak relations along federal lines, with precise demarcation of competencies of state and national bodies. On 26 May 1945, the Slovak National Council approved directives regarding talks with the government and representatives of Czech political life. The first three points expressed support for the federal principle of constitutional organisation of the Czechoslovak Republic, while preserving the unitary state. The state was to have one head of state (president), a Czechoslovak parliament and a Czechoslovak government. There were to be Czech and Slovak national institutions: a Czech Diet (Snem) and government,

---

[4] Czech political parties had three ministerial posts each, Slovak political parties four each.

and a Slovak Diet and government. Further parts of the directives dealt with questions regarding competencies.

The issue of a federation was abandoned at a joint meeting of the government and the Presidium of the Slovak National Council in Prague from 31 May to 2 June 1945. The representatives of the Czech political parties rejected the idea outright. The Slovak Communists, until then the most consistent supporters of federalism, abandoned the idea on the instructions of the Prague-based leadership of the Communist Party of Czechoslovakia. Only the representatives of the Democratic Party continued to support the resolution of the Slovak National Council, issued on 26 May 1945, but even they relinquished the plan once they realised their isolation.

Thus an asymmetrical model for the constitution emerged from these discussions. It was asymmetrical in the sense that there were central state bodies and Slovak national bodies, but no Czech national bodies. The Slovak National Council had no equivalent on the Czech side. The result was an anomaly: what was Czech was also Czechoslovak, but what was Slovak concerned only the Slovaks. Slovaks participated in the administration of Czech matters, because they were represented in the central government and in parliament after it was elected, but Czechs could not (at first) really, and (later) be seen to, intervene into Slovak matters. This situation led to criticism of Slovak 'privileges' and an effort to cover the widest possible range of questions as matters of importance to the whole state, and to subordinate the Slovak national bodies to the central institutions. The asymmetrical model contained within it the danger that the interests of the smaller nation might be suppressed, with a tendency to reduce the jurisdictional powers of the Slovak national bodies.

The First and Second Prague Agreements

The joint session of the government and Presidium of the Slovak National Council only discussed the question of apportioning areas of competency. The result was the First Prague Agreement, signed on 2 June 1945; it defined which matters concerned the whole state, that is, which fell within the competency of the state legislative body. The Slovak National Council retained significant powers. It was responsible for legislative activity in relation to Slovakia, temporarily participated in the creation of legislation for the whole state by approving presidential decrees concerning Slovakia, and decided all personnel questions in Slovakia. Central governmental power in Slovakia was executed through the Board of Commissioners. The position of Slovakia in this period can be described as a sort of autonomy within a united state with temporary elements of federalism or confederalism, which disappeared after formation of the Temporary National Assembly and the creation of a unified currency in the autumn of 1945.

The efforts of the Slovak politicians to put Czech–Slovak relations on a firm constitutional basis were not wholly successful. This question had therefore to be addressed in the new constitution. Until then, Czech–Slovak relations were regulated by means of political agreements, and these depended on power relationships between political groupings. However, the Constitutional Act on the Constitutional National Assembly of 11 April 1946 contained an important article that prevented Slovaks from being disadvantaged on the basis of a simple majority (of votes). Not only was a majority of three-fifths required to pass a constitutional act concerning the constitutional position of Slovakia, but the agreement of the majority of attending Slovak members of the Constitutional Czechoslovak Assembly was also necessary for such legislation to be approved.

On 11 April 1946, the government and Presidium of the Slovak National Council adopted the Second Prague Agreement, which supplemented that concluded in June 1945. On the basis of this agreement, the president regained his powers in Slovakia, which the Slovak National Council had appropriated during the final days of the war. These included the right to appoint university professors and to grant amnesties.[5] A further change in the position of the Slovak National Council and the Board of Commissioners came after the parliamentary elections held in 1946.

Parliamentary elections of 1946 and the Third Prague Agreement

The first post-war parliamentary elections were held in Czechoslovakia on 26 May 1946. They were considered free, fair and, in the conditions that then existed, democratic. Eight political parties – four in Slovakia and four in Bohemia, Moravia and Silesia – contested the election. The Democratic Party won the election in Slovakia with 62 per cent of the vote. The Communist Party of Slovakia gained the support of 30.4 per cent of the electorate in Slovakia. The Freedom Party and the Labour Party suffered an electoral fiasco: 3.7 and 3.1 per cent respectively.

[5] J. Barto, *Riešenie vzťahu Čechov a Slovákov (1944–1948)* [Attempts to find a solution to the relations between the Czechs and Slovaks (1944–1948)] (Bratislava, 1968), pp. 136–47.

The Communist Party of Czechoslovakia was victorious in the Czech Lands, where it gained 40.2 per cent of the vote. The other parties achieved the following results: the Czechoslovak National Socialist Party, 23.6 per cent, the Czechoslovak People's Party, 20.2 per cent, and the Czechoslovak Social Democratic Party, 15.6 per cent.

The differences between the election results in Slovakia and in the Czech Lands can be broadly interpreted in two ways:

(1) Slovak society was more politically polarised. The Communist Party and its voters were on one side, while almost all the non-communists and anti-communists were grouped under the banner of the Democratic Party. In the Czech Lands, votes were more evenly distributed between the parties, although the differences between them, especially between the Communist Party of Czechoslovakia and the other parties, were significant.

(2) In the Czech Lands, the Communist Party of Czechoslovakia and those parties on the left of the political spectrum gained predominance. The Communists and Social Democrats together gained 55.8 per cent of the vote. In Slovakia, the Democratic Party, which declared a centrist position, predominated.

These elections did more to divide the two nations than to bring them closer together. The events that followed further complicated these Slovak–Czech disputes. The Communists were alarmed by the victory of the Democratic Party and began to react. They used, and misused, the so-called April Agreement between the Protestants and Catholics in the Democratic Party, which had contributed to the party's victory and had enabled Catholics to participate in politics.[6] As political Catholicism was associated with the now banned Hlinka's Slovak People's Party, the Communists described the April Agreement as a union with the enemies of the Czechoslovak state and the people's democratic regime. The Czech bourgeois parties were also disturbed by the ramifications of the agreement, so they accepted the Communists' claims about the danger of Slovak separatism at face value, and did not realise that the Communists' ultimate aim was to divide the democratic forces. This manoeuvre left the Democratic Party at the mercy of the Communists

---

[6] The April Agreement was actually signed on 31 March 1946. The public was informed in April, hence its name. It introduced the principles that Catholics and Protestants would be represented in all party bodies in a proportion of seven to three, and in lists of candidates for elections in a proportion two to one. The Catholic Church supported the agreement. For more details, see M. Barnovský, *Na ceste k monopolu moci. Mocensko-politické zápasy na Slovensku v rokoch 1945–1948* [On the road to monopoly power. Power-political struggles in Slovakia 1945–1948] (Bratislava, 1993), pp. 72–82.

and strengthened their demands to limit the institutional powers of the Slovak national bodies.

Communist parties consistently followed the principle that the national question was subordinate to the question of class conflict, which in this case meant its subordination to the struggle for power. In the spring of 1945, the Slovak Communists became convinced that Slovakia was, and would remain, the prime moving force behind the revolution, so they demanded sweeping powers for the Slovak national institutions. For the same reason, the Czech Communists were more favourable to the demands of the Slovak National Council than the other Czech parties. When this did not work out, Slovak and Czech Communists completely reversed their positions.

The Czech non-communist parties supported a unitary, centralised state for other reasons. They feared that the autonomy of Slovakia could lead to renewed separatism and the break-up of the state. They also clung to the idea of Czechoslovakism – the concept of a unitary Czechoslovak nation. They did not want to come into conflict with public opinion in Czech society, which was not disposed towards the autonomous efforts of the Slovaks. Lastly, they did not need to make concessions to the Slovaks because they were not after Slovak votes. They were active only in the Czech Lands and, apart from the Social Democrats, they had no sister parties in Slovakia.

Slovakia paid for the Democratic Party's success, when the competencies of both the Slovak National Council and the Board of Commissioners were reduced, as the Democrats had an absolute majority in these bodies. To negate the influence and power of the Democratic Party, the leaders of the Communist Party of Czechoslovakia and the Communist Party of Slovakia devised restrictive conditions for its participation in government. They included a new adjustment of the competencies of the Slovak national bodies. After long talks, the Communists gained tacit support within the National Front for their proposals, from the Czech non-communist parties and the two marginal parties from Slovakia (the Freedom Party and the Labour Party).

The Third Prague Agreement, adopted on 27 June 1946, radically reduced the competencies of the Slovak national bodies. Preliminary government control over the activities of the Slovak National Council was established. The council had to submit proposed decrees to the government first for scrutiny of whether they fit with the government's agenda. Thus, the government, as the executive authority, gained the right to limit or stop completely the legislative activity of the Slovak National Council – the Slovak legislative body – which was anomalous from the legal point of view. The Board of Commissioners was also placed under government supervision. The Presidium of the Slovak National Council still appointed its members, but only after approval by the central government and taking an oath to the prime minister of Czechoslovakia. The board retained original government and executive power within the framework of the legislative activity of the Slovak National Council, but was subordinate to the central government. The commissioners were made individually responsible to the appropriate state ministers, who had a mandate to make decisions regarding Slovakia through their ministerial bodies. The Third Prague Agreement therefore degraded the Slovak national bodies into powerless institutions and in effect was unconstitutional.[7]

After the 1946 parliamentary elections, the two communities – the Czechs and the Slovaks – were drifting apart, as a Czech nationalist bloc had emerged as a consequence of the emergence of the Slovak national bodies, and fears of Slovak separatism were being revived in public. Anti-Czech sentiments were re-emerging in Slovakia, and many people began to believe that the Slovaks were being deprived of what belonged to them and that promises were being broken. For many people, the bodies in Prague presented a double danger – centralism and left-wing radicalism.

On 2 July 1946, President Beneš appointed a new government headed by Klement Gottwald (1896–1953), the chairman of the Communist Party of Czechoslovakia. The government had twenty-six members. The individual political parties were represented according to the number of seats they held in parliament, plus two ministers who were not party members.[8] Slovakia was represented by seven members. The Slovak National Council and Board of Commissioners were reconstructed according to the results of the elections in Slovakia to the Constituent National Assembly. Representatives of the Democratic Party had an absolute majority in both bodies.[9]

---

[7] K. Kaplan, *Pravda o Československu 1945–1948* [The truth about Czechoslovakia 1945–1948] (Prague, 1990), pp. 182–4.

[8] The ministers without party membership were the foreign minister, Jan Masaryk, and the minister of defence, General Ludvík Svoboda.

[9] The chairman of the Slovak National Council was Jozef Lettrich, and the chairman of the Board of Commissioners was Gustáv Husák, a member of the leadership of the Communist Party of Slovakia. The Slovak National Council had a hundred members, of which the Democratic Party had sixty-three, the Communist Party of Slovakia thirty-one, the Freedom Party three and the Labour Party three. In the Board of Commissioners, the Democrats had nine members and Communists five. The commissioner for the interior was the non-party member, Mikuláš Ferjenčík.

Communist campaigns against the Democratic Party

Political development in Slovakia from the 1946 elections to the February takeover of 1948 were characterised by a Communist campaign against the Democratic Party. The aim of these activities was to break up the Democratic Party, deprive it of its majorities in the Slovak national bodies and exclude it from political life eventually. At first, the Communist leadership placed great hope in the trial of Jozef Tiso, a Catholic priest and former president of the Slovak Republic, who had pursued a policy of collaboration with Nazi Germany during the war. They expected that, after Tiso's execution, many Catholics would turn away from the Democratic Party and the party would split. The National Court announced its verdict on 15 April 1947, and Tiso was executed three days later. Although the execution provoked some discontent among Catholics, the Democratic Party remained functional. Its leadership remained in control because the overt Communist threat united it.

From then on, the Communists did not rely on the internal collapse of the Democratic Party. Instead, they began to prepare a dual offensive that combined the mobilisation of a 'people's movement' from below with administrative power-political interventions against it from above.[10] Political and police actions were interwoven. The difficulties in supplying the population with food and industrial consumer goods, compounded by the bad harvest of 1947, the growth of the black market and slow implementation of land reform, created favourable conditions for the organisation of mass unrest. Although the Communist Party of Slovakia was just as much a government party as the Democratic Party, the Communists blamed the Slovak Democrats for the adverse situation. They drew all the special interest organisations under their control into this political offensive. The Union of Slovak Partisans resolutely campaigned for the removal of Ľudák activists from positions of influence in politics, the economy, culture and so forth; the trade unions called for a solution to supply problems; the Peasant-Farmers' Commissions demanded consistent implementation of the land reform. State Security (the secret police), also controlled by the Communists, had the task of obtaining evidence of the Democratic Party's unreliability with regard to state security. To achieve this goal, it fabricated a so-called anti-state conspiracy in Slovakia.

The Commissionership for the Interior issued an official report in mid September 1947 about this alleged 'anti-state conspiracy'. More

---

[10] J. Lettrich, *History of Modern Slovakia* (New York, 1955), part IV, ch. 2.

revelations soon followed. The Congress of Works Councils met in Bratislava on 30 October 1947 and demanded the resignation of the Board of Commissioners and the creation of a new one. The next day, the chairman of the Board of Commissioners, Gustáv Husák, four Communist commissioners and the commissioner for the interior (not a party member) offered their resignations. This series of events led to political crisis in Slovakia, and the dispute between the Communist Party of Slovakia and the Democratic Party intensified. The crisis was resolved by a compromise some eighteen days later. The Democratic Party lost its positions in Slovakia's executive body, which it had gained by winning the election. It lost three seats on the Board of Commissioners, and thus no longer had an absolute majority.[11] The Democratic Party's influence was further weakened by police and administrative interventions. Two of its general secretaries, J. Kempný and M. Bugár, were accused of anti-state activity and arrested. However, the Democrats kept their majority position in the Slovak National Council and in the national committees and remained the most influential party in Slovakia. The Communist Party of Slovakia had failed in its original aims and had not extended its own power base in the country. Nor was the Democratic Party destroyed, excluded from the government, eliminated from political life or significantly weakened. Only partial success was achieved: the Democratic Party was deprived of its majority on the Board of Commissioners.

The political crisis in Slovakia in autumn 1947 exerted its own influence on Czech–Slovak relations and political groupings in the state. A supplement to the Third Prague Agreement was adopted on the initiative of the Communist Party of Czechoslovakia, which enabled the government to revoke and appoint the Board of Commissioners under certain conditions. This was proof of further interference with the competencies of the Slovak national bodies.

The Communist offensive against the Democratic Party and the fabrication of an 'anti-state conspiracy' had two different effects. On the other hand, these moves heightened the Czech public's distrust of Slovakia, and created a distorted image of the country as being chaotic and full of anti-state elements. However, they also led to the break-up of the Czech nationalist bloc. The invented accusations levelled against

---

[11] The Freedom Party and the Labour Party gained one seat each on the new Board of Commissioners at the expense of the Democratic Party. A legal expert held the position of commissioner of justice. For more details on the autumn political crisis in Slovakia of 1947, see K. Kaplan, *Der kurze Marsch. Die kommunistische Machtübernahme in der Tschechoslowakei 1945–1948* (Munich, 1981), pp. 154–70.

several Democratic Party functionaries did not have the effect the Communists expected on the Czech bourgeois parties. Instead, the leading representatives of the Czechoslovak National Socialist Party and the Czechoslovak People's Party were soon well aware of the Communists' objectives. They gradually realised that the Communists were stirring up trouble for their own political ends, and that the attack on the Democratic Party was also an attack on democracy. Therefore, they began to defend the Democratic Party, although not very bravely or effectively. An anti-Communist bloc, formed by three political parties (the Czechoslovak National Socialist Party, the Czechoslovak People's Party and the Democratic Party) began to emerge. The lessons the Communists learnt in autumn 1947 were soon put to good use across the entire state. In this sense, the autumn offensive in Slovakia of 1947 proved to be a dress rehearsal for the decisive power struggle to come.

The new constitution was supposed to solve definitively the Slovak question. Preparations for the drawing up of a constitution began in the second half of 1946, but as a result of the differing views of the political parties, the parts concerning the position of Slovakia were not drafted and discussed by the parliamentary Constitutional Committee until February 1948. At first, the Democratic Party prepared a proposal for the constitutional settlement of Czech–Slovak relations along federal lines. When it realised that the proposal would not be ratified in parliament, it worked out a new variant based on the asymmetrical model. It planned to widen institutional powers for the Slovak national bodies to the level proposed in the First Prague Agreement and to strengthen the position of the president. The Czech non-communist parties supported a territorial organisation with three political administrative units – Bohemia, Moravia and Silesia, and Slovakia.[12] The Communist Party of Czechoslovakia and the Communist Party of Slovakia worked out a joint proposal based on the Third Prague Agreement. It involved an asymmetrical constitutional structure with limited powers for the Slovak National Council and Board of Commissioners.

In this context, it is necessary to note that, in contrast to the situation in 1945, the Communist Party of Slovakia already attached greater importance to the economic aspect of the Slovak question than to the constitutional aspect. It emphasised the need for rapid industrialisation

---

[12] However, it was not an exact replica of the pre-war situation. The Land Diets and executive bodies were to have wider jurisdictional powers than the former Land representations and committees. See J. Rychlík, *Češi a Slováci ve 20. století. Československé vztahy 1945–1992* [The Czechs and Slovaks in the twentieth century. Czech–Slovak relations 1945–1992] (Prague and Bratislava, 1998), p. 56.

in Slovakia in order to raise its economy up to the same level as that in the Czech Lands. This idea was also incorporated into the programme of Gottwald's government. The political parties submitted their proposals on the constitutional settlement of Czech–Slovak relations at the beginning of February 1948. They were supposed to be discussed by the National Front and then by the parliamentary Constitutional Committee at the end of February. By that time, events intervened; they were to be pivotal in the post-war history of Czechoslovakia.

The road to the Communist takeover

By the end of 1947 and the beginning of 1948, Czechoslovakia was the last remaining country in the Soviet sphere of interest in Central and South-Eastern Europe where the question of power had not been finally decided in favour of the Communists. Moscow made it clear that it was time to eliminate this weak link. Preparations for the decisive power struggle were by now underway. From the end of May 1946, the leadership of the Communist Party of Czechoslovakia associated the establishment of a Communist monopoly on power with gaining more than 50 per cent of the votes in the next elections, planned for May 1948, but during the second half of 1947 other options were considered in the event of a political crisis.

As a result of Communist activities in the autumn of 1947, societal tensions increased and disputes in the National Front deepened. When the Communist minister of the interior, Václav Nosek, refused to implement a government resolution of 13 February 1948 on stopping security personnel transfers in favour of the Communists, twelve ministers from the three bourgeois parties (the Czechoslovak National Socialist Party, the Czechoslovak People's Party and the Democratic Party) submitted their resignations on 20 February. They assumed that their resignations would either force the Communists to retreat or lead to the fall of the government and the calling of early elections, in which the bourgeois parties would gain more votes than they had in 1946.

This strategy was fatally flawed, because the Social Democrats and the foreign minister, Jan Masaryk, did not resign. Only a minority of ministers resigned, so the government did not fall. However, this was not the cause of the defeat of the democrats. The leadership of the Communist Party of Czechoslovakia did not regard solution of the government crisis as its most important task. It was only an excuse and an opportunity to make basic changes in the political area. The Communists used this event to launch a decisive bid for power. Communist functionaries in the Czech Lands and in Slovakia mobilised all Party members, and immediately put a repressive mechanism into action. They began to create Action Committees of the National Front, the purpose of which was 'to purge public and political life of all reaction'. This process meant excluding opponents of the Communist Party of Czechoslovakia and Communist Party of Slovakia from political life.

On 22 February, the Congress of Works Councils supported the demands of the Communists. The next day, the minister of the interior ordered the National Security Force on an increased level of alert, and selected units were transferred to Prague. The political parties of the resigning ministers were then forbidden to hold public assemblies. The people's militias – Communist armed units – were formed. A one-hour general strike was held on 24 February. By then, the Communists were already masters of the situation.

The speed of events surprised the bourgeois parties. They were not prepared for these extra-parliamentary activities, and they organised no counter-responses. Their activity was paralysed after the administrative interventions on 23 and 24 February. President Beneš, fearing societal disintegration and repressions, capitulated on 25 February 1948. He accepted the resignation of the ministers and signed the decrees appointing new members of the government. The government of the so-called regenerated National Front had twenty-four members, twelve of them Communists. The new non-communist members of the government obediently carried out the instructions of the Communist Party. After being purged, the bourgeois parties were reduced to the status of pseudo-parties. The first changes in the Board of Commissioners were made on 23 February, when its chairman, Gustáv Husák, unlawfully dismissed the commissioners drawn from the Democratic Party. On 6 March 1948, the Presidium of the Slovak National Council appointed eight new members of the Board of Commissioners. The Communists held ten posts in Slovakia's fourteen-member government and executive body.

The February takeover ended the brief post-war period of political plurality and limited democracy. The era of Communist dictatorship had begun. These events also put paid to the solution to the Slovak question. Further work on the new constitution henceforth took only Communist proposals into consideration. The objections of the Slovak Communists, designed to moderate centralisation somewhat, were frustrated by the leadership of the Communist Party of Czechoslovakia. With the abolition of the ban on the Czech majority imposing its will on Slovakia, the Slovaks formally lost the ability to influence the character of the constitutional status of Slovakia, since they had fewer members of parliament than did the Czech Lands. The new constitution adopted by the Constitutional National Assembly on 9 May 1948 gave the Slovak national bodies even fewer jurisdictional powers than they had enjoyed under the Third Prague Agreement.

The question of the constitutional settlement of relations between the Czechs and Slovaks lost its significance after the Communist monopoly of power was established, because a Communist regime is essentially centralist and totalitarian, regardless of whether the state is unitary or federal. All important decisions were henceforth taken at the Communist Party headquarters. In effect, the Communist Party of Slovakia became a branch of the Communist Party of Czechoslovakia in August 1945, when Viliam Široký (1902–1971) became its chairman. In September 1948, it formally united with the Communist Party of Czechoslovakia. The leadership of the Communist Party of Czechoslovakia in Prague became the sole authority of the Party. The totalitarian regime and rigid centralisation along Party and state lines prevented the implementation, or even any expression, of the national efforts of the Slovaks for many years to come.

16   Czechoslovakism in Slovak history

Elisabeth Bakke

The concept of 'Czechoslovakism' can be regarded as being both an ideology, which holds that the Czechs and the Slovaks comprise one nation, and a political programme designed to result in the unification of both nations in one state.[1] Czechoslovakism as a political programme was first formulated during the First World War by the independence movement abroad, in order to justify the establishment of a Czechoslovak state, comprising the Czech Lands and Slovakia. The idea that the Czechs and Slovaks were twin aspects of a single nation had a far older pedigree, going back to the national revivals of the late eighteenth and early nineteenth centuries. Czechoslovakist ideology had its heyday during the First Czechoslovak Republic (1918–1938), when it became the state doctrine, and it was officially abandoned after the Second World War. Czechoslovakism also existed in two versions: the first version held that Czechs and Slovaks jointly comprised a Czechoslovak nation formed from two tribes, Czechs and Slovaks; the second maintained that the Slovaks were actually less developed Czechs.[2]

During the First Republic, the theory of a unitary Czechoslovak nation was closely associated with administrative centralism. While there was little Czech opposition to official Czechoslovakism, Slovakia's political elite were split over this issue and the majority opposed their imposition.

The purpose of this chapter is to examine the ideological composition of Czechoslovakism, and to give an overview of the role of Czechoslovakism in Slovak history. The main focus of this chapter will be on the inter-war period, but I will also trace the roots of Czechoslovakism and briefly discuss the status of the ideology during the Communist period and after its demise in 1989.

[1] D. Kováč, *Slováci a Češi Dejiny* [Slovak and Czech history] (Bratislava, 1997), pp. 118–119.
[2] See E. Bakke, 'Doomed to Failure? The Czechoslovak National Project and the Slovak Autonomist Reaction 1918–1938', unpublished Ph.D. thesis, University of Oslo (1999).

Antecedents: Czechoslovak reciprocity

The idea that a sense of unity existed between the Czechs and Slovaks preceded Czechoslovakism and played an important, albeit varied, role in the national revivals of both peoples. The situation of the Czechs and Slovaks was very different in the period preceding their joint expressions of nationhood. While an awareness of being Czech existed early in the Middle Ages (albeit confined to the upper strata of society), Slovak national consciousness was a more complex affair. Until the turn of the nineteenth century, the Slovaks were referred to as 'Slavs of Hungary' (or even 'Bohemian Slavs') just as often as 'Slovaks', suggesting that Slovak identity was as yet undefined.[3] Moreover, the Slovaks lacked a literary language of their own, a tradition of their own state and – consequently – a tradition of narrating national history through chronicles.

Over the course of both revivals, Czechoslovak reciprocity was associated with the idea of a larger Slavic nation. From the beginning of the *Czech* revival, Slavism (and the related idea of Czechoslovak reciprocity) served the interests of the Czech nation-to-be, and was conditional on the development of a Czech national consciousness.[4] Conversely, in the *Slovak* case the idea of a Slavic nation was a premise, a starting point for wider revival efforts. There were, in fact, two currents in the Slovak national revival: one was Slovak-Catholic, the other Czechoslovak-Protestant, and the two disagreed about whether the Czechs and Slovaks were one or two separate tribes within the Slavic nation.

Czechoslovak reciprocity thus assumed varying forms among the Czech and Slovak 'awakeners' from the start. The Czechs tended to see the Slovaks as a part of the Czech nation and the Slovak language as a sub-group of Czech dialects. They generally viewed the Slovaks as their poor relatives, and this attitude did not change significantly over the course of the national revival. The Czechoslovak-Protestant sections of the Slovak revival regarded themselves as a part of the Czechoslovak tribe of the Slavic nation, not as Czechs, and most of them had some notion of Slovak individuality. Central figures in both national revivals were Ján Kollár and Pavol Jozef Šafárik, Slovaks by birth and staunch defenders of the idea of a Czechoslovak tribe of the Slavic nation.

Questions of language and identity were closely intertwined in both national revivals, a result of the prevailing linguistic conception of

---

[3] See P. Brock, *The Slovak National Awakening* (Toronto and Buffalo, 1976), p. 3; Bakke, 'Doomed to Failure?', pp. 136–7, 265.

[4] V. Šťastný (ed.), *Slovanství v národním životě Čechů a Slováků* [Slavdom in the national life of the Czechs and Slovaks] (Prague, 1968), p. 95.

nationhood. If the language is the soul of the nation, it follows logically that there must be one nation for each (literary) language, and one (literary) language for each nation. In the Slovak case, this led to a linguistic split, with the one strand adhering to a Slovak literary language while another remained faithful to the old Czech biblical language of the sixteenth century. The Czech revivers tended to see the Slovaks as a part of the Czech nation and were thus opposed to the establishment of a separate Slovak literary language.[5]

After the second codification of Slovak in 1843, as undertaken by the Protestant Ľudovít Štúr, the Czechoslovak idea became secondary and no longer implied linguistic unity, yet the idea of cultural kinship was not abandoned. Czechoslovak reciprocity in this diluted form had a renaissance among the Czech and Slovak elite in the years prior to the First World War. The focus was on aiding the Slovaks in cultural and economic matters, not on political co-operation. This process found its expression among Czechs through the society Czechoslav Unity (Českoslovanská jednota, 1896). Among the Slovaks, the Prague student association Detvan and the circle around the journals Hlas (The voice, 1898; adherents were referred to as Hlasists) and Prúdy (Currents, 1909) were the chief advocates of Czech–Slovak reciprocity.

Czechoslovakism and war-time propaganda

The foundations of Czechoslovakism were laid during the First World War, as a part of the propaganda effort to convince the Allies that a Czechoslovak state should be carved out of the Habsburg monarchy. Tomáš G. Masaryk had begun contemplating an independent Czechoslovak state by the autumn of 1914, and from 1915 this was the official policy of the independence movement abroad. The Czech and Slovak political leaders at home were, however, far more reluctant. In fact, the Czech politicians at home did not demand an independent state until January 1918, and the Slovaks followed suit only in May.

The independence movement was soon divided along two lines of argument. On the one hand, historical state rights were used to justify independence for the Czech Lands. The starting point was that the Kingdom of Bohemia, though linked since 1526 with the Kingdom of

---

[5] See D. Short, 'The Use and Abuse of the Language Argument in Mid-Nineteenth-Century "Czechoslovakism": An Appraisal of a Propaganda Milestone', in R. B. Pynsent (ed.), *The Literature of Nationalism. Essays on East European Identity* (London, 1996), pp. 44–54; P. Bugge, 'Czech Nation-Building, National Self-Perception and Politics 1780–1914', unpublished PhD thesis, University of Aarhus (1994).

Hungary and the hereditary Austrian dominions in a personal union under the Habsburg ruler Ferdinand I (1503–1524), had never surrendered its rights. The right to statehood still applied, and a Czechoslovak state would thus be a 're-establishment of Bohemia as an independent state', with the addition of Slovakia. On the other hand, the principle of national self-determination was invoked to justify the inclusion of Slovakia. Czechoslovakism constituted the ideological link between these two divergent opinions.

In essence, it was argued that the Czech Lands had a historical right to independence, and a natural right to include Slovakia, the latter based on the premise that the Czechs and Slovaks were one nation. Masaryk was the driving force behind this particular thesis. The Slovaks were presented as a part of the Czech nation and their language as an (archaic) Czech dialect. Slovakia was presented as the core of Great Moravia, the shared state from which Slovakia 'was torn away by the Magyars in the tenth century'.[6]

Whereas, until 1917, Czechoslovakist rhetoric was largely confined to the independence movement operating abroad, Czech leaders at home maintained an exclusively Czech focus. When references to the Slovaks did begin to appear, they were presented as having originated from the Slovak branch of the Czech or 'Czechoslav' nation. A decisive shift in terminology occurred only in the summer of 1918, with the establishment of the Czechoslovak National Committee in Prague. The Slovaks at home were relatively silent during the war, but in two semi-official declarations from 1918 Slovak leaders referred to their nation as the Slovak branch of the Czechoslovak tribe or nation. Reference to a 'Czechoslovak nation' was conspicuous by its absence from the two Czech–Slovak agreements signed by émigré organisations in the United States of America – the Cleveland Agreement of 1915 and the Pittsburgh Agreement of 1918.[7]

---

[6] T. G. Masaryk had in 1905 already expressed the view that the Slovaks were a part of the Czech nation. See T. G. Masaryk, *Problém malého národa* [The problem of a small nation] (Prague, 1990), p. 17. For the Czechoslovakist interpretation, see Masaryk's memorandum on 'Independent Bohemia' of 1915, in J. Rychlík, T. D. Marzik and M. Bielik (eds.), *R. W. Seton-Watson and His Relations with the Czechs and Slovaks. Documents 1906–1951* (Prague and Martin, 1995), p. 229; Masaryk's memorandum 'The Future Bohemia' [1917], reprinted in Czech as *Budoucí Čechy* (Prague, 1925); T. G. Masaryk, *The new Europe* [1918], reprinted as *Nová Evropa* (Brno, 1994), p. 150; 'Declaration of Independence of the Czechoslovak Nation by Its Provisional Government', 18 October 1918 (Prague, 1933); see also Bakke, 'Doomed to Failure?', pp. 154, 182–91.

[7] *The Czech Declaration of 6 January 1918* (New York, 1918); *The Slovaks and the Pittsburgh Pact* (Chicago, 1934), pp. 16, 27; E. Beneš, *Světová válka a naše revoluce III. Dokumenty* [The world war and our revolution III. Documents] (Prague, 1929); T. Čapek, *The Origins of the Czechoslovak State* (New York, 1926), pp. 99–101.

There is every reason to believe that the Czechoslovakism of the independence movement abroad as well as that of the home front were tactically motivated. The underlying rationale was 'strength-through-unity', which was explicitly expressed by the likes of T. G. Masaryk. The Czech national leaders wanted to include Slovakia in their proposals so as to offset the large German minority contained within the historical Czech Lands, while Slovak national leaders preferred becoming part of a Czechoslovak state to the alternative, which was to remain under Magyar rule. National self-determination was the tune of the day, and Czechoslovakism fitted that score.

Official Czechoslovakism

In the first official statements released by the Czechoslovak state in November and December 1918, Czechoslovakist rhetoric was far less pronounced than in war-time documents. Yet, it did not take long for the concept of Czechoslovakism to return to the fore; early in 1919 it was clearly identifiable in speeches in parliament, and by 1920 it was well on the way to becoming the official doctrine of the First Republic.[8] This means that it was applied across a variety of official documents, from the constitution, laws and government decrees, to official statistics and school textbooks. It was further expressed in scholarly works and in the press. A concerted effort was made to rewrite history in order to fit the concept of a Czechoslovak nation with two branches.

Official Czechoslovakism was, however, opposed by Slovak autonomists, who argued that the Slovaks were a *separate* nation; they instead advocated a form of Slovak autonomy. The Slovak elite was split along lines similar to those that had existed during the national revival. These scholars had played the most important role on the Czechoslovakist side of the struggle. In terms of parties this autonomist wing was made up of the (Catholic) Slovak People's Party (Ľudáks) and the small (Protestant) Slovak National Party. Generally, Czech and Slovak parties were firmly Czechoslovakist, apart from the multi-national Communist Party of Czechoslovakia, which abandoned its support for the concept of a unitary Czechoslovak nation in 1924. The two other left-wing parties, the Czechoslovak Social Democrats and the Czechoslovak National Socialists, were no less Czechoslovakist than the bourgeois parties – the

---

[8] Bakke, 'Doomed to Failure?', pp. 192–5, 277–79. See also the parliamentary shorthand reports in *Těsnopisecké zprávy o schůzích Národního shromáždění československého* [Stenographic notes of the Czechoslovak National Assembly meetings] (Prague, 1918–1919).

Agrarian Party, the Czechoslovak National Democrats, the Czechoslovak People's Party (appealing to the Catholic vote) and the Czechoslovak Small Traders' Party.

Two matters are of particular interest here. First, I will address how, and to what extent, Czechoslovakism was expressed in various official documents. The main emphasis will be on the constitution, official statistics and school textbooks. The second objective is to pinpoint aspects of Czechoslovakist ideology that may help explain why a part of the Slovak national elite rejected this concept, and why there was so little *Czech* opposition to it. Here the main emphasis will be on the scholarly debate, with a quick side glance at the political debates held in parliament. Among the matters of dispute in the current scholarly debate about Czechoslovakism is whether it was based on a political or a cultural concept of 'nation', and whether or not it implied assimilation or had other negative consequences for the Slovaks. Finally, the overall evaluation of Czechoslovakism as a historical phenomenon varies: I will return to this aspect later in the chapter.

Czechoslovakism in official documents

The constitution of 1920 marked a watershed in the vocabulary of official rhetoric, although the 'Czechoslovak nation' is mentioned only twice in the text, both times in the preamble. The constitution as such made no mention of a Czechoslovak nation (or a Czech and Slovak nation for that matter) but this was clearly implied by the references to a 'Czechoslovak language' in § 131, and in the Language Act, which gave 'the Czechoslovak language' status as the official state language.

The preamble reads as follows:

We, the Czechoslovak nation, desiring to consolidate the perfect unity of our nation, to establish the reign of justice in the Republic, to assure the peaceful development of our CzechSlovak homeland, to contribute to the common welfare of all citizens of this state and to secure the blessings of freedom to coming generations, have in our National Assembly on 29 February 1920 adopted the following constitution for the Czechoslovak republic. In doing so, we, the Czechoslovak nation, declare that we will endeavour to carry out this constitution as well as all the laws of our country in the spirit of our history as well as in the spirit of the modern principles embodied in the slogan of self-determination; for we want to take our place in the community of nations as a cultivated, peace-loving, democratic and progressive member.[9]

---

[9] This quotation is based on the English translation in *The Constitution of the Czechoslovak Republic* (New York, 1944), except in the cases where the translation was inaccurate or linguistically awkward. For example, the second reference to the Czechoslovak nation was missing. See also *Sbírka zákonů a nařízení státu československého* [Collection of laws and decrees of the Czechoslovak state] (Prague, 1920), p. 255.

As Eva Broklová has noted, the phrase 'We, the Czechoslovak nation' provides an obvious parallel to the preambles of the American and French constitutions. Her claim that it must therefore be interpreted in terms of a political nation is, however, less convincing.[10] The Czechoslovak nation was certainly not a political nation in the classic Western sense, where membership in the nation is tied directly to citizenship, and where the nation is seen as a community of people bound together by shared rights and obligations, regardless of cultural affiliations. On the contrary, the national minorities were excluded. This is also quite clearly expressed in the constitution. First, where the entire population was mentioned, the constitution referred to 'citizens' and also to 'inhabitants' of the Czechoslovak Republic, not to the Czechoslovak nation. Second, a political interpretation of 'nation' is unreasonable, especially in light of the second reference to the phrase 'We, the Czechoslovak nation'. The 'spirit of our history' and 'the modern principles embodied in the slogan of self-determination' that appear in the following sentence hardly refer to the citizens of the newly formed Czechoslovak state. On the contrary, it is consistent with the war-time propaganda aimed at securing Czech and Slovak independence. The Czechoslovak nation can therefore be regarded as a political nation *only* in the sense of a *state-forming nation*, i.e. a political subject.

Third, the references to a 'Czechoslovak language' point to a cultural conception of nationhood, and this impression is strengthened by the debate about the Language Act that occurred both in the Constitutional Committee and in parliament. In the committee, it was argued quite explicitly that the Czechs and Slovaks formed one nation in a cultural and even a racial sense, and that Czech and Slovak were two dialects of the same language.[11] At the same time, however, both literary versions were recognised, and the Language Act thus privileged both Czech and Slovak vis-à-vis the other languages spoken by the national minorities.

From the Slovak point of view, the problem was that the Language Act did not give the Slovak language as much protection as the Czech language. Article 4 pronounced that 'as a rule', state offices should 'use the Czech language in [the Czech Lands], and the Slovak language in Slovakia'. This formal equality worked to the disadvantage of the Slovaks and the Slovak language because of the difference in size and

---

[10] E. Broklová, *Československá demokracie* [Czechoslovak democracy] (Prague, 1992), p. 148.

[11] See Antonín Švehla's and Isidor Zahradník's speeches in the Constitutional Committee, quoted in Eva Broklová, *Československá ústava* [The Czechoslovak constitution] (Prague, 1992), pp. 72–3; see also Bakke, 'Doomed to Failure?', pp. 336–8.

the gap in cultural development between the two nations.[12] Not only did the Czech intelligentsia dominate the central administration, but it also made up a large share of the public employees in Slovakia (about a fifth of the total).[13] Czech was thus commonly used in Slovakia, while Slovak was rarely used in the Czech Lands. This was not due to discrimination; initially, the Slovak intelligentsia was simply too small to fill the vacancies, and during the economic crisis of the 1930s it was not possible to dismiss Czechs in order to employ Slovaks.

Czechoslovakism was most consistently applied in statistics. The Czechs and Slovaks were habitually presented as one nation in the statistical information pertaining to nationality published during the period of the First Republic. This applies to statistical handbooks, yearbooks and even the population censuses. (The only exceptions are cases where the figures were based on foreign or pre-war statistics – Austrian or Hungarian.) In these handbooks and yearbooks, the Czechoslovak category was used without a clear definition of what 'Czechoslovak nationality' meant in practical terms. For this reason the guidelines for the gathering of population census data are of particular interest.

Two full censuses were carried out during the period of the First Republic, the first in 1921, the second in 1930. In the first census, a subjective definition of nationality was applied; only in cases where an individual indicated two nationalities or no nationality at all was the census official allowed to determine the nationality on the basis of mother tongue. In the subsequent census, nationality was determined, as a rule, according to the mother tongue of the individual.

The 1921 census guidelines listed 'Czechoslovak (Czech or Slovak)' as one of the alternatives in the column for nationality, adding that 'nationality should be understood by tribal affiliation, the main external mark of which is usually the mother tongue'.[14] This explanation may at first seem contradictory: Czechoslovak was defined as a form of nationality, even though Czech and Slovak were clearly separate languages. The answer is again that Czech and Slovak were regarded as two literary forms of the same language. In both censuses, most statistics pertaining

---

[12] For the Language Act, see J. A. Mikuš, *Slovakia. A Political and Constitutional History with Documents* (Bratislava, 1995), pp. 196–8.

[13] A. Boháč, 'Češi na Slovensku' [Czechs in Slovakia], in *Statistický obzor* [Statistical survey] (Prague, 1935), pp. 184, 188–90; see also Bakke, 'Doomed to Failure?', pp. 410, 416.

[14] *Sčítání lidu v republice československé ze dne 15. února 1921* [Census in the Czechoslovak Republic of 15 February 1921] (Prague, 1924), vol. I, p. 13; *Sčítání lidu v republice Československé ze dne 1. prosince 1930* [Census in the Czechoslovak Republic of 1 December 1930] (Prague, 1934), vol. I, p. 17.

to nationality registered people of Czech or Slovak origin as being 'Czechoslovaks', regardless of what answer they had given. When this process was criticised in parliament, the government referred back to the constitution.[15]

School history textbooks are interesting sources for two reasons. First, they are the one place where you would expect to find official attempts to establish a historical foundation for a Czechoslovak identity. Second, a review of school textbooks will give us an idea of how consistently a Czechoslovak national project was advocated. To my surprise, many of the books conveyed very little about a Czechoslovak identity at all. Perhaps even more surprisingly, Czech and Slovak textbooks (especially those for primary school) differed in terms of their description of Czechoslovakist tendencies.[16] Slovak textbooks for primary schools were the ones that most closely matched my original expectations, but even these texts did not consistently advocate a Czechoslovak consciousness. Even in the most Czechoslovakist of these books, the main focus was inevitably on the separate histories of the Czechs and Slovaks, and the terms 'Czech' and 'Slovak' were found to occur far more often than 'Czechoslovak'.

All the Czech textbooks I surveyed, even those written in the 1930s, were very Czech-centred. What was conveyed was a Czech identity: 'Czech' and 'Czechoslovak' were all too often used interchangeably. The Slovaks were, like their history, treated as a mere extension to or an appendix of the Czech nation.

Strikingly, not a single Slovak book was particularly Slovak-centred or conveyed a strong sense of a differentiated Slovak identity. Moreover, in the Slovak books, the Czechoslovakist rhetoric reflected the idea that Czechs and Slovaks jointly comprised a Czechoslovak nation with two branches, and not that the Slovaks were part of the Czech nation. While the Czech and Slovak secondary school textbooks proved more similar than their primary school counterparts, they were still closer to the Czech than the Slovak tradition. Slovak history received a shockingly low level of attention even in the Slovak textbooks for secondary schools. This was probably due to the fact that all the Slovak books I surveyed

---

[15] See Tisk 173 (interpellation) and Tisk 255 (answer) in *Tisky k těsnopiseckým zprávám poslanecké sněmovny, Národního shromáždění republiky československé* [Printings relating to shorthand reports of the Czechoslovak National Assembly, Chamber of Deputies] (Prague, 1930), vol. II.

[16] Detailed findings regarding Czechoslovakism in school textbooks may be found in Bakke, 'Doomed to Failure?', ch. 9. A Slovak version was also published: Bakke, 'Čechoslovakizmus v školských učebniciach (1918–1938)' [Czechoslovakism in school textbooks (1918–1938)], *Historický časopis*, 47 (1999), 2, 233–52.

were based on Czech originals, except one – and this was again closer to
the Slovak primary school textbooks in tendency and emphasis.

So what exactly did Czechoslovak nationhood consist of according
to these textbooks? The features that were seen as uniting the two
were kinship or blood relations, language and culture, and spirit – or what
we might term 'national character', although that term was used by only
one author.[17] The Czechoslovak nation was thus conceived as a *cultural-
linguistic* community based on the closeness of the two languages, and/or a
kinship community based on blood relations. Their shared Slavic origin
underpinned all this, even though it was not always explicitly cited.

Constructing a historical narrative that could serve to unite the
Czechs and the Slovaks was obviously no easy task. Though Great
Moravia belongs to Czech and Slovak history, it is incorrect to regard
it as the first common state of the Czechs and Slovaks. It is from 1526 to
1918 that the Czechs and Slovaks lived in a common state – the
Habsburg monarchy. But they shared little political history, so the
Czechoslovak 'nation-builders' had to use Czech–Slovak contacts, over
the centuries, as they conceived it.

Thus the historical events emphasised in these school textbooks as
having united the Czechs and Slovaks were: their shared Slavic forefathers; Great Moravia as the first Czechoslovak state (more common in
Slovak books); Czech–Slovak contacts resulting from Hussitism[18] and
the Reformation (including the diffusion of Czech in Slovakia); but
especially the national revival and the founding of the Czechoslovak
Republic. These features were especially apparent in Slovak primary
school textbooks, where the 'strength-through-unity' theme was common;
the message was that the Czechs and Slovaks needed to stand together
against their enemies, the Germans and the Magyars. In this historical-
political line of argument, Great Moravia was viewed positively, and
its demise seen as a disaster. On the whole, primary school books
were generally anti-German and/or anti-Magyar, while the textbooks
for secondary school were far more balanced.

[17] See Dejmek, Kratochvíl and Šimko, *Po stopách ľudstva. Dejepis pre 6.–8. školský rok
ľudových škôl slovenských* [On the tracks of mankind. History for the sixth to eighth
classes of Slovak elementary schools] (Prague, 1927), p. 119.
[18] Hussitism was a Czech religious movement of the fifteenth century with social and
national dimensions, named after Jan Hus (a martyr who was burnt at the stake, after
the Council of Constance pronounced him to be a heretic in 1415). It is often seen as a
forerunner of Lutheranism. The Catholic Church regarded Hussitism as a heresy,
and several crusades were organised against the Czech Lands, by Emperor Sigismund
of Luxemburg, King of Rome and Hungary (which included the territory of
contemporary Slovakia). Probably no other period in Czech history has been more
important for Czech self-identity. See Bakke, 'Doomed to Failure?', pp. 89–93.

A struggle over national identity

The officially endorsed Czechoslovakist ideology was opposed by a number of Slovak autonomists, who argued that the Slovaks were a separate nation. On both sides, the national concept was predominantly regarded as being *cultural*. Yet, the Czechoslovakists leaned more towards a subjectivist view of the nation, while a natural concept of nationhood was not uncommon among Slovak autonomists. While the Slovak autonomists generally took the existence of a Slovak nation for granted, the Czechoslovakists often regarded a Czechoslovak nation as a project.

With the exception of some individuals such as the philosopher Emanuel Rádl, who was openly critical of Czechoslovak unitariness,[19] few people advocated a purely political concept of 'nation', i.e. a nation comprising all Czechoslovak citizens regardless of their cultural background. Admittedly, the Slovak politician Milan Hodža gradually changed his conception of Czechoslovak unity from being a linguistic and cultural unity via spiritual unity to a 'Czechoslovak political nation'. But even this concept comprised Czechs and Slovaks, and the criterion of inclusion into the Czechoslovak nation was thus still implicitly cultural. This is also obvious from Hodža's focus on Great Moravia, the Czech federation proposal in 1849, and the joint war-time efforts for liberation as historical foundations of Czechoslovak political kinship.[20]

The scholarly debate that surrounds this subject is of interest because it shows how different interpretations of the same historical events can be used to support two different national projects. The Czechoslovakist point of departure was the idea of Czechoslovak *national* unity as the original and, by implication, natural situation. In contrast, the Slovak autonomists regarded Czechoslovak unity merely as a *tribal* unity that had long since served its purpose. There were two critical junctures in the Czechoslovakist interpretation of history: the demise of Great Moravia (in 907) represented a political separation, and the codification

[19] E. Rádl, *Válka Čechů s Němci* [The war between Czechs and Germans] (Prague, 1928), pp. 140–4.

[20] These date from 1922, 1926 and 1928 respectively: M. Hodža, *Články, reči, štúdie, sv. VII, Slovensko a republika* [Articles, speeches, essays, vol. VII, Slovenia and the republic] (Bratislava, 1934), pp. 61, 144, 190; 'Moderný nacionalizmus' [Modern nationalism] [1932], reprinted in Hodža: *Federácia v strednej Európe a iné štúdie* [Federation in Central Europe and other essays] (Bratislava, 1997), p. 57; Hodža, 'Nie centralizmus, nie autonomizmus, ale regionalizmus v jednom politickom národe' [No centralism, nor autonomism, but regionalism in a single political nation] (1934), in R. Chmel (ed.), *Slovenská otázka v 20. storočí* [The Slovak question in the twentieth century] (Bratislava, 1997), pp. 183–8.

of the Slovak language (in the eighteenth and nineteenth centuries) signified a linguistic separation of the two 'branches of the Czechoslovak nation'.

The writings produced by the independence movement abroad during the First World War portrayed an independent Czechoslovak state as the re-establishment of the historic Czech kingdom, with the addition of Slovakia. This was the predominant view on the Czech side, where Great Moravia was regarded as being of secondary importance. Conversely, Slovak Czechoslovakists regarded Great Moravia as the first Czechoslovak state, and thus as the historical predecessor of the Czechoslovak Republic. The Slovak autonomists, however, saw Great Moravia as a predominantly Slovak state, not least as a Czech state had existed alongside it. They also blamed the Czechs for its eventual collapse.[21]

What was needed from the Czechoslovakist point of view was an explanation of how Czechoslovak unity could survive 1,000 years of political separation. From a Slovak autonomist point of view, what needed to be explained was the extent of Czech influence in Slovakia despite the severed tribal ties – and especially the use of the literary Czech language.

On the Czechoslovakist side, all contacts between the Czechs and Slovaks were cited as proof that Czechoslovak unity had been preserved over the centuries. The Hussite period played an especially important part in these projections (it was argued that Hussitism brought the Slovaks into direct and lively contact with the Czechs, and that it led to the diffusion of Czech culture and language). In addition to these features, Czech Protestant exiles in Slovakia, the national revival and the joint liberation efforts – the founding of the Czechoslovak Republic – were all regarded as being central.

Scholarly works advocating Czechoslovakism shared many of the features of the school textbooks mentioned above, but these were more elaborate and some new elements were added. Thus the conversion of Bořivoj to Christianity at the court of Svätopluk of Great Moravia, the first member of the Přemyslid dynasty to be documented, around 880, was emphasised. Enhanced importance was attributed to Prague University (where the Slovaks formed part of the *natio Bohemica*), as was German colonisation (which brought Czechs and Slovaks into contact with the same Western influences). This positive evaluation of the German colonisation differs somewhat from the way this issue was presented in schoolbooks.

---

[21] Bakke, 'Doomed to Failure?', pp. 197–8, 246–7.

Both sides agreed that the establishment of Prague University in 1348, where students from Slovakia came into contact with the Czech language, contributed to the increased use of Czech in Slovakia. Likewise, both sides agreed that the immigration of Czech Protestants into Slovakia following the Battle of the White Mountain in 1620 strengthened the use of literary Czech in Slovakia but, while Czechoslovakists emphasised the positive effects of this process, Slovak autonomists argued that it was detrimental to the development of literary Slovak. There were also nuances within the Czechoslovakist camp itself: Hodža emphasised Slovakia's role in providing shelter for Czech Protestants during the Counter-Reformation, as opposed to Czech scholars who generally placed the Slovaks unequivocally as the party who benefited most.[22]

Slovak autonomists also objected that the Czechoslovakist interpretation of history did not clearly distinguish between Czech–Slovak contacts in general and those that may have served to unite the Czechs and the Slovaks, while it neglected those aspects that set Czechs and Slovaks apart. These same autonomists argued that Christianity and German colonisation did not serve the cause of Czechoslovak unity, and claimed that the visits of the Hussites and Protestants had a religious rather than a national meaning. Jozef Škultéty (1853–1948), Professor at Comenius University of Bratislava, went further and argued that Hussitism probably served to separate Czechs from Slovaks.[23] In the conception of the Slovak People's Party, the Hussites were plunderers who burned and looted, while Jan Hus himself was regarded as a heretic.

Finally, while the Czechoslovakists regarded the use of literary Czech as a proof of Czechoslovak national unity, Slovak autonomists argued that the use of Czech was accidental; that it was detrimental to the codification of Slovak; and that the use of literary Czech did not prove anything with respect to the national awareness of the Slovak people. On the contrary, they maintained that Czech performed the same function as Latin or German, and that only the upper classes used it.

Conversely, both sides agreed that the differences between the Czechs and Slovaks were the result of the long separation between them, but where the Czechoslovakists saw regional differentiation as being of a temporal nature, the Slovak autonomists saw it as a permanent *national* differentiation. There were also further nuances within the

[22] M. Hodža, 'The Political Evolution of Slovakia', in R. W. Seton-Watson (ed.), *Slovakia Then and Now. A Political Survey by Many Slovak Authors* (London and Prague, 1931), pp. 66–7.
[23] See especially D. Rapant, 'Národ a dejiny' [The nation and history], *Prúdy*, 8 (1924), 474–5; J. Škultéty, *Sto dvadsaťpäť rokov zo slovenského života, 1790–1914* [One hundred twenty-five years of Slovak life, 1790–1914] (Turčiansky Sv. Martin, 1920), pp. 72–3.

Czechoslovakist camp. On the Czech side, the differences between Czechs and Slovaks were interpreted on a cultural level; alleged Slovak cultural backwardness was attributed to the split with Czech culture and the negative influences of the Magyar (by implication barbarian) culture. This was also Masaryk's view.[24] Hodža represented a Slovak alternative to this position: he argued that it was the Czechs who had been influenced (contaminated) by the Germans, while Slovak culture and language remained more authentic (but lagged behind), due to its isolation. The Magyar influences were limited to the Slovak elite, according to Hodža.

The Slovak autonomist interpretation was that the Slovaks had influenced – even civilised – the Magyars, not the other way around, and that the Slovaks were a nation in their own right, both of which views were in line with the conception of the Slovak national revival. They also downplayed the importance of the demise of Great Moravia.[25]

The second critical juncture in the Czechoslovakist interpretation of history was the codification of the Slovak language. In Czech literary history, there was a long pre-war tradition of interpreting the codification of Slovak as a separation from its Czech roots. This view was also expressed in some school textbooks. Since the cultural and linguistic conception of the nation predominated, it is perhaps not surprising that the interpretation of the Slovak 'national revival' became a matter of dispute.

From a Czechoslovakist point of view, the problem was the traditional linkage between language and nationhood, according to which a nation could only have a single, predominant national language. One strategy was to play down the importance of language and emphasise how national unity had survived despite linguistic separation. Another strategy was to portray linguistic separation as artificial, initiated for extra-linguistic reasons. The point of departure was (once again) that

---

[24] An interview T. G. Masaryk gave to *Le Petit Parisien* in September 1921 is quite illuminating: 'There is no Slovak nation, said Masaryk, this is an invention of Magyar propaganda. The Czechs and Slovaks are brothers. They speak two tongues, between which there is less difference than between north and south German. They understand each other perfectly. All that separates them is cultural level – the Czechs are more developed than the Slovaks, because the Magyars kept them in the dark. We are building schools in Slovakia. It is necessary to await the results; in one generation there will be no difference between the two branches of our national family' (cited in T. G. Masaryk, *Cesta demokracie II* [The way of democracy II] (Prague, 1934), pp. 78–9).

[25] M. Hodža, *Československý rozkol* [Czechoslovak schism] (Turčiansky Sv. Martin, 1920), pp. 14, 358; Hodža [1928], 'Slovenské veci' [Slovak affairs], in Hodža, *Slovensko a republika*, pp. 191–2. See also J. Škultéty, *Slovensko v minulosti* [Slovakia in the past] (Prague, 1926), p. 5; Bakke, 'Doomed to Failure?', pp. 246–62.

Czechoslovak linguistic unity was regarded as being the norm. This position was based on the claim that the differences between the spoken idioms were negligible and merely a matter of dialect, combined with references to a number of 'authorities' (mostly earlier 'awakeners') who happened to agree that Czech and Slovak constituted one language.

The interpretation of the motives behind the codification of the Slovak language varied within the Czechoslovakist camp. Some saw it as a reaction to pressures of Magyarisation, while others argued that the 'awakeners' had made the move for political reasons, or else were motivated by Panslavism. The argument that proved to be particularly galling to the Slovak autonomists was the insinuation that Anton Bernolák and Štúr were under Magyar influence. This was the analysis presented by Albert Pražák (a Czech professor at Comenius University in Bratislava, whose name was later used as an insult by Slovak autonomists).[26]

It should be noted that even though the Czechoslovakists interpreted the codification of Slovak as a form of linguistic separation, they did not see the existence of literary Slovak as contrary to the principle of Czechoslovak unity. By the 1920s, nobody advocated that the Slovaks should give up their own language in favour of Czech, not even in scholarly writings, a suggestion that Masaryk had made back in 1897.[27] Given the circumstances, this was probably a wise course of action.

The Slovak autonomists argued that there had been no perception of Czechoslovak unitariness prior to the 'revival', that the codification of Slovak only was the final step in a natural process and that the Slovak 'national revival' had served to bring the Slovaks closer to the Czechs. Their own view was that the 'awakeners' were motivated by a desire to save the Slovaks from national annihilation, and, in Škultéty's words, they rushed to codify literary Slovak in 1843 as a preventative measure.

As the preceding summary demonstrates, the Czechoslovakist reinterpretation of history proved to be primarily a reinterpretation of *Slovak* history. For a significant proportion of the Slovak political and cultural elite, Czechoslovakism ran contrary to the principles of Slovak national identity, and it contradicted the traditional Slovak interpretation of

---

[26] See A. Pražák, *Dějiny spisovné slovenštiny po dobu Štúrovu. Knihy zkušenosti a úvah* [History of literary Slovak up to Štúr's era. Books of experiences and reflections] (Prague, 1922), pp. 68–9, 131–3, 147–8, 391–2.

[27] Z. Urban, 'K Masarykovu vztahu ke Slovensku před první světovou válkou' [On Masaryk's attitude to Slovakia before the First World War], in J. Opat, M. Tomčík and Z. Urban, *T. G. Masaryk a Slovensko* [T. G. Masaryk and Slovakia] (Prague, 1992), p. 82.

history in certain important areas. For the Czechs, the new identity was *complementary*: Czech and Czechoslovak amounted to much the same thing. Czech history remained basically the same, with an additional sentence or two about Slovakia and the Slovaks.

The main difference between the scholarly and the political debates was that the latter were less preoccupied with the interpretation of history and more instrumental. The main autonomist argument was that the Czechoslovak nation was a fiction, that it was a threat to the existence of the Slovak nation, and that it ran contrary to Slovak interests. Czechoslovakist rhetoric argued that Czechoslovak unitariness had a long pedigree, and accused the autonomists of being pro-Magyar. A conspicuous feature of this political debate was a high level of mutual recriminations, especially between Slovak politicians, who accused each other of treason to Slovak cause on the one hand, and to the Czechoslovak cause on the other.

Part of the reason why the Czechoslovak national project failed probably lies in the ideology itself. Not only were Slovak nationalists accused of being renegades and of having (covert) pro-Magyar sympathies, but Czechoslovakist ideology contained a strong Czech bias. This situation placed the Slovaks in the role of passive receivers of Czech (positive) and Magyar (negative) cultural influences. The role of Hussitism was exaggerated out of all proportion, and was presented as an ideal, whereas Catholicism (the religion professed by the majority of Slovaks) was evaluated negatively and as being symptomatic of pro-Hungarian attitudes. All things Slovakian were regarded as having resulted from Magyar influences, and seen as a deviation from the Czech standard. These attitudes were not conducive to cementing unity, to put it mildly.

On the other hand, creating a new Czechoslovak nation out of the individual Czech and Slovak nations was never going to be easy, even under the most favourable of conditions. And the circumstances were far from ideal: the inherited socio-economic gap between the Czech Lands and Slovakia was profound, and the economic constraints on government action were severe, especially during the economic crisis in the early 1920s and the 1930s. Equally fateful was the difficult situation in which young Slovak intellectuals found themselves in the 1930s. When the Slovak intelligentsia finally became numerous enough to run Slovakia, vacancies were at a premium.[28]

---

[28] See Bakke, 'Doomed to Failure?', chs. 11, 12, 13 and the conclusion, for a full examination of this issue.

From Munich to Košice: sealing the fate of Czechoslovakism

By the mid-1930s, it was quite obvious that the official line on Czechoslovakism had failed to take root. Part of the reason why it was not abandoned earlier was probably the interdependence between two opposing claims. On the one hand, there was the claim of the Czechoslovak state to independence on the basis of the existence of a unitary Czechoslovak nation, made up of two branches: Czechs and Slovaks. On the other, there was the claim of a separate Slovak nation to political autonomy. In both cases, the principle of national self-determination provided the link between the question of national identity and that of state organisation. Official Czechoslovakism therefore served two purposes. In the first place, it helped legitimise Czechoslovakia as a nation-state and as a superior alternative to the old Austrian 'prison of the nations'. Second, it utilised the Slovak population to swell the numbers of Slavs in the state in comparison to the German minority, while at the same time the Czechs helped to offset the number of Magyars in Slovakia.[29]

On the Czechoslovakist side, apart from the pro-Magyar card, there is every reason to believe that the main priority was to maintain *state* unity in the face of the strong German minority. As for the autonomists, they invoked a number of war-time documents that 'guaranteed' the Slovaks' right to autonomy, notably the Pittsburgh Agreement. This was a document signed by representatives of Slovak and Czech organisations in the United States and T. G. Masaryk on behalf of the Czech–Slovak National Council. It had functioned as the representative political body of the Czechs and Slovaks abroad since 1916. The Pittsburgh Agreement envisaged an autonomous Slovakia within a democratic Czecho-Slovak state. But the details of the constitutional arrangements were a matter for the liberated Czechs and Slovaks and their mandated spokesmen.

While the autonomists saw in autonomy the 'cure' for all Slovakia's ills, the Czechoslovakists did not yield to this request. Official Czechoslovakism was abandoned only after the fateful Munich Agreement of 1938, when the autonomists forced the government to accept the autonomy proclaimed in Žilina on 6 October 1938.

---

[29] Czechoslovakia was of course not nationally homogeneous but, without the Slovaks, the Czechs would have barely been in a majority, with 50.8 per cent. According to the census of 1921, there were 13.4 million Czechoslovak citizens. Czechs and Slovaks together comprised 65.5%, Germans 23.4%, Magyars 5.6%, Ruthenians 3.5%, Jews 1.4%, Poles 0.6% and 'others' 0.2%. See *Sčítání lidu v republice 1921*, vol. I, pp. 60, 66.

The relevant documents here are the constitutional amendment of 1938, promulgated on 22 November, which also brought an end to the First Czechoslovak Republic. Hlinka's Slovak People's Party had filed their third autonomy proposal in August 1938, and after Munich seized the opportunity to push it through parliament. The constitutional amendment of 1938 recognised Slovak individuality, introduced autonomy for Slovakia, and stated in the preamble that 'the Czecho-Slovak republic originated through an agreement of the sovereign will of two equal nations'.[30] The (Second) Czecho-Slovak Republic survived only until 14 March 1939, when the Slovak Diet declared independence. Slovakia then became a puppet state of Nazi Germany, while the post-Munich remains of the Czech Lands became a German protectorate.

The Czechoslovak government-in-exile, based in London and led by President Edvard Beneš, had not given up hope of re-establishing Czechoslovakia and of returning to the pre-Munich status quo. The concept of unitariness was regularly recalled in declarations that referred to the 'sovereignty of the Czechoslovak nation'. Beneš refused to abandon the notion of a Czechoslovak nation, declaring this to be his 'scientific view'. He still presented the Slovaks as Czechs, and Slovak as a Czech dialect.[31] In contrast, it would appear that most Slovak politicians of the former Czechoslovakist government parties at home realised that it would be necessary to reassess Slovakia's position and introduce some sort of limited autonomy in order to re-establish Czechoslovakia.

Internal opposition to the rule of the (now quasi-fascist) Hlinka's Slovak People's Party was organised around the Slovak National Council. At first this body was composed of Communists and former Agrarians, but later other factions joined. In the Christmas Agreement of 1943, the Slovak National Council claimed to be 'the only representative of the political will of the Slovak nation at home', and declared its goal to be that 'the Slovak nation and the Czech nation, as the most related Slav nations, work out their future destiny in the Czech-Slovak Republic, that is, in a joint state of the Slovaks and Czechs, and on the basis of

---

[30] The Constitutional Act of 22 November 1938 concerning the autonomy of Slovakia is printed as Appendix O in D. H. El Mallakh, *The Slovak Autonomy Movement, 1935–1939: A Study in Unrelenting Nationalism* (Boulder, 1979), p. 234f.

[31] J. Slávik, *Československo. Zemský ráj – nacistické peklo* [Czechoslovakia. Earthly paradise – Nazi hell] (London, 1943); V. Kulíšek, 'Úloha Čechoslovakismu ve vztazích Čechů a Slováků' [The role of Czechoslovakism in the relationship between Czechs and Slovaks], *Historický časopis*, 1 (1964), 56; V. Bakoš, *Question of the Nation in Slovak Thought* (Bratislava, 1999), pp. 116–19; J. Barto, *Riešenie vzťahu Čechov a Slovákov* [The solution of the Czech–Slovak relationship] (Bratislava, 1968), pp. 10–11; S. Faľtan, *Slovenská otázka v Československu* [The Slovak question in Czechoslovakia] (Bratislava, 1968), pp. 78, 174, 333–4.

equality'. In all later declarations, the Slovak National Council took the Slovak nation for granted, and envisaged some sort of post-war federation in Czechoslovakia.[32]

Negotiations between the Slovak National Council, the Czechoslovak government-in-exile and the Communist Party of Czechoslovakia, based in Moscow, ended in a compromise in March 1945. Official Czechoslovakism was abandoned for good, but centralism was not. Admittedly, the Košice Government Programme proclaimed on 5 April 1945 gave the Slovak national bodies wide-ranging powers in Slovakia as well as at the federal level, but Slovak institutions were gradually stripped of their executive powers through the three subsequent Prague agreements.[33] Gradually the identity question was thus divorced from the issue of state organisation. The constitutions of 1948 and 1960 were both relatively centralist and asymmetric, placing Slovak national bodies under centralised control; the 1968 constitution was federal in name only.

In section VI of the Košice Government Programme, the government recognised the Slovaks as a separate nation, putting an end to old controversies. At the same time, the government promised to re-establish the republic, 'as the shared state of two nations with equal rights, the Czech and the Slovak', and stated that the Slovaks would be the masters of Slovakia.[34]

Remnants of Czechoslovakism remained in place in political circles even after this date: the Czechoslovak People's Party advocated 'full national unity between the Czechs and Slovaks' in their programme; the chairman of the Czechoslovak National Socialist Party openly subscribed to a unitary Czechoslovak nation in parliament; and the leading Slovak Social Democrat, Ivan Dérer, was ardent in his Czechoslovakism.

---

[32] The quotation is from the English translation in Mikuš, *Slovakia*, p. 241; see also documents in J. Chovanec and P. Mozolík, *Historické a štátoprávne korene samostatnosti Slovenskej Republiky* [Historical and constitutional roots of the Slovak Republic's independence] (Bratislava, 1994), pp. 108f.

[33] The three Prague agreements are printed as appendixes in Chovanec and Mozolík, *Historické a štátoprávne*, pp. 114–22; the third also appears in English translation in Mikuš, *Slovakia*, pp. 250–1; see also J. Rychlík, *Češi a Slováci ve 20. století. Československé vzt'ahy, 1945–1992* [Czechs and Slovaks in the twentieth century. Czech–Slovak relations, 1945–1992] (Bratislava, 1998), pp. 27–51; M. Barnovský, 'Tri pražské dohody' [The three Prague Agreements], in M. Melanová (ed.), *Československé vzt'ahy – Slovensko-české vzt'ahy* [Czech–Slovak relations – Slovak–Czech relations] (Liberec, 1998), p. 119f; see also Barnovský's chapter in this volume.

[34] *Program prvé domácí vlády republiky vlády národní fronty Čechů a Slováků* [Programme of the first domestic Czech and Slovak national front government] (Prague 1945), pp. 16–17; see also an English translation of article VI (about the status of Slovakia), in Mikuš, *Slovakia*, pp. 242–3.

Another Social Democrat and former teacher in Slovakia, the Czech Josef Jirásek, maintained that 'we are a Czechoslovak nation also in a linguistic sense'. Elsewhere, Dérer advocated that the preamble of the 1920 constitution should be kept on, including the opening words 'We, the Czechoslovak nation'.[35]

If we turn now to the Communist period, none of the three post-war constitutions contained any reference to a Czechoslovak nation. In the 1948 constitution, the introductory phrase 'We, the Czechoslovak nation' from the 1920 constitution was turned into 'We, the Czechoslovak people'. In the 1960 (socialist) constitution this became 'We, the working-class people of Czechoslovakia', while the federal constitution of 1968 opened with 'We, the Czech and Slovak nations'. All three constitutions recognised the Slovaks as a separate nation, and defined Czechoslovakia as the united (and, after 1968, federal) state of 'two equal brotherly [in 1948, Slavic] nations, the Czechs and Slovaks'. The emphasis varied slightly in each. The preamble of the 1948 constitution referred to the Czechs and Slovaks as 'two brotherly nations', who had already lived 'a thousand years ago jointly in a single state' (clearly Great Moravia) and who had accepted Christianity from the East. There are also positive references to the Hussite revolution. Here one gets the feeling that 'tribe' has been changed into 'nation'; otherwise the rhetoric is much the same.[36] According to the preamble of the 1960 constitution, 'both nations, the Czechs and the Slovaks, lived in fraternal concord', while the preamble of the 1968 constitution stated that 'our modern history is permeated by the mutual will to live in a common state'.[37]

In the population censuses, the practices employed in the First Republic were totally reversed. The first incomplete census after the war in 1946 and 1947 did not contain any references to nationality at all. In the population censuses conducted under communism (in 1950,

---

[35] I. Dérer, *Slovenský vývoj a ľudácka zrada* [Slovak development and the Ľudak betrayal] (Prague 1946); J. Jirásek, *Slovensko na rozcestí 1918–1938* [Slovakia at the crossroads] (Brno, 1947), p. 10; Kulíšek, 'Úloha Čechoslovakismu', 56; Barto, *Riešenie*, pp. 113–14, 196–9.

[36] An interesting example of the same is *Od srdce k srdci. Literární pásmo o družbě českého a slovenského národa* [From heart to heart. A literary ribbon about the friendship between the Czech and Slovak nation] (Prague, 1959).

[37] *Ústava Československé republiky* [Constitution of the Czechoslovak Republic] (Prague, 1948), pp. 5–6, 9; *Ústava Československej socialistiskej republiky z 11. júla 1960* [Constitution of the Czechoslovak Socialist Republic from 11 July 1960] (Bratislava, 1960); *Ústava Československé socialistiské republiky. Ústavní zákon o československé federaci ze dne 27. října 1968* [Constitution of the Czechoslovak Socialist Republic. Constitutional Act on Czechoslovak Federation from 27 October 1968] (Prague, 1972), pp. 46–7; an English translation of each may be found in Mikuš, *Slovakia*, pp. 255–87, 294–307, 312–51.

1961, 1970 and 1980), the 'Czechoslovak nationality' category was omitted, and if anybody put down 'Czechoslovak' nationality this was not mentioned. In all these censuses, nationality was defined in terms of a combination of subjective and cultural criteria ('belonging to a cultural and working fraternity') and, according to the guidelines, each individual was free to put down the nationality he wanted 'without regard to mother tongue'. However, when the mother tongue was cross-tabulated with nationality, the correspondence was high (over 95 per cent for the largest groups).[38]

Post-Communist reinterpretation

After the Velvet Revolution in 1989, the practice as well as the interpretation of Czechoslovakism changed once more. In the first post-Communist census (1991), 'Czechoslovak nationality' was reintroduced as a category, but subsumed under the heading 'others'. In the Czech Lands, 3,464 subscribed to being of Czechoslovak nationality, of which 1,339 lived in Prague. In Slovakia, the corresponding figure was fifty-nine Czechoslovaks. This is not very impressive, especially since there were 307,004 mixed marriages across Czechoslovakia, nearly two-thirds of which were marriages between Czechs and Slovaks.[39] The potential

[38] *Soupis obyvatelstva v Československu v letech 1946 a 1947* [Census of population in Czechoslovakia 1946 and 1947] (Prague, 1951); *Sčítání lidu a soupis domů a bytů v republice československé ke dni 1. března 1950* [Census of the population and inventory of houses and flats in the Czechoslovak Republic to 1 March 1950] (Prague, 1957), vol. I, pp. 24–7; *Sčítání lidu, domů a bytů v Československé Socialistické Republice ke dni 1. březnu 1961* [Census of the population, houses and flats in the Czechoslovak Socialist Republic to 1 March 1961] (Prague, 1965), vol. I, pp. 17, 54; *Sčítání lidu, domů a bytů ČSSR 1970* [Census of the population, houses and flats in the Czechoslovak Socialist Republic 1970] (Prague, 1975), pp. 104, 203, 213; *Sčítanie ľudu, domov a bytov k 1.12.1970. Tabuľky za SSR* [Census of population, houses and flats to 1 December 1970. Tables for the Slovak Socialist Republic] (Bratislava, 1974), p. 57; *Sčítání lidu, domů a bytů 1980, ČSSR* [Census of population, houses and flats 1980, Czechoslovak Socialist Republic] (Prague, 1982), pp. 88, 192; *Sčítanie ľudu, domov a bytov 1.11.1980. Obyvateľstvo, domy, byty a domácnosti SSR* [Census of population, houses and flats to 1 November 1980. Population, houses, flats and households in Slovak Socialist Republic] (Prague and Bratislava, 1982), p. 28.
[39] See *Sčítání lidu, domů a bytů 1991. Pramenné dílo* [Census of population, houses and flats 1991. Source materials] (Prague, 1994), pp. 17, 57; *Sčítanie ľudu, domov a bytov k 3.3.1991. Obyvateľstvo, domy, byty a domácnosti. Republika Slovenská* [Census of population, houses and flats to 3 March 1991. Population, houses, flats and households. Slovak Republic] (Prague and Bratislava, 1992), vol. II, p. 19; *Lexikón slovenských dejín* [Dictionary of Slovak history] (Bratislava, 1997), p. 196; L. Edelsberger, 'K československé vzájemnosti' [On Czechoslovak reciprocity], in S. Kučerová (ed.), *Československství – středoevropanství – evropanství* [Czechoslovakism – Central Europism – Europism] (Brno, 1998), p. 283.

for a Czechoslovak national identity in terms of people with a dual heritage (the offspring of these relationships) was thus much higher than the actual number of individuals who subscribed to this category in the census.

There have been no serious attempts to revive the idea of a Czechoslovak nation since 1989; the Czechoslovakist ideology is today regarded as a historical phenomenon, and few people regret its passing. In fact, several Slovak participants in the 1990 'hyphen debate' in parliament argued that it was necessary to insert a hyphen in the name 'Czecho-Slovak' Republic in order to remove all remnants of Czechoslovakism. One deputy, the offspring of a mixed marriage, defined himself as a Czechoslovak, but he preached tolerance rather than Czechoslovakism.[40] In the ensuing debate in Slovakia the term 'Czechoslovakism' was mostly used in a pejorative sense, and there were not many traces of it apart from the occasional newspaper article.[41] As for the interpretation of Czechoslovakism after the Velvet Revolution, it came to be presented in a more balanced way, but it was still regarded as a fiction and remained a relatively unpopular topic.[42]

[40] The hyphen debate was triggered by a presidential proposal to remove the word 'socialist' from the name of the state, which was only one of many proposed constitutional amendments designed to bring the constitution more in line with reality. As it turned out, a major point of dispute was whether the name should be the 'Czechoslovak Republic' or the 'Czecho-Slovak (Federal) Republic'. In the end, it became 'The Czech and Slovak Federal Republic'. See 'Zpráva o 26. společné schůzi Sněmovny lidu a Sněmovny národů' [Report on the 26th Chamber of the People and the Chamber of the Nations joint meeting], in *Federální shromáždění Československé socialistické republiky. V. volební období* [Federal Assembly of the Czechoslovak Socialist Republic. Fifth electoral period] (Prague, 1990), pp. 254, 265, 269–70, 287, 305.

[41] See M. Dvořák, 'Co mám dělat se svým čechoslovakismem?' [What should I do with my Czechoslovakism?], *Gemma*, 5 (1992), 1–2.

[42] See M. John, *Čechoslovakismus a ČSR, 1914–1938* [Czechoslovakism and the Czechoslovak Republic] (Beroun, 1994), p. 58; Bakoš, *Question of the Nation*, pp. 103, 105, 120; Chovanec and Mozolík, *Historické a štátoprávne*, p. 23; on this subject Kováč, *Slováci a Česi*, is also pertinent.

17 The Magyar minority in Slovakia before and after the Second World War

Štefan Šutaj

Viewed from a Slovak historical perspective, the Slovak–Magyar and Slovak–Czech relationships were undoubtedly the most important ones for the nation. One of the key features of the relationship between the Magyar and Slovak inhabitants of the old Kingdom of Hungary was the forcible Magyarisation of the Slavic population under the influence of state administrative measures, especially in the final years of the nineteenth century and first decades of the twentieth century. When the Slovak–Magyar frontier was determined after the First World War, the Slovak–Magyar ethnic, or linguistic, border was not clearly defined and remained fluid. As a consequence, Magyars in the Czechoslovak Republic were demoted from the position of the ruling nation to that of a minority.

The Magyar population of Czechoslovakia after 1918 had therefore to adjust to its new minority status. Part of this population perceived the decision of the great powers, which had made them a minority, as an injustice, and they demanded that the frontiers be revised once more. In this way, they came into conflict with the integrity of the new state in which they lived as well as into conflict with the power of the state. Measures enacted by the Czechoslovak state, such as land reform and granting of citizenship, led many Magyars to suspect that the republic was not their home. After the creation of the Czechoslovak Republic, part of this population left its territory (some 105,000 persons by the end of December 1920), and about another 45,000 persons failed to receive Czechoslovak citizenship.[1] The Citizenship Act of 1920 linked the granting of citizenship with a series of conditions (right of domicile, place of residence, employment, birthplace) that made it difficult for

---

[1] Gy. Popély, 'A magyarság számának alakulása az 1921 és 1930 évi csehszlovákiai népszámlálások tükrében' [The development of the Magyar population as reflected by Czechoslovak population censuses from 1921 and 1930], *Századok* (1989), Nos. 1–2, 44–75.

members of minorities to gain citizenship. The state, not the person affected, decided the citizenship of people on the basis of the act.[2]

On the basis of the international agreements guaranteeing the establishment of the state, the Czechoslovak government had to introduce legal norms regulating the position of ethnic minorities on its territory. The principles concerning national minorities included in the Treaty of Saint-Germain of 10 September 1919 were regulated by the Constitution of the Czechoslovak Republic of 29 February 1920. The Constitutional Charter also included the Second Language Act of 29 February 1920 (Act 122/1920 col.).[3] The 'Czechoslovak language' was declared to be the official language, and in communities where at least 20 per cent of the population belonged to a national minority, the minority language was also made an official language. As a result, the official census acquired a special importance. According to the first Czechoslovak census, held in 1921, 650,597 people (that is, 21.7 per cent of the population of Slovakia) declared Magyar nationality. This census demonstrated the results of the Magyarisation policy of the Kingdom of Hungary and post-war instability. In the 1930 census, 585,434 inhabitants of Slovakia (that is 17.6 per cent of the total population) declared Magyar nationality.

The fact that the border regions of southern Slovakia, where the majority of those who had declared Magyar nationality were concentrated and which lay on the periphery of the investment plans made by businesses in Czechoslovakia, had a negative effect on the development of this region. Overpopulated villages, over-reliance on seasonal work and large extended families were typical of southern Slovakia.[4] The population suffered from unemployment and a low level of health care, factors that strengthened dissatisfaction with the new state and reinforced tendencies towards irredentism, fed by domestic and foreign sources.

Land reform had a great impact from the point of view of the socio-economic position of the Magyar minority. The objective of these reforms was to undermine the powerful position of land-owning strata of other (especially non-Czech) nationalities. Another goal was to settle the southern frontier with colonists, who would be politically reliable. On the basis of the Land Confiscation Act of 16 April 1919, some 1,396,135 hectares of land (that is, 28.51 per cent of all agricultural

[2] J. Purgat, *Od Trianonu po Košice* [From Trianon to Košice] (Bratislava, 1970), pp. 19–20.
[3] P. Mosný, 'Medzinárodné zmluvy a československý menšinový problém po prvej svetovej vojne' [International treaties and the Czechoslovak minority problem after the First World War], in J. Nováková (ed.), *Vedecké informácie Spoločenskovedného ústavu SAV*, 1 (1987), 5–32.
[4] See Purgat, *Od Trianonu*.

land in Slovakia) was confiscated. This affected some 957 owners.[5] In the areas of major Magyar settlement, 325,852 hectares of land were confiscated, and 130,250 hectares (39.99 per cent) were redistributed to new owners. From the total number of 184,806 inhabitants of Magyar nationality, only 12,177 persons received about 27,833 hectares of land, an average of 2.2 hectares per person.[6]

The peace treaties and legislation of the pre-Munich Czechoslovak Republic, as well as the Slovak Republic of 1939–1945, ensured that Magyar retained a place in the education system. Although the proportion of schools where Magyar remained the language of instruction declined during this period, this fact can be attributed to the educational system in the old Kingdom of Hungary, which forced pupils to attend schools using the Magyar language, as well as to lower population growth among Magyars during the war. The Second Language Act legislated that schools set up for members of national minorities could teach in their own language, and associated cultural institutions would be administered in the minority language. A national (primary) school had to be established in every village with at least forty children of school age. The problem of secondary schools and teacher training colleges was finally solved by Act no. 123 of 8 June 1923. The state language became an obligatory subject, while the minority language could be an obligatory or an optional subject.[7]

In 1921, the Magyar minority in Slovakia had fifty-eight nursery schools, containing 4,084 children, 845 primary ('people's') schools with 114,940 pupils, 19 secondary modern schools (meštianky), 10 continuation schools with a vocational orientation, and 2 secondary vocational schools. In addition by 1922, there were four gymnasia and one teacher training college. At this time, seventy newspapers, magazines and periodicals were published in Magyar, and there were more than 400 cultural societies.[8] By 1926, there were 695 schools where Magyar was the

---

[5] J. Voženílek, Předběžné výsledky československé pozemkové reformy. Země Slovenská a Podkarpatskoruská' [Preliminary results of the Czechoslovak land reform. Slovakia and Subcarpathian Ruthenia] (Prague, 1932), p. 28; P. Horváth, Príručka hospodárskej štatistiky Slovenska [Handbook of economic statistics of Slovakia] (Bratislava, 1935), p. 67.

[6] P. Komora, 'Maďarské buržoázne strany na Slovensku (1919–1929)' [The Magyar bourgeois parties in Slovakia (1919–1929)], Zborník Filosofickej fakulty Univerzity Komenského Historica, 20 (1969), 105. According to J. Borsody, 26,863 hectares of land were assigned to people of Magyar nationality: Magyarok Csehszlovákiában 1918–1938 [The Magyars in Czechoslovakia 1918–1938] (Budapest, 1938), p. 85.

[7] Purgat, Od Trianonu, p. 40.

[8] V. Fábry, Kultúra maďarskej menšiny na Slovensku [Culture of the Magyar minority in Slovakia] (Bratislava, 1998), p. 9.

language of education, with 66,260 pupils, and 17 secondary modern schools. The decline in the number of pupils reflects the reduced number of children born during the war, the movement of part of the population who adopted Slovak nationality and administrative measures imposed by the state.

The Magyar minority established its own political parties, which were represented in parliament. The strongest of these were the Országos Kereszténysocialista párt (National Christian Socialist Party) and the Magyar Nemzeti párt (Magyar National Party). In 1920, the parties took part in the election separately, but later (1929–1936) they formed various electoral groups with each other and with some of the German parties. Some Magyar inhabitants joined mainstream Czechoslovak political parties.

Under political pressure from Budapest and due to internal developments, the strongest political parties of the Magyar minority endeavoured to form a single party. After declaring their intentions in the newspaper *Prágai Magyar Hirlap* (Prague Magyar news) in January 1936, the voice of all Magyar political parties, support for this idea strengthened. A conference to discuss the merger was held on 21 June 1936, in Nové Zámky (southern Slovakia), and it was agreed to form the United Magyar Party. In 1938, the policy of the United Magyar Party demanded that the territory inhabited by people of Magyar nationality should be re-united with Hungary.[9]

Following the Munich Agreement in September 1938, pressure from Hungary led to Slovakia losing its southern regions.[10] This occurred under the terms of the Vienna Arbitration (2 November 1938), when Germany and Italy awarded part of southern Slovakia, inhabited by 272,000 Slovaks, to Admiral Horthy's Hungary. This change was calculated on the basis of the 1910 census, which had been manipulated by the ruling Hungarian bureaucracy. Of the 279 villages transferred to Hungary, 170 had Slovak majorities. After the creation of the independent Slovak state on 14 March 1939, the Hungarian army, with the agreement of Germany, marched beyond the frontier agreed in Vienna and occupied a further seventy-four villages in eastern Slovakia and Subcarpathian Ruthenia.[11]

[9] L. Deák, 'Zjednotenie maďarských opozičných strán roku 1936 na Slovensku' [The unification of the Magyar opposition parties in Slovakia in 1936] *Historický časopis*, 46 (1998), 583–7.
[10] For more details, see L. Deák, *Slovensko v politike Maďarska v rokoch 1938–1939* [Slovakia in the politics of Hungary in 1938–1939] (Bratislava, 1990); Deák, *Hra o Slovensko* [The game regarding Slovakia] (Bratislava, 1991), pp. 149–74.
[11] L. Deák, *Slovensko v politike Maďarska*, p. 123; D. Čierna-Lantayová, *Podoby česko-slovensko-maďarského vzťahu 1938–1949* [The modes of Czech–Slovak–Magyar

This loss of territory substantially reduced the number of Magyars in Slovakia, but even this did not solve the minority problem. A Magyar minority of 65,000 people remained in the territory of autonomous and later independent Slovakia. During this period the Magyar minority had one elected deputy in the Diet, János Esterházy, while the Magyar National Party continued the political activity begun by the United Magyar Party. The Magyar nationality retained thirty-five primary schools, two secondary modern schools, one (two-year) commercial school, one (four-year) commercial academy, one *gymnasium* and ten Magyar newspapers and magazines.[12]

During the Slovak National Uprising, the Magyar National Party was dissolved. The Slovak National Council, the legislative body of the uprising, decreed on 6 September 1944 that Magyar and German schools were allowed to operate only if they existed before the declaration of Slovak autonomy on 6 October 1938. After the end of the Second World War, the Czechoslovak government tried to resolve the situation of the Magyar minority in Slovakia by a rapid reduction in its size. The post-war situation in the liberated territories was characterised by the enacting of radical measures against minorities, who were considered to be partly responsible for the break-up of the Czechoslovak Republic.

The basic strategic policy of the Czechoslovak government-in-exile was to remove the German and Magyar minorities from the country. The preferred solution was some form of population transfer. In relation to Hungary, an exchange of populations was proposed, an idea that had already been considered for the German minority. Armistice talks with Hungary began in January 1945 and proved to be an important milestone in the search for a possible solution to the position of the Magyar minority in Slovakia. These talks indicated the demands that Czechoslovakia would make against defeated Hungary, and how these proposals might be co-ordinated with the victorious powers in Central Europe.[13]

relationships, 1938–1949] (Bratislava, 1992); Deák, *Malá vojna. Vojenský konflikt medzi Mad'arskom a Slovenskom v roku 1939* [The little war. The military conflict between Hungary and Slovakia in 1939] (Bratislava, 1993), p. 20. Following the Treaty of Saint-Germain (1919), Subcarpathian Ruthenia (formerly a Hungarian province) became Czechoslovakia's easternmost part (Eds.).

[12] Fábry, *Kultúra*, pp. 9–10.

[13] For more details, see K. Kaplan, *Československo v letech 1945–1948* [Czechoslovakia from 1945 to 1948] (Prague, 1991); Čierna-Lantayová, *Podoby*; Purgat, *Od Trianonu*; K. Jánics, *A hontalanság évei* [The years of statelessness] (Budapest, 1989); Kaplan, *Pravda o Československu 1945–1948* [The truth about Czechoslovakia 1945–1948] (Prague, 1990).

The final armistice agreement was signed on 20 January 1945; with reference to Slovakia it included the recognition of the pre-Munich Slovak–Hungarian frontier, the removal of Magyar officials and soldiers from its territory, reparations for war damage, the annulment of all decrees relating to the annexation of the occupied territories, and the return of all looted materials and valuables taken from these territories.[14] After the liberation of southern Slovakia, about 32,000 people who had come to the region from Hungary after 1939 and who were not Czechoslovak citizens, left this territory.

The first measures enacted by the Slovak National Council in the liberated territories did not contain measures affecting the Magyar minority as a whole. The Manifesto of the Slovak National Council, issued in February 1945, made reference to the departure of Hungarian officials who did not have Czechoslovak citizenship in 1938 and to the granting of minority rights to the inhabitants of Magyar nationality. This action allowed Magyarised Slovaks to return to their ethnic roots and assume their original Slovak nationality. At the time this process was referred to as 're-Slovakisation'. However, the legislation enacted after the war did have a generally anti-Magyar character. On the local level, 'revolutionary' solutions to certain problems were applied in connection with the inhabitants of Magyar nationality, the use of the Magyar language was curbed, and scores were settled. Injustices which Slovaks felt they had suffered at the hands of Magyars in the occupied territory were 'corrected', and in this way new injustices were created.

Slovakia was liberated before Bohemia, and so measures affecting the inhabitants of German and Magyar nationality, including traitors and collaborators of Slovak nationality, had already been adopted in Slovakia before the so-called Beneš (presidential) decrees. These included the Decree of the Slovak National Council no. 4, issued on 27 February 1945 on the confiscation of agricultural property larger than 50 hectares belonging to Magyars, Germans, traitors and collaborators. Further measures regarding land reform and the confiscation of agricultural property of Magyar inhabitants of Slovakia were also enacted by decrees of the Slovak National Council, and not by presidential decrees.

The representatives of the bourgeois and communist Czechoslovak resistance movement, at home and abroad, unified their positions on the Magyar question during their talks on governmental policy held in Moscow in March 1945. From the adoption of the first programme of

---

[14] Ministerstvo inostrannykh del SSSR [Soviet Foreign Ministry], *Sovetsko-vengerskie otnosheniya 1945–1948* [Soviet–Hungarian relations 1945–1948] (Moscow, 1969); Čierna-Lantayová, *Podoby.*

the Czechoslovak government – the Košice Government Programme – the relationship between the restored state administration and the Magyar minority changed dramatically. The effort to transfer the population of Magyar nationality out of Czechoslovakia became the central pillar of new Czechoslovak policy. The changes in relation to the Magyar minority, confirmed by the Moscow talks of March 1945, were expressed in section VIII of the Košice Government Programme. This policy towards the German and Magyar minorities was apparently based on the principle of collective guilt. The Košice Government Programme issued a political declaration that the Magyars and Germans had lost the right to be citizens of Czechoslovakia; Presidential Decree no. 33 of 2 August 1945 on Czechoslovak citizenship legislated on this decision. Another important change was that a decree passed by the Slovak National Council nationalised all schools in Slovakia and made their staff state employees. Teachers in southern Slovakia had to submit applications for their re-acceptance into state service. The school inspectorate verified their political and national reliability. In line with the plan to solve the Magyar question, no new Magyar schools were opened, and teaching in existing schools gradually came to an end. In spite of this, some schools that taught in Magyar did complete the school year.[15]

In southern Slovakia measures directed against the Magyar minority gradually began to affect not only the economic but also the social sphere. This region suffered from limited investment, stagnation of rebuilding activities and limitations placed upon culture and education. On the basis of a decree issued by the Slovak National Council in July 1945, German and Magyar clergymen were dismissed from their posts. A resolution passed by the Board of Commissioners decided that social aid to the population was also dependent on having Czechoslovak citizenship and Slovak or Czech nationality.

Unilateral Czechoslovak proposals for the transfer of the Magyar minority out of the republic were not accepted by the great powers during talks regarding the armistice with Hungary, held at Yalta and Potsdam. Hence, Czechoslovakia and Hungary agreed to sign a treaty on the exchange of population on 27 February 1946, after a complex series of negotiations and under international pressure. As a result, Czechoslovakia oriented its internal policy towards other ways of resolving the Magyar question. Essentially, this meant steps to reduce the numbers of persons of Magyar nationality in southern Slovakia. These

---

[15] S. Gabzdilová, *Maď'arské školstvo na Slovensku v druhej polovici 20. storočia* [The Magyar school system in Slovakia during the second half of the twentieth century] (Dunajská Streda, 1999), p. 12.

included 're-Slovakisation', the moving of Magyars into Bohemia, and the transfer of population within Slovakia. Land reform, the activities of the people's courts and educational reorganisations also targeted Magyars, and these measures were clearly discriminatory towards this group.

During the immediate post-war period, Czechoslovak–Hungarian relations were supervised by the Soviet Union, a regime with a history of using the resettlement of populations to solve 'problems'. The idea of transferring the whole Magyar minority out of Slovakia proved to be unrealistic, especially due to the lack of international support from West European countries and the USA. In addition, the unilateral resettlement of Slovakia's Magyar minority was roundly rejected by Hungary. The exchange of populations was also considered an inappropriate method, and the agreement on an exchange of populations was seen as having been imposed. The Czechoslovak side perceived Hungary's refusal to accept the exchange as a prerequisite for a future revisionist policy, favoured by keeping a Magyar population in Slovakia as close to the boundary as possible. It understood the agreement as the first step to profound changes in the nationality structure of southern Slovakia.[16]

Czechoslovak diplomacy now concentrated on the implementation of the signed agreement with Hungary on a partial exchange of populations, although achieving this goal also proved to be problematic. According to this agreement, signed on 27 February 1946, the Magyar inhabitants of Czechoslovakia, identified as such by government officials, were to be transferred to Hungary in exchange for Slovaks who volunteered to move out. Hungary signed the agreement under international pressure, demonstrating its intention to resolve the problem of Slovak–Hungarian relations. At the same time, this was a preventive move against possible attempts to transfer the whole Magyar minority out of Slovakia. Hungary was in effect blocking the full implementation of the population exchange by imposing further conditions before proceeding with it. In fact, the exchange belatedly began in 1947.

The exchange was beset with problems. The resettled Slovaks sometimes, for example, spoke more fluent Magyar than they did Slovak. Whole generations had lived in a Magyar milieu and had been educated in Magyar schools. According to a report undertaken by the Czechoslovak Ministry of Foreign Affairs in 1958, when these matters were already definitively closed, 89,660 Magyars were resettled from

---

[16] Record of a meeting of the Slovak National Committee, on questions connected with talks with Hungary, 4 October 1945, box 38, Slovak National Archive (SNA), Bratislava.

Czechoslovakia to Hungary during the immediate post-war period, while 71,787 Slovaks were resettled from Hungary to Czechoslovakia.[17]

The adoption of the act that removed citizenship from Magyars and Germans (Presidential Decree no. 33, 2 August 1945) and the preparations for the population exchange between Czechoslovakia and Hungary required the problem of Magyarised Slovaks to be dealt with. That is, re-Slovakisation began when the state formally enabled inhabitants who had previously adopted Magyar nationality to declare themselves Slovak. Parents were now sending their children to Slovak schools, street names were changed from Magyar to Slovak and so on.[18]

Bilingualism was an obvious precondition for such changes to occur. The Board of Commissioners, the highest executive government body in Slovakia, adopted a directive on re-Slovakisation at a session held on 2 April 1946, and the Commissionership for the Interior (*poverenictvo vnútra*) issued a declaration on 17 June 1946 which became the basis for further re-Slovakisation. The directives in this declaration classified those who could apply for re-Slovakisation into two categories: first, persons of contested ethnic origin, who had given conflicting information about their nationality in different censuses, and according to this directive could be regarded as Slovaks; second, persons of Slovak nationality by origin who could prove their Slovak or Slavic origin, but had previously declared themselves to be Magyar.

Moreover, these directives on re-Slovakisation acknowledged the possibility to declare oneself a Slovak not only for ethnic, but also for political reasons, on the basis of a re-evaluation of one's relationship to the Czechoslovak state, or opposition to the Slovak or Hungarian profascist regime during the war. A condition for granting Slovak nationality was that the person had committed no offence against the Act for Defence of the Republic during the war, had not been prosecuted according to the Decree of the Slovak National Council no. 33, issued

---

[17] For more details, see Š. Šutaj, *Maďarská menšina na Slovensku v rokoch 1945–1948* [The Magyar minority in Slovakia from 1945 to 1948] (Bratislava, 1993); Šutaj, 'Ungarische Minderheit in der Slowakei während der Nachkriegsentwicklung', in R. G. Plaschka, H. Haselsteiner, A. Suppan and A. M. Drabek (eds.), *Nationale Frage und Vertreibung in der Tschechoslowakei und Ungarn 1938–1948. Aktuelle Forschungen* (Vienna, 1996), pp. 81–7.

[18] For more details on the problem of re-Slovakisation, see Š. Šutaj, *Reslovakizácia. Zmena národnosti časti obyvateľstva Slovenska po II. svetovej vojne* [Re-Slovakisation. Change in the nationality of part of the population of Slovakia after the Second World War] (Košice, 1991); Šutaj and V. Bačová, 'Reslovakisation. The Changes of Nationality and Ethnic Identity in the Historical Development of the Slovak–Hungarian Environment' in S. Devetak, S. Flere and G. Seewann (eds.), *Small Nations and Ethnic Minorities in Emerging Europe* (Munich, 1993), pp. 239–43; K. Vadkerty, *A Reslovakizácio* [Re-Slovakisation] (Bratislava, 1993).

on 15 May 1945 on people's courts, and had not been a functionary of a Magyar political party or organisation. There was a clear difference between these directives and Presidential Decree no. 33 of 2 August 1945. According to this decree, Czechoslovak citizenship could be granted only to those Magyars who had actively participated in the anti-fascist movement. Officials in the state administration estimated the number of people who could be considered for re-Slovakisation under these criteria to be 150,000 to 200,000.

The aim of re-Slovakisation was to change the ethnic structure of southern Slovakia. Many people accepted re-Slovakisation to protect themselves from the repressive measures now being applied against Magyars. The process was also affected by the intervention of the two strongest political parties in Slovakia. The Communist Party of Slovakia supported the class principle of re-Slovakisation, that is, the acceptance of applications from the poorest sections of the population. In contrast, the Democratic Party emphasised the ethnic or national principle. This meant re-Slovakising those who could prove Slovak ethnic origin, demonstrated by objective criteria: knowledge of the language, Slovak relations, surname, membership of Slovak societies, and other indicators without regard to their property status.

The Czechoslovak government, led by Klement Gottwald, accepted the proposals of the Slovak Communists. It issued directives on re-Slovakisation on 9 August 1946, which included the selection principle according to property circumstances and so-called settlement zones; class and state security criteria were therefore paramount. These directives mandated that consideration of applications for re-Slovakisation was not to undermine the possibility of removing 100,000 Magyars from the republic. Moreover, persons regarded as traitors and collaborators, especially those from the ranks of the intelligentsia, persons living in the settlement zones of southern and south-eastern Slovakia (border areas to be settled only by Slovaks) and owners of more than 5 royal yokes of land[19] would not be re-Slovakised. Other persons were to be treated benevolently. Thus, re-Slovakisation, a state-organised action to change nationality, became part of the measures discriminating against the Magyar minority population.

By 1948, 452,089 persons had applied for re-Slovakisation. The applications of 84,141 people were rejected because they did not fulfil the preconditions. In the case of 41,269 persons, applications for re-Slovakisation were not completed for reasons such as death or

[19] Equal to 5.75 hectares or 14.2 acres.

emigration.[20] The reappearance of a significant proportion of the re-Slovakised population as Magyars in the censuses of 1950 and 1961 illustrates that, although some were Magyarised Slovaks, the majority were Magyars who applied for re-Slovakisation for fear of repression.

A special type of solution to the Magyar question, imposed after the Second World War, was the transfer of Magyars to work in Bohemia.[21] On the basis of Presidential Decree no. 88/1945 related to labour obligations, Magyars, largely drawn from the socially weaker groups, and who were likely to be assimilated in a foreign environment, were transferred to work in Bohemia. However, they were not settled in the area's abandoned farms following the transfer of the Germans, but employed in Czech farms in border areas and in the interior of the country. From November 1946 to February 1947, 44,129 Magyars were transferred to Bohemia within the framework of centrally organised recruitment of labour. The mass movement of Magyars was intended to be one of the ways of forcing the Hungarian government to start the exchange of population on the basis of the February 1946 agreement. However, the Hungarian government used the fact that the Czechoslovak government was transferring Magyars to Bohemia as an argument to prevent the exchange from taking place. It emphasised that the Czechoslovak side was breaking the agreement and not respecting the supplement to the protocol about the exchange of population, which banned the transfer of population on an ethnic basis.

Apart from considering all the technical, internal political and international aspects of this action, the most controversial issue was simply how it was carried out. It was done in winter, with the assistance of military and security forces, in cold wagons, and sometimes in dramatic circumstances, with some people identified for transfer attempting to escape; this violated humanitarian principles.

The transfer of Magyars to Bohemia became a trump card for both sides. The Hungarian side refused to implement the exchange until the transfer of Magyars to Bohemia ended, but the Czechoslovak side was not willing to change its internal policy towards the Magyar minority.

---

[20] Report on re-Slovakisation for the Presidium of the Central Committee of the Slovak Communist Party, 1950, SNA, Bratislava.

[21] For more details, see Š. Šutaj, 'Zwangsaustausch bzw. Aussiedlung der Madjaren aus der Slowakei – Pläne und Wirklichkeit', in D. Brandes, E. Ivaničková and J. Pešek (eds.), *Erzwungene Trennung. Die Vertreibung und Aussiedlungen in und aus der Tschechoslowakei 1938–1947 im Vergleich mit Polen, Ungarn und Jugoslawien* (Essen, 1999), pp. 251–71; Šutaj, 'A Dél-akció. A szlovákiai magyarok 1949 évi csehorsági kitelepítese' [The southern action. The ejection of Magyars from Slovakia to Bohemia in 1949], *Regio*, 2 (1992), 93–113.

Secret talks held between the Hungarian foreign minister János Gyöngyösi and Czechoslovak representatives were unsuccessful. The Hungarian side protested about the Czechoslovak policy. In response, the Czechoslovak representatives demanded that a larger number of persons be transferred to Bohemia, because the current total of 43,000 people was considered insufficient. From the economic point of view, the transfer caused irreparable losses for Magyars, who often had to sell part of their property for a fraction of its true value. But the people who received the vacated property also experienced problems.

The Hungarian side believed that the forthcoming Paris Peace Conference (designed to draw up the surrender settlements with Germany's allies) would recognise Hungarian reservations about the population exchange. The conference lasted from 29 July 1946 to 15 October 1946. The Czechoslovak side proposed that the peace treaty with Hungary should include an article authorising Czechoslovakia to move 200,000 people of Magyar origin from its territory. The Hungarian delegation regarded this proposal as the greatest threat to Hungarian interests at the Peace Conference.[22] The Peace Conference rejected the transfer of populations as a way of resolving the dispute and did not accept Hungarian claims for territorial changes and the introduction of a minority statute. Therefore both sides regarded the decision as a partial failure.

However, by the end of 1947, signs of a new approach towards the problem of the Magyar minority in Slovakia began to appear as a result of the Paris Conference and the 'leftward' shift in the political scene in both Czechoslovakia and Hungary. There were already signs that Czechoslovakia might modify its policy towards the Magyar minority, and that communist circles in Budapest were already speaking of a changed attitude of the Soviet Union towards the problem of the Magyar minority in Slovakia.

The political regime in Czechoslovakia changed at the end of February 1948 due to the Communist takeover. Apart from interference by the Soviet Union, this event had a profound influence on future developments in the republic.[23]

A proposal to resolve the status of the Magyar minority was submitted to a meeting of the Presidium of the Central Committee of the

---

[22] S. Kertész, *The Last European Conference: Paris 1946 – Conflict of Values* (Lanham, 1985), p. 38.

[23] For more details, see K. Kaplan, *Československo v letech 1948–1953* [Czechoslovakia from 1948 to 1953] (Prague, 1991); M. Barnovský, *Na ceste k monopolu moci* [On the road to monopoly power] (Bratislava, 1993).

Communist Party of Czechoslovakia on 8 July 1948. The main principle adopted indicated the policies the Party wished to pursue: they proposed to grant Magyars full civil rights and to create parallel Magyar-medium schools at all levels; at the same time, they did not plan to introduce a special minority statute or to allow the creation of any Magyar political organisation. At a meeting between representatives of the Communist Party of Czechoslovakia and Hungarian Communists held on 23 and 24 July 1948, the Czechoslovak side declared that it was possible for the Communist Party to resolve the Magyar question by granting civil rights and citizenship to its Magyar inhabitants. The joint declaration contained the proposal regarding the resolution of the whole spectrum of the status of the Magyar minority in Czechoslovakia.

Following these decisions, the government and legislative organs of Czechoslovakia took steps to remove some of the discriminatory measures levelled against the Magyar population. On 30 September 1948, the Czechoslovak government decided that persons of Magyar nationality who were Czechoslovak citizens as of 1 November 1938, who had later lost their citizenship and who were permanent residents on Czechoslovak territory would regain Czechoslovak citizenship, provided they had not offended against the Czechoslovak Republic and its people's democratic regime.

The discrimination against the population of Magyar nationality carried out in 1945–1947 came to an end in 1948, but its consequences and influence continued for a longer period. The last transport of people to be resettled in Hungary left on 21 December 1948. The last Slovak family to be resettled in Slovakia left Hungary on 1 January 1949. In spite of the changes in government policy in Hungary and Czechoslovakia, the basic tendency of the policy towards the Magyar minority remained. Czechoslovakia endeavoured to hold the course and to complete the population exchange, while the Hungarian side prioritised ceasing any further exchanges. On 12 September 1948, the Board of Commissioners adopted a measure securing an organised return of the 'labour force of Magyar nationality from Bohemia'. According to a government resolution issued on 30 September 1948, persons who had acquired Czechoslovak citizenship after 1 May 1949 were exempt from work in Bohemia. The settlement of property losses was postponed until 1950 and gradually merged with the collectivisation of agriculture, which was rapidly proceeding across southern Slovakia.

Economic processes that took place after 1948 had an important influence on ethnicity in the villages of southern Slovakia. Widespread industrialisation absorbed a great number of people, who went to towns in different parts of Slovakia or to Bohemia. The collectivisation of agriculture drove a large part of the original population from their villages. While the first stage of collectivisation was practically completed (90 per cent) in the returned territory by 1949–1953, it was only beginning to be implemented in the rest of Slovakia in that period. Villages with predominantly Magyar populations generally entered co-operatives during the first few years of collectivisation, because of fear of further repression. In 1961, more than 95 per cent of the agricultural land in the southern districts of Slovakia was collectivised. Migration increased, especially in the period after 1970. The large number of people leaving agriculture, and the building of new industrial enterprises, brought about profound changes in the rural way of life: a noticeable reduction in the number of multi-generational families, the utilisation of the advantages of centrally directed housing policy, changes in the structure of employment and professional orientation of the population, and rising levels of education all influenced the population density and ethnic composition of the villages of southern Slovakia.

After 1948, schools with Magyar as the language of instruction were revived; a cultural society, Csemadok, was established; papers, magazines, periodicals and books began to be published in Magyar once more; and a professional theatre ensemble was established in Komárno and later also in Košice. The number of Magyar schools, publications in Magyar, Magyar theatre ensembles, members of parliament of Magyar nationality and so on increased, and these developments were under the control of the Communist Party.

The re-organisation of public and state administration and national committees in the southern districts of Slovakia during 1950–1951 led to the proportional increase of Magyars in these areas. Gradually they included members of the Slovak and Magyar nationality in proportion to their numbers in the local community. The Magyar language could be used in official business.

The physical enlargement of districts (*okresy*) under district national committees in 1960 affected the Magyar minority in southern Slovakia. The change was introduced against the will of the population, as it increased the distance to district centres and reduced the representation of Magyars in district bodies. Difficulties with employing school leavers soon appeared, and critics pointed to the fact that the enlargement of districts also reduced the possibilities for the use of bilingualism. For example, after the territorial re-organisation, local houses of 'public education', which had been centres for the cultural activities of the population, were closed. Communist propaganda at the beginning of the 1960s claimed that the abolition of small districts with mainly Magyar populations and the creation of larger districts with a lower proportion of Magyar inhabitants was a positive step, which would bring the members of the Slovak and Magyar nationalities closer together. In 1968, representatives of the Magyar minority campaigned for a return to the original districts.

The Constitutional Act on the Situation of Nationalities in the Czechoslovak Socialist Republic, no. 144/1968, characterised the nationalities as entities that formed the Czechoslovak state, together with the Czech and Slovak nations. In contrast to the Constitution of the Czechoslovak Socialist Republic from 1960, where national rights were bound to individuals, the Constitutional Act of 1968 designated nationalities as state-forming entities. It gave nationalities the right to representation in organisations in proportion to their numbers, to education in their own mother tongue, to general cultural development, to use their language in official business in areas inhabited by them, and to the news and information in their native language. But the legislative norms detailing the implementation of these rights were never adopted. In this period, the Slovak National Council and Federal National Assembly had Magyar members in line with their proportion within the population of Slovakia. They were chosen by the Communist Party and elected on the single list of candidates. Roughly similar representation continued until 1989.

The Magyar minority experienced complex development from 1918 up until the Velvet Revolution in 1989. Still, at the end of this period, it remained a strong, cohesive group with close internal ties within the community and links to the mother nation in Hungary. A strong sense of ethnic consciousness, preference for the Magyar language in communication and orientation towards Magyar culture remained among its basic characteristics.[24]

---

[24] For more details on the state of the Magyar minority in the post-Communist period, see A. Zeľová, V. Bačová, S. Hadušovská, M. Homišinová, M. Olejník, V. Paukovič, Š. Šutaj and J. Výrost, *Minoritné etnické spoločenstvá na Slovensku v procesoch spoločenských premien* [Minority ethnic communities in Slovakia in the processes of social change] (Bratislava, 1994).

18 The establishment of totalitarianism in Slovakia after the February coup of 1948 and the culmination of mass persecution, 1948–1953

Jan Pešek

The Communist takeover of Czechoslovakia, in February 1948, began a period of the transformation of Slovak society in line with Communist ideology and the Soviet model of socialism. The central pillar of this new political system was the Communist Party, which became a 'state-party' and monopolised political power. The Party began to take over the economy of the state. All industrial and other enterprises, foreign trade and wholesale trade gradually came under its remit. The economic liquidation of the majority of privately owned crafts and trades followed. In the villages, most land was in the possession of the peasant-farmers, but from the beginning of 1949 mass collectivisation commenced. It was formally voluntary, but in reality pressure and intimidation prevailed.

These forcible interventions fundamentally altered the social structure of Slovak society. Private ownership of the means of production was largely abolished. Practically all citizens became employees of the state. In practice, this also included the collectivised peasant-farmers, who lost their claims to their own land. The Communists controlled the state from the centre to the districts, towns and enterprises. The new regime was not satisfied with a monopoly of power, but aimed at total state control of all aspects of society, including the spiritual sphere and personal life of every individual. Historical literature calls the period of extraordinarily extensive social changes the 'founding period of the totalitarian regime' or the 'hot phase of the totalitarian process'. This phase lasted until 1953.

These basic changes in Slovak society, including some limited levels of economic, social and cultural growth, were introduced during a period of increased hostility between East and West, the Cold War, which constantly threatened to escalate into all-out conflict, and within the framework of a unitary and strictly centralised Czechoslovak Republic. The planning of these changes originated with the Party in Prague, and the process of implementing them was enforced equally across the Czech Lands and in Slovakia. Each part of the republic had its own specific features as a result of these developments, but the basic aim of the new regime was to maintain and strengthen its monopoly of power and to effect the basic transformation of all aspects of society.

These changes were accompanied by mass persecution, violence and illegality; indeed, their widespread use underpinned the implementation of the aims of the Communist dictatorship. After the takeover by the Communist Party, political persecution became part of official policy, an accompanying feature of and condition for the existence of its monopoly of power. It was a useful measure for the control of society, and an important instrument and support for the regime. A central feature of the regime was that it sought to establish a general atmosphere of fear. The Party's monopoly of power was built upon this fear. It was not its only means of support, but it was certainly one of the most important. Political persecution was one way of solving conflicts between the Stalinist regime and the rest of society, which rejected or disagreed with some of its policies. It was used to dominate the whole of society, and so helped to lay the political foundations of the regime, but it was also wielded against particular groups and individuals, depending on the interests of the regime at any particular time.

This persecution was especially concerned with the eradication or limitation of basic civil rights and the freedoms of citizens; these included freedom of the press, of movement, of thought and religion, and of assembly and association, as well as labour rights and the right to trade union membership. In addition, they wanted protection of private property, independence for the judiciary and free elections. Elections on the basis of the 'united list of candidates of the National Front' were held, but these were not 'free' elections as the results were falsified. The intensity of suppression changed over the lifespan of the Communist regime, but the Party could never totally abandon this policy because doing so would have undermined the foundations on which it was built.

The deliberate, targeted persecution of specific social, political and professional groups and individuals played a decisive role in the introduction of the Communist social system. These actions directly affected certain groups as well as families and individuals. It was directed against all those who opposed totalitarian power and against those suspected of opposition by the representatives of the regime.

The system of political persecution enabled the regime to apply total political and administrative domination over the whole of social, economic and cultural life, over the state, society and the individual citizen.

The Communist regime created a high level of political persecution which was almost perfectly systematic, in the sense that the citizen, who was persecuted, had no possibility of escape. For example, s/he could not escape into a private company, because these were nationalised, or into another institution, because they all belonged to the state or were connected with it. S/he could not defend himself or herself, because no institution would listen to him/her or support his/her rights.

The period 1948–1953 witnessed the greatest wave of political persecution during the whole existence of the Communist regime in Czechoslovakia, including Slovakia. The new regime felt insecure, and it encountered various forms of opposition to and disagreement with its policies and methods. The Party reacted with mass persecution, which passed through a number of different stages.

The first stage occurred immediately after February 1948, and its aim was to secure and justify the takeover. The second stage began in autumn 1948, when the basic political purpose was to secure the Party's monopoly of power in all areas of society. The third, culminating phase of persecution began around the end of 1949 and beginning of 1950. Its aim was the total reconstruction of society according to Soviet practice.[1]

The forms of persecution varied: from purges affecting social organisations, through bans on certain forms of employment and study and limitations of personal freedom, to imprisonment on the basis of staged political trials or even without trial. Persecution affected all social classes, not only those considered 'hostile' to the Party, but also those that the regime proclaimed as its social support, that is, the workers and peasants.

The Communist Party of Slovakia had already used violence and persecution during its seizure of power in February 1948. On 20 February 1948, the Party leadership used the resignation of ministers from the People's, National Socialist and Democratic Parties from the Czechoslovak government in Prague to declare that this automatically meant the resignation of the representatives of the Democratic Party from the Board of Commissioners in Slovakia. Gustáv Husák, a member of the Communist leadership and chairman of the Board of Commissioners, announced this on the radio the next day. This was clearly an illegal decision, and the Democratic commissioners refused to accept it; they considered it completely invalid. On Monday, 23 February, the commissioners from the Communist Party of Slovakia, their

---

[1] K. Kaplan, *Political Persecution in Czechoslovakia 1948–1972* (Cologne, 1983); Kaplan, *Report on the Murder of the General Secretary* (Columbus, 1990).

supporters from other departments and Communist-controlled security personnel went to the offices that had until then been administered by the Democrats and forced the Democratic commissioners to leave. Officials loyal to the Democrats were also thrown out and replaced with Communists.[2]

The Democratic Party, as the main opponent of the Communist Party of Slovakia, more or less disintegrated under this pressure during the February crisis. The Communists, helped by security forces and armed partisans, occupied its central secretariat and prevented it publishing, its leadership lost its ability to act, and some functionaries began collaborating with the Communists. Already shaken by the autumn crisis of 1947, the Democratic Party proved unable to stand up to the events of February 1948.

Immediately after seizing power, the new Communist regime began further persecution campaigns. Action Committees of the Slovak National Front, which the Communists and their supporters began to form during the February coup, organised purges across the non-communist political parties, mass organisations, public administration, state and economic apparatus and cultural institutions. Under pressure from the Communists and with the mediation of their supporters in the disintegrating Democratic Party, Action Committees were created within the party. On 12 March 1948, the first session of the Slovak National Council was held, by which date the mandates of twenty-five Democratic members had been removed. A further three Democratic members then resigned, the Communist Party removed one 'unreliable' member of their own, and a member for the Social Democratic Party also resigned. Thus, the number of members of the Slovak National Council was reduced from 100 to 70. Other members (sixty-four of them), who attended the session of the Slovak National Council on 23 March, voted to approve the new, now entirely pro-Communist, Board of Commissioners.[3]

The Communists took control of the districts, towns and villages by means of the Action Committees of the Slovak National Front. On 2 March, the Commissionership for the Interior, controlled by the Communists, instructed the district national committees to subordinate themselves to the decisions of the Action Committees. The national

---

[2] No. 03/110, box 1, Ústřední výbor Komunistické strany Československa [Collection of the Central Committee of the Communist Party of Czechoslovakia], Státní ústřední archív [Central State Archives], Prague.

[3] M. Barnovský, *Na ceste k monopolu moci. Mocenskopolitické zápasy na Slovensku v rokoch 1945–1948* [On the road to monopoly power. Power-political struggles in Slovakia 1945–1948] (Bratislava, 1993), p. 246.

committees (local government bodies), in which the Democratic Party had a majority, were dissolved and replaced with temporary administrative commissions headed by Communists. The result was that, of 3,348 communities in Slovakia, only 1,136 retained their local national committees. Only six of seventy-nine districts retained their original national committees. When the post-February purges were complete, apparently 26,332 members of national committees belonged to the Communist Party of Slovakia, 8,421 were not members of any party, 1,506 were members of the Party of Slovak Renewal, formed from the remnants of the Democratic Party, and 337 were members of the Freedom Party.[4]

The purges were principally aimed against those who disagreed or were thought to disagree with the new regime. The extraordinarily wide and indefinite criteria enabled the persecution of a very wide range of people. They were labelled 'unreliable for the people's democratic regime'; this announcement was followed by dismissal from work or re-assignment to work at a lower level. Failure to participate in the one-day general strike, organised by the Communist-controlled Revolutionary Trade Union Movement on 24 February 1948, often had the same result. Such a failure was classified as a violation of trade union unity. After the formal retrospective legalisation of the purges, it was possible to appeal against the decision of the Action Committee or works council of an enterprise, but this had no delaying effect. When the affected appealed, the penalisation remained valid, with a few exceptions.

To quantify precisely the number of persons struck by the post-February purges is very difficult. A later evaluation by the regime gave names of 1,573 victims, about half of whom lost employment. The others were suspended, re-assigned or pensioned off. However, these are only the names of persons from central institutions (commissionerships, army and police commands, broadcasting and so on); the extent of the purges was substantially wider. About 25,000 representatives of the non-communist parties were deprived of their membership of national committees. It is also necessary to add the victims of purges in organisations, university students excluded from study and others. The total number of people affected by the post-February purges in Slovakia can be estimated at 35,000–40,000; this does not include

---

[4] Box 131, file Povereníctvo vnútra [Collection of the Office of the Commissioner for the Interior], Sekretariát PV [Secretariat of the Commissioner for the Interior], Slovak National Archives (SNA), Bratislava.

[5] Box 86, Ústredný akčný výbor Slovenského národného frontu [Collection of the Central Action Committee of the Slovak National Front], SNA, Bratislava.

the owners of land and businesses who lost their property in the post-February land reform and nationalisation. In addition, many members of their families were branded for life.

The Communists also used the February 1948 coup to settle accounts with their pre-February political opponents, especially on the pretext of dealing with 'participants in the anti-state conspiracy' of autumn 1947. On 27 February 1948, leading functionaries from the Democratic Party were charged with slandering State Security (the political police controlled by the Communists) in autumn 1947. However, the majority successfully fled the country. It proved to be worse for those arrested before February 1948 but not tried before the coup. Compensating for this earlier 'failure', they could now be rapidly tried 'under the reliable direction' of the new regime. In April 1948, Ján Ursíny, former deputy prime minister of Czechoslovakia, was put on trial, followed in May 1948 by the former general secretaries of the Democratic Party, Jozef Kempný and Miloš Bugár. The Communists used these trials to prove that a conspiracy really had existed in autumn 1947, and was successfully defeated thanks to the firm measures employed by the Party, including the February coup.[6] These activities had yet to reach the intensity of the later round of political trials, especially because the Communist regime had still not sufficiently perfected the mechanism of preparing them.

Great political trials, a phenomenon typical of this period, began to be prepared in Slovakia around the end of 1948 and the beginning of 1949. They were part of the Party's 'firm course against reaction', that is, against persons and social groups opposed to communism. These political trials had both internal and international dynamics, which overlapped and influenced each other. Each 'domestic trial' also had an international dimension, and vice versa. There was a historical aspect to them as well, especially in connection with real and fictitious supporters of the Ľudák regime in Slovakia during the Second World War, but above all to the political practice of the time, and with reference to 'discovering the enemies of socialist construction'. The trials were held on both a national and a local level. They were so numerous in the so-called founding period of the totalitarian regime – that is, up to 1953 (with some continuation into 1954) – that only some of the most important can be mentioned.

[6] K. Kaplan, 'Czechoslovakia's February 1948', in N. Stone (ed.), *Czechoslovakia: Crossroads and Crises 1918–1988* (London, 1989), pp. 147–68; J. Lettrich, *History of Modern Slovakia* (New York, 1955).

The first political trials were connected with accusations of having links with Ľudák exiles and the pre-February 'anti-state conspiracy'. State Security arrested a group of almost sixty people on these charges by the beginning of 1949. Their prosecution was based on the accusation that, from 1947 to the time of their arrest, they had developed anti-state activity in the service of Ľudák exiles and the US Central Intelligence Agency (CIA). They were accused of obtaining economic information (for example about Danubian trade via Bratislava and about the railway trans-shipment facilities at Čierna nad Tisou on the Soviet frontier), political information about State Security, military information about security along the eighty kilometres of the Austrian frontier and other matters. The accused were primarily charged with leaking the sort of information that all states, regardless of their political system, kept secret and thus were committing a crime. But they also were charged with leaking information not considered sensitive in democratic states, though treated as such in Czechoslovakia, such as concerning relations within the leadership of the Communist Party of Slovakia, the causes of economic difficulties, the situation in the trade union movement and the composition of the national and Action Committees.[7] Albert Púčik, Anton Tunega and Eduard Tesár, the main representatives of the group, were tried in 1950 and sentenced to life imprisonment. However, after an appeal by the prosecutor, they were sentenced to death and executed in February 1951. The others received long prison sentences.

The so-called White Legion had a special place among the groups connected with the Ľudák exiles. In 1948, but especially in 1949, organisations and groups with anti-communist aims emerged in Slovakia, especially in the central and eastern regions. There was no centrally directed organisation, but rather a loose-knit collection of independent groups. The members expressed their opposition to the regime, from passive opposition, through intelligence activities, to attempts at armed resistance. The activities of these groups were inspired by exiles, both post-war (that is, Ľudák), and post-February (that is, democratic), and from spring 1950 also by the White Legion radio station, broadcasting from the American occupation zone in Austria. State Security described the White Legion as a mass paramilitary terrorist organisation, directed from abroad. State Security infiltrated some of these groups and even directed or provoked criminal activity. From spring 1951 to early 1952,

---

[7] Box 2147, file Ústredný výbor Komunistickej strany Slovenska, Generálny tajomník [Collection of the Central Committee of the Communist Party of Slovakia, General Secretary], SNA, Bratislava.

the White Legion groups were gradually eliminated and their members tried. Hundreds were arrested and almost a hundred were convicted in a series of trials. Four received the death penalty.[8]

Further trials were connected with contacts with post-1948 political exiles. After the Communist takeover, a large number of persons went into exile, especially leading functionaries of the Democratic Party. State Security closely monitored their political activities. The prosecution of Živodar Tvarožek and his associates was one of the most significant of these political trials. Tvarožek was accused of meeting Michal Zibrín, a former deputy for the Democratic Party, at Frankfurt am Main. Allegedly, Zibrín then sent him back to Slovakia to obtain economic information. In fact, Tvarožek had only been in Germany by accident, when an aeroplane *en route* from Bratislava to Prague was hijacked and landed in Munich. In January 1949, State Security arrested Tvarožek, and in June 1949 he was sentenced to death. After an appeal, the sentence was reduced to long-term imprisonment.[9]

Co-operating with anti-communist exiles was also one of the main accusations in the trial of Juraj Dlouhý, Vladimír Velecký and associates held in the middle of 1951. This trial was connected with 'uncovering espionage activity' emanating from the office of the French consul general in Bratislava, Manuel E. Manach, and implicated him personally. In 1949, State Security succeeded in infiltrating two of its agents into the consulate, so gaining access to diplomatic codes. On the basis of this success, State Security identified a group of people who opposed the Party and maintained contacts with political personalities in exile. State Security kidnapped the secretary of the consulate, Jean Fakan, a naturalised French citizen of Slovak origin, and forced him to testify about the 'espionage activity' conducted by the consulate. Dlouhý and Velecký were condemned to death in a public show trial and executed; others received long prison sentences.[10]

The prosecution of former partisan commanders, almost all Communists, had a specific place in the framework of these major political trials. These activities were connected with the conflict between the

---

[8] K. Bacílek, box 2304, file no. P 10/3, inventory number 16, Archív Ministerstvo vnútra Slovenskej republiky Nitrianska Streda [Archives of the Ministry of the Interior of the Slovak Republic at Nitrianska Streda], file Ústredný výbor Komunistickej strany Slovenska, SNA, Bratislava.

[9] J. Pešek, *Odvrátená tvár totality. Politické perzekúcie na Slovensku v rokoch 1948–1953* [The dark face of totalitarianism. Political persecution in Slovakia in the years 1948–1953] (Bratislava, 1998), p. 89.

[10] No. 4, SPt III. 61/51, Štátna prokuratúra Bratislava [Collection State Prosecution Service], State Regional Archives, Bratislava.

Soviet bloc and Yugoslavia. State Security started from the claim that the former partisans in Yugoslavia, who now held power, maintained contacts with the former partisans in Czechoslovakia, especially in Slovakia, and supported their efforts to seize power. The precedent for this policy was the constructed trial of the Yugoslav vice-consul in Bratislava, Šefik Kevič, and his associates in late August and early September 1950. Among the specific trials of partisan commanders, the trial of Viliam Žingor and his associates in autumn 1950 attracted the most attention. State Security used a group of agents provocateurs against Žingor, and invented a large group of 'enemies', who aimed to 'overthrow the people's democratic regime'. Žingor and two others were condemned to death and executed. The others were given long prison sentences.[11]

The trial of the so-called Slovak bourgeois nationalists proved to be the most important of the whole post-1948 period. Preparations began in 1951, but the prosecutions did not take place until April 1954. Leading functionaries from the Communist Party of Slovakia, headed by Gustáv Husák, were accused of 'bourgeois nationalism'. That is, they were charged with succumbing to the influence of the Slovak bourgeoisie and weakening links with the working class and Communist Party in the Czech Lands. After partial rehabilitation in 1963, Husák became the leading representative of the so-called normalisation regime of the 1970s and 1980s. His final fall from power came with the collapse of communism in Czechoslovakia at the end of 1989.

The trial was originally to be held earlier, but 'priority' was given to the trial of the 'Anti-State Conspiratorial Centre' headed by Rudolf Slánský at the end of 1952. A further reason for delaying the trial was that Husák, the most important person accused, refused to 'confess' to his crimes. The trial finally opened at the beginning of the 'thaw' following Stalin's death in March 1953, and after the removal of one of the main instigators of these show trials across the Soviet bloc, Lavrenti Beria. The chief prosecutor proposed the death penalty for Husák, but the court 'generously' reduced his sentence to life imprisonment. The others accused received prison sentences ranging from ten to twenty-two years.[12]

The regime made extensive use of political trials against organised religions, which represented a serious obstacle on the road to controlling all spheres of social life. This applied mainly to the Catholic Church, the

[11] No. 27, file no. P 10/1, inventory number 27, Archív Ministerstvo vnútra Slovenskej republiky.
[12] *Pravda*, 25 April 1954.

largest and best organised of the churches in Slovakia. Catholicism exerted a significant influence on the Slovak public, and tenaciously opposed pressure from the totalitarian regime. Ordinary priests and lay people were subjected to judicial persecution, but major trials of members of the Church hierarchy proved to have decisive political importance. The most important in Slovakia was the show trial of the 'traitor bishops', Ján Vojtaššák, Michal Buzalka and the Greek Catholic (Orthodox) Pavol Gojdič. In mid 1950, the leadership of the Communist Party of Czechoslovakia set out the basic political objectives of the trial: to deal with the actual accused, but also to intimidate and warn other members of the hierarchy, priests and lay people. The trial was held in January 1951 and convicted the bishops as 'typical representatives of the reactionary Church hierarchy and agents of the Vatican agents in Czechoslovakia'. Buzalka and Gojdič were sentenced to life imprisonment and Vojtaššák to twenty-four years.[13]

Thousands of people were affected by the political trials at the beginning of the totalitarian regime in Slovakia. Their number gradually increased from 1948. In 1948, 388 people were convicted for political reasons, in 1949, it was 2,111 persons, in 1950, 3,456, and in 1951, 2,949. Judicial persecution peaked in 1952, with 5,149 persons convicted of political 'crimes'. Almost the same number – 5,081 – were convicted in 1953, but in the following years the intensity of judicial repression and the number of convicted persons began to decline. A total of 19,134 people were convicted for political reasons in Slovakia during the period 1948–1953.[14] This was, and is, disturbing evidence of the character of the Communist regime during this period. However, even this large number of convicted persons was not the final total, since not all cases were successfully documented. The real final figure affected by judicial persecution was undoubtedly even larger.

Losing personal freedom by means of manipulated and deliberately held judicial proceedings was only one method of getting put in prison during this period. An inconvenient person or group of persons could also suffer this fate on the basis of non-judicial proceedings, for example,

[13] Ministry of Justice, *Proces proti vlastizradným biskupom Jánovi Vojtaššákovi, Michalovi Buzalkovi, Pavlovi Gojdičovi* [The trial of the traitorous bishops Ján Vojtaššák, Michal Buzalka and Pavol Gojdič] (Bratislava, 1951), p. 223.

[14] F. Gebauer, K. Kaplan, F. Koudelka and R. Vyhnálek, *Soudní perzekuce politické povahy v Československu 1948–1989. Statistický přehled. Sešity ÚSD AV ČR, sv. 12* [Judicial persecution of a political nature in Czechoslovakia 1948–1989. A statistical overview. Publications of the Institute of Contemporary History of the Academy of Sciences of the Czech Republic, vol. 12] (Prague, 1993), pp. 90–1, 122–4, 178–81.

via decisions made by national committees, security or military
authorities and the so-called ecclesiastical commissions. Assignment
to forced labour camps or auxiliary units of the army and internment
(especially of priests and religious figures) did not involve a formal
conviction, but in reality they also meant imprisonment and loss of
personal freedom, often for several years.

Assignment to a forced labour camp was used as a form of persecution
for those people who had not committed punishable offences, according
to the existing legal norms, but who were regarded as enemies of the
regime because of their social origins or political past. A period in a
forced labour camp, established on the basis of Act no. 247 issued on
25 October 1948, was recognised as a form of punishment. The regime
wanted to put 'class enemies' in these camps, by which they meant
former political opponents and state officials, owners of nationalised
companies, members of the free professions, bigger tradespeople and
others. However, in reality more than half of those sent to these camps
were workers, peasant-farmers and craftsmen. The reason behind this
decision was that many of the people the regime wanted to incarcerate
and 're-educate' knew of its intentions and so were cautious in their
opposition, while workers and peasant-farmers reacted to actions of the
regime more emotionally and openly. Commissions of regional and
district national committees decided on assignments for periods from
three months to two years. These commissions also had the power to
ban people released from forced labour camps from returning to
their original places of residence, to allocate new places of residence,
to order expulsion from flats and to take away permission to make a
living as a trader.[15] However, the main 'assigners' to forced labour
camps were the organs of State Security. They identified 'hostile persons' and the appropriate commissions approved the proposals, though
this was only a formality. In reality they were merely executive bodies
for State Security.

The number and location of forced labour camps in Slovakia changed
over the course of their existence. The best known were at Nováky, Ilava
and Ruskov near Košice. The Ruskov camp was the last to operate,
finally closing in June 1953. Perhaps 23,000 to 24,000 people passed
through the labour camp system in Czechoslovakia, with about 7,000 of
these in Slovakia.[16] These people directly experienced the harsh living
and working conditions of the camps, given by their character as coercive

[15] Box 104, file Poverenictvo vnútra, Pracovné tábory [Labour camps], SNA, Bratislava.
[16] Box 201, file Poverenictvo vnútra, Sekretariát PV, SNA, Bratislava.

facilities and by the arbitrary management of the camps, including cases of violence. However, it was not only those people in the camps who suffered, but also their families. Camp inmates feared for their relatives' well-being, since the forced labour camps provided only limited possibilities to earn money and support families. Payments for accommodation, food, equipment and so on were deducted from the wages of the inmates, and only part of what remained reached their families. However, the existence of forced labour camps affected more than just this relatively limited group of people. Assignment to camps, or even the threat or possibility of assignment, was taken into account by everybody and helped to foment an ever present atmosphere of fear.

Assignment to the 'auxiliary technical battalions' of the army was an even more drastic form of punishment without trial. Their formation began in the autumn of 1950, after the appointment of a new minister for defence, Alexej Čepička. They were disciplinary or punishment units, intended to isolate politically unreliable soldiers during their basic or reserve service, but in the end people freed from military service were also sometimes assigned to them. Under the pretext of re-education through work, they served as a source of cheap labour for the needs of the army and the wider economy.

The battalions were divided into two types: light, intended mainly for work in construction, and heavy, for work in mining. Men assigned to the mining battalions found themselves in the harshest working conditions, and those working on the construction of barracks, airports, stores and other buildings were little better off. The members of auxiliary technical battalions had a right to wages corresponding to the pay of a civilian worker, but they were usually assigned to the worst-paid work, which nobody else wanted. Payment for accommodation, food and clothing, income tax, medical insurance and a charge of 30 per cent of the net wage to support the military administration were deducted at source. The soldiers received only half the remainder; the rest was paid into a deposit account, which they could not use freely.

Apart from 'politically unreliable' persons, people with unsatisfactory class origins, such as the sons of former owners of large properties, people affected by the post-February purges and so on were also assigned to the auxiliary technical battalions. In addition, the majority of recruits of German or Magyar nationality, considered 'nationally unreliable', were assigned to these battalions, as were the Roma, illiterate soldiers and 'anti-social elements', that is, criminals. Apart from them, conscripts from the mining and construction professions were assigned to the appropriate auxiliary technical battalions even if they had not committed a political crime. The decisive criterion for assignment for political reasons was the classification E – politically unreliable. It has been estimated that about 5,500 Slovaks were assigned to these battalions because of the E classification before these units began to be phased out in 1953 and were finally dissolved in the spring of 1954. Across all of Czechoslovakia, some 25,000 people served in such battalions.[17]

The use of imprisonment without trial or internment was often used against Catholic priests and other religious leaders, and formed part of the Party's campaign against organised religion. It was connected with the political trials of Church members and it supplemented the larger persecution of the Church. The disbandment of the male religious orders in the spring of 1950 caused a great wave of internments. The decisive action occurred on the night of 13/14 April 1950, and the final dissolution of these orders was completed overnight 3/4 May 1950. More than a thousand monks were removed from their monasteries in Slovakia and interned in several so-called concentration (internment) monasteries, where they were to be 're-educated'.[18] Those monks who seemed to be less 'dangerous' were gradually released and some were allowed to undertake pastoral work, but the great majority refused to co-operate with the regime and were interned for several years. The younger ones were assigned to the auxiliary technical battalions. Younger priests were also moved there from pastoral work, although previously they had been free from the obligation to perform basic military service. In the middle of 1950, the seminaries were brought under state control and their number was drastically reduced; few students were able to complete their studies. According to the law, basic military service lasted two years, but for monks and priests it was extended to three years or more.

It was not only monks and priests who were put in the internment monasteries, but also parish priests considered 'reactionary' by the regime. Internment was used when people could not be dealt with via the judicial route, that is, when there were simply no laws justifying conviction. Therefore, it was enough for a state or security official to accuse somebody of 'becoming hostile to people's democracy and of organising opposition to it', and his fate was decided. At first, such people were assigned to forced labour camps, but this did not suit the regime, because they could influence others and, after some time in

[17] J. Bílek, *Pétépáci aneb Černí baroni uplně jinak* [Members of the auxiliary technical battalions or Black Barons with a difference] (Plzeň, 1996), p. 117.
[18] Box 5, file Slovenský úrad pre veci cirkevné [Collection of the Slovak Office for Ecclesiastical Affairs], SNA, Bratislava.

any case, they had to be released from the camp. It was more convenient to place them in internment monasteries, where they were isolated and could be held for as long as the authorities wanted.[19] The authorities attempted to 're-educate' or at least intimidate them, so that they would not cause trouble in future, but would rather submit to the interests of the regime.

The varying forms of persecution mentioned here are by no means exhaustive; many others were also employed by the regime during the first stages of its existence, against both real and potential opponents. Other forms included resettlement of 'undesirable' people from towns to the country, eviction of people from their homes, the forcible resettlement of owners of larger holdings from Slovakia to the Czech Lands, pressure on peasant-farmers to join agricultural co-operatives (so-called collectivisation) and persecution for national reasons, especially against the remnants of the ethnic German population. Persecution of various forms affected hundreds of thousands of people in Slovakia in the period 1948–1953. They were subjected to political and ideological pressure, as well as social and economic coercion. Many threatened citizens chose to emigrate due to fear of further persecution. From 1953, the intensity of persecution abated, but it did not stop completely. To varying extents it accompanied the Communist regime until its collapse in 1989.

The policies of persecution employed by the Communist Party after its seizure of power meant that the population could observe its methods at first hand. The Communists had many supporters in Slovakia after the war. They had lost the election in 1946, but they still received 30 per cent of the popular vote. Many citizens, who had been regaled with fine promises, were sobered by several years of Communist government, but it was too late. The totalitarian regime supported by the Soviet Union was determined not to share power, and had no intention of holding democratic elections.

The Communists still endeavoured to gain the people's support and therefore introduced some advantageous social measures. Unemployment did not formally exist, a social security system was introduced, and in the 1950s the standard of living was still not dramatically different from that in Western Europe. The Communists commenced a programme of industrialisation in Slovakia. They built some large and middle-sized enterprises, which provided new job opportunities.

---

[19] Box 211, file Slovenský úrad pre veci cirkevné [Collection of the Slovak Office for Ecclesiastical Affairs], SNA, Bratislava.

However, it gradually became clear that a centralised, planned economic system, without the operation of a free market and competition, was not capable of competing with the developed world. Production gradually stagnated and the standard of living declined. After the trials of the 1950s, this aspect of the Communist system became the target of popular criticism from and the cause of dissatisfaction on the part of the population. This finally led to many Communists concluding that the Communist system needed to be reformed, especially the economy.

19 Slovakia and the attempt to reform socialism in Czechoslovakia, 1963–1969

Stanislav Sikora

The reforms of socialism in Czechoslovakia and the subsequent so-called Prague, or Czechoslovak, Spring are usually associated, especially abroad, with the years 1968–1969. However, this social (and now historic) movement also had its origins in a 'pre-spring', the beginnings of which can be traced back to the earlier period of 1962–1963. At this juncture, the leading political force in Czechoslovakia – the Communist Party of Czechoslovakia (CPC) – was obliged to react to numerous pressures that emanated from an interconnected series of internal and international developments. In terms of the domestic situation, a number of pressing problems had developed in the economic, political and cultural spheres. Among a range of foreign influences, it was impossible for the Communists to ignore the consequences of the 22nd Congress of the Communist Party of the Soviet Union (October 1961), the Second Vatican Council (1962–1965) and a variety of cultural developments outside the Soviet bloc: in philosophy, literature, film, theatre and art as well as in the vibrant arena of popular music. The central problem lay, however, in the economic sphere, and these influences affected the whole social system in Czechoslovakia. How could the Party accept, and functionally transplant, Western scientific and technological advances into the socialist economic system? It was believed, with some justification, that this issue had to be tackled or the countries of the socialist community would be unable to continue to compete economically with the capitalist world.[1]

The first attempts at de-Stalinisation

The rehabilitation in 1963 of the persons wrongfully convicted in the staged political trials held between 1949 and 1954 proved to be a great

---

[1] R. Richta, *et al.*, *Civilizácia na rázcestí* [Civilisation at the crossroads] (Bratislava, 1966), p. 16; published in English as R. Richta and a research team, *Civilization at the Crossroads: Social and Human Implications of the Scientific and Technological Revolution*, 3rd expanded edition (Prague, 1969).

stimulus for further reform. The leadership of the CPC and the president of Czechoslovakia, Antonín Novotný (1904–1975), had already to contend with the second wave of de-Stalinisation in the Soviet Union that started with the 22nd Congress of the Communist Party of the Soviet Union. Naturally enough, this was an awkward situation for Novotný and his supporters, many of whom, including the president himself, had personally participated in the preparation of the show trials. From their perspective, it would have been best if the rehabilitation commission headed by Drahomír Kolder (the Kolder Commission was established in September 1962) had confirmed the justification for the trials, as the earlier Barák Commission had done in 1955–1957.[2] In the face of pressure from the highest Soviet Party and state functionaries, and in harmony with the tradition of the political subordination of Czechoslovakia to the Soviet Union, this situation could no longer be allowed to continue.[3] The Kolder Commission finally decided that all the political trials of members of the CPC from 1949 to 1954, including the notorious show trial of Rudolf Slánský and his associates, had been staged, and the victims were rehabilitated civically and largely also by the Party.[4] The commission's final report was submitted to the Party leadership at a session of the CPC Central Committee at the beginning of April 1963.

The fact that Novotný and his supporters could no longer impose and maintain their support for the show trials caused a significant decline in their political prestige. Nevertheless, Novotný was a skilful political operator, who shifted the blame on to other CPC representatives, such as Alexej Čepička, Rudolf Barák and Karol Bacílek, to name a few.[5] The resignation of Bacílek from the position of first secretary of the Central Committee of the Communist Party of Slovakia (CPS) in April 1963 proved to have significant consequences for Slovakia.[6] This was not least

---

[2] The Barák Commission was named after Rudolf Barák, a member of Politburo of the Communist Party of Czechoslovakia; Kolder was a secretary of the Central Committee of the CPC.

[3] K. Kaplan, *Kořeny československé reformy 1968* [The roots of the Czechoslovak reform of 1968] (Brno, 2000), p. 26.

[4] *Potlačená zpráva (Zpráva komise ÚV KSČ o politických procesech a rehabilitacích v Československu 1949–1968)* [The suppressed report (Report of the Commission of the Central Committee of the Communist Party of Czechoslovakia on the political trials and rehabilitations in Czechoslovakia 1949–1968)] (Vienna, 1970), pp. 160–1.

[5] J. Rychlík, *Češi a Slováci ve 20. století*, 2. díl, *Česko-slovenské vztahy 1945–1992* [The Czechs and Slovaks in the twentieth century, vol. II, Czech–Slovak relations 1945–1992] (Bratislava, 1998), p. 192.

[6] In Czechoslovakia there existed an 'asymmetric' model of government. The CPC existed in Slovakia alongside a Communist Party of Slovakia, which was subordinated to the CPC and had limited competency; there was not, however, a Communist Party of the Czech Lands.

as he was replaced by Alexander Dubček (1921–1992), who is closely associated with the partial liberalisation of the political regime in Slovakia several years before the Prague Spring began.

Alexander Dubček as head of the Communist Party of Slovakia

The results of the work of the Kolder Commission evoked great indignation in Slovakia. This was because the so-called bourgeois nationalists from the Communist Party of Slovakia – Gustáv Husák, Ladislav Novomeský, Daniel Okáli, Ladislav Holdoš, Ivan Horváth and others, who had advocated equality between the Slovak and Czech nations after the Second World War, in accordance with the Košice Government Programme of April 1945 – had not been fully rehabilitated by the Party. They continued to be branded as adherents of what was termed 'nationalist deviation', a serious crime in Communist eyes. Essentially, this meant that any effort to enhance the jurisdictional powers of the Slovak national bodies was still regarded as a political and ideological deviation. This position was rejected by a working group within the Kolder Commission that was concerned with the activity of the 'bourgeois nationalists in the Communist Party of Slovakia' – to no avail.[7]

Intense political pressure from Slovakia, where Dubček was already installed as first secretary of the CPS Central Committee and thus was the leading figure on the Slovak political scene, resulted in the establishment of a new commission, named the Barnabite Commission after the former Barnabite monastery in Prague where it met from July 1963.

Its findings were unambiguous: the whole affair of 'bourgeois nationalism in the Communist Party of Slovakia' was fabricated and all those who had been persecuted on the basis of this accusation were innocent. At the beginning of December 1963, the Barnabite Commission submitted its report to the Presidium of the Central Committees of the CPC and CPS. It recommended that the members of the leadership of the CPS convicted in 1950 should be cleared of any guilt and all persons unjustly sentenced should be fully rehabilitated. In addition to the

---

[7] On 22 March 1963, the Slovak members of the Kolder Commission sent the chairman of the Slovak National Council, J. Lenárt, a letter stating that the conclusions of the commission's report, which would be submitted to the plenary session of the CPC Central Committee in April 1963, were 'not in harmony with the conclusions reached by our working group, in the end unanimously, on the basis of long-term study and thorough discussions'. See V. Plevza, *Československá štátnosť' a slovenská otázka v politike KSČ* [Czechoslovak statehood and the Slovak question in the policy of the CPC] (Bratislava, 1971), p. 227.

Slovak 'bourgeois nationalists' listed earlier, Vladimír Clementis (1902–1952), former foreign minister of Czechoslovakia sentenced to death at Slánský's trial, and Karol Šmidke, former chairman of the CPS during the Slovak National Uprising (1944) and for a short time after the liberation, were also cleared of all guilt. The CPS Central Committee approved the report on 18 December 1963, and the CPS Central Committee followed suit the next day. Thus, a reprehensible chapter in the history of the CPC was formally brought to a close. Yet in reaching these conclusions, the Barnabite Commission had further undermined Novotný's position. He reacted the same way he had after the announcement of the results of the Kolder Commission: by identifying a person to bear the blame. That is, he immediately dismissed the prime minister of Czechoslovakia, Viliam Široký, who had been chairman of the CPS during the show trials and the main participant in the campaign against the 'Slovak bourgeois nationalists'.[8]

Naturally, the rehabilitation of these Slovak Communist politicians and intellectuals was also a rehabilitation of their efforts to secure jurisdictional powers for the Slovak national bodies, in line with the principle of equality between the Czech and Slovak nations based on the Košice Government Programme. Immediately after liberation from fascism, they, together with the representatives of the Democratic Party in the Slovak National Council, reiterated this principle by demanding the introduction of a federal system in Czechoslovakia.

The struggle for Slovak emancipation

By 1963, it was time to renew the struggle for Slovak national autonomy. It is worth noting that the Constitution of the Czechoslovak Socialist Republic, enacted in July 1960, had granted the Slovak national bodies only negligible jurisdictional powers. This fitted with the views of Slovak historian Miloš Gosiorovský, who stated at the end of March 1963 that 'the ethnic territory of the four million strong Slovak nation (49,000 km^2) contains no national state institution, so that the Slovak nation is the only Slavic nation (and even the only nation in the socialist camp) which on its territory possesses no national institutions of socialist state power'.[9] Slovak representation within the central bodies of the

---

[8] A. Dubček, *Nádej zomiera posledná. Z pamäti* (Bratislava, 1998), p. 102; translated into Slovak from the English-language original, *Hope Dies Last. The Autobiography of Alexander Dubček* (New York, 1993).

[9] Rychlík, *Češi a Slováci*, p. 194. The quotation is from M. Gosiorovský's *On Some Questions Concerning Czech–Slovak Relations in the Policy of the Communist Party of Czechoslovakia*, published in samizdat form.

Czechoslovak Socialist Republic was at best symbolic. After 1960, 14,000 persons worked for them, but only 521 of these had declared Slovak nationality.[10]

This situation was again the result of manipulation undertaken by Novotný and his supporters in the Party and state institutions. They skilfully exploited the weaknesses of the Slovak national institutions and the wave of subjectivist utopianism that was promoted by Nikita S. Khrushchev (1884–1971) and his political group around 1960. The idea was rapidly to catch up with and then overtake the capitalist states, and to build up communism, which would be accompanied by the rapid withering away of the state, including the development and the coming together (even fusion) of nations and nationalities.[11] In Czechoslovakia, this was expressed through a Communist-led revival of the discredited idea of political Czechoslovakism drawn from the inter-war period.[12]

In spite of expectations, an official Slovak autonomy movement, directed towards strengthening the powers of the Slovak national bodies and the establishment of a federation, did not begin until 1968. Gosiorovský's study, *On Some Questions Concerning Czech–Slovak Relations in the Policy of the Communist Party of Czechoslovakia*, evoked a political storm within the CPC and especially in Slovakia. This was not simply because he had raised the taboo issue of demanding a federation, but also because the concept itself had completely disappeared from the vocabulary of official Slovak representatives for several years.

Consequently, the official Slovak political leadership, headed by Dubček, found itself in a difficult situation. On the one hand, the CPC under Novotný, which included several Slovak politicians (among them the new prime minister of Czechoslovakia Jozef Lenárt and the chairman of the Slovak National Council, Michal Chudík), endeavoured to maintain the current status of the Slovak national bodies under the existing constitution of 1960. On the other hand, a group of Slovak intellectuals led by Gustáv Husák, which included journalists, especially the editors of the weekly *Kultúrny život* (Cultural life), research workers in the Slovak Academy of Sciences – historians, lawyers, economists, sociologists and others – were pushing for the emancipation of the Slovak nation. This corresponded to the aim of federalising Czechoslovakia

---

[10] Rychlík, *Češi a Slováci*, p. 186.
[11] The leading Slovak historian, Ľ. Lipták, commented ironically on this phenomenon in 1968: 'the Slovak national bodies began the withering away of the state in a worldwide context, to an extent that surpassed the ambitions of any Slovak politician' (Ľ. Lipták, *Slovensko v 20. storočí* [Slovakia in the twentieth century] (Bratislava, 1968), p. 337).
[12] *Ibid.*, p. 338.

along the lines set out after 1945. The official leadership of the CPS, especially Dubček and Vasil' Bil'ak, found it difficult to tolerate the existence of this group, especially as it developed into a kind of an unofficial opposition.

Given this situation, the leaders of the CPS and Slovak National Council pursued a policy of 'small steps' towards gradually strengthening the jurisdictional powers of the Slovak national bodies, within the framework of the asymmetrical constitutional model and in harmony with the existing constitution. The result of these efforts was a joint resolution of the CPC and CPS Central Committees entitled 'For a fuller assertion of the authority of the Slovak National Council' (7 May 1964).

In essence, this document aimed at co-ordinating the activities of the Slovak National Council and its commissions and departments with those of the central state parliament (the National Assembly) and its ministries. The central and Slovak institutions were jointly to prepare legislative norms and together secure their implementation. The resolution also proposed that the central Czechoslovak institutions would transfer part of their jurisdictional powers to the Slovak National Council – a move designed to increase their initiative in the process of preparing and implementing legal norms, and of curbing what was seen as excessive subordination to the central government institutions in Prague. From the legislative point of view, these changes were based on Act no. 93 passed in 1964, the provisions of which included renaming the executive bodies of the Slovak National Council commissionerships, as they had been called prior to 1960.

Before 1968, the culmination of these efforts was the passing of the Act on National Committees on 29 June 1967, under the terms of which the Slovak National Council regained the right to participate in directing 'national committees', that is, the local governmental institutions in Slovakia. This development strengthened the position of the Slovak National Council and its commissioners within the state administration. In reality, however, these new jurisdictional powers were purely formal. Power remained in the hands of the leaders of the CPC, an unrepentant group of centralists in both thought and deed. The state authorities were only executive, dependent instruments with their jurisdictional powers granted from above.[13] This situation was an entirely characteristic feature of a Soviet-type socialist political system, and involved the application of the basic theory that gave the leading role to the Communist Party.

[13] *Ibid.*, p. 329.

However, the struggle for emancipation of the Slovak nation in the 1960s (before 1968) also occurred on another level. The aforementioned thesis of the development and the drawing together of nations and nationalities as part of the building of socialism had been announced at the 22nd Congress of the Communist Party of the Soviet Union, and was also officially adopted at the 12th Congress of the Communist Party of Czechoslovakia, convened at the beginning of December 1962. The aims and dialectical relationship between these two 'apparently' contradictory phenomena, development on the one hand and the coming together of nations and nationalities on the other, were analysed by numerous conferences of historians and philosophers, which arrived (or had to arrive) at the desired theoretical results. Problems arose, however, when the politicians representing these nations and nationalities attempted to put these theoretical ideas into political practice. Moreover, another important issue (and for many nations and nationalities a dangerous one) was the fact that this coming together of nations and nationalities, including the 'overcoming of linguistic differences',[14] had to occur in the very near future.

The subjectivism of Khrushchev's leadership of the Communist Party of the Soviet Union rewrote the timeline for the 'transition to communism', which it was now believed could be achieved within the lifetime of the current generation. This revised objective meant that closer integration over such a short period was often understood as a sort of merger. This attitude led political representatives of nations struggling for national emancipation to emphasise development rather than the convergence advocated by ruling nations.

Despite the fact that the theses of joint development and of convergence of nations and nationalities were supposed to be understood in the sense of the dialectical unity of its components, in practice they soon dissolved into two mutually isolated opposites: that is, the development of nations and nationalities on the one hand and their ultimate convergence (merger) on the other. After Dubček came to power most Slovak political representatives cautiously, but unambiguously, oriented themselves towards the concept of the development of nations, especially the Slovak one. The Czech side, which controlled the central Party and state institutions, laid more stress on convergence. It was precisely this issue that fuelled growing differences between Dubček's leadership of the CPS and Novotný's leadership of the CPC, which affected the economic, cultural and other spheres of social life. Novotný's Party leadership

---

[14] *XXII. zjazd Komunistickej strany Sovietskeho zväzu* [The Twenty-Second Congress of the Communist Party of the Soviet Union] (Bratislava, 1961), p. 311.

Figure 16 Alexander Dubček

was unwilling to grant concessions on this issue or on the matter of the jurisdictional powers of the Slovak national bodies.

The struggle waged by Slovak political representatives for the 'development of nations and nationalities', that is, of the Slovak nation, also included the creation of space for objective research into recent Slovak history (within the limiting framework of Communist ideology). Thus, it enabled the study of important events in modern Slovak history, such as the Slovak National Uprising.[15]

The emphasis was on the compatibility of national consciousness and national identity with socialism. These activities by representatives of Slovak political life, headed by Dubček (Fig. 16), ran into strong opposition from Novotný and his supporters in the CPC leadership. Disputes

[15] In this regard, the following works were of great importance: G. Husák, *Svedectvo o Slovenskom národnom povstaní* [Testimony about the Slovak National Uprising] (Bratislava, 1964), and V. Prečan, *Slovenské národné povstanie. Dokumenty* [The Slovak National Uprising. Documents] (Bratislava, 1965).

about the interpretation of the thesis on the development and coming together of nations and nationalities thus became one of the driving forces behind the Prague Spring of 1968.

An economic and social crisis

Societal developments in the Czechoslovak Socialist Republic and in Slovakia at the beginning of the 1960s were also shaped by paradoxical tendencies and events, particularly in the economic sphere. On the one hand, there was outlandish propaganda about how the socialist world was rapidly catching up with, and overtaking, the capitalist states in terms of industrial production and the rapid building of communism. On the other hand, the Czechoslovak Socialist Republic experienced a deep economic crisis at the beginning of the 1960s that had a significant effect on the living standards of the population.[16]

This economic crisis clearly demonstrated that the possibilities for further extensive economic growth (the construction of more factories drawing their labour force from agriculture within the framework of so-called socialist industrialisation, while retaining the existing levels of equipment) were at best limited, and revealed the inability of the central administrative planning system to run the national economy in such a way as to satisfy the requirements of the population. In 1962–1963, economic losses amounted to billions of crowns, and the average annual growth rate of the national income in the period 1961–1965 was the lowest of the whole decade. The third Five-Year Plan, launched during this period, proved to be a complete failure. Moreover, the Czechoslovak econ-omy fell even further behind in its rate of modernisation – computerisation, the radical reduction of material and energy demands for production pro-cesses, the improvement of ecological conditions – which had been in process in Western countries for far longer. Put simply, the economic system being employed in Czechoslovakia could not deal with the scientific-technical revolution.

This situation led a group of economic theorists, headed by Ota Šik, to attempt to reform Czechoslovakia's planned economy. The ultimate objective was to loosen the centralised administrative planning system and the acceptance of certain free market principles. In other words, it was an attempt to synchronise, if this was at all possible, economic categories such as the social ownership of the means of production, the

---

[16] Two Prague-based protest singers, J. Paleček and J. Janík, described this situation in the refrain of one of their songs as follows, 'Coloured carpet woven of complicated plans – grey mats of certain facts'.

planned economy and the regulated market. The principles of the 'main directions for the perfection of the centrally planned economy and the work of the Party', were finally accepted at a session of the CPC Central Committee in January 1965.

In spite of their limitations, these reforms opened up real possibilities for change within the political system in at least three areas:

(1) They reduced the need for a huge Party and state apparatus that directly controlled every aspect of economic life. Within the apparatus of the CPC Central Committee two-thirds of personnel were involved in economic planning.[17]

(2) The transformation of socialist enterprises into relatively independent economic units, which were now obliged to show some respect for the laws of the market and efficient production, along with the growth of the role of professionally qualified personnel. This change then led to a preference for employees with relevant qualifications, rather than 'political consciousness'. This move threatened to undermine the mechanisms for the application of the 'leading role of the Party' in enterprises and works and thus in the entire national economy.

(3) The economic reform also brought to the fore the question of the role of trade unions and works collectives. They were to return to their original function – the defence of the economic and social interests of employees. The workers in state enterprises also wished to participate in a more autonomous style of management.

These developments ran contrary to the power-political interests of the ruling Party-state bureaucracy, which strongly opposed the economic reform. As a result, some important economic measures designed to enable transition to the new system of management were blocked at a session of the CPC Central Committee held at the beginning of May 1967. Consequently, economic reform came to a halt. This situation finally convinced reformist-minded Czechoslovak economists and politicians that, without basic reform of the political system, there could be no reform of the economy.[18]

Unfortunately, the economic reform concentrated primarily on the economic situation in the Czech Lands. Yet Slovakia was affected too,

---

[17] Z. Mlynář, *Mráz přichází z Kremlu* [Frost comes from the Kremlin] (Prague, 1990), p. 92; originally published as Mlynář, *Nachtfrost. Erfahrungen auf dem Weg vom realen zum menschlichen Sozialismus* (Frankfurt am Main, 1978).

[18] V. Kural, J. Pauer, J. Valenta, J. Moravec, F. Janáček, J. Navrátil and A. Benčík, *Československo roku 1968, obrodný proces* [Czechoslovakia in 1968, the regeneration process] (Prague, 1993), vol. I, p. 19.

especially by the restructuring of the wholesale prices of materials and goods, which was an inherent part of the reform. Wholesale prices had a direct effect on the majority of industrial enterprises in Slovakia, which produced mainly raw materials and semi-finished products for the Czech Lands. Such products sold for lower prices than the finished articles; at the same time the existing system of state subsidies was being abolished. This change therefore reduced the profitability of Slovak enterprises, and increased the differences in pay between industrial workers in the Czech Lands and Slovakia. There was also the problem of integrating large numbers of the Slovak labour force into production in the Czech Lands.[19]

In the light of these problems, Slovak reformist Communists and economists, such as Hvezdoň Kočtúch, Viktor Pavlenda and others, endeavoured to secure more investment for Slovakia in the interests of developing a more balanced economy across both halves of the state. In particular, they wanted to establish far more enterprises involved in making finished products in Slovakia, instead of semi-finished products destined to be completed in the Czech Lands.[20] They also pointed out that the Slovak national bodies should shape economic development in Slovakia through expert-directed legislation, resolutions and directives, while preserving the unity of the Czechoslovak socialist economy. In addition to Husák and his opposition group, these Slovak economists formed another section of the Slovak intellectual community that supported a federative re-organisation of Czechoslovakia. Unfortunately, Slovak and Czech economists did not reach any accord on this question. In Czech intellectual circles, the objections and suggestions put forward by these Slovak economists were regarded as being old-fashioned, dogmatic positions proposed by discontented provincials.[21]

The cultural elite as a driving force behind democratisation

The political changes of the early 1960s also influenced developments in other areas of social life, especially in culture and journalism. Dubček recalled in his memoirs that freedom of the press was one of the three main arenas of conflict in his struggle to liberalise Soviet-style socialism

---

[19] M. Štefanský, 'Spory o postavenie Slovenska v 60. rokoch' [Disputes about the situation of Slovakia in the 1960s], in M. Barnovský (ed.), *Slovenská otázka v dejinách Česko-Slovenska, 1945–1992* [The Slovak question in the history of Czecho-Slovakia, 1945–1992] (Bratislava, 1994), p. 46.

[20] Dubček, *Nádej*, p. 116.

[21] Lipták, *Slovensko v 20. storoči*, pp. 345–6.

in Czechoslovakia, together with the economy and Czech–Slovak relations.[22] The congress of the Union of Journalists held in May 1963 provided a powerful stimulus to reform the press in Slovakia. At first, this debate centred on topics discussed in Slovak journalism, especially in *Kultúrny život* and the CPS's central organ *Pravda*, such as the rehabilitation of Slovaks convicted in the show trials of 1949–1954 and wider Czech–Slovak relations. Over time these topics were widened to include discussions about the basic problems of socialist democracy, socialist realism as an artistic method, and questions of the cultural and political relations between East and West.

Among other things, a dialogue began between the Slovak writer Ladislav Mňačko and the German dramatist Rolf Hochhuth,[23] which stimulated a wide-ranging discussion. This dialogue eventually included leading Slovak writers and commentators, Edo Friš, Ladislav Novomeský, Miroslav Kusý, Eugen Löbl, Ján Uher, the Pole L. Lewandowski, Zoltán Fábry, a Magyar author living in Slovakia, and many others. While these exchanges in 1964 and 1965 contributed to the development of critical and creative writing in Slovakia during the second half of the 1960s, they irritated leading politicians in the CPC, especially Novotný and his allies. It is worth noting here that the majority of members of the CPS leadership, headed by Dubček, covered up for or defended many of the 'offences' and 'misdemeanours' committed by Slovak journalists.[24] Prior to 1968, the press in Slovakia enjoyed quite a high level of freedom. A good many Czech writers were envious and regularly contributed articles (which were unpublishable in the Czech Lands) to *Kultúrny život*.[25]

A congress of the Union of Slovak Writers held in April 1963 proved to be highly influential. After it, writers working in various genres intensified their efforts against the ideological and political control of the CPC, challenged its 'leading role' in culture, and criticised the dogmatic imposition of socialist realism as an artistic method.

[22] Dubček, *Nádej*, p. 114.

[23] This dialogue began when Slovak exiles wanted to publish Mňačko's *Oneskorené reportáže* [Delayed reportages] (Bratislava, 1963) in Germany. He did not allow its publication abroad to avoid its being politically misused – similarly to R. Hochhuth's ban on performances of his play *Der Vertreter* (The deputy) in the countries of the Soviet bloc.

[24] For more details, see J. Fabian, 'Analýza masových oznamovacích prostriedkov, 1967–1970' [Analysis of the mass media, 1967–1970], in *Slovenská spoločnosť v krizových rokoch 1967–1970* [Slovak society in the years of crisis 1967–1970] (Bratislava, 1992), vol. II, pp. 116–84. This volume was produced by the Governmental Commission for the analysis of historical events, 1967–1970.

[25] Dubček, *Nádej*, p. 106.

A plurality of different poetic forms and attitudes was characteristic of Slovak literature during the 1960s.[26] The older generation of writers, such as Vladimír Mináč, Alfonz Bednár, Ladislav Mňačko and Vojtech Mihálik, usually did not doubt the justification for the existence of socialism. What they sought to show was that the problems in society were not caused by the system, but by the individual. A possible exception was Ladislav Ťažký and his novel *Pivnica plná vlkov* (A cellar full of wolves), which was devoted to the problematic collectivisation of agriculture.

Existentialist philosophy appeared in some prose works (such as those of Dominik Tatarka and Ján Johanides). Many creative artists also rejected any ideological determination of their work. These efforts led to an international exhibition of young Slovak artists, called Danuvius' 68, held in Bratislava. While Slovak cinema never enjoyed the international successes of the Czech 'new wave', changes were occurring. From 1960, descriptive and schematic films, especially those heavily influenced by the constraints of socialist realism, became less popular. Existentialist and 'absurd' theatrical pieces by Slovak authors (P. Karvaš, J. Bukorčan) reflected the transformation that had swept the cultural landscape. The range of stage works of foreign provenance changed significantly, with plays by J.-P. Sartre, E. Albee, R. Hochhuth and others appearing in the repertoire of leading theatres. But it was the platforms of small theatres (a new phenomenon) that resounded with criticisms of the existing regime.

Youth culture in Czechoslovakia and Slovakia during the 1960s was heavily influenced by popular music. The new musical forms from the West – especially rock and roll – made young Slovaks aware of music affecting Western youth, experiencing a way of life that differed from the officially laid-down admonitions and directives of intellectual and cultural life they were familiar with in a totalitarian Communist regime. Many domestic pop and rock groups were formed, and some achieved international success. This penetration of alternative Western values into Slovakia, which emphasised individual freedom, caused great problems for the official youth organisation, the Czechoslovak Union of Youth. Even before 1968, a significant proportion of young people developed activities outside this union, forming various informal groups.

The beginning of the reforms

The on-going disputes between the Slovak and Czechoslovak (mostly Czech) political representation, characterised in the phrase 'Dubček

[26] For details, see D. Kováč, *et al.*, *Kronika Slovenska II. Slovensko v dvadsiatom storočí* [Chronicle of Slovakia II. Slovakia in the twentieth century] (Bratislava, 1999), p. 414.

versus Novotný', finally came to a head in the summer and autumn of
1967. At the end of August 1967, on an official visit to Slovakia,
Novotný stage-managed a confrontation with representatives of Slovak
culture. His purpose was to highlight what he regarded as the inadequacies in the implementation of the political line on the convergence and
merging of nations, and to intimidate the Slovak political leadership
with the threat of consequences in the Presidium of the CPC Central
Committee.[27] The conflict continued at the next session of the CPC
Central Committee, held on 30–31 October 1967, when Dubček criticised internal Party conditions for excessive centralisation and the
method of implementing of its 'leading role' in society, as well as inadequate investment into Slovakia's economy. The conflict culminated
in December 1967 and at the beginning of January 1968. By this time,
the majority of the CPC Central Committee had turned against
Novotný, and he failed to receive support from Leonid I. Brezhnev, the
general secretary of the Communist Party of the Soviet Union. These
events led to Novotný being removed from his post as first secretary
at a session of the CPC Central Committee on 3 to 5 January 1968,
when Dubček was elected as his successor.

After a hesitant beginning following Dubček's accession to power,
the process of democratising the Czechoslovak Socialist Republic, commonly referred to as the Prague Spring, began in earnest.[28] A number of
previously banned newspapers and magazines began to re-appear. The
publication of the Czech cultural weekly *Literární noviny* (Literary news),
banned after the Fourth Congress of the Union of Czechoslovak Writers
at the end of June 1967, was started again in mid February 1968. These
developments were widely regarded as the unofficial abolition of censorship, which was officially enacted on 26 June 1968. An avalanche of
critical articles began to uncover the realities of the totalitarian Communist regime and led to the rebirth of civil society in Czechoslovakia.
Thus, the cultural sphere became a driving force for social change. The
new, largely reformist leadership of the Communist Party of Czechoslovakia endeavoured to keep up with these developments. At the beginning
of April 1968, it adopted an Action Programme.

Compared to the situation that had existed before January 1968, the
Action Programme contained some revolutionary proposals, such as the

---

[27] Štefanský, 'Spory', p. 48.
[28] With regard to the development of Slovak society in the period 1968–1969, see
Slovenská spoločnosť' v krízových rokoch 1967–1970, I–III [Slovak society in the crisis
years 1967–1970, I–III] (Bratislava, 1992); and a selection of documents, *Slovensko v
rokoch 1967–1970* [Slovakia in the years 1967–1970] (Bratislava, 1992).

democratisation of the CPC, partnerships with non-communist parties and social organisations within the framework of the National Front. In addition, plans were laid to secure basic civil rights, to introduce a federal system, to democratise economic management through workers' councils and to create space for entrepreneurship, to permit privatisation in the service sphere, and to pursue a more active foreign policy in Europe. However, in spite of all these initiatives, the Action Programme came too late, because society was already concentrating on a new set of problems.

The resurgence of civil society began to create political organisations outside the framework of the National Front. These included the Club of Engaged Non-Party Members (KAN), K 231 (an organisation of people persecuted by the Communists, named after the number of the act under which they had been prosecuted) and its Slovak counterpart, the Slovak Organisation for Defence of Human Rights, led by Emil Vydra. The Social Democrats, absorbed by the Communists in 1948, also demanded their right to re-engage in the political process. This move was problematic for the reformist Communists, in view of old disputes about the leadership of the working-class movement, and profoundly negative reactions from the other socialist states led by the Soviet Union.

There was also a vigorous revival in religious life, especially in Slovakia. The Roman Catholic Church put an end to the Peace Movement of the Catholic Clergy, an organisation imposed by the regime, and replaced it with the Work of Concilar Renewal (whose name echoed the Second Vatican Council). The Greek Catholic Church, which had merged with the Orthodox Church under strong political pressure in 1950, was re-established. At the end of November 1968, there were also attempts to restore monastic life.

Soviet tanks – the end of the democratisation process

While these reforms did not move beyond Soviet-type socialism, the turbulent democratisation of all sections of society in the Czechoslovak Socialist Republic drew a very negative response from the other states in the Soviet bloc, with the exception of Romania. After various serious warnings, Czechoslovakia was invaded by the armies of the Warsaw Pact on 21 August 1968.[29]

[29] See Kováč, *Kronika*, p. 418; 300,000 foreign troops, more than 6,000 tanks and armoured vehicles, 4,000 cannons and 1,000 aircraft entered the territory of Czechoslovakia.

To begin with, opposition from the citizens of Czechoslovakia prevented Warsaw Pact forces from achieving their primary objectives of establishing a 'worker and peasant-farmer' government and revolutionary tribunals to deal with the 'counter-revolutionaries'. The Moscow Protocol, released after talks held in Moscow on 23–6 August 1968, raised the possibility of maintaining these democratic developments. However, time was against the reformers, and these delays favoured their foreign and domestic opponents. A group of 'realists' – Ludvík Svoboda (president of the state), Husák, Lubomír Štrougal (prime minister) and others – finally emerged. The members of this group soon realised that their explicit submission to Soviet pressure would ensure that they received positions of power in the state administration.

Husák's position caused great surprise in Slovakia, because before the occupation he had been the informal leader of the Slovak reformist Communists. Nevertheless, it was Husák in whom the Soviet Party leadership placed their trust. After he replaced Dubček as first secretary of the Central Committee of the Communist Party of Czechoslovakia in April 1969, Husák initiated a process now known as 'normalisation'. Thus Husák, a Slovak, replaced another Slovak, Dubček, but wider society, especially in the Czech Lands, perceived this change negatively. The aim of normalisation was to extinguish the democratisation process and return Czechoslovak society to the state of affairs before January 1968, or, if possible, as of April 1963. The Communist Party was thoroughly purged of all reformers in 1970, and a fifth of its 1,535,537 members were summarily expelled.[30] They found themselves forced on to the margins of society and remained humiliated and persecuted until the Velvet Revolution of 1989.

This process of democratisation occurred across most of Czechoslovakia, although it is necessary to emphasise that, after January 1968, it was Czech society – its political and intellectual elites took the initiative – that became the moving force. Developments in Slovakia differed from those in the Czech Lands primarily because democratisation proceeded less intensively. However, many Slovaks were very interested in the federal re-organisation of the state. Their demands for the federalisation of Czechoslovakia gradually became a central component of the democratisation process, often to the detriment of other, perhaps more significant aspects.

---

[30] In Slovakia 53,206 Communist Party members were expelled, that is, 17.5 per cent of the membership: *ibid.*, p. 437.

20 Slovakia's position within the Czecho-Slovak federation, 1968–1970

Jozef Žatkuliak

In 1968, a series of social reforms began in Czechoslovakia with the aim of creating a democratic form of socialism. This process has since been variously described as 'socialism with a human face', the 'Prague Spring' or the 'regeneration process'. The reform movement was directed 'from above', because it was implemented by reformist representatives of the Communist Party. But both the Czech and Slovak halves of the country supported these reforms. In January 1968, Alexander Dubček, the Slovak politician, was elected first secretary of the Communist Party of Czechoslovakia (CPC), and this event is commonly regarded as the beginning of this process; other reformist Communists also secured a range of further political and state positions.

Slovakia's role in the social reforms

The basis of the constitutional settlement between the Czech and Slovak nations was the concept of the mutual recognition of expressions of their national sovereignty. The settlement of relations between the Slovak and Czech nations was predicated upon the principle of national equality (*rovný s rovným*, or 'like with like'), but this principle of recognition of Slovak self-rule was not applied after 1945. As a result, many Slovaks demanded that this situation should be corrected by means of the federalisation of the state.

Federalisation soon became one of the constituent components of the wider reform process, and settling the constitutional relations between the Czech and Slovak nations thus became a priority. This process not only presupposed a sense of political symmetry, but also (state) equality, equal rights and self-determination of both nations. The Slovak and Czech question had therefore to be solved on the basis of mutual respect for national interests. As a result of their historic experiences, Slovaks also had a clear natural interest in the political and constitutional rehabilitation of the Slovak question. This issue also related to the persecution of the churches in Slovakia by the Communist regime. By raising both the

315

national and the religious questions, Slovaks had widened the scope of these on-going reforms, giving them a deeper democratic character. While Slovak reformers emphasised the demands for federalisation, Czech reformists viewed this issue as something 'additional' to the wider reform movement. Although at first Czech society did not fully accept this concept of national and state self-realisation as being advantageous, by the summer of 1968 it had come to support the principle of federalisation.

The limitations on the federalisation of the state

The federalist reformers faced three types of limitations in trying to implement their proposals: the first of these was the totalitarian political system and the entrenched position of the Communist Party, which predetermined just how far the federalisation of the state could proceed. Perhaps unsurprisingly, the Communist Party viewed federalisation as a threat to its monopoly on power, especially as this plan would have shared authority out between several political and state centres, and because it presupposed the federalisation of the Party and the whole political system. Moreover, the relatively independent administration granted to each half of the new federation would have undermined the centralist principles of Communist political power.

The second limitation the reformists faced was the transformation of the unitary Czechoslovak state into a more complex state formation. With the exception of the remaining national minorities, the common state contained two main state-forming nations – the Slovaks and the Czechs – who shared numerous social, historical, political and economic connections, although they had some fundamental differences. Slovakia had only half the population and economic strength of the Czech Lands (Bohemia and Moravia). Constitutionally the way forward was the thoroughgoing federalisation of the Czechoslovak state.

The third limitation was the different ways in which the two peoples understood the concepts of national and state identity. In the Czech nation, these identities were often identified with Czechoslovakism and the Czechoslovak state. This was not how most Slovaks felt. They wished to achieve their statehood against the background of their history of national emancipation and identification. Consequently, it proved difficult to promote the idea of federation and Slovak national interests in Czech society. This problem was compounded by the fact that by 1960 the political centralisation of the Czechoslovak state had already been achieved. This was a sensitive point because it involved the elimination of the jurisdiction of the Slovak national institutions – the Slovak National Council, which was the legislative body, and the Board of Commissioners (the Slovak government).

The origins of the Constitutional Act on the formation of a Czecho–Slovak federation

In March 1968 the Slovak National Council, proposing settlement of bilateral constitutional relations on the basis of the principles of equality, equal rights and national self-determination, stated that it appreciates 'with deep satisfaction, that an inseparable part of the democratisation process is the task of consistently equalising the positions of our two state-forming nations – the Czechs and Slovaks – and the appropriate constitutional expression of this measure'.[1]

Also, the Action Programme of the Communist Party of Czechoslovakia took into account other Slovak ideas and demands. The government of the Czechoslovak Socialist Republic committed itself to establishing a federal system as well. The possibility of one nation using its majority to impose its will on the other where basic questions were concerned had to be excluded by the constitution. The gradual removal of any remaining asymmetry in relations between the Czechs and Slovaks and the establishment of full equality had also to be accomplished. On this issue, the initiative of the Presidium of the Slovak National Council was of particular importance, especially the fulfilment of its resolution no. 38, issued on 11 March 1968, designed to develop various proposals for the future federalisation of the state.

In the wake of the government's resolution of 15 May 1968, a 75-member political committee was established to draft a 'Proposed Constitutional Act on a new solution of the constitutional relations between the Czechs and Slovaks'. Its chairman was Prime Minister Oldřich Černík. This committee consisted of representatives of the political parties and the government, members of parliament and representatives drawn from Czech and Slovak scientific and cultural spheres. A thirty-member governmental commission of experts headed by Deputy Prime Minister Gustáv Husák was also formed to prepare the Constitutional Act on the Czechoslovak federation.

Various other sub-commissions were created within this framework, each with its own chairman and deputy chairman: Karol Laco and Pavol

---

[1] 'Zápisnice zo zasadaní pléna, 1944–1968, stenografická správa zo 14–15.3.1968' [Records of Plenary Sessions 1944–1968, shorthand report from 14 to 15 March 1968], file SNR [Slovak National Council Collection], inventory number 864, box 4, pp. 226–9, Slovak National Archives (SNA), Bratislava.

Pešek in the constitutional legal sub-commission, and Antonín Červinka and Viktor Pavlenda in the economic sub-commission. The government also established an expert commission to examine solutions to the economic problems raised by the new constitutional organisation of the republic. This commission was headed by Deputy Prime Minister Ota Šik. The creation of these working commissions made possible progress towards the federal re-organisation of the state.

A number of other important factors also influenced this process; in the first place, on 24 June 1968, the National Assembly approved Constitutional Act no. 77/1968 on the preparation of the federal organisation of the Czechoslovak Socialist Republic. This act established the Czech National Council as a temporary institution, tasked with the constitutional and political representation of the Czech nation. This body was empowered to carry out activities connected with preparation of the federation, to express the Czech national political position, to prepare the system of Czech state bodies, and to participate in the devising of the Constitutional Act on the Czechoslovak federation. The Czech National Council was to elect the National Assembly, on the proposal of the National Front, from among the deputies of the National Assembly elected in the Czech Lands and other important representatives of the Czech nation. In addition, Act no. 77 established the constitutional basis for the legal reconstruction of the unitary (asymmetrical) Czechoslovak state into a symmetrical and federal entity.

Problems with the federalisation of the state

From the outset, the significance of federalisation within the wider reform movement was underestimated. The idea that democratisation (which in the Czech Lands related to the political system) and federalisation (which in Slovakia pertained to the state) were inherently contradictory processes hindered the preparations. This is how Petr Pithart, one of the Czech experts active in 1968, later highlighted the unfortunate division regarding Czechs as democrats and Slovaks as federalists: 'The principle of federation was and needed to be an inseparable part of all the democratic strategies. Democratic reforms that avoided the problem of the equality of the two nations would not have been democratic reforms'.[2] Thus this division between the processes of democratisation

---

[2] P. Pithart, *Osmašedesátý* [The year 1968] (Prague, 1990), p. 116; Z. Jičínský, *Vznik České národní rady v době Pražského jara 1968 a její působení do podzimu 1969* [The origin of the Czech National Council in the period of the Prague Spring of 1968 and its activity until autumn 1969] (Prague, 1990), pp. 31–3.

and federalisation complicated the relations between the two nations and the progress of the reforms themselves.

Moreover, although the Czech representatives in these negotiations were committed to reforming the state, they also displayed an excessive attachment to the preservation of the country as a single unit, thus upholding the identity of a Czechoslovak rather than a Czech state. Therefore, the Czech side, represented by the lawyers Zdeněk Jičínský, Jiří Grospič and others, proposed the creation of a 'centralist federation'. Put simply, a significant proportion of the Czech representatives were not prepared to accept justified Slovak proposals regarding the coexistence of the two state units.

Reaching a mutually acceptable agreement on the expression of the principle of equality between the Czechs and the Slovaks also proved to be easier said than done. Slovak experts, including Karol Laco, Vojtech Hatala, Viktor Pavlenda, Hvezdoň Kočtúch and others, proposed that the National Assembly, as the highest state body in the federative state, should be divided into a 'Chamber of the People' and a 'Chamber of the Nations'. In the second chamber, the two nations would each have an equal number of representatives.

Similar problems surfaced regarding the structure of the executive bodies, especially the division of competencies between the federal and national bodies. It had been agreed that only the areas of national defence, foreign policy, the currency, federal administration, state reserves and international treaties would fall under the exclusive remit of the federal institutions. The interior (home affairs), mining, education, health and a further twenty-five areas would fall under the exclusively national remit. Finally, finance, planning, foreign trade, technology, prices, labour and social affairs, statistics, transport, communications, customs and the federal currency-issuing institution (bank) would fall under joint remit (though there were to be national issuing banks).

Husák submitted disputed topics to the Presidium of the government of the Czechoslovak Socialist Republic for further consideration on 26 July 1968. It decided that the federal parliament was to have two chambers, with the principle of general democracy applying to the first chamber and the principle of national parity applying in the second. The Chamber of the People was to have 200 members, elected in proportion to the total population of the state, while the Chamber of Nations was to have 200 members, divided equally between the two nations. The two chambers would have equal rights and would vote on a simple majority basis, except in the cases when legislation came under the ban that limited the Czechs using their majority to impose their will.

Agreement was also reached on the content of the Constitutional Act on the federation. It was to be a comprehensive act detailing the structure of the federal and national bodies, and their federal, national or joint competencies. The principle of parity was not to be applied mechanically inside the federal government; instead there were to be state secretaries within all federal ministries, and federal committees were to be formed on the basis of the principle of parity.

But disagreements persisted between the Slovak and Czech members of the government commission, especially in reference to some key aspects of the proposed constitution of the federation. The Slovak representatives took it for granted that the economic reform could be put into effect only after the introduction of the federal system. At the same time, the economic competencies of the national states within the federation were to be clearly demarcated. In particular, they were each to have the necessary economic instruments to manage and finance industry in their respective territories. Therefore, the economy of the Czechoslovak Socialist Republic was henceforth to be composed of two national economies.

The Slovak view of how this re-organisation of the state should progress was set out by the Slovak National Council in June 1968: 'With the implementation of the demand that the federal organs should have primary judicial authority we would come into conflict with the theory of the sovereignty of the nation with all kinds of unfavourable consequences ... The bearers of original jurisdictional powers are the national state units, which transfer part of their jurisdictional powers, in equal degree, to the federal state and its institutions'.[3]

National sovereignty was to become primary, operating together with the sovereignty of the federal state, as part of a whole. This emphasis on the national principle in state and economic decision-making was a substantial shift away from the guiding principles of the previous centralist regime. But Czech economists, headed by Ota Šik, who opposed the federalisation of the Czechoslovak economy, were thinking of an economic reform covering Czechoslovakia as an entity.

There was a further problem. Although the government commission of experts agreed on a bilateral federation based on the national principle, representatives from Moravia and Silesia proposed that they become a third constituent member of the re-organised state. The alternative was

[3] Zápisnice zo zasadaní pléna, 1944–1968 [Records of Plenary Sessions, 1944–1968], Stenografická správa zo 17. schôdze SNR 27.6.1968 [Shorthand report from 17th meeting SNR 27.6.1968], inventory number 864, box 4, p. 46, file SNR, SNA, Bratislava.

to retain the two-member system in which Moravia and Silesia's position would be secured on the basis of a provincial constitutional structure. At first, Moravian and Silesian representatives pleaded for the tripartite option. However, after the so-called Moravian Day, held in June 1968 at Koloděj castle (the 'seat' of the government commission of experts) they had to accept the plan for a bipartite federation based on the national principle that secured Moravia's and Silesia's position within the territorial administration of the (Czech) state.

The agreements that emerged from the discussions held by state and political organs resulted in the 'Proposed principles of the federal organisation of the Czechoslovak Socialist Republic', which the expert commission submitted to the government on 7 August 1968. This document contained the political, legal and economic principles of the Czechoslovak federation. It emphasised that the federation was to be based on the national principle and that the political and economic principles had to be congruent.

21 August 1968 and the end of democratic conditions

The occupation of Czechoslovakia, on 21 August 1968, by the armies of five Warsaw Pact countries substantially changed the conditions for putting the finishing touches to the Constitutional Act of the Czecho-Slovak federation, and further reform of Slovak and Czech society. The military invasion violated the sovereignty of the Czecho-Slovak state, and henceforth Moscow began to intervene directly in its internal political development. It became obvious that the federalisation of the state was dependent on reforming the political system. The Kremlin, however, strictly rejected plans for the federalisation of the Communist Party and any 'revision' of its position in the political system.[4] The Moscow Protocol of August 1968, in effect a dictat recalling the Munich Agreement in the way it was worded, was the beginning of 'normalisation' (the official term was 'consolidation'), that is, the re-imposition of the neo-Stalinist system and the suppression of democratic and autonomous

---

[4] J. Vondrová and J. Navrátil, *Mezinárodní souvislosti československé krize 1967–1970. Září 1968–květen 1970* [The international connections of the Czechoslovak crisis of 1967–1970. September 1968–May 1970] (Prague and Brno, 1997), pp. 116–35. For more details on the period, see V. Kural (ed.), *Československo roku 1968* [Czechoslovakia in 1968], vol. I *Obrodný proces* [The renewal process] (Prague, 1993); M. Bárta, O. Felcman, J. Belda and V. Mencl, *Československo roku 1968*, vol. II, *Počátky normalizace.* [The beginning of normalisation] (Prague, 1993); G. Golan. *Reform Rule in Czechoslovakia: The Dubček Era 1968–1969* (Cambridge, 1973); Z. Hejzlar and V. Kusin (eds.), *Czechoslovakia 1968–1969. Chronology, Bibliography, Annotation* (New York, 1975).

elements across all areas of Czech and Slovak society. Basically, this was a return to the situation that had existed before 1968.

In spite of these events, preparations for the federalisation of the state continued even after the occupation. An explanatory report on the proposed Constitutional Act on the Czechoslovak federation was produced on 26 September 1968. It was largely based on the submissions made by the Slovak National Council to the government commission of experts and its key document 'The proposed principles of the federal organisation of the Czechoslovak Socialist Republic' of 7 August. The report noted that the creation of a federal state union, made up of two self-governing and sovereign nations, originated in their right to self-determination and their common interest to live together. It went on to emphasise the 'inseparable' connection of the federation with the ideas of 'socialist democracy'. That is, 'the federation can only properly function within a democratic political system' if the federal principle is fully adopted by the National Front, the Communist Party and other social organisations. The report continued: 'The meaning and purpose of the Czechoslovak federation are a democratic settlement of the constitutional relations between the Czech and Slovak nations'.[5]

But by then the leading Slovak Communist, Gustáv Husák, contended that a unified political and state leadership, as well as a unified political system, was necessary, because the leading role of the Communist Party required it. When he acceded to power in April 1969, he abandoned the original conception of the federation as a union of two national states. In ruling political circles he promoted neither the federalisation of the Communist Party nor economic reform within the federalised state, since the latter would have caused the 'disintegration' and weakening of the Communists' hold on political and state power.

The invasion of Czechoslovakia brought to an abrupt end the 'Czecho-Slovak Spring', the essence of which had been to reform the Soviet model of socialism and develop a more democratic and humane model of society. By putting an end to the democratisation process, the invasion sapped the very foundations of a Czecho-Slovak federation.

---

[5] Osobný fond Vojtecha Hatalu. Dôvodová správa k návrhu ústavného zákona ... z 26.9.1968 [Personal collection of Vojtech Hatala. Explanatory report on the proposed Constitutional Act of 26 September 1968], SNA, Bratislava pp. 1–2. On the proposed act, see J. Žatkuliak, *Federalizácia československého štátu, 1968–1970. Vznik česko-slovenskej federácie roku 1968* [The federalisation of the Czechoslovak state, 1968–1970. Origin of the Czecho-Slovak Federation 1968] (Prague and Brno, 1996), vol. I, pp. 256–300.

It is not true, as is sometimes alleged, that the arrival of Soviet tanks granted federation to the Slovaks as compensation for the loss of democratic socialism with a human face.[6] Such a claim ignores the nation-state aspirations of Slovak society at least from 1945, its attitude to the reform process and especially its civil resistance to the occupiers of the homeland in August. At that time Slovak society did not concentrate on federalisation, but understood what was at stake: the defence of the reform process, human rights and state sovereignty as a whole.

The Constitutional Act on the Czecho-Slovak federation

The basis for the proposed Constitutional Act on the federation of September 1968 was federative organisation of the state along national principles. This was to be an expression of mutual agreement between the national-political representations of the Czech National Council and Slovak National Council. The political foundation of this federation was to be socialist democracy. The division of responsibilities distinguished between areas of exclusively federal functions (national defence, foreign affairs and the like), joint tasks (foreign trade, planning, finances) and exclusively national competencies (industry, construction, education, health, the Supreme Court and the General Prosecutor's Office). The Czechoslovak economy was to be regarded as a synthesis of the two national economies. A further important feature of the proposals was the general democratic principle of parity, derived from the idea of the two states being equal and bearing equal rights. This presupposed a ban on the imposition of majority decisions on pivotal legislative acts.

A complex variant of the Constitutional Act on the federation was discussed at talks between the Presidia of the Slovak National Council and Czech National Council on 30 September 1968. The political 'Committee for the preparation of the new constitutional organisation', the government commission and the expert commission also discussed this document on 1 October. In spite of the existing complex political situation, the report from the government talks emphasised that 'the purpose and aim of the Czechoslovak federation are a democratic settlement of the constitutional relationship between the Czech and Slovak nations. Therefore the federation is based on the national principle; it originates from conditions that exist in Czechoslovakia

---

[6] See M. Kusý, 'Slovenský fenomén' [The Slovak phenomenon], in R. Chmel (ed.), *Slovenská otázka v 20. storočí* [The Slovak question in the twentieth century] (Bratislava, 1997), p. 473.

and fully respects them. Its specific feature is that it is composed of two equal national participants'.[7]

The remaining unresolved issues were decided on 17 October by a political commission made up of members drawn from the Presidium of the Central Committee of the Communist Party of Czechoslovakia. The participants were Prime Minister Oldřich Černík, First Secretary Dubček, Chairman of the National Assembly Josef Smrkovský, Deputy Prime Minister Husák, Deputy Prime Minister Peter Colotka, Chairman of the Slovak National Council Ondrej Klokoč, and Chairman of the Czech National Council Čestmír Císař. The commission supported the completion of the Constitutional Act, because the existing political situation had to be settled, including the outstanding disputes between the Czechs and Slovaks. It therefore decided that the two chambers of the Federal Assembly would have equal rights, and the national councils would delegate members to the Chamber of Nations.

Constitutional Act no. 143/1968, of 27 October 1968, on the federation was approved by a plenary session of the National Assembly. A signing ceremony was performed at Bratislava castle by the president of Czechoslovakia, Ludvík Svoboda, on 30 October. This legislation brought changes in the structure of the state and its organs, in the mechanisms for the functioning of the state, in its character and in its territorial organisation. More importantly, the Constitutional Act marked the formation of the Czechoslovak federation, in which the Czech and Slovak nations realised their right to self-determination and self-government in the form of national statehood, as represented by the Czech Socialist Republic and Slovak Socialist Republic, united together in a single federative state. It made clear that the basis of the new state was a voluntary union of the two republics. The act was the result of compromises reached between Czech and Slovak representatives, but many questions remained unresolved because of the internal political situation after the invasion of the Czechoslovak Socialist Republic.

The implementation of the federative system

On 1 January 1969, the Slovak Socialist Republic and Czech Socialist Republic were duly established. The national councils and national governments became the highest institutions of state and executive power respectively within each national state. The two-chamber Federal

---

[7] V. Plevza, *Československá štátnosť a slovenská otázka v politike KSČ* [Czechoslovak statehood and the Slovak question in the policy of the CPC] (Bratislava, 1971), pp. 336–7.

Assembly, the highest institution of state power of the Czechoslovak Socialist Republic, applied the principle of 'like with like' within the Chamber of Nations. However, the 'federative' Czecho-Slovak Republic was established in a peculiarly undemocratic way. The term 'federative' had been omitted from the official title because Czech representatives had rejected it. Furthermore, the two chambers of the Federal Assembly – the Chamber of the People and Chamber of Nations – were established by a public show of hands. Parliamentary elections were supposed to be held in November 1968, but the Communist regime was concerned about the outcome and did not allow them to proceed.

The chairman of the Slovak National Council was Ondrej Klokoč, and Čestmír Císař was chairman of the Czech National Council. The Slovak and Czech prime ministers were Štefan Sádovský and Stanislav Rázl. The Slovak government appreciated the formation of the national state proclaiming:

Thus, after 120 years of struggle by the Slovak nation for its own statehood, we are joining the nations of Europe and the world as their self-governing and equal partner. The formation of the Czechoslovak federation, and the Slovak Socialist Republic within it, is an event of historic importance in the complex and, at times, painful history of our nation. Slovakia's own state structure is the culmination of its struggle for economic, cultural and general human progress ... Slovak statehood is at the same time also the natural fruit of an age-old effort at mutual understanding and accord between the Czech and Slovak nations.[8]

From the point of view of the Slovak National Council, as the supreme legislative organ in Slovakia, it was important that the Constitutional Act on the Czechoslovak federation included articles nos. 37 and 38, which enabled it to utilise the jurisdiction of the Federal Assembly when the affairs of the republic and its legislation were concerned. Apart from this, the Slovak National Council could submit its proposals for legislation directly to the Federal Assembly of the Czechoslovak Socialist Republic. The Slovak National Council could utilise this procedure in the interest of national sovereignty and the rights of Slovakia. It could also use its legislative initiative in cases of joint competencies of the federation and Slovakia. Thus, a balanced relationship and an equal position in relation to the Federal Assembly were achieved by the application of the principle of 'like with like' at the state level as well.

[8] J. Žatkuliak, 'Realizácia ústavného zákona o československej federácii od októbra 1968' [The implementation of the Constitutional Act on the Czechoslovak federation after October 1968], *Historický časopis*, 40 (1992) 3, 356–69.

From its establishment in January 1969, the Slovak government experienced many problems. It had to struggle to enforce some of its rightful powers, and to ensure that specific conditions in Slovakia were taken into account. Slovakia was also at a disadvantage because both the federal and the Czech national bodies were based in Prague. Problems arose primarily regarding those responsibilities that were shared jointly between the federal and the national bodies, especially in the economic area. The greatest problem lay in the general demarcation of these competencies. Constitutional Act no. 43 had shifted them in favour of the federation, although the Slovak side opposed this position; Constitutional Act no. 171/1968 further widened the activities of the federal ministries and the Federal Assembly. In the event, disagreements over joint competencies continued from 1969 to 1989.

'Normalisation' of the Czecho-Slovak state

The principle of equality within the federation also became a matter of enduring disputes. The principle was violated in the cases of legislative loopholes and the problematic division of competencies between the federal and national bodies. It was Alexander Dubček, the symbol of the Czecho-Slovak Spring, who drew attention to this state of affairs. Removed in April 1969 from the leadership of the Communist Party as part of the 'normalisation' process, he occupied the post of chairman of the Federal Assembly. In his speech to the Slovak National Council in July 1969, it is clear that he was well aware of the political pressures designed to recentralise the state. While he accepted these pressures, he continued to call for the observance of laws, civil rights and freedoms.

It was after Husák replaced Dubček as first secretary that an unambiguous policy designed to centralise state power in the hands of the Communist Party was rigorously applied. Empowering Act no. 117 passed in October 1969 and the so-called Party interviews led to purges across state institutions. The position of the federal bodies was strengthened, but not those of the constituent republics. Decisive power remained with the political and state centre. This course of action conflicted with the establishment of the federation and the enactment of national statehoods. Quite simply, the Communist Party of Czechoslovakia retained complete 'supervision' over the implementation of the Constitutional Act.

Moscow did not require three equal state centres for its policy in Czechoslovakia. The Soviet's primary consideration was the reimposition of the 'all-embracing and all-powerful' leading role of the Communist Party of Czechoslovakia and the restoration of 'real socialism'. In practice, Moscow decided on all policies in the non-sovereign Czechoslovak state. But the fact that the Czechoslovak federation exceeded the Soviet model of state organisation was an obstacle.[9] The model had also been undermined by prior political rehabilitations, the abolition of censorship, the relaxation of state control over religion and the like.

To the neo-Stalinist regime a real federation was not desirable. The state reforms could not be carried out as originally hoped, because they were based on the democratic principle of equality between the two state-forming nations of Czechoslovakia. By the spring of 1969, the regime was already seeking ways to diminish the federation's *raison d'être*. It did this by distorting the principle of equality within the federation in favour of the political monopoly by the Communist Party, a move that directly contradicted the earlier democratic settlement of relations.

The legislative initiatives undertaken by the Federal Assembly, underpinned by the Constitutional Act, were a demonstration of centralising pressures. Although in 1969 the Slovak National Council was approving legislation or discussing proposals related to Slovakia (economic plans, the Constitutional Court, national radio and television, the position of the nationalities, civil rights, the Supreme Auditing Office, territorial (regional) division and the system of national committees and so on), increasingly it participated only when important acts were under consideration. In effect, article no. 38 of the Constitutional Act regarding joint legislative activity was being breached.

Thus the Slovak national bodies were unable to function in the national interests of Slovak society. The earlier violation of Czechoslovakia's state sovereignty and the Warsaw Pact's lack of respect for its frontiers further complicated the situation. While the position of the Slovak National Council as the representative of national sovereignty and Slovak self-rule had been accentuated, its task, that is, the preparation of a Slovak constitution, was foiled by the internal political situation.

Apart from its involvement in the work on the new constitution respecting the equality of the Czech and Slovak nations, the activities of the Slovak National Council during the 'crisis years' of 1968 and 1969 were appraised by the new Communist Party leadership as having been

---

[9] M. Štefanský, 'Slovenská spoločnosť v roku 1968' [Slovak society in 1968], in M. Púčik and M. Stanová (eds.), *Armáda a spoločnosť na Slovensku v kontexte európskeho vývoja 1948–1968* [Army and society in Slovakia in European developmental context 1948–1968] (Bratislava, 1997), p. 226. For more details, see V. Kusin, *From Dubček to Charter 77. A Study of Normalisation in Czechoslovakia, 1968–1978* (New York, 1978).

'counter-revolutionary'. The Slovak National Council's Action Programme of 1968 and the activity of the 'rightists' in its ranks were also
severely criticised. They included the former deputy prime minister of
Czechoslovakia Samuel Falt'an, the former prime minister of Slovakia
Jozef Zrak, and two of the creators of the federation, the lawyer Vojtech
Hatala and the economist Hvezdoň Kočtúch. When an avalanche of
'normalisation measures' was unleashed at the end of 1969, the Slovak
National Council's anti-occupation declarations were annulled for being
non-Marxist and politically incorrect. In accord with Constitutional
Act no. 117 of October 1969, the Slovak National Council deprived
six deputies of their seats while a further twenty-nine 'voluntarily' gave
them up. The Empowering Act became an instrument of normalisation
policy across all state institutions. Prime Minister Štefan Sádovský and
Deputy Prime Minister Jozef Zrak, plus Ministers Štefan Brenčič,
Štefan Šebesta, Mária Sedláková and others, had to leave the Slovak
government. In Slovakia almost 9,000 people – about 15 per cent of
the total – left the local bodies of state power and administration, the
national committees.

From May 1969 measures were brought in that especially affected the
economic sphere and strengthened the powers of the federal government
at the expense of the national government. Key industries were
reclaimed by federal departments, much to the detriment of Slovakia's
economic requirements. The economic policies of the Communist Party
of Czechoslovakia, which were based on central planning and directives
from Moscow, excluded other directing centres.

In a conversation with the Hungarian Communist leader János Kádár,
Husák mentioned that his administration was re-evaluating Czechoslovakia's experiences with the federation, 'with the aim of strengthening
the integrity of the whole state and the role of the federal government,
all of which are connected with the renewal of the directive system of
planning'.[10] What prevailed was the integration of the economy and the
dominance of the federal government to the disadvantage of the national
governments. But, officially, it was demagogically claimed that the interests of both republics and the federation as a whole were being safe-
guarded. The economic reforms based on combining a market economy
with economic planning and private ownership were altogether rejected.

---

[10] Stenografický záznam ... zo 17.12.1969 [Shorthand record ... from 17 December
1969], p. 7, Zbierka komise vlády ČSFR [Collection of the Government Commission
of the Czecho-Slovak Federal Republic], inv. no. D III/138, Institute for Contemporary
History, Academy of Sciences of the Czech Republic, Prague.

In October 1970, further amendments to Constitutional Act no. 143/ 1968 were made, dealing with the federation itself, and to no. 171/1968 that dealt with the activities of the federal ministries and committees. The amendments to Constitutional Acts nos. 125 and 133, plus other measures, strengthened the economic powers of the federation and restructured the relevant state mechanisms. They also finally abolished the federal committees, which had served as an expression of the parity between the two nations within the state, while establishing new federal ministries that removed even more powers from the national governments. The effects of these acts deformed the structures and integrity of the federation, the last keystone of the earlier round of reforms.[11] The normalisation process culminated in December 1970 with the issuing of a document entitled *The Lesson from the Period of Crisis in the Party and Society after the XIIIth Congress of the Communist Party of Czechoslovakia*, which denounced the entire reform movement of 1968 as a counter-revolution.

Constitutionally, a unitary system of state organisation operated in Czechoslovakia from 1948 to 1968; while the federative system that was brought into being in 1969 lasted until 1989, it existed in fundamentally undemocratic conditions.[12]

---

[11] J. Žatkuliak, 'Deformácie ústavného zákona o československej federácii po októbri 1968' [Deformations of the Constitutional Act on the Czechoslovak Federation after October 1968], *Historický časopis*, 40 (1992), 4, 473–486. See also, K. N. Skoug, *Czechoslovakia's Lost Fight for Freedom, 1967–1969. An American Embassy Perspective* (Westport, 1999).

[12] J. Rychlík, *Češi a Slováci ve 20. století. Česko-slovenské vztʼahy 1945–1992* [The Czechs and Slovaks in the twentieth century. Czech–Slovak relations, 1945–1992] (Bratislava, 1998); J. Musil (ed.), *The End of Czechoslovakia* (Budapest, London and New York, 1995); J. Žatkuliak, 'Slovakia in the Period of "Normalisation" and Expectation of Change (1969–1989)', *Sociológia – Slovak Sociological Review*, 30 (1998), 3, 251–68.

21 Slovakia under communism, 1948–1989: controversial developments in the economy, society and culture

Miroslav Londák and Elena Londáková

Forty years of communism have had a controversial influence on the Slovak economy and society. On one hand, the industrialisation of the country after 1948 changed the Slovak economy from an agrarian into a quasi-industrial one. Before 1948, the majority of the population worked in agriculture, but by the end of the Communist period only 13 per cent of all employees continued to do so. New employment opportunities were created, and the country was rapidly urbanised. That having been said, industrialisation was oriented towards the common market of the countries of the Council for Mutual Economic Assistance (COMECON); large industrial works were constructed, often to the detriment of the local environment. The Communist regime provided people with basic social security and a low, but nevertheless quite tolerable standard of living.

However, levels of development were limited; the economy was not capable of further natural growth and fell behind the dynamically developing economies of the Western world. The standard of living of the population also lagged behind those enjoyed to the west of the Iron Curtain. The Communist regime invested significant resources in science, education and culture, but the controlling power of the Communist Party was consistently manifested across the intellectual sphere. Science and culture, as represented by the leading figures in the field, gradually came into opposition with the Communist dictatorship, the so-called Marxist-Leninist ideology applied by it and the narrow understanding of art imposed through socialist realism, the only form of artistic expression that the regime permitted.

The economic sphere

As early as 1945 to 1947, there were moves to change Czechoslovakia's market economy into a planned economy. After the takeover of February 1948, nothing stood in the way of the new Communist administration continuing this process, together with the introduction of 'social engineering'.[1] Over the subsequent period, the national economy of the Czechoslovak Republic was directed by the state in line with the principles of Marxist-Leninist economic theory: industry was national-ised, thousands of tradesmen and craftsmen were expropriated, and private agricultural production was collectivised, often through the use of various coercive methods. An homogeneous one-sector socialist planned economy gradually developed, with the mechanical adoption of Soviet methods of management, which had to be implemented in line with Moscow's interests.

These developments unfolded in Slovakia quite differently than they did in the Czech Lands, not least because the process of 'socialist industrialisation' began in Slovakia, where there was more scope to reconfigure the work force. The existence of a relatively large and easily mobilised reserve of labour was regarded as one of the main precondi-tions for the industrialisation of Slovakia, and since at this time almost 50 per cent of the total population (3,327,000) worked in agriculture (at a low intensity of production), such a work force was easily achieved. The existing level of development of the Slovak economy was characterised by the low percentage of the population employed in industrial and craft production (only 22.7 per cent), but also by the low proportion of factory workers among this total. This situation contrasted with that in the Czech Lands, where the number of people working in industry or crafts was higher than that employed in agricul-ture.[2] The level of political development determined that Slovakia started on the path of socialist industrialisation in the non-market conditions of a planned economy, directed from the centre of a unitary, centralised Czechoslovakia.

The ability of the Slovak national bodies to exert an influence over the running of the national economy was, at best, very limited. Opportun-ities did arise from time to time for Slovak institutions to increase their control over the economy, but the state's central authorities unambigu-ously rejected any such attempts.[3] The central institutions viewed the national economy of Czechoslovakia as a united and homogeneous

---

[1] See P. Johnson, *Dějiny 20. století* (originally published as *History of the Modern World 1917 to the 1980s*) (Prague, 1991).

[2] Although the data vary to some extent, in the period before February 1948 about 50% (according to some data almost 60%) of the economically active population of Slovakia were employed in agriculture, forestry and fishing, while just over 20% were employed in industry and productive trades. In the Czech Lands, the proportions were reversed, with about 40% of the population working in industry and about 30% in agriculture.

[3] Although the federalisation of Czechoslovakia in 1968 was an important development, when it comes to running the Slovak national economy.

whole. On the other hand, economic policy in Slovakia included an effort to bring its economy and society up to the level of the Czech Lands.

The whole national economy was directed through five-year plans, but these were changed so often that in reality the economy was directed by annual development reviews. Industrial enterprises were told their production targets, products, suppliers, number of employees and so on by superior bodies. They were separated from real markets, and all investments in individual areas of industry, regions and so on were centrally determined. In spite of these many disadvantages, this direct method of management achieved positive results in economic growth, not least in quantitative terms; this was due in particular to the increase in the industrial work force.

The period of the first Five-Year Plan (1949–1953) saw vigorous growth of industrial production in Slovakia in comparison with the previous period. A whole series of new works were constructed.[4] Over five years, production increased by 128 per cent. Slovakia's share of the state's industrial production rose from 13.2 per cent to 15.6 per cent, while its share of overall investment in Czechoslovak industry increased to 25 per cent. However, the relatively rapid growth of industry across Czechoslovakia, a consequence of the Party's aspirations to become a world player in engineering and due to Soviet interest in and support for its arms industry, was achieved at a high price. Both the agricultural sector and the standard of living suffered because they received a very low inward flow of investment. Consequently, a catastrophic shortage of consumer goods resulted, combined with a growth of totally unusable purchasing power among the population, so much so that the leadership of the Communist Party and state decided to reform the currency in 1953.

The Communist leadership attempted to justify the currency reform as being a 'final blow against the former capitalists, the definitive liquidation of their economic power'. However, it was not only old deposits that were converted to the new currency levels at the very disadvantageous rate of 50:1, but also money deposited after 1948. The population paid for this reform with its savings, as well as with a corresponding decline in the standard of living; the overall direction of the economy was unfavourable, and inefficiency across all aspects of management increased. Many citizens, including workers, lost their entire life savings

---

[4] For example, the engineering works at Snina, Bánovce, Krompachy and Košice; the wood-processing works at Zvolen, Banská Bystrica and Topoľčany; the furniture factory at Spišská Nová Ves; and the hydro-electric power stations at Kostolná, Nové Mesto nad Váhom and Dobšiná.

in these reforms. As a result, mass dissatisfaction with the regime appeared for the first time, and there were strikes and protests.

During the second half of the 1950s, the rapid development of Slovakia's industrial base continued, in spite of a moderate decline in the proportion of Czechoslovak investment going to Slovakia. Slovakia received 29.5 per cent of total investment in the national economy and 24.3 per cent of investment in industry; thirty-eight new works were constructed in Slovakia, and forty-three were reconstructed.[5] Nevertheless, more than 75 per cent of industrial investment still went to the Czech Lands, which remained at a higher level of industrialisation.[6]

The agrarian sector in Slovakia lost 356,056 workers in the period 1948–1960, while industry created just 173,376 new jobs. In the Czech Lands, employment in agriculture declined by 414,615, while industry offered 446,811 new jobs. This means that, in contrast to Slovakia, the already highly industrialised Czech economy was able to absorb employees from the agricultural sector, and created an additional 32,196 jobs in industry. A further paradox of economic development in Czechoslovakia was that the number employed in material production fell by 72,694 in Slovakia, while in the Czech Lands the numbers grew by 280,717.[7]

The widespread redistribution of property after the takeover in February 1948 caused a radical reshaping of the social structure of Slovakia. Capitalists – that is, the former owners of the means of production – who numbered approximately 30,000 in 1946 (not including their families), completely disappeared. The number of employees in the capitalist sector before February 1948 was estimated at 265,000, and the capitalist owners held 15 per cent of agricultural land.[8] Small businessmen or tradesmen also almost completely disappeared as a stratum. By the end of 1948, 68,267 small enterprises were registered in Slovakia, with 150,000 people working in them.[9] They often employed only a few

---

[5] There were mostly the large projects, demanding high level of investment, e.g., the five hydroelectric power stations on the Váh river (Nosice, Skalka, Krpel'any, Sučany, Madunice) and the Hričov–Mikšová–Považská Bystrica cascade; big factories such as the aluminium works at Žiar nad Hronom or Slovnaft (oil refinery) in Bratislava; and the beginning of construction of works such as Duslo Šal'a (fertilisers) and the East Slovakia Ironworks in Košice (see Fig. 17).

[6] For statistics, see *Historická statistická ročenka ČSSR* [Historical statistical annual of the Czechoslovak Socialist Republic] (Prague, 1985), pp. 169, 684; see also M. Londák, *Otázky industrializácie Slovenska* [Questions regarding the industrialisation of Slovakia] (Bratislava, 1999), p. 133.

[7] Data calculated on the basis of *Historická statistická ročenka ČSSR*, 1985.

[8] M. Barnovský, *Sociálne triedy a revolučné premeny na Slovensku v rokoch 1944–1948* [Social classes and revolutionary transformations in Slovakia, 1944–1948] (Bratislava, 1978), pp. 29, 159–60.

[9] P. Zelenák, *Socializácia živností na Slovensku* [The socialisation of trades in Slovakia] (Bratislava, 1988), pp. 52, 53, 71.

people. Furthermore, enforced collectivisation radically altered the social structure of the agricultural sector, with peasant-farmers practically disappearing as a result.

At the beginning of the 1960s, three main groups could be identified in Slovak society: first, workers in state organisations (employees); second, workers in co-operative organisations; and, finally, independent producers. From the point of view of the social structure, the first group was dominant. It consisted of people engaged in regular manual or non-manual work. In 1961 they formed 79 per cent of the population. The second group worked mainly in agriculture, especially in the unified agricultural co-operatives. In 1961 they formed 14 per cent of the population. The remaining 7 per cent were independent producers, especially in agriculture and to a much smaller extent in other trades and crafts. A tiny group of members of the free professions need to be added to this total. However, the value of the property owned by the independent producers was very small, and the number of members of this group constantly declined. In 1950 they made up 37 per cent of the population; by 1967, the figure was less than 5 per cent.[10] Slovakia reached a significant turning point in about 1963 or 1964, when, for the first time in its history, the number employed in industry began to exceed the number employed in agriculture.[11] The primary task of industrialisation was thus fulfilled, and Slovakia began to acquire the character of a country that was more industrial than agrarian (Fig. 17).

In the early 1960s, Czechoslovakia entered a deep economic crisis. In 1963, national income suffered a serious decline compared to the results from the previous twelve months. An economic crisis of such dimensions, which included a real decline in national income, had no parallel in the post-war development of the socialist countries, not to mention the development of the developed Western states.[12] The real and substantial causes of the economic crisis were not immediately clear to the authorities. It took some time before economic theory began to reveal its connection with the Stalinist form of socialism and the centrally administered and directed system of planning.

[10] R. Roško, 'Premeny v sociálnej štruktúre Slovenska (1945–1970)' [Transformations in the social structure of Slovakia (1945–1970)], *Sociológia*, 4 (1970), 345–6.

[11] In 1963, 461,573 workers were employed in industry in Slovakia, and in 1964 it was 471,247; 476,724 worked in agriculture in 1963, and 462,897 in 1964: data from *Historická štatistická ročenka ČSSR*, 1985, p. 661.

[12] The post-war period from the beginning of the 1950s to the oil crisis (1973) is said to have been a phase in which a worldwide economic miracle occurred. The French economist Jean Fourastié refers to the 'thirty glorious years' (*les trentes glorieuses*). See J. Fourastié, *Les Trentes Glorieuses ou la révolution invisible de 1946 à 1975* (Paris, 1979).

Figure 17 Industrialisation (1954–1960): the East Slovakian Iron
Works at Košice

Here was the beginning of the road to wider economic reform. The
agenda for such reform was devised in Prague, by a group of experts led
by Ota Šik, and, with various difficulties, was approved step by step by
the Party bodies and put into practice from January 1965.[13] The essence
of the reform was to be a combination of state planning and the market,
and much wider use of economic categories (prices, interest rates, credit
and so on) in economic management, while preserving the socialist
character of the state.

Slovakia's role in the preparation of the reform was determined above
all by its political position within the structure of the state.[14] The central
institutions in Prague were rarely receptive to various suggestions formulated in Slovakia. Slovakia's status was circumscribed by the 1960
constitution, which further limited the jurisdiction of the Slovak national
bodies, and offered it no leverage to pursue its own economic interests.

[13] For more detail on the state's economic reforms, see Z. Šulc, 'Stručné dějiny
ekonomických reforem v Československu (České republice) 1945–1995' [A brief
history of economic reforms in Czechoslovakia (Czech Republic) 1945–1995], *Studie
národohospodářského ústavu Josefa Hlávky* (1996); K. Kaplan, *Kořeny československé
reformy 1968* [The roots of the Czechoslovak reform of 1968] (Brno, 2000).
[14] For more detail, see M. Londák, 'Príprava ekonomickej reformy a Slovensko v rokoch
1963–1967' [Preparation of the economic reform and Slovakia, 1963–1967], *Historický
časopis*, 49 (2001), 635–54.

For this reason, Slovak opinions were seldom heard. The economists preparing the reform in the centre treated the national economy of the state (from 1960 called the Czechoslovak Socialist Republic (ČSSR)) as a homogeneous whole. They endeavoured to solve the most serious problems, caused by the dogmatic application of socialist political economy, by the application of economic mechanisms in management. Consequently, solutions of regional problems or questions of economic growth in Slovakia and bringing it up to the level of the Czech Lands were not a priority in the reform process.

This economic crisis of the early 1960s and the way reform was applied in Slovakia slowed down its catch-up with the Czech Lands. Moreover, the restructuring of wholesale prices on 1 January 1967 (an important element of the economic reform) proved disadvantageous to Slovak enterprises, which produced mainly raw materials and semi-finished goods for Czech industry. By summer 1967, the leadership of the Communist Party of Slovakia under Alexander Dubček (he had become head in the spring of 1963) had obtained a number of reports that detailed the negative impacts of the economic reform on Slovakia.[15] Employing this evidence, Dubček gave a speech, which had not been authorised in advance, to a session of the Central Committee of the Communist Party of Czechoslovakia in September 1967. The speech was unusually critical for such a high Party forum. He evaluated the recent economic developments in Slovakia and, among other things, drew attention to the expectation of a mass migration of Slovak workers moving to the Czech Lands in search of work.[16] This speech exacerbated the dispute regarding the work of the Party between Dubček and the leader of the Communist Party of Czechoslovakia, Antonín Novotný. It deepened at a further session of the Central Committee of the Communist Party of Czechoslovakia in October 1967, when Dubček's critique also impinged upon the political sphere, which eventually led to the Prague Spring.

By 1968, preparations for economic reform reached a new level; laws regarding socialist enterprises and workers' councils were to move events forward more radically, affecting also the progress towards democratisation. But the occupation of Czechoslovakia by the armies of the Warsaw Pact forcibly brought this whole process to an end. In Slovakia, at least, the hope remained that the federalisation of Czechoslovakia would give the Slovak national bodies new opportunities to participate positively in the national economy.

---

[15] For more detail, see *ibid.*, 648.   [16] *Ibid.*, 653.

The cultural sphere

Cultural developments formed a crucial part of the dramatic path Czechoslovakia followed after 1945. The processes occurring in the economic and social spheres had their parallel in the intellectual sphere. Cultural developments replicated and reflected the key political excesses of this period. The close connection between culture and politics flowed from the demands made by the totalitarian regime that culture play an ideological role, and that it had a propagandist and 're-educational' mission to help build a new communist society. The radical transformation of the old culture of a Central European country occurred in a context of increasing limitations imposed on cultural life by the regime. The official form of culture was obliged to follow predetermined ideological contours set out by the regime, and artworks had to conform to a single 'correct' (that is, permitted) form: socialist realism.

After the takeover of 1948, Czech and Slovak societies were in a similar, but not entirely identical, situation. Their historical and cultural traditions, together with their recent and different experiences of the war, contributed to a range of differences between the two halves of the country.[17] These factors influenced their differing attitudes not only at the beginning of the new Communist regime, but also in their perceptions of the subsequent course of its rule. The situation in Slovak culture was characterised by a historical disproportion between the creative potential of a relatively narrow Slovak artistic intelligentsia, which laid the foundations for Slovak modern art in the 1930s, and an inadequate material and institutional infrastructure.[18] The positive social and educational programme of the Communist Party intended to help secure the completion of the infrastructure necessary for the development of culture, and to make it accessible to all groups in the population.

---

[17] While the Czech Lands were paralysed by being turned into a German protectorate (1939 to 1945), Slovakia experienced a period as a controversial independent state, the foundation of a broad anti-Hitler coalition and the Slovak National Uprising. The latter created a good initial political and economic position for Slovakia when it returned into the common state although it was gradually eliminated. See J. Lettrich, *Dejiny novodobého Slovenska* [A history of modern Slovakia] (Bratislava, 1993); M. Barnovský, *Na ceste k monopolu moci* [On the road to monopoly power] (Bratislava, 1993).

[18] The commissioner for schools and education, the well-known Slovak poet Ladislav Novomeský (1904–1976), reported an absolute shortage of schools (only three university-type institutions, at which only 7 per cent of the students who completed secondary school could study) and a shortage of textbooks and teachers. Moreover, the latter were insufficiently qualified. In 1953, 30 per cent of elementary school teachers and 20 per cent *of gymnasium* teachers lacked qualifications. See L. Novomeský, *Nový duch novej školy* [The new spirit of the new school] (Bratislava, 1974), p. 23.

Though initially received with distrust in Slovakia, it was, however, eventually viewed more favourably than in the Czech Lands, which enjoyed incomparably better conditions at the outset.

In a way, Slovakia provided an ideal model platform for Communist cultural policy, first outlined at the legendary Ninth Congress of the Communist Party of Czechoslovakia in 1949. Initiated under the slogan of 'socialist cultural revolution', it dominated Czecho-Slovak culture for the next half-century. Eminent Slovak intellectuals, both Communist and non-communist, were sympathetic to its basic social goals. Their active participation was considered as natural. Indeed, owing to the underdeveloped political landscape, Slovak intellectuals in the past had acted as spokesmen for the body politic.

The ideals propagated by the Communists, of building a new, socially just world, blinded many intellectuals to the totalitarian practices employed by the regime, especially in the initial period. A high political position was accepted by the Communist poet Ladislav Novomeský, who became commissioner for schools and public education. High departmental collaborators were the Christian-oriented poet and translator Emil Boleslav Lukáč, the philosopher Ladislav Szantó, the educational theorist Ondrej Pavlík, and the journalist and writer of popular best-sellers Peter Jilemnický. The writer Daniel Okáli became commissioner of the interior in 1948; the journalist Ladislav Holdoš became commissioner for church affairs in 1950; the noted prose writer Ivan Horváth moved from being commissioner for social services to the post of deputy chairman of the Slovak National Council; and so on.[19]

The Communist Party used the traditional interest in 'work for the nation' to win the support of part of the cultural community for its aims. This was a process that had begun during the struggle for power before February 1948. At this time, the Party promised both comprehensive state financing for cultural activities and respect for freedom of artistic expression; the general secretary of the party, Štefan Bašťovanský, made this pledge at the Congress of Cultural Workers of the Communist Party of Slovakia in Martin, 20–21 April 1946. Michal Chorváth declared at the same gathering that the management of culture should be placed fully in the hands of its creators. A guest at the congress, Minister

[19] Among others, it is worth mentioning the prominent journalist Edo Friš (1912–1978), who held the post of secretary of the Central Committee of the Communist Party of Slovakia from 1945 to 1947, and then became editor-in-chief of the daily *Pravda*; Eugen Klinger, who was the head of a department at the Ministry of Foreign Affairs; the literary critic Michal Chorváth, who was commissioner for information; and Ivan Pietor, who was minister of internal trade for a time. Best known was the journalist and lawyer Vladimír Clementis (1902–1952), who became minister of foreign affairs.

of Information Václav Kopecký (later unpopular in Slovakia for his chauvinist anti-Slovak attitudes) went further with his own theory that the Communist Party of Czechoslovakia would secure 'complete under-standing of Slovak ideas' and ensure the principles of equality with the Czech side.[20] However, more observant listeners could not fail to notice his less emphatic, yet still clearly identifiable ideas about art's role in political agitation, about artists' duties towards society. For the time and place he made an unusually open statement that the livelihood of artists would depend on their attitude to 'social' demands, which was to prove to be a somewhat fateful reference given future developments.

This, then, was the essence of Communist cultural policy during all four decades of its rule. The cultural community was given a comfort-able livelihood, and in return it was required to produce muzzled art that conformed to Communist ideology, fulfilling the regime's goal of the 're-education' of the people. The gradual destruction of the private and confessional sphere of culture accompanied the building of the new society. The traditional artistic societies gradually disappeared[21] and were replaced by Communist-dominated artistic unions.[22] Behind the scenes the union's 'primary organisation' (lowest Party body) of the Com-munist Party of Czechoslovakia was active and 'responsible' to the higher Party bodies for the conflict-free operation of the union. The existence of two parallel, directed systems of management became a permanent feature, as in all other areas of society. The unions were 'selective' and work opportunities for individuals were conditional on membership. After 1948, culture began to be increasingly directed by the ideological depart-ments of the Central Committees of the Communist Parties of Slovakia and Czechoslovakia.

Control of the media

For the Communist regime, it was very important to obtain control over the media. Rigid totalitarianism was first imposed with the passing of an act on the publication of newspapers and magazines in 1950. A ban on

---

[20] L. Grešík, *Slovenská kultúra v revolúcii (1944–1948)* [Slovak culture in revolution (1944–1948)] (Bratislava, 1977), p. 160.

[21] According to Karel Kaplan, around 700 societies remained from a total of 60,000 social organisations and associations in existence before February 1948. For details, see K. Kaplan, *Československo v letech 1948–1953* [Czechoslovakia in the years 1948–1953] (Prague 1991), vol. II, p. 25.

[22] The professional union of journalists and librarians was founded in 1946, those for writers and composers in 1949 and fine artists in 1950. Actors formed their union in 1956. The unions covered the whole state. Their Slovak sections were granted formal independence by the first half of the 1960s.

importing foreign press titles was introduced by a decision of the Central Committee of the Communist Party of Czechoslovakia on 24 February 1948. The disappearance of opposition and 'ideologically unsound' publications also secured a selective supply of information. In all, sixty-one periodicals were stopped from appearing by the first quarter of 1949. A further ninety-two periodicals gradually disappeared as a result of 're-organisation'.[23] At the same time, a rigorous system of censorship was introduced. To begin with, these measures were co-ordinated by the Press Department of the Central Committee of the Communist Party of Czechoslovakia (1948). In due course these processes were essentially legalised in a more sophisticated form by unpublished Government Decree no. 17/1953, which established the Office for Supervision of the Press, technically designated as a 'preventive' measure, but which had legal powers.[24] Every editorial office had its own 'censor', who reported daily decisions and without whose approval no article, radio programme, theatrical performance or exhibition was allowed.

Nor did the Communist regime forget to scrap inappropriate books and continuously to add to the list of forbidden works. The 'purge' of all libraries, bookshops, stores and second-hand bookshops was conducted in several waves. During the first one in 1948, about half the book collections of Czechoslovakia, that is almost fourteen million titles were to go. Relentless attacks were launched on the works of John Steinbeck (whose reminiscences on the Soviet Union (1946 to 1947) were especially irritating), along with those of Karl Kautsky and André Gide, non-communist philosophers and sociologists.[25] This was in addition to assaults on scientists opposed to the theories of T. D. Lysenko and Olga Lepeshinskaya, or historians and writers positively evaluating leading feudal or bourgeois personalities and other 'trash'; these attacks continued with equal intensity during the years 1951 to 1953. No publication or periodical (even local ones) could appear without written permission from the appropriate Party bodies.

In spite of these new forms of organisational support for culture, complete with methods of uncompromising ideological control, Slovak artists did receive a secure livelihood, which became an effective form of political pressure. In addition, a new method of state control was also

---

[23] L. Šefčák and Z. Duhajová, *Dejiny slovenského novinárstva 1918–1968* [The history of Slovak journalism, 1918–1968] (Bratislava, 1999), p. 144.

[24] J. Weiser, 'Novinárska organizácia na Slovensku 1945–1989' [The organisation of journalists in Slovakia, 1945–1989], unpublished manuscript, Institute of Political Science of the Slovak Academy of Sciences in Bratislava, pp. 28–34.

[25] Sociology as a whole was strictly rejected by the regime for years as a 'pseudoscience'. The official rehabilitation of sociology came only at the beginning of the 1960s.

being introduced at this time, the pseudo-artistic method of 'socialist realism' that intervened directly in the heart of artistic creativity. Although the Communists had occasionally mentioned this concept prior to 1948[26] (always in the sense of an alternative aesthetic concept of what art should be), the situation changed after the Communist seizure of power. When the Union of Czechoslovak Writers was inaugurated in Prague in 1949, art was described as being 'in the service of the socialist reconstruction of society and the re-education of the people'. Henceforth, this statement formed the basis for the Stalinisation of all other areas of creative endeavour.

The First Congress of Slovak Painters, Sculptors and Architects, at which the principles of the 'new' art were declared, took a similar, if slightly less pompous, line. The inaugural first exhibition of the 'Czechoslovak people and its country in life, work and struggle' was held in Prague in spring 1949. Another exhibition opened soon after, entitled 'An artist among miners'. Many notable artists (Vincent Hložník, Peter Matejka and others) spontaneously exhibited pictures depicting the working lives of ordinary people, influenced by their own roots and affiliations to this theme, just as various writers were equally attracted by the possibility of finally re-aligning old ideals (such as František Hečko, Vladimír Mináč, Dominik Tatarka and others).[27] It only gradually became apparent that ideological supervision hindered the free development of other forms of artistic expression.

Prior to the growth of television as a mass medium, film was the most important propaganda vehicle and was generously supported by the state, which churned out one schematic work after another. From the many films produced during this period, a few cult works of socialist realism should be mentioned: the film *Drevená dedina* (Wooden village) (directed by Andrej Lettrich), based on a novel by the well-known author František Hečko; *Kozie mlieko* (Goat's milk) (directed by Bořivoj Zeman); *Lazy sa pohli* (Mountain pastures are stirring) and *Priehrada* (The dam) (both directed by Pal'o Bielik; and *Pole neorané* (Uncultivated field) (directed by Vladimír Bahna), based on a novel by Peter Jilemnický.[28]

[26] File Povereníctvo informácií a osvety (PIO), 1953, boxes nos. 4 and 5, Slovak National Archives, Bratislava.

[27] Some years later the writer and journalist L. Mňačko (1919–1994) reminisced in an interview for *Literárny týždenník* (Literary weekly) about the wonderful elevated atmosphere of opportunity during this period: 'there were equal opportunities for everybody in the world, without regard for race or religion. I told myself that now we must win and then it will be a springboard to communism' (*Literárny týždenník*, 1989, nos. 51/52, 14).

[28] M. Forrayová, *Slovenské filmy 1945–1964. II. diel. Filmografia tvorcov a hercov* [Slovak films 1945–1964. Part II. Filmography of creators and actors] (Bratislava, 1987), pp. 88–99.

For musicians 'Through music to musicalness' was the fatal slogan of the day, foretelling a one-dimensional future for Slovak composers and musicians. This phrase not only dictated an orientation towards ordinary people and their folklore traditions, but also the end of 'wild experimentation' and 'anti-music', in the interest of 'mass comprehensibility'. Radio stations, school classrooms and public performances were soon saturated with 'inspirational' songs and marches relating to the construction of the new socialist order. Choral works that placed collectivism above bourgeois individualism were preferred. Art took on a pathetic monumentalism, whether in sculpture, painting or architecture, all designed to represent the desired picture of the totalitarian state, its power based on the citizens' faith in the great ideas of equality and communism.

The Communist machinery was somewhat slower to turn its attention to the world of fine art, which it did, after some delay, after 1949. After the Communists came to power, their original perception of socialist culture as an alternative stream now became the orthodox canon, violations of which were strictly punished, either by exclusion from public life, by not being allowed to publish or exhibit, or through expulsion from the artists' union. Thus, the creative modernism of Mikuláš Galanda,[29] Ľudovít Fulla, Koloman Sokol, Miloš Bazovský and others was condemned. Official 'art criticism' without hesitation rejected it for its formalism and cosmopolitanism.

Plays by world classics and domestic authors were regarded as ideologically 'inappropriate' and removed from the repertoire of theatres nationalised in 1948.[30] One of the first to be affected was Leopold Lahola's *Atentát* (Assassination), which was withdrawn immediately after its premiere. The play was soon described pejoratively in the press as being existentialist and cosmopolitan. The author understood the situation, and he soon emigrated.[31] Some authors fell silent under

---

[29] M. Galanda (1895–1938) gained his place in the history of Slovak fine art not only for his highly evaluated work (he is regarded as a co-founder of modern Slovak painting), but also for publication of his 'Private Letters' (1930, 1932), in which he and Ľ. Fulla (1902–1980) declared their support for the European avant-garde.

[30] The act providing for this (no. 32/1948) also established the Council for Theatre and Drama, which operated from 1948 to 1953 as an instrument of the permanent ideological intervention in the running of theatres and planning of performances.

[31] L. Lahola (1918–1968), whose works included the scenario for the successful film *Vlčie diery* (Wolf holes) (1948), joined the second post-war wave of emigration of writers along with the graphic artist K. Sokol. The motivation for the first wave was connected with the involvement of the writers with the war-time Slovak Republic (A. Žarnov, Tido J. Gašpar, V. Beniak, Š. Gráf, J. C. Hronský, R. Dilong, S. Mečiar, K. Strmeň and others) and opposition to the new Communist regime. But after 1948 artists left mainly for another reason: they were seeking the creative freedom denied to them by the regime.

these circumstances, and the dark cloud of totalitarianism spread over culture unusually quickly. In exhibitions, theatres, commissions overseeing the ideological purity of textbooks, film scenarios, radio commentaries, theatre plans: in all these cases, anonymous persons, often former workers and clerks, now decided which academic painters, architects and writers were 'good' and which were not acceptable.

The harshest period of totalitarianism (1950 to 1953) affected Slovak cultural life intensely. Many cultural representatives, paradoxically leftist members of the Communist Party, were accused of 'bourgeois nationalism' from the platform of the Ninth Congress of the Communist Party of Slovakia. At the beginning of 1950, many were arrested and became victims of fabricated 'show trials', which excluded them from civil life for many years. These included Ladislav Novomeský, Ladislav Holdoš, Daniel Okáli and Ivan Horváth, who all lost their positions and their basic civil rights, with confiscation of property in some cases. The well-known Communist activist and politician Vladimír Clementis was accused of high treason. He was removed from his post as the Czechoslovak minister of foreign affairs, taken straight to a prison cell and, following a show trial, to his execution.

The aim of this campaign, instigated by the Communist Party of Czechoslovakia, was to actively participate in the internationally organised Communist hunt for the enemy within. It also provided the leadership of the Communist Party of Czechoslovakia with a justification for stemming the chronic discontent in Slovakia by gradually curtailing the powers of the Slovak government bodies. The climate of fear extended to the pages of the Slovak press. Some periodicals could finally be closed down: *Tvorba* (Creative activity), run by Emil Boleslav Lukáč, in 1950; Gustáv Husák's *Nové slovo* (New word) in 1952. The content of the weekly *Kultúrny život* also changed: it had previously been relatively liberal, but soon became a faithful mouthpiece of the Party.[32]

The temperature of this destructive campaign was raised when the head of the Culture and Propaganda Section of the Secretariat of the Central Committee of the Communist Party of Slovakia, Július

---

[32] The magazine, which was to become legendary, originated in 1946 as the press organ of the Council for Art and Science, constituted at the first congress of artistic and scientific workers in Banská Bystrica, convened on the occasion of the first anniversary of the Slovak National Uprising in August 1945. According to the keynote speech by Novomeský, the council supported the ideals of humanism and democracy and intended to represent the professional interests of artists and scientists, to defend their freedom to pursue creative and scientific work, and to promote the activities of their associations. The council was dissolved in 1951, while in 1949 its weekly journal had been transferred to the Slovak section of the newly founded Union of Czechoslovak Writers.

Šefránek, addressed a meeting of Communist writers, members of the Slovak section of the Union of Czechoslovak Writers, in Bratislava (30–31 March 1951). He not only strongly condemned people who had already been imprisoned,[33] but also widened the net to include the likes of the literary scholar Michal Chorváth, the noted literary critic Alexander Matuška, the art critic and scholar Mikuláš Bakoš and the writers Vladimír Mináč and Dominik Tatarka. Thus, he launched an avalanche of condemnations in the pages of *Kultúrny život*, which led to many people losing posts in professional organisations and editorial offices.

A first relaxation of this hard-line position began after Stalin died in 1953. Thus, a debate about the problems of the new art took place at the conference 'On some conceptual and artistic questions' in June 1953. The conference of the Union of Czechoslovak Writers, held in April 1954, had already openly opposed the official 'universal method' of socialist realism. The Second Congress of Czechoslovak Writers, held 22–29 April 1956, proved to be historic because of the open conflict which erupted between the writers and the Party delegation. The Czech writers František Hrubín and Jaroslav Seifert demanded the right to free creative activity and the abolition of censorship. By doing so, they crossed the boundary of what was permitted and unwittingly opened the floodgates to general discontent with the regime.

While the writers were promoting themselves as the 'conscience of the nation', students and journalists also began to formulate their demands. At first, the Party leadership reacted relatively calmly by quickly diverting this undesirable 'public discussion' towards economic questions. Subsequent Party interviews in 1957 silenced critics, who were 'ahead of their time'.[34] What followed was a period of apparent calm, when social ferment was pushing Slovak culture to the centre of social events over the subsequent decade.

Slovak painters and sculptors were among the first to be imbued with the spirit of the Second Congress, mobilising them to disregard both the condemnations of their exhibitions in the press and orders banning their work from being shown. In 1957 the young generation, drawn together in Nástup (Line-up) 1957, declared its allegiance to the best

---

[33] He reproached them for activities in the organisation of left intelligentsia DAV (Crowd), influential during the period of the First Czechoslovak Republic. He had himself, at least in 1933, participated in their activities by publishing articles in the magazine of the same name.

[34] Thus Academician O. Pavlík, co-founder of the Communist school reforms of 1948, was expelled from the Communist Party. A senior lecturer, P. Pollák, suffered Party punishment. The editor-in-chief of *Kultúrny život* from 1956, J. Špitzer, and the poet I. Kupec were also dealt with in a similar way.

traditions of Slovak modernism and publicly rejected previous criticism of this movement. A second generation of young artists, concentrated in the Nástup 1961 group, developed this initiative and attempted to depict the 'internal world of the contemporary person via modern means'. The route to non-figurative art, freed from traditional means of expression, was thus opened. During the 1960s, Slovak painters and sculptors engaged with the European cultural context, achieving success at numerous foreign exhibitions.[35]

Slovak writers and journalists supported the golden age of Slovak culture in the 1960s not only with their writings,[36] but also at their congresses held in the spring of 1963. Here they demanded the complete rehabilitation of those Slovaks labelled 'bourgeois nationalists' by the regime. The journalists Miro Hysko and Roman Kaliský raised questions about Slovakia's equality within the common state, the adaptation of industrialisation to Slovak realities, changes in the method of running the state, free expression and creative activity.[37] These changes in Slovak culture also influenced a much resigned Czech cultural community, which began to struggle with 'its' orthodox Party leadership. Relentlessly delving into the nature of this system, the writers formulated not only professional but also hard political questions at their 1967 congress.[38]

It was the sphere of culture, therefore, which felt the lack of freedom as a particular limitation, and which began to break through the barriers with which the political totalitarian system enclosed the whole society. Thus the cultural movement merged with the wider dissatisfaction with the regime, flowing from the country's economic problems. This overall social movement led to the brief Czecho-Slovak Spring of 1968, when

[35] R. Matuštík, *Moderné slovenské maliarstvo 1945–1963* [Modern Slovak painting 1945–1963] (Bratislava, 1963), p. 172.

[36] With his first work *Sklenný vrch* (Glass hill) (1954) and collection of short stories *Hodiny a minúty* (Hours and minutes) (1956), Alfonz Bednár pioneered the move away from heroism to a psychological confrontation between the war-time generation and the reality of building socialism. Magazines published *Démon súhlasu* (Demon of consent) by D. Tatarka, the novel *Smrt' sa volá Engelchen* (Death is called Engelchen) (1959) by L. Mňačko, his well-known *Oneskorené reportáže* (Delayed reportages) (1963) from the background of the political trials, and *Ako chutí moc* (How does power taste) (1967). The poet Milan Rúfus began to publish in 1956 with the collection *Až dozrieme* (Until we mature) by which 'he gained the right to grieve'. The theorist Milan Hamada defined the new alternative literature returning to man and his being. For more detail, see J. Hvišč, V. Marčok, M. Bátorová and V. Petrík, *Biele miesta v slovenskej literatúre* [Blank spaces in Slovak literature] (Bratislava, 1991), pp. 75–80.

[37] *1. zjazd slovenských novinárov v r. 1963. Výpis z protokolu* [The 1st Congress of Slovak journalists in 1963. Extract from the minutes] (Bratislava, 1968), pp. 69–117.

[38] For more detail, see D. Hamšík, *Spisovatelé a moc* [Writers and power] (Prague, 1969); K. Kaplan, *Všechno jste prohráli!* [You have lost everything!] (Prague, 1997).

hope for reform and a freer, more democratic society ('socialism with a human face') activated the citizens of Czechoslovakia. The military invasion by the Warsaw Pact countries in August 1968 dramatically ended this reform and the democratic process.

After 1968

After the occupation of Czechoslovakia, little remained of the many aims set out by the authors of the economic reform of the 1960s. Their efforts to direct the economy by means of economic instruments and involving market regeneration were not fulfilled. Probably the only permanent result of the 'regeneration process' was the federalisation of the state, which had some consequences for the process of managing the national economy in Slovakia. However, this was seriously limited by the lack of federalisation at the Party level, so that the real decisive jurisdictional powers in the area of economic management remained centralised. In the main, the centrally administered and directed national economy prevailed until 1989.

As a result of economic development during the 1970s and 1980s, Slovakia continued to evolve as an industrialised country. Its energy base was being developed, as was the chemical industry; a series of technically demanding areas of production were mastered and some extremely large enterprises were built up. A positive feature was that there was no longer a great difference between the support for heavy and light industry. In comparison with earlier periods, relatively sizable levels of resources flowed into agriculture, and the supply of goods to the population improved. Although the regime did not allow real amends for the injustices suffered during of the period of collectivisation, thanks to the continual flow of financial resources into agriculture, the immense differences between the standards of living and life styles of the rural and urban population were eliminated.

By the end of the 1980s, few differences between the national economies of Slovakia and the Czech Lands remained, although some quantitative disparities did persist. In 1989, Slovakia produced 31% of the national income, 30% of industrial output and 33% of agricultural production. For comparison: in 1948 the figures for national income and industrial output were 19% and 14% respectively. Slovakia's production of weapons and arms in 1985 accounted for almost 60% of the whole state's output (of tanks and armoured personnel carriers).[39]

---

[39] Data from *Štatistická ročenka ČSSR 1989* [Statistical yearbook of the Czechoslovak Socialist Republic 1989].

The qualitative change of character in the Slovak economy naturally also affected employment. In 1989, industry and construction employed almost 1.1 million persons, compared to 315,000 in 1948. In the same period, the number employed in agriculture declined from more than 900,000 to 300,000, but agricultural output increased by 250 per cent. In this context, it is necessary to note that the provision of a relatively fixed percentage share of Slovakia's total investment in the development and construction of industry and infrastructure represented positive discrimination in favour of Slovakia, which would not have been possible without direct state intervention in the economy. Such results could not have been achieved under market economy conditions.

In spite of these positive developments, the socialist economy in Slovakia and across the whole of Czechoslovakia performed poorly during the 1970s and 1980s. These difficulties could not easily be corrected, because they were mainly connected with the type of ownership of the means of production. More often than not, newly constructed works failed to utilise the most modern production techniques, and many other problems with the overall quality of production were overlooked. While the socialist economy offered employment to many thousands of people, it could not overcome the problems related to the application of the latest technology. The application of the results of the Scientific-Technical Revolution, and the transition to an information-based society, proved to be beyond its ability. The gradual development of domestic production was not sufficient to keep pace with the dynamically developing styles of production in the Western world. Technological backwardness was combined with continually decreasing standards of living. Since the Communist regime could not totally insulate the population from the outside world, this backwardness stiffened opposition to the regime.

A range of creative small and medium-sized companies with private capital were needed to produce change in manufacturing processes, but the Communist regime did not intend to allow this to happen. Understandably, this state of affairs had a wider political context caused by the West's embargo on the export of modern technologies, on the one hand, and the gradual orientation of Czechoslovak exports towards less-demanding markets, on the other. All this led to increasing uncompetitiveness and wastefulness across the whole Czechoslovak economy and an underlying demand for real 'revolutionary change'.

The active participation of the cultural community in the regeneration movement incurred a heavy price after the invasion of the Warsaw Pact armies, even though the consequences were not immediate. Many artistic projects and activities continued until 1970–1971. For example, the group of Conceptualists, devotees of action-painting, endeavoured 'to preserve a zone of free art' by transferring their exhibitions from public galleries to private studios. But Jozef Jankovič, Andrej Rudavský, Milan Laluha and others were prevented from displaying their work. Slovak film-makers, who had achieved Europe-wide fame in the 1960s,[40] managed to complete the films they had started work on. These included Elo Havetta's *Slávnost' v botanickej záhrade* (Celebration in the botanical garden) (1969) and Juraj Jakubisko's *Vtáčikovia, siroty a blázni* (Little birds, orphans and madmen) (1970), *Zbehovia a pútnici* (Deserters and pilgrims) released 1970, and the unfinished *Dovidenia v pekle priatelia* (See you in hell, friends). Dušan Hanák produced his first work in 1969: the film *322*.

While the drastic 'normalisation' of society did not prevent the publication of some important literary works in the relatively freer atmosphere before 1972, a membership purge of the artistic unions began at the turn of 1969/1970. Administrative intervention closed *Kultúrny život* on 6 September 1968. In 1969 new selective artistic unions were formed. These bodies established fresh membership lists, which enabled them to reject previous members branded as 'unsuitable', starting with Ladislav Mňačko, who had by then emigrated. In 1971, thirty-seven former members were expelled from the new Union of Slovak Writers. Their names were dropped from textbooks, expert periodicals and monographs. Soon afterward, their works were purged from libraries. The Second Congress of the Union of Slovak Writers in 1972 proclaimed the reincarnation of socialist realism. The avant-garde literary magazine *Mladá tvorba* soon disappeared, and the editors of other magazines were replaced. Consolidation followed an almost identical course in the key posts of artistic life. Ľubomír Kára, editor-in-chief of *Výtvarný život* (Creative life), and Vincent Hložník, Rector of the Academy of Fine Arts, were forced from their posts. On losing their union membership, internationally known artists were forbidden to exhibit their works. Some works were destroyed, for example, a sculpture by Jozef Jankovič that stood in front of the monument to the Slovak National Uprising at Banská Bystrica.

After 1968, cultural life in Slovakia was controlled by three men: the minister of culture Miroslav Válek, the ideological secretary Ľudovít Pezlár, and the head of the department for art and culture of the Central Committee of the Communist Party of Slovakia, Miroslav Hruškovič.

---

[40] The film *Slnko v sieti* (Sun in a net) (1962) by Š. Uher. M. Forman called it the John the Baptist (or forerunner) of the Czech new wave. The film *Obchod na korze* (Shop on the high street) (1965) by E. Klos and J. Kádar won an Oscar.

Between them they were responsible for preventing 'anti-socialist artistic diversion' in any shape or form. However, political power alone was insufficient to silence totally the inventiveness and inspirational effects of the Slovak arts of the 1960s. There were authors willing to collaborate with the regime, but much art moved into partial illegality, and remained there until the end of the 1970s. A new generation of artists was formed in the 1980s who took advantage of the partial relaxation of censorship in that period and, among other innovations, pioneered the use of audio-visual media.

All the leading figures in the Slovak film industry were removed in 1969. Juraj Jakubisko, Eduard Grečner and Peter Solan could no longer make films, and the Oscar winner, Ján Kádar, emigrated. A commission of the Ministry of Culture prevented many Slovak films from the 1960s from being screened. While Dušan Hanák's film *Obrazy starého sveta* (Pictures of the old world) and Elo Havetta's *Ľálie poľné* [Field lilies] were complete, others were not so lucky. Hanák managed to return to making films only in 1976, with *Ružové sny* (Rose-tinted dreams), while Jakubisko could devote himself only to documentary film making. By the beginning of the 1980s a new generation of young directors was emerging, which came into its own by the end of the decade.[41] Literature showed the same vitality, with a group of talented writers growing up in spite of the unfavourable environment of that period.

It may appear paradoxical that Slovak culture experienced its most fruitful period under a totalitarian regime, which did not favour free creative activity. However, in spite of the Marxist view that the spiritual and intellectual spheres are dependent on the material and political worlds, the free space created by culture in the periods of 'relaxation' showed great persistence. Put plainly, creativity could not be simply banned. The results of the Communist period were controversial because, on the one hand, Slovak culture received greater material support than ever before but, on the other hand, the regime invested less in culture than other comparable European countries. While several generations of the Slovak intelligentsia grew up under an ideological regime, it retained a sense of independence.

Education was the key to Slovak cultural growth. Its principles, state provision, unification and democratisation (Act no. 95/1948) limited the differentiation of schools, but secured free education for all without regard to social status. Slovakia used this advantage to the maximum extent, in spite of many reforms and political deformations of education

---

[41] See *Encyklopédia slovenského filmu* [Encyclopaedia of Slovak film] (Bratislava, 1998).

policy. The undervaluing of education[42] meant that the system was not able to satisfy the growing demand for university education from the large number of young people born after the war. Educational results were comparable to those of other countries in Europe.

In the inter-war period, Slovakia had one university with three faculties, and in the 1950s the proportion of the population completing secondary or higher education was still lower than in the Czech Lands. However, by about 1970 the proportion of Slovaks who received a university education (3%) was almost equal to that of Czechs (3.4%). The proportion of women in university education was 1.9% in the Czech Lands, and 1.8% in Slovakia.[43] By 1989, Slovakia had thirteen institutions of higher education with a total of forty-three faculties. In spite of the problems in academic education, which provided more encyclopaedic than practical knowledge, it is possible to say that the graduates of Slovak schools and universities achieved a high degree of success in the world 'beyond the Iron Curtain'. This point was especially apparent after 1989. The fall of the Iron Curtain also meant a transition to a new quality of education, science and culture.

---

[42] While Japan (still comparable in the 1950s) invested 12% of its national product in education, the USSR 10.1% and Western countries an average of 7 to 9%, Czechoslovakia generally invested less than 4 to 5%. See A. Kamiač, *Ekonomika vzdelávania* [The economics of education] (Bratislava, 1971), p. 104.

[43] J. Průcha, *Vzdelávání a školství ve světe* [Education and schools in the world] (Prague, 1999), p. 274.

22 The fall of communism and the establishment of an independent Slovakia

Michal Štefanský

The entry of five Warsaw Pact armies on to Czechoslovak soil in August 1968 prevented the continuation of the country's social reforms. After the intervention the Soviet leadership, in co-operation with other Warsaw Pact leaders, continued to pressure the leadership of the Communist Party of Czechoslovakia (CPC), the government and the parliament to prevent further reforms. These pressures led to the Moscow Protocol, which defined Czechoslovakia's new limited sovereignty.[1] The *Agreement on the Stationing of Soviet Forces*, which gave no date for their departure, legitimised their presence on the territory of Czechoslovakia until the eventual collapse of the Communist regime.[2] The leaders of the Warsaw Pact, with the support of conservative and pro-occupation forces, then planned to expel the representatives of reformist communism from leading positions in the CPC, government and parliament.

---

[1] The Moscow Protocol was the formal summary of a number of agreements reached by the delegation of the Union of Soviet Socialist Republics and the Czechoslovak Socialist Republic. It was signed in Moscow on 26 August 1968 and contained fifteen points. The Soviet leadership demanded that the Czechoslovak government withdraw the question of military intervention from the UN Security Council; declare the invalidity of the Fourteenth Congress of the CPC; introduce censorship; ban certain organisations; and carry out personnel changes; while retaining in their positions representatives of conservative Communist forces who were accused of personally inviting foreign military intervention. The protocol was published in the book, J. Navrátil (ed.), *The Prague Spring '68. A National Security Archives Documents Reader* (Budapest, 1998), pp. 477–80. The issues of the intervention and occupation have been discussed in a great number of works, including: J. Pauer, *Prag 1968. Der Einmarsch des Warschauer Paktes* (Hamburg, 1995); V. K. Volkov, *Konflikty v poslevoennom razvitii vostochnoevropeĭskikh stran* [Conflicts in the post-war development of East European countries] (Moscow, 1997); F. Leoncini and Carla Tonini (eds.), *Primavera di Praga e dintorni* (Venice, 2000); F. Fejtö and J. Rupnik (eds.), *Le Printemps tchécoslovaque* (Brussels, 1999).

[2] The Czechoslovak parliament approved a treaty on the 'temporary stay' of Soviet forces without much opposition. On the basis of the treaty, 75,000 Soviet soldiers were stationed in Czechoslovakia. See Navrátil, *The Prague Spring '68*, pp. 533–36.

The era of 'normalisation'

By the autumn of 1968, the campaign led by domestic conservative Communists was primarily directed at Josef Smrkovský, who was the chairman of parliament. As a result of Soviet pressure the leadership of the CPC did not repropose Smrkovský for the post at the end of 1968. The campaign unleashed to discredit Smrkovský was, at the same time, discrediting reformist communism in general. The second victim of Soviet pressure was Alexander Dubček, who was forced to resign as first secretary of the Central Committee of the CPC in mid April 1969.

With Gustáv Husák's assumption of the top position in the Communist Party, the era of 'normalisation' got underway.[3] At first, Husák (Fig. 18) denied that he would use repression against the reformist Communists. But in August 1969, when mass demonstrations against the occupation were held throughout the state, the CPC leadership ordered the use of the army, police and militia against the demonstrators. In addition, a special act was adopted, enabling the prosecution of any participant in such demonstrations.

In September–October 1969, under Husák's leadership, the Communist Party annulled the anti-occupation documents produced in August 1968. The lower Party bodies, state institutions and social organisations were also encouraged to annul their anti-occupation proclamations. At the same time, the Central Committee of the CPC and the Central Committee of the Communist Party of Slovakia (CPS) expelled their reformist members and appointed ideologically acceptable representatives of conservative forces in their place. The CPC's Action Programme of 1968, which contained a complete short-term plan for social reform, was declared invalid. At the end of August 1969, the highest representative of the CPC, Husák, in agreement with other Warsaw Pact leaders, henceforth described the military intervention as 'international assistance'. Reformist Communists were dismissed not only from elected positions on the Central Committees of the CPC and the CPS, but at lower levels of the Party and state bodies as well. In retrospect, the changes in the elected bodies of the CPC in autumn 1969 were preparations for the mass purges of 1970.

The stimulus for interviewing ('screening') all members of the CPC came from a session of the Central Committee held at the end of January 1970. Formally, the reason for screening was the replacement of Party membership documents. The real reason was, however, to exclude from

---

[3] The expression 'normalisation' is ironic, because Gustáv Husák referred to the period after 1969 as the time for a 'return to normal life'.

Figure 18 Gustáv Husák

the CPC reformist Communists and those who took a critical view of the policies of Husák's leadership after April 1969. Screening procedures were designed to secure the agreement of Party members for the military intervention and support for its rationale, that is, preventing a counter-revolutionary takeover in Czechoslovakia.

The mass screening of CPC members was combined with the screening of non-Party members and members of parliament; it included everyone with a leading position in the state and economic apparatus and social organisations as well as the representatives of the small non-communist parties. Expressions of disagreement with the military intervention, or with Husák's leadership, resulted in dismissal from work. Employment in the state or economic apparatus was now increasingly judged on political, rather than professional, criteria.

The screening of non-communists was undertaken by special commissions, composed of heads of offices or enterprises, representatives of the CPC, trade unions, and the personnel department of the office or enterprise. Tens of thousands of professionals were dismissed from their jobs for political reasons. The federal government of the Czechoslovak Socialist Republic and the governments of the Slovak Socialist Republic and Czech Socialist Republic were the supreme organs that directed the screening of the non-communists.

The screening of the members of the Communist Party was centrally directed by the Presidia of the CPC and CPS Central Committees. These bodies evaluated the progress of these endeavours in weekly or bi-weekly cycles, and directed the activity of the various screening commissions. Their task was to prove that this or that member of the Party was a 'rightist opportunist' or a 'revisionist', and supported or belonged to counter-revolutionary forces. The most commonly asked question during screening was the interviewee's attitude towards the military intervention. Screening commissions also used newspaper articles and public speeches from 1968 as evidence of counter-revolutionary or rightist-opportunist activity. Since it was problematic to prove hostile activity on the basis of such arguments, the screenings of many members were repeated several times, often without the participation of the screened person.

Mass screening of CPC members had been completed by the beginning of December 1970, as confirmed by a session of the CPC and CPS Central Committees. According to documents from this session, 326,817 members had been expelled from the Party, representing 21.7 per cent of the total membership. More Party members were expelled in the Czech Lands than in Slovakia. This is shown by the following figures: in the Czech Lands, 273,607 members, 23 per cent of the total, were expelled; but in Slovakia, the total was 53,206 members or 17.5 per cent. In addition, the number of members declined by about 150,000 as a result of resignations in protest against the Party's policies.

It was the ranks of the intelligentsia within the CPC that were most affected by these screenings. With 135,164 expellees from the Party across Czechoslovakia, the highest percentage of members driven out were artists, cultural, scientific and technical workers.[4] Expulsion from the CPC affected professionals at various levels of the state apparatus, representative bodies, education, culture and the armed forces. The greatest difference between the Czech Lands and Slovakia lay precisely in this group of intellectuals. Whereas in the Czech Lands 34.7 per cent of people belonging to it (including artists and journalists) were expelled, in Slovakia the figure was 15.8 per cent.[5] A large proportion of those who were forced out of the Party in Slovakia were aged from twenty-six to forty-five. A significant number were excluded for reasons of religious faith.

The tragedy of the mass screening of CPC members and non-Party members lay in the fact that their expulsion from the Party or dismissal from a job led to far-reaching social consequences. Journalists could not publish, scientists could not work in scientific institutes, and teachers could not teach. The affected people could only carry out manual work, usually as labourers or foresters, or in water management. The Party purges excluded more than 300,000 citizens from full political, management, scientific and cultural life, including the managerial sphere. The effects on those expelled from the CPC extended to the next of kin. The children could not go to selective schools or universities, or hold more important positions in the state apparatus, in economic enterprises or in schools. In this way, these political issues created a category of 'second-class citizens', who could work, but could not fully realise their abilities. They could not be elected to public office or apply for management positions.

The CPC was concerned that the people expelled might become radicalised; it therefore developed a plan to introduce a unified central record of the officially designated 'exponents of the right'. The Presidium of the CPC Central Committee ordered the keeping of these records at the beginning of 1971, and the lower Party bodies were to provide the names to be included in the record. By the end of 1971, the central record of 'exponents of the right' embraced 9,700 persons from the ranks of the reformist Communists and members of various associations, among them more than 500 who came from Slovakia. The purpose of

[4] The data on the purges are taken from 'Stenografický záznam Zasadania Ústredného výboru Komunistickej strany Československa 11.–12. decembra' [The shorthand record of the session of the Central Committee of the Communist Party of Czechoslovakia of 11–12 December]. It is included in V. Menzel (ed.), *Československo roku 1968* [Czechoslovakia in the year 1968], vol. II, *Počátky normalizace* [The beginnings of 'normalisation'] (Prague, 1993), p. 99.

[5] J. Maňák, *Čistky v Komunistické straně Československa 1969–1970* [The purges of the Communist Party of Czechoslovakia, 1969–1970] (Prague, 1997), p. 68.

this record was to ensure that these people did not hold public office and could not publish their views. The difference in the numbers of people expelled from the Party and then monitored in the two parts of Czechoslovakia throws light on the later development of the dissident and opposition movement in the Czech Lands and Slovakia.

The reformist Communists played an important part in the proclamation of Charter 77 by a group of Czech intellectual oppositionists (1 January 1977). The general weakness of the dissent in Slovakia is documented by the fact that when it originated, Charter 77 was signed by more than a thousand people in the Czech Lands, including many of well-known individuals, but by only ten in Slovakia. This situation becomes more understandable when one considers the fact that another form of 'normalisation' was used in Slovakia, one that was not as severe as it was in the Czech Lands. A certain passivity and the avoidance of direct confrontation with the regime continued in Slovakia until the middle of 1989. Therefore, the fall of communism came as a surprise to the majority of inhabitants, because it came without long-term conceptual and organisational preparations.[6]

The leaders of reformist communism were under police supervision from 1970 until the collapse of the Communist regime in 1989. Dubček later provided an eyewitness account of being kept under surveillance by State Security in his memoirs.[7] According to his account he was watched by security agents on his journeys into work, while at work, and in his free time; his house in Bratislava was constantly monitored.

About one-fifth of members of the Communist Party were affected by these purges, and once again more people came under suspicion in the Czech Lands than in Slovakia. This disparity evoked a certain amount of anti-Slovak sentiments in the Czech Lands. Part of Czech society associated the purges in the CPC and across society exclusively with Slovak politicians, not least Gustáv Husák and Vasil' Bil'ak (1917–), and their policies in the 1970s, and with the anti-democratic course and renewal of the hard-line political system. The influence these politicians had on this anti-democratic course was obvious, but Czech society also included radicals in the CPC and state institutions, who demanded strict treatment of the people expelled from the Party. The 'Communist Internationalists' were a special pressure group of radicals who demanded political trials of reformist Communists. These were older

---

[6] Ľ. Lipták, *Storočie dlhšie ako sto rokov* [A century longer than a hundred years] (Bratislava, 1999), p. 149.

[7] Alexander Dubček, *Nádej zomiera posledná* [Hope dies last] (Bratislava, 1993), contains a detailed description of his attitude to the Soviet occupation up to 1989.

members of the CPC who strongly opposed the reformist Communists, in co-operation with Soviet political representatives in Czechoslovakia.

In 1970, a special commission of high functionaries of the CPC was created to prepare a document on the causes of the military intervention and the Warsaw Pact's subsequent occupation, explaining the counter-revolutionary situation in Czechoslovakia, and assigning the blame for creating the situation in 1968 to the reformist Communists. This document was approved at a session of the CPC Central Committee in December 1970 under the title *Lesson from the Period of Crisis in the Party and Society after the Thirteenth Congress of the Communist Party of Czechoslovakia*. The final version of the document, drafted in consultation with the Soviet leadership, aimed at complying with the standpoint of the Soviet Union, the countries of the Warsaw Pact and the international communist movement regarding the military intervention. The document described the decision to intervene militarily in Czechoslovakia as international assistance and as the only option available to save socialism in Czechoslovakia. The document did not give the names of the CPC functionaries who asked the Soviet leadership to launch military intervention in letters in July–August 1968. The reason was because Husák, the chairman of the Federal Government Ľubomír Štrougal (1924–) and other leading Party and state figures were not among the signatories requesting a military intervention.

The document was the manifesto of neo-Stalinism in Czechoslovakia. Its content was obligatory reading for pupils and students in all schools. It was used to discredit the reformist Communists until the collapse of the regime in 1989. The document had catastrophic consequences for the social sciences in Czechoslovakia and especially for the interpretation of contemporary history. Accounts of history after 1945, that did not follow the dogmas contained in the document were banned. It was translated into Russian and, except for Polish, published in the languages of the Warsaw Pact states that had participated in the military intervention.

The CPC leadership under Husák also approved further measures to reinforce the neo-Stalinist policy. The 'cadres departments', defunct during the Prague Spring, were re-activated. These were offices that checked employees for job competency and political soundness. In November 1970, the Presidium of the CPC Central Committee approved the criteria for the evaluation of cadres. Political criteria such as full agreement with CPC policy, class consciousness and support for friendship with the Soviet Union were established as prerequisites for holding a responsible job. Professional expertise languished in second place. Such criteria for evaluating personnel opened the door for career advancement to the people who had recently participated in the purges of the CPC and society. The system of selection, assignment and control of the leading cadres in the state administration and economic apparatus, schools and cultural institutions, armed forces, and other areas of society according to political criteria continued until the collapse of the regime in 1989.

Under Husák, the CPC resumed centralisation of the economy in the years 1969–1971. The enhanced powers of federal ministries and the reined-in powers of the national governments strengthened centralism. This trend evolved from the amendment, in 1971, to the Act on the Czechoslovak federation of 1971. The changes significantly affected Slovakia, since engineering, arms production and energy production became the joint responsibility of the federal institutions. Thus, the Slovak government lost authority over the most important branches of its industry.

Investment in the industrial development of Slovakia remained high, especially in the 1970s. In spite of many problems – some in structural development, some in effectiveness, and some in the production of finished consumer goods – Slovakia approached the Czech Lands in various important indicators of production and standard of living during the 1970s and 1980s.[8] Almost full employment and a generous pension system created a feeling of social security across society. The gradual orientation towards a consumer society, tacitly supported by the Communist leadership from the beginning of the 1970s, was to prevent the merging of the political crisis with an economic one.

Social support for young married couples and pensioners and the relatively high standard of living in comparison with Poland, Hungary and the Soviet Union helped blunt dissatisfaction with the regime. However, in the longer term, the Czechoslovak economy and services were not able fully to satisfy the need of the citizens for high-quality and newly developed consumer goods, comparable to those available in advanced countries. Investment in the food processing, chemical and car industries in the 1970s and 1980s did not fulfil the targets either in terms of quantity or quality of their products. As a result, the black market economy and corruption were increasing. They existed with the tacit agreement of the regime, since they dampened discontent with the inadequacies of supplies to the internal market.

Following the oil crisis of the mid 1970s, the continuation of the old programmes and methods of managing the economy by the Communist

---

[8] For more detail on the question of the Slovak–Czech economic equalisation, see J. Musil (ed.), *The End of Czechoslovakia* (Budapest, 1997), pp. 62, 70.

leadership increasingly came into conflict with new trends in the developed industrial countries. The CPC leadership failed to recognise the significance of these changes and redirect social processes. Thus, it missed its last chance to change the long-term inefficiency of the Czechoslovak economy. The growth of negative phenomena such as the misappropriation of state property, the reporting of untrue and exaggerated economic results, the black market economy and corruption were factors that slowly eroded the regime from within.

'Really existing socialism', as the neo-Stalinist system of the 1970s and 1980s was officially designated, had the following characteristics: ideology became a set of signs and directives, by which the regime indicated what views were required from people; failure to give the required sign was punished. Really existing socialism completely failed in its great propaganda campaign designed to link socialism with the Scientific-Technical Revolution worldwide. While the supposed superiority of the socialist political system over the capitalist system remained an idea on paper, the regime gradually exhausted the possibilities for lasting stabilisation.

Opposition to the neo-Stalinist regime

The everyday life of citizens in the 1970s and 1980s took a variety of forms. As a result of almost full employment, the number of people living below the minimum standard of living was much lower than in the developed countries, but problems existed in other areas. Citizens faced difficulties with shortages of certain kinds of goods and low-quality services, with the black market economy profiting from this situation. Attempts to eliminate these problems proved unsuccessful because the regime proceeded in reverse order – it was not removing the causes but the effects. Apart from this, various corruption scandals traumatised society in Slovakia: the investigations were long-drawn-out and ended with the punishment of lowly functionaries, while the main offenders escaped prosecution. The majority of people were powerless to improve the increasingly negative aspects of society, and this heightened their distrust of the ruling establishment.

Opposition to the neo-Stalinist regime under Husák at the beginning of the 1970s crystallised around representatives of the intelligentsia harmed by the Party purges. Effectively they had been badly harmed by the revival of censorship and the limitation of freedom of scientific and artistic activity. As noted earlier, once they lost their previous jobs, they earned their living by manual labour. The situation of the opposition was different from that in Poland because it did not have support among the workers and peasant-farmers. Since the regime reintroduced state supervision of the churches, they were unable to give political and moral support to the opposition in Czechoslovakia at the beginning of the 1970s.

In 1972, the regime staged political trials against representatives of the opposition, who came largely from the ranks of the Czech intelligentsia. The stimulus to hold political trials came from the Soviet leadership, which urged the Czechoslovak government to silence the opposition and prevent reports of violations of civil and human rights spreading abroad before the beginning of the proposed Conference on Security and Cooperation in Europe (CSCE).

The political trials of 1972 aimed to silence the activity of individuals, especially reformist Communists. After the imprisonment of forty-seven members of the opposition, its ranks were seriously depleted and weakened for several years. As a result, an atmosphere of immobility and political passivity emerged. Fear of repression strengthened the conviction that the socialism in Soviet-type societies was not reformable.

Alexander Dubček occupied a special place in the opposition. Since he was under strict police supervision, he decided to protest against CPC policy in letters addressed to the Presidium of the Central Committees of the CPC and the CPS, Gustáv Husák, the federal and Slovak parliaments, representatives of the Warsaw Pact states which had participated in the military intervention, and representatives of the Italian and French Communist Parties. His letters openly criticised the CPC's policy and representatives.

Dubček's letters from 1969 to 1975 contained sharp criticism of the situation of the reformist Communists and all those given the status of 'second-class citizens' by the regime. He gave a detailed description of his own position in what he regarded as a police state, where the security services dominated life. In October 1974, Husák reacted to Dubček's criticisms in a letter to the federal parliament. In a public speech, Husák described Dubček's platform as being anti-state and treasonable. This public criticism was intended to intimidate and silence Dubček, as well as to warn other reformist Communists. Before a European conference of communist parties due to be held in Berlin, Dubček sent a letter to the leaders of the Polish and East German Communist Parties, demanding that the Berlin conference should concern itself with the position of the members expelled from the CPC, since they were subjected to oppression and social inequality. He emphasised that there was a campaign in the socialist countries against the violations of human rights by General Augusto Pinochet in Chile, but that the communist states closed their eyes to persecution and violation of human rights in Czechoslovakia.

Dubček could not be arrested and convicted in 1975, because the Communist regime in Czechoslovakia wanted to avoid complete isolation prior to the signing of the Final Act of the Conference on Security and Cooperation in Europe in August.

New dynamics in society in the second half of the 1980s

After Mikhail S. Gorbachev (1931–) became general secretary of the Communist Party of the Soviet Union in 1985, Slovak and Czech society observed the development of *perestroika* and *glasnost* with great interest. Many people hoped that the neo-Stalinist regime in Czechoslovakia would not only declare its support for these policies, but that it would also change its own policy. These expectations flowed from the fact that, on various occasions, Gorbachev adopted a critical stance towards the previous form of relations between the Soviet Union and the states of the Soviet bloc. A declaration by Gorbachev on the independent decision-making power of the communist parties of the Soviet bloc countries and an indication that the Soviet leadership would not intervene in their internal affairs were regarded as being especially important. The Soviet leadership had made it clear that the development of individual states was down to the free play of domestic forces, without regard for their relationship to Soviet *perestroika*.

Dubček viewed these Soviet reforms as a process similar to that which had emerged in Czechoslovakia in 1968. After Gorbachev came to power, Dubček once more protested against Husák's leadership in letters sent to the Presidiums of the Central Committees of the CPC and the CPS, to Soviet representatives, the Hungarian leader János Kádár and the Italian Communists, in which he defended the Czechoslovak reforms of 1968. The CPC leadership declared its verbal support for *perestroika*, but did not allow renewed public discussion of the reforms of 1968.

Gorbachev's first official visit to Czechoslovakia took place in April 1987, and raised many people's expectations. The warm welcome that the inhabitants of Prague and Bratislava gave Gorbachev was associated with hope that the Soviet leader would denounce the 1968 military intervention. But this did not happen. During his visit, Gorbachev spoke of Czechoslovakia as a country with a high standard of living, and in doing so he actually lent support to Husák's leadership of the Communist Party of Czechoslovakia. His support for the conservative politicians in Czechoslovakia came as a great disappointment for the population.

In January 1988, Dubček gave the Italian paper *L'Unita* an extensive interview, in which he demanded that the CPC re-evaluate the events of

1968. However, during a visit by Husák's successor as general secretary of the CPC Central Committee, Miloš Jakeš, to Moscow in January 1988, Gorbachev said that there was no reason to re-evaluate the events and individuals of 1968. Jakeš then accused Dubček of wanting to exploit Soviet *perestroika* to conduct a political campaign against the CPC leadership. The belated condemnation of the military intervention in Czechoslovakia by the Soviet leadership on 4 December 1989 came only after the collapse of the Communist regime.

The opposition and dissident movements in Slovakia developed among the activists connected to Charter 77 and other independent civic groups. The original number of signatories from Slovakia was rather small; they worked towards the same goals of promoting human and civil rights. Its members were drawn from the ranks of former reformist Communists and belonged to the intelligentsia (teachers, writers and research workers). Over the course of the 1980s, members of the Catholic Church also developed activities in defence of religious freedom. At various religious celebrations, they decried the limitation on and violation of the right of citizens to express their religious freedom. Environmental activists formed a green group, which campaigned for greener policies. They criticised the ruling establishment for the pollution of the environment at various localities in Slovakia. The publication of the Bratislava Greens, *Bratislava nahlas* (Bratislava aloud), received a remarkable response both at home and abroad. The authors criticised pollution of the atmosphere in Bratislava and the lack of care for historic monuments.

In the second half of the 1980s, previously unknown dissidents and opposition civic groups gained support from other social groups. The atmosphere in society was ever more influenced by their activity, especially after jamming of Voice of America and Radio Free Europe ended, and other information barriers were removed. The regime unwittingly increased public interest in the activity of the dissidents and civic groups when it demanded unambiguous condemnation of its documents and appeals without releasing information about their content.

At first, the Communist regime regarded the dissident movement and civic groups as the work of the intelligentsia and not of particular significance. Until the mid-1980s, the highest Party and government circles held the view that not publishing the documents relating to the activities of the dissident movements, together with supervision of its members by State Security, was sufficient to keep such groups under control. This situation changed after 1985 with the arrival of *perestroika* and *glasnost*. The Communist regime now observed the growth of the opposition movement with some apprehension.

The ruling establishment in Slovakia was especially disturbed by the growing underground activities of the Church, the lay movement within the churches, and the Pacem in terris movement, plus the growing number of pilgrims attending religious celebrations; these all showed the weakening of state influence over the religious sphere.[9] Until the collapse of the regime, State Security provided the Party and state leadership with reports on the security situation in Czechoslovakia. These reports contained disturbing information about how the dissident and civic groups were beginning to unite and undertake co-ordinated activities. Reports on foreign support for the dissident and civic groups were also regarded with alarm.

The regime launched media campaigns against the dissidents, their organisations and other groups, calling this a 'struggle against anti-socialist forces', but these actions were not successful because the regime was losing the support of social strata that had traditionally supported it, and the young generation was inclined to a system of values different to those propagated by the Communist regime.

A variety of problems accumulated in a range of socio-economic developments that emerged during the period 1970–1989, none of which the regime could solve. The citizens felt growing dissatisfaction and had increasing reservations about the inefficient economic system and the resulting low levels of pay. All previous attempts to solve the economic and social questions had proved unsuccessful. The regime had prevented, primarily for ideological reasons, any reforms allowing elements of a market economy. The CPC feared that even small-scale private business and free competition would weaken its position. However, the social situation prior to the fall of communism was not bad enough directly to cause the collapse of the regime.

The collapse of the Communist regime

The collapse of the Communist regime in Czechoslovakia began on 17 November 1989, primarily for political reasons, which included the inability of the regime to liberalise the political system, and hence to safeguard the provision of human and civil rights. It also proved impossible for the Party to end the centralisation of decision-making processes, to legalise a plurality of political groupings and to remove its power monopoly over society. One of the leading Slovak dissidents, Milan Šimečka (1930–1990), said in connection

---

[9] Pacem in terris was a religious pro-regime organisation of priests that was not recognised by the Holy See.

with the fall of communism that November 1989 was a revolution for freedom, human rights and dignity.

Over the course of six weeks, beginning on 17 November, the decisive political forces – Občanské fórum (the Civic Forum, CF) in the Czech Lands and Verejnosť proti násiliu (Public Against Violence, PAV) in Slovakia – succeeded in taking over the key departments of executive power, including the federal presidency. The handing over of functions from the representatives of the Communist Party to representatives of the CF and PAV was accompanied by tensions in parliament and across all of society. This happened because at the time of their formation both the CF and PAV lacked clear ideas about how to take over the legislative and executive power of the state. They continued exerting political pressure on the leadership of the CPC, the ministries and parliament by organising demonstrations, including a general strike, in large towns statewide. University students played an important role as a vocal pressure group. The decisions about how best to form the new government and federal parliament and elect the new president were finally made by a small number of persons representing the CF and PAV.

At the beginning of December 1989, the determining political forces – the CF and PAV – decided to participate in political power. They held negotiations with the CPC leadership regarding the composition of a new federal government led by the Slovak Marián Čalfa.

By means of a negotiated transfer of power, the CF and PAV succeeded in bringing about changes in key state posts by the end of December 1989. In addition to Čalfa, who headed the federal government, they proposed Alexander Dubček for the post of chairman of the federal parliament and Václav Havel (1936–) for the presidency of Czechoslovakia. These changes, together with other reforms in the governments of the Czech and Slovak Republics and their parliaments, created important conditions for a stable transition from the communist to the democratic system. This transition was not a matter of the regeneration of 'reformed socialism' from 1968, but of a return to a democratic system that had existed before communism, but in a new modified form.

On the road to the 'velvet divorce'

The collapse of the Communist regime in 1989 revealed a multitude of accumulated problems in the economic sphere and issues related to the constitutional relations within the federation. The legacy of the Communist regime, which had been in place since the takeover in February 1948, also had to be overcome in other areas of social life. The CF and

PAV had no specified plans for the transition period. The legitimacy of the government of national understanding (the federal parliament and national governments only lasted until the elections held in June 1990) was too short to work out long-term programme changes.

The representatives elected in the parliamentary ballot of 1990 and 1992 endeavoured to resolve the constitutional relations between the Czechs and Slovaks. The complex talks over three years can be divided into three phases according to the dominating themes and the main participants.

The first phase concerned amendment of the Constitution of the Czechoslovak Socialist Republic and the Constitutional Act on the Czechoslovak federation. The articles related to the monopoly of the CPC, the ideology of Marxism-Leninism, the planned economy and other issues were removed. These changes occurred at the end of 1989. The first complications in Czech–Slovak relations arose in connection with choosing a new name for the state. In March 1990, the adjective 'socialist' was removed from the name Czechoslovak Socialist Republic. President Havel proposed that the new name of the state should be the 'Czecho-Slovak Republic', that is the name from the period 1918–1920. The inclusion of a hyphen into the name provoked opposition in the Czech Lands. The name Czecho-Slovak Republic was not accepted by the Federal National Assembly, and at the beginning of April 1990 they agreed on the name the 'Czech and Slovak Federative Republic', which was to remain the final name of Czechoslovakia until its demise. The hyphen provoked differences of view and emotions on both sides of the federation. Displays of nationalism were dangerous because they made the negotiations more difficult. This phase also involved moves to strengthen Slovak national symbols, including the state emblem, the flag and the anthem.

However, during the final phase of these talks the main subject of the Czech–Slovak talks was the division of powers between the federal and national bodies. Conducted by representatives of the executive, the talks led to the revised Constitutional Act of 12 December 1990. It defined the jurisdiction powers of the federal bodies in eleven separate areas, with other competencies being given to national institutions. In effect, this act renewed the division of powers as they were originally defined in 1968, when the federation was first formed. It repealed a series of articles from the years 1970–1972 that strengthened the central federative institutions at the expense of the national ones. During this phase, the Czech and Slovak sides were willing to co-operate and agree on the continued preservation of the federation in spite of various disputes.

The second stage consisted of negotiations regarding a new state treaty that was to determine the division of powers between the federation and national republics. The sphere of activity of the federation was to be reduced from eleven areas to three: foreign affairs, defence and the internal market. The main reservations about the state treaty proposed by the Slovak representatives came from the Czech Lands. Their fears and reservations were based on the concern that such a constitution would go beyond the framework of the federation and would change it into a confederation. This would require basic changes to the federal constitution. The negotiations between the Slovak and Czech representatives became increasingly tense during the run-up to the parliamentary elections in spring 1992. The compromise treaty was not accepted, because it was not approved by a vote in the Presidium of the Slovak parliament. After the rejection of the treaty by the Slovak parliament, the Czech side refused to hold further talks about constitutional questions with the Slovaks.

It was the winners of the 1992 parliamentary elections who effectively initiated the third phase; these included: the Civic Democratic Party (CDP) in the Czech Republic and the Movement for a Democratic Slovakia (MDS) in Slovakia. After the elections, the leaders of these parties – Václav Klaus (1941–) of the CDP and Vladimír Mečiar (1942–) of the MDS (see Fig. 19) – expressed differing views on the future constitutional relations between Czechs and Slovaks. But they finally agreed on a division of the federation into two independent states. The talks between Klaus and Mečiar were designed to tackle the question of how to divide the federation, including the dismantling of the federal establishment; constitutional aspects of this division; and the allocation of federal property and obligations between the successor states of the federation. Shortly before the division, further talks were held on the future form of relations between the Czech and Slovak Republics. The two sides agreed that mutual relations were to develop on the basis of international treaties and agreements, so that good neighbourly relations could extend to all spheres; they also ruled out tight restrictions for moving across their common border.[10]

The acceptance of the Declaration of Sovereignty of the Slovak Republic on 17 July 1992 and of the Constitution of the Slovak Republic

---

[10] An expert legal view can be found in E. Stein, *Česko-Slovensko, konflikt, roztržka, rozpad* (Prague, 2000). The book is a translation from English into Czech. The original version is E. Stein, *Czecho/Slovakia. Ethnic Conflict, Constitutional Fissure, Negotiated Break-up* (Ann Arbor, MI, 1997). Stein uses the following periodisation for 1990–1992: reforms, restructuring, new forms of coexistence (pp. 247–50).

Figure 19 The two politicians who dissolved the Czech and Slovak Federative Republic (1992): Václav Klaus and Vladimír Mečiar (first and second from left)

on 1 September 1992 constituted important milestones on the road to the division of the federation. In the autumn of 1992, the Federal National Assembly adopted measures ensuring that the dissolution of the federation was legal and civilised, thus avoiding the violent conflict that had consumed the former Yugoslavia. Despite calls for a referendum on the federation's future, and about 2.5 million Czechoslovak citizens (of 15.6 million) supporting the idea, no referendum took place. Both the CDP and MDS rejected the concept of holding one because they feared the outcome.

The members of the Federal National Assembly voted on 25 November 1992 to accept Constitutional Act no. 542 on the Dissolution of the Czech and Slovak Federative Republic, to be implemented on 31 December 1992, and the Succession of the Czech and Slovak Republics to the Federation. The seventy-four years of the coexistence of the Slovaks and Czechs in a common state came to an end.

The federation, as it was implemented in 1969, had never been fully functional, and resembled the administrative division of the state into two units, rather than a functioning federative organisation. The causes of the federation's dissolution, therefore, need to be sought elsewhere.

Economic factors are often present in ethnic conflicts, but they can be considered secondary in the case of the break-up of Czechoslovakia. In 1989, macro-economic data from the Czech Lands and Slovakia were broadly similar. Changes began after 1990, when unemployment grew rapidly as a result of the conversion of the arms industry in Slovakia. This issue influenced Slovak voters in the 1992 parliamentary elections, because the nationalistically oriented political parties used it to spread anti-Czech propaganda.

Ethnic conflicts usually have a deeper genesis. In the case of Czechoslovakia, we can say that its origins lay in the different historical developments of the Czechs and Slovaks prior to the formation of Czechoslovakia in 1918. Moreover, it was constituted from entities that differed economically, socially and culturally. These differences were reflected in the political conceptions of the relationship between the Czechs and Slovaks. The Czech political representatives in 1918 generally supported the conception of a Czechoslovak political nation, combined with the preservation of a separate cultural identity for the Slovaks. In Slovakia, a significant proportion of politicians supported autonomy for Slovakia within the framework of Czechoslovakia, and later a federative system. These different political conceptions re-emerged in 1990–1992, when a new constellation of political forces and leaders took power after the fall of communism. Important parts of the political elite in both parts of the state stimulated nationalist feelings, which they used in public arguments about division of the federation. The political ambitions of the leaders of the CDP and MDS, who used the situation to their advantage, also played an important role in the state's eventual dismemberment. Some Czech and Slovak politicians developed the idea of the separate integration of the Czech and Slovak republics into European structures. While external factors influenced the break-up of the federation, direct foreign influence can be excluded.

The peaceful division of Czechoslovakia had its own internal and external rationale. The linguistic closeness of the two nations, and close contacts between them, strengthened by numerous mixed marriages and family relationships, resulted in a peaceful separation. Historical experience of mutual relations was also associated with this.[11] During a thousand years of history, the Czechs and Slovaks had never fought each other in wars or in local conflicts. Past relationships between Czechs and Slovaks usually had been mutually supportive. Importantly, there were

---

[11] D. Kováč, *Slováci. Češi. Dejiny* [Slovaks. Czechs. History] (Bratislava, 1997).

no outstanding territorial issues because the Czech–Slovak borders had long been accepted by both sides.

The peaceful constitutional division of the state was not achieved without some disquiet among the population. This was confirmed by sociological research in the Czech and Slovak Republics in 1993, a year after the independence of the two republics. According to this research, the percentage of the population opposed to the break-up of the state were 48 per cent in Slovakia and 44 per cent in the Czech Republic.[12]

The attitude of Western countries to the peaceful division of Czechoslovakia was also important. At first the Western countries, including the USA, Britain and Germany, did not favour the division, especially because they feared that it would complicate the integration of these successor states into a number of important world and European organisations. The British prime minister, John Major, one of the strongest supporters of a united Czechoslovakia even after the June 1992 elections, expressed the view that the state should not be divided for these reasons.

The first change in the position of the Western states came about after a meeting between President George Bush *père* of the United States and President Havel of Czechoslovakia at the third summit of the Conference on Security and Cooperation in Europe in Helsinki on 9 and 10 July 1992. Havel emphasised that the split was unavoidable and would not destabilise Central Europe; precisely the reverse: it was the way to avoid a crisis situation that could lead to instability.[13] President Bush accepted the arguments of President Havel and issued a declaration in which the USA accepted the division. After this declaration, other Western states and members of the North Atlantic Treaty Organization (NATO) also changed their positions. In the summer and autumn of 1992, Czechoslovak diplomacy began to seek international recognition for both successor states.

---

[12] R. Roško, *Slovensko na konci tisícročia* [Slovakia at the end of the millennium] (Bratislava, 2000), p. 275.

[13] M. Beblavý and A. Salner, *Tvorcovia obrazu a obraz tvorcov. Vnímanie Slovenska v západných krajinách 1989–1999* [Creators of an image and the image of the creators. The perception of Slovakia in Western countries 1989–1999] (Bratislava, 1999), p. 49.

23 Afterword: Slovakia in history

Mikuláš Teich

I

Until the dissolution of Czecho-Slovakia (31 December 1992/1 January 1993) Slovakia was largely associated with the ending of the words Czechoslovakia/Czecho-Slovakia. Czech or Slovak? What's in a name? Many English speakers remain uncomfortable with this question or, for that matter, with differentiating between Slovakia and Slovenia.

As documented in this volume, Slovaks and Czechs are two closely related nations, sharing many things in the spheres of language and culture. While the short history of Great Moravia (833–907) belongs to Czech and Slovak history, there are gaps – due to a paucity of sources – in our understanding of its decline and the ensuing incorporation of the territory of contemporary Slovakia into the Hungarian state. This has provided the impetus for misrepresentations of the Slovak–Magyar coexistence, which lasted 1,000 years. Not confined to dubious perceptions on the part of the general public, myths and half-truths have been a disturbing element in national historical works authored by Slovak and Magyar scholars.[1]

Slovakia in History parallels *Bohemia in History*.[2] Both collections offer accounts of key moments and themes in the history of Czechs and Slovaks and thus allow for comparisons between them. What attracts attention, in the Czech case, is the relative early rise of Czech national consciousness and statehood.

From the tenth century, the history of Slovaks and Czechs unfolded differently. Slovaks constituted themselves ethnically within the Hungarian state, and politically as a nation during the nineteenth century. Then the Slovak spokesmen adopted a political programme demanding autonomy within the framework of the Hungarian state. This goal resurfaced after the establishment of the Czechoslovak Republic in 1918. The

---

[1] For a recent discussion of this subject, see R. Holec, 'Aký príbor potrebujeme?' [What kind of cutlery do we need?], *Listy*, 38 (2) (2008), 36–40.
[2] M. Teich (ed.), *Bohemia in History* (Cambridge, 1997).

demand for autonomy was continuously advocated by sections of the Slovak polity and entailed a dramatic complication of Slovak political history after it was unilaterally proclaimed on 6 October 1938, in the wake of the Munich Agreement – dramatic in the sense that within fifty-four years Slovakia's constitutional status changed five times: autonomy, statehood by proxy, asymmetry in influencing affairs of the state, federalisation, independent statehood. Conspicuously, it is the period 1938 to 1992 which is addressed most fully in *Slovakia in History*. Eleven of twenty-one contributions focus upon it, whereas in *Bohemia in History* it is covered in three of eighteen.

Whatever the divergences in style and emphasis, the authors agree on the oppressiveness of the political systems introduced by Hlinka's Slovak People's Party and the Communist Party of Czechoslovakia/Slovakia – denoted as 'totalitarian'. The term goes back to the 1920s when Italian fascists employed it to define their system. During the Cold War period, in the West, it became part and parcel of the description of the nature of the communist regimes.[3] The historians who accept the usefulness of the term argue that fascism and communism were two sides of the same coin. In essence, what is common to both systems, they stress, is the one-party rule in conjunction with overall state control of people's lives. Put like that – making them equivalent – it sounds logical enough. But when it comes to Slovakia, we have only to glance at the contributions dealing with the clerico-fascist period (1939–1945) and the Communist era (1948–1989) to see that, even where there is broad agreement on the totalitarian nature of the Communist regime, there are variants in positions taken on it. Here a Slovak historian's comment deserves to be cited:

The theory of totalitarianism regarding the common roots and anti-democratic nature of fascism and communism (as two antipodes of the same phenomenon), brought to absurdness, eradicates differences between aggression and defence. In this way the *raison d'être* of the very fight against fascism and for the national liberation, and the results of the whole war, is called in question.[4]

---

[3] Communist/communist regimes; Communism/communism etc. To capitalise, or not to capitalise: that is the question – answered in a variety of ways. Cf. T. Bottomore (ed.), *A Dictionary of Marxist Thought* (Oxford, 1983); A. Brown, *The Rise and Fall of Communism* (London, 2009).

[4] J. Korček, 'K dezinterpretáciám charakteristiky politického systému a režimu Slovenskej republiky 1939–1945' [On misrepresentations of the nature of the political system and regime of the Slovak Republic 1939–1945], in P. Juriga (ed.), *Nezodpovedané otázky. K spochybňovaniu odboja a SNP v našich národných dejinách* [Unanswered questions. On calling into question the resistance movement and the Slovak National Uprising in our national history] (Banská Bystrica, 1998), p. 41.

II

When eleven years ago Cambridge University Press was considering the proposal for *Slovakia in History*, it was provided with three reports. While one was enthusiastic, two were sceptical, even hostile. Among others, the notion 'Slovakia' was questioned – it was argued that it did not exist before 1918. Responding in a letter (18 October 1999), I pointed out that names of localities – Slovenská Lupča, Slovenské Pravno and others – give the lie to such suppositions. Further drawing on my scholarly interests, I put forward two instances of earlier use.

First, trivially but none the less factually, 'Slovakian' barley was widely known and sought after by brewers in Germany. But of more significance is Isaac Newton's employment of 'Sclavonia' – the Latinised form of Slovakia – in a famous letter known as the 'Aston letter', dated 18 May 1669. For one thing, 'it is the only personal letter to or from a peer in Cambridge in the whole of Newton's correspondence'.[5] For another, its interpretation became one of the issues in the historiography of science, debated between 'externalists' and 'internalists': that is, to what extent, if at all, external social influences played a role in Newton's work. What cannot be gainsaid is that 'about 1669 Newton began to read extensively in alchemical literature'[6] which, inevitably, led him to pay attention to mining and metallurgy. He certainly became an expert assayist which stood him in good stead in his association with the administration of the Mint, first as Warden and then as Master, from 1696 to his death in 1727.

Among the most studied metallic transmutation by alchemists was that of iron into copper. It was believed to occur when iron objects dipped into 'vitriolate waters' (copper sulphate solutions) precipitated copper in the process. Known to be practised in European mining regions, Newton urged Aston to find out whether at Schemnitium in Hungary (where there were mines for gold, copper, iron, vitriol, antimony and so on) they changed iron into copper by dissolving it in a 'vitriolate water' that they found in the cavities of rocks in the mines and then melted the slimy solution in a fierce heat before cooling it to reveal the copper.

Newton was also interested in the extraction of gold by means of amalgamation and he asked Aston:

---

[5] R. S. Westfall, *Never at Rest. A Biography of Isaac Newton* (Cambridge, 1984), p. 193. Like Newton, Francis Aston (1645–1715) was a Fellow of Trinity College Cambridge. Before departing for Europe, Aston asked Newton for advice on what to observe etc. Newton's response is reprinted (with notes) in H. W. Turnbull (ed.), *The Correspondence of Isaac Newton*, vol. I, *1661–1675* (Cambridge, 1959), pp. 9–13.

[6] Westfall, *Newton*, p. 290.

Whither in Hungary, Sclavonia, Bohemia neare the town Eila [Jílové], or at ye mountains of Bohemia neare Silesia there be rivers whose waters are impregnated with gold; perhaps ye Gold being dissolved by som corrosive waters like *Aqua Regis* & ye solution carried along wth ye streame that runs through ye mines. And whither ye practise of laying mercury in the rivers till it be tinged with gold & then straining ye mercury through leather ye gold may stay behind, bee a secret yet or openly practised.

Schemnitium is the Latinised Schemnitz – the German rendering of Slovak Banská Štiavnica.[7] Sclavonia, as noted, is the Latinised Slovakia – Slovensko. Seemingly, there is no information whether Aston took up any of Newton's suggestions. What is certain that another Englishman, the physician Edward Brown(e) visited Štiavnica and other mining localities in central Slovakia in 1672. His detailed account provides a vivid picture of contemporary mining and metallurgic operations therein. It includes the manner in which

the Miners direct themselves underground by a compass not of thirty-two points (such as is used at sea) but by one of twenty-four, which they divide as we do the hours of the day into twice twelve.

The account contains also a good deal about the change of iron into copper. Thus

They make also very handsome Cups and Vessels out of this sort of Copper, and we drank out of one of them which was gilded over, and had a rich piece of Silver-Ore, fastned in the middle of it; and this Inscription graved on the outside:

> *Eisen war ich, Kupfer bin ich*
> *Silber trag ich, Gold bedeckt mich.*
> Copper I am, but Iron was of old,
> Silver I carry, cover'd am with Gold.[8]

---

[7] In 1959, unbelievably, the editor of Newton's correspondence maintains that 'Schemnitz (Selmeczbánya) . . . is still the mining centre of Hungary.' For historical reasons the place-names referred to appear in literature under different guises:

Slovak	German	Magyar
Banská Štiavnica	Schemnitz	Selmeczbánya
Kremnica	Kremnitz	Körmöczbánya
Banská Bystrica	Neusohl	Beszterczebánya
Gelnica	Göllnitz	Gölniczbánya
Levoča	Leutschau	Löcse
Nová Baňa	Königsberg	Ujbánya
Skleno/Sklenné Teplice	Glasshütte	Skleno Fürdö
Smolník	Schmölnitz	Szómolnok

[8] E. Brown, *A Brief Account of Some Travels in Hungaria . . . Friuli etc.* (London, 1673), pp. 99, 110; reprint K. Nehrig (ed.) (Munich, (1975).

III

The relatively advanced state of mining and metallurgy in early modern Slovakia (conjectured by Newton and testified to by Brown) prompts a question: why did these favourable conditions not become a starting point for the country's industrialisation? Before attempting to answer it, we should recall briefly the historical background. Since the Middle Ages the mountainous regions of Slovakia, which belonged to the Kingdom of Hungary, were among the leading Central European mining centres. Ever since 1526, regarded as the year of the birth of the Habsburg monarchy with the union of Austria, Bohemia and Hungary, the Viennese court had come to regard the production of gold, silver and copper in Slovakia as a major contribution to the state economy.

There were two large mining areas, one situated in the central part of Slovakia and the other further to the east. Whereas first in importance among the 'Lower Hungarian Mining Towns' in the central part were Banská Štiavnica (silver), Kremnica (gold) and Banská Bystrica (copper), the principal among the 'Upper Hungarian Mining Towns' in the east were Gelnica and Smolník, chiefly known for their copper.

From the middle of the fifteenth century, bronze guns were preferred to iron ones. As copper is the most important ingredient of bronze, the significance of trade in 'Hungarian copper' grew. Spain, for example, obtained a supply of copper mostly from Slovakia until the middle of the sixteenth century. As confirmed by V. Segeš, a major player in the European copper trade was the Thurzo-Fugger Commercial Company. It was set up jointly by a native of Levoča in east-central Slovakia, Ján Thurzo (1437–1505), a gifted technician and entrepreneur, and the Fuggers, the great south German entrepreneurs. The financial resource for the copper trade was the silver produced in the process of refining the crude copper.[9]

The Austrian Habsburgs, continually short of money, supported various attempts to increase the production of gold and silver in territories under their rule, which included the mining and exploitation of metals in

---

[9] As noted by V. Segeš, there is a collection of studies on the subject by M. Marsina (ed.), *Banské mestá na Slovensku* [Mining towns in Slovakia] (Martin, 1990); C. M. Cipolla, *Guns and Sails in the Early Phase of European Expansion 1400–1700* (London, 1965), still provides a good background. See also T. Sokoll, 'Das ungarische Garkupfer und die Fugger-Thurzo-Gesellschaft', in Sokoll, *Bergbau im Übergang zur Neuzeit* (Idstein, 1994), pp. 55–6. It relies on older literature: P. Ratkoš, 'Das Kupferwesen in der Slowakei vor der Entstehung der Thurzo-Fuggerschen Handelsgesellschaft', in I. Bog (ed.), *Der Aussenhandel Ostmitteleuropas 1450–1650. Die ostmitteleuropäischen Volkswirtschaften in ihren Beziehungen zu Mitteleuropa* (Cologne and Vienna, 1971), pp. 584–99; J. Vlachovič, 'Produktion und Handel mit ungarischem Kupfer im 16. und im ersten Viertel des 17. Jahrhunderts', *ibid.*, pp. 600–27.

Slovakia. This resulted in the introduction of new techniques, such as the cracking of rock with the aid of gunpowder (1627), the setting up of the first Newcomen engine outside Britain (1721–1722) and the construction of impressive water-pressure engines for the draining of mines (in the 1750s and 1760s).[10] Another aspect of the efforts to raise the mining and metallurgical standards was the recognition of the need to train mining and metallurgical personnel. From 1735 an educational system for specialists in mining and metallurgy gradually developed, culminating in the establishment of the Mining School at Banská Štiavnica (1762–1764). The first higher educational institution of its kind in Europe, it changed its name to Mining Academy in 1770.[11]

By the latter part of the eighteenth century, however, production of precious metals in central Slovakia was in decline. These were then the external circumstances which encouraged Ignaz (Inigo) von Born (1742–1791) to investigate the possibility of bringing amalgamation for silver production back to the Old World and also of establishing that low-grade ores could be treated in that manner. His amalgamation process was examined at an international gathering of experts in mining and metallurgy, possibly the first of its kind, held at Skleno/Sklenné Teplice in 1786. Here also a short-lived society for mining sciences, the Societät der Bergbaukunde, was founded.[12]

It is natural to inquire whether the innovations actuated in the region of Banská Štiavnica had repercussions in Slovakia similar, for instance, to Scotland, where a close relationship between the economy, technology and education existed in the eighteenth century. For one thing, the lack of suitable coal affected negatively any further contemplation of its

[10] See M. Teich, 'Diffusion of Steam-, Water-, and Air-Power to and from Slovakia During the Eighteenth Century and the Problem of the Industrial Revolution', in M. Daumas and R. Taton (eds.), *L'acquisition des techniques par les pays non-initiateurs. Colloques internationaux du CNRS, no. 538* (Paris, 1973; reprinted in S. Pollard (ed.), *The Metal Fabrication and Engineering Industries* (Oxford, 1994)); M. Teich, 'The Early History of the Newcomen Engine at Nová Baňa (Königsberg). Isaac Potter's Negotiations with the *Hofkammer* and the Signing of the Agreement on 19 August 1721', *East Central Europe/ L'Europe du Centre-Est*, 9 (1982), 24–38.

[11] See J. Vlachovič, 'Die Bergakademie in Banská Štiavnica (Schemnitz) im 18. Jahrhundert', in E. Amburger, M. Cieśla and L. Sziklay (eds.), *Wissenschaftspolitik in Mittel- und Osteuropa Wissenschaftliche Gesellschaften, Akademien und Hochschulen im 18. und beginnenden 19. Jahrhundert* (Berlin, 1976), pp. 206–20.

[12] M. Teich, 'Born's Amalgamation Process and the International Metallurgic Gathering at Skleno in 1786', *Annals of Science*, 32 (1975), 305–40. Born, a representative figure of the Bohemian and Austrian Enlightenment, was a man of many facets: scientist (Fellow of the Royal Society), technologist, collector of minerals, civil servant, publisher, editor, organiser of science, Freemason and anti-clerical ideologist. Remarkably, no comprehensive account of his life and work exists. See H. Reinalter (ed.), *Die Aufklärung in Österreich. Ignaz von Born und seine Zeit* (Frankfurt am Main, 1991).

use in fuelling Newcomen engines and, of course, hampered a transition to Watt steam engines. For the Habsburgs, the mining of precious metals in Slovakia was primarily a means of bolstering the notoriously shaky financial position of the Austrian state. Joachim von Sternberg (1755–1808), a shrewd Bohemian aristocrat and an entrepreneur of considerable scientific-technical ability, observed that if the profits yielded by mining at Štiavnica were used for the replacement of commercial losses, exhaustion would inevitably result.[13]

The economic development of the regions across the river Leitha was also influenced by an interplay of circumstances created by the Habsburgs and the Hungarian aristocracy. In their centralisation efforts, the Habsburgs were bent on forcing the Hungarian aristocrats to pay taxes by applying a customs policy which, in effect, favoured the industrial development of the western parts of the monarchy. On the other hand, the Hungarian aristocrats were much less prepared to turn their attention to industry than their counterparts in Austria and Bohemia. In reality, the feudal structure of agriculture and the still medieval organisation of handicrafts and trades in the towns were not conducive to economic and technical advances. Despite promising features, Slovakia remained a backward country for a long time. Mining and metallurgy did not become a nucleus of further economic, technical, educational and, alas, national progress in the country.[14]

IV

Thus, by 1800, it was through mining and metallurgy that Sclavonia/Slovakia became perceptible in other countries – but not the Slovaks. Here it is apt to point to the observation by a knowledgeable Austrian journalist, Karl-Peter Schwarz, that the Slovaks kept alive their identity during a thousand years of foreign rule as no other people in Europe, under comparable historical circumstances, had done. Broadly, according to Schwarz, this had to do with the late dissolution of the feudal Hungarian state, activated by the reforms of Maria Theresa and Joseph II (addressed by E. Kowalská). This included the elevation of German

---

[13] J. von Sternberg, *Reise nach den ungarischen Bergstädten* (Vienna, 1807), pp. 33–4.

[14] This also has to do with the history of German colonisation in Slovakia, which intensified in the wake of the Mongol (Tatar) invasion (1241). The significant effect of the settlement of a large number of German-speaking colonists (including miners) was to change the national composition of urban population but not that of the countryside. A judicious study of the 'German' dimension in the history of Slovakia is badly needed.

as the 'official language' (*Amtssprache*) as a means of communication throughout the multilingual Habsburg lands.[15]

This measure met with opposition from the Hungarian 'political nation' – essentially the nobility and gentry. With this came their growing inclination to see in Magyarisation the instrument of political cohesion in a country in which a mixture of ethnic groups was real.[16] It is within this framework that the problem of Slovak ethnicity began, after 1800, to claim the attention of (still only) a few intellectuals thinking about the Slovak past. As examined especially by Ľ. Haraksim, a feeling of closeness with other Slavic peoples played an essential part in the ethnic identification and acquisition of a national consciousness by the Slovaks. A component of the notion of togetherness was the idea of creating a common Slavic language. It inspired the publication of works, such as *Elementa universalis linguae slavice e vivis dialectis eruta et sanis logicae principiis suffulta* (1826). Authored by the Slovak J. Herkeľ, the book should be remembered by the fact that it was the locus from which the term 'Panslavism' began its controversial world voyage.

In the process, it acquired a connotation opposed to the one it had when it originated in Slovakia. While Slovak intellectuals rhapsodised about Slavic reciprocity and a common Slavic language, Panslavism became a spectre – not unlike that of communism, famously invoked by Marx and Engels at the beginning of the *Communist Manifesto* (1848). An inappropriate juxtaposition? Perhaps. Just the same, recall that Ľ. Štúr wrote a year earlier in an article 'Panslavism and Our Country' in his newspaper *Slovenskje národňje novini*:

Suddenly an outcry about Panslavism has swept through Europe; this word has produced an echo and has been uttered with alarm among nearly all European nations; hundreds and hundreds of periodicals have discussed it.[17]

We may note here that the *Oxford English Dictionary* quotes B. Jowett, the renowned English philosopher, writing in 1846: 'My balance of power would be ... France and England against Panslavism and despotism.' Nor is the reference dated 1860 more sympathetic: 'The Panslavic invasion, which will be the next source of danger to the civil and

---

[15] K.-P. Schwarz, *Tschechen und Slowaken. Der lange Weg zur friedlichen Trennung* (Vienna and Zurich, 1993), p. 49. This is a brief integrated history of the Czechs and the Slovaks, interpreted from an anti-communist position.

[16] Even questionable statistics of 1880 confirm this situation. While the Magyars constituted the largest proportion of the total population, they were not the majority (41.2%). They were followed by the Romanians (15.4%), Germans (12.5%), Slovaks (11.9%). The remainder were Ruthenians, Serbs and Croats. See *ibid.*, p. 51.

[17] Cited by V. Clementis, *Panslavism Past and Present* (London, 1943), p. 24.

intellectual liberty of Christendom.' What we are dealing with here is the fear of tsarist Russia which, in fact,

never had a Slav programme; it sometimes suppressed the Slav sympathies in Russia, and sometimes it used, or rather, misused them for its own purposes, connected with either home or foreign policy.[18]

While in Slovakia the traditional appeal of Russia as the mighty sustainer ('oak') of Slavic interests declined, it did not disappear completely before 1914.

Slavophilism/Russophilism revived in the war in which Austria-Hungary and Germany, and Serbia and Russia, were involved on opposite sides. It found reflection in desertions of Slovak soldiers, and Slovak prisoners of war volunteering for the Czechoslovak Legions in Russia. That they were set up was in no small measure due to M. R. Štefánik, who was able to arouse interest in and win sympathy of the tsar and the Russian military for the idea of a Czechoslovak force in Russia.

As to Soviet Russia, because of its multi-ethnic and multi-national make-up in the 1920s and 1930s, it did not become a vehicle of Panslavism. After the German invasion in 1941, while expressly eschewing the idea of Panslavism, the Soviet regime invoked Slavic solidarity as an ideological weapon in the fight against the German armies and Nazism. The Hitlerite intent, among others, to subjugate the 'racially inferior' Slavs was not merely rhetoric. Neither were the appeals for Slavic solidarity which went out from All-Slav Congresses at Moscow during the Second World War. It had a part in the defining national and international moment of modern Slovak history – the Slovak National Uprising of 1944.

V

The Slovak National Uprising covers a two-month period from the end of August to the end of October 1944. It was during this span that bodies of the Slovak resistance movement wielded power on the territory in central Slovakia, liberated through the actions of Slovak military and armed partisan combatants. This episode in the history of the European resistance movement has virtually been ignored by non-Slovak historiography, except for informed specialists. In Slovakia, 29 August remains a public holiday marking the beginning of the uprising, which reveals that there is a consensus, officially sanctioned, about the landmark significance of the uprising in the history of Slovakia. None the less, this leaves questions of (mis)representation, as indicated earlier.

[18] *Ibid.*, p. 52.

When on 14 March 1939 Slovakia effectively became a German client state, it provided

the most important jumping-off point for the invasion, and indeed the Slovak government actually sent some units to fight their way into Poland alongside the German troops, lured by the promise of a small amount of extra territory once Poland had been defeated.[19]

But even Slovaks, who greeted the establishment of the Slovak state, were under no illusion that its creation 'came to pass by the grace of Hitler'. While the Slovak public admired German industrial, technical, scientific and cultural achievements, it was not Germanophilist.

Neither the public nor the army was enthusiastic about Slovak participation in the war against the Soviet Union under the banner of anti-Bolshevism. Though the ruling party was Roman Catholic, the number of Protestant officers holding positions of responsibility was far greater than the numerical strength of the Protestants in the country would warrant. This had to do with the historically strong support from Slovak Protestants for the foundation of the Czechoslovak Republic. It was Slovak Protestant families who encouraged their sons to join an army with a largely Czech officer corps.[20] This is how it came about that they occupied posts in the Slovak army, which allowed them to set up an underground centre to provide critical support for the uprising. It was

[19] R. E. Evans, *The Third Reich at War* (London, 2008), p. 4. To recall: in the wake of the Munich Agreement, the Slovak autonomous government was forced to cede territory in northern Slovakia (276 km^2), inhabited by about 4,000 persons. Apart from regaining it, Slovakia was enlarged by twenty-five communes in northern Slovakia as well, conjoined to Poland after the First World War.

[20] The history of the Protestant element in the Czechoslovak–Slovak army goes back to the Czechoslovak Legions in Russia, Italy and France in the Great War. Štefánik, who helped to organise them, was the son of a Protestant pastor. General F. Čatloš, who fought in the Czechoslovak Legion in Russia and held the post of minister of defence throughout the existence of the Slovak state, was a Protestant, as was the Italian legionary General R. Viest, who was sent to Slovakia from London to command the insurgent armed forces. So were three brothers prominent in the uprising, Major Milan Vesel, Lt-Col Mirko Vesel and Major Miloš Vesel. Milan led the delegation which flew on 4 September 1944 to the Soviet Union to inform authorities about the military situation in Slovakia. Mirko was a member of the delegation of the Slovak National Council that flew to London on 7 October 1944. Miloš was the commander of the garrison in Ružomberok, which went over to the partisans, who liberated locally incarcerated political prisoners on 26 August 1944. Here I draw on J. Jablonický and M. Kropilák, *Slovník Slovenského národného povstania* [Dictionary of the Slovak National Uprising], 2nd edn. (Bratislava, 1970), pp. 309–10. For relevant observations on Slovak Protestant officers, see P. Čarnogurský, *14. marec 1939* [14 March 1939] (Bratislava, 1992), pp. 35–6. The author, a prominent autonomist, wants to show that he had patriotic reservations regarding the complete subordination of the Slovak state to Hitlerite Germany.

a unique event in the history of the Second World War. No other Axis state changed sides so dramatically or in the same way as Slovakia did in 1944. The campaign was fought by a truly international cast on all sides. Americans, Britons, Frenchmen, Czechs, Germans, Hungarians, Poles, Slovaks, Russians, Ruthenians, Ukrainians and even five Jewish parachutists from Palestine were involved. Escaped French prisoners of war fought alongside Soviet partisans, American Special Forces and the Slovak infantry. Some SS [Schutzstaffel, protection squad] divisions contained French and Ukrainian volunteers, and local ethnic Germans joined Slovaks still loyal to Tiso's regime. Antiquated Slovak bi-planes and homemade armoured trains were pitted against the latest German technology. Soviet fighter planes, flown by Czechoslovak pilots, patrolled the skies, while American B-17 bombers flew in OSS [Office of Strategic Service] agents and some supplies.[21]

No other regular army of a friendly state attacked the German might from the rear. Moreover, as J. Rychlik and V. Prečan show, the military resisters, entering into an alliance with the communist and bourgeois resisters as equal partners, acknowledged the primacy of the civilian centre of the uprising. The tripartite anti-fascist communist–bourgeois–military coalition, embarking on the strategy of armed struggle, made the Slovak National Uprising a one-of-a-kind event in the history of the European resistance.

Originally, according to the Slovak military historian V. Štefanský, the chief point in planning the uprising was for the eastern divisions of the Slovak army to secure Slovak territory for one month, after which the Soviet armed forces were to arrive. Why this was not achieved has been the subject of debate, with answers embedded in various theses. They include the view that the Slovak National Uprising was left in the lurch because of underlying East–West strains. After examining British files, M. D. Brown finds

the persistent myth that direct parallels can be drawn between Soviet behaviour during the Warsaw Uprising and their behaviour towards the Slovaks can be firmly rejected, as can the suggestion that the Soviets refused British requests to use their airfields for resupply flights. Consequently, the reasons why the Uprising failed can only be comprehended with reference to the military and logistical context on the ground in Slovakia, and not, as has so frequently been suggested over the past sixty years, solely in regards to deteriorating east–west relations.[22]

And yet there can be little doubt that frictions existed and became a prevailing factor in domestic and world politics. As to the military importance of the uprising, Štefanský remonstrates

[21] M. D. Brown, 'SOE and the Failure of the National Slovak Uprising', *History Today*, 54 (12) (2004), 40.
[22] M. D. Brown, *Dealing with the Democrats. The British Foreign Office and the Czechoslovak Émigrés in Great Britain 1939–1945* (Frankfurt am Main, 2006), p. 347.

the insurgent army, even though the eastern divisions failed to operate, held on to a contiguous insurgent territory for a period of two months which, when all is said and done, cannot be regarded as a complete fiasco.[23]

In the short run, the significance of the Slovak National Uprising lies in a nexus of political, military and moral factors. In the long run, the Slovak National Uprising provides a clue to the course of history leading to the Prague Spring and, ultimately, to the collapse of Czecho-Slovakia.

VI

The Slovak National Council as the supreme body of the national liberation struggle during the uprising supported the restoration of the Czechoslovak state. But it was to be based on the principle of the equality of the Czechs and the Slovaks in their mutual relations. As the contributions by M. Barnovský, J. Pešek and S. Sikora variously bring home, the principle was accepted in theory but it did not operate in practice (1945–1968). The retreat was triggered off by the unexpected setback for the Communist Party of Slovakia in the parliamentary elections in May 1946.

Fearing the revival of the Right, supported by former members of the Hlinka's Slovak People's Party, the leaderships of the Communist Party of Czechoslovakia and the Communist Party of Slovakia opted to pursue policies that weakened Slovak statehood and strengthened Prague centralism. By 1960, after the introduction of the socialist constitution when the Czechoslovak Republic was declared to be the Czechoslovak Socialist Republic, the jurisdictional powers of the Slovak national bodies were effectively done away with.

The dramatic dimension of this phase of Czechoslovak/Slovak history is personified by the co-founder of the illegal Slovak National Council, Gustáv Husák. After 1945, as a leading state and Communist Party functionary, he helped to institute an arbitrary repressive regime, including manipulated trials of individuals suspected as enemies of the system. Designated as the head of Slovak 'bourgeois nationalists' within the Communist Party of Slovakia, he eventually became its victim. After being sentenced to life imprisonment in 1954, Husák was granted amnesty in 1960, partially rehabilitated in 1963 and appointed deputy chairman of the government in 1968. In the same year he became

---

[23] V. Štefanský, 'K niektorým problémom povstaleckej armády ako rozhodujúcej ozbrojenej sily povstania' [On certain problems of the insurgent army as the decisive armed force of the uprising], in Juriga, *Nezodpovedané otázky*, p. 150.

head of the Communist Party of Slovakia, a year later first secretary of the Communist Party of Czechoslovakia, and president of the republic in 1975.

Although by 1960 the Czechoslovak economy was stagnating, Slovakia's accelerated industrialisation was accompanied by undeniable progress in education, culture, health and housing. By then, upward social mobility for workers and peasant-farmers had become a prominent feature of social conditions in Slovakia as it was in the Czech Lands. 'Income distribution in Czechoslovakia by the early Sixties', writes an uncompromising critic of the Soviet bloc, 'was the most egalitarian in Soviet Europe'.[24]

The centrally administered planned economy was not capable of co-ordinating the processes of economic life. This engendered widespread dissatisfaction with politics and economics which came to engage the Communist rank and file. Among the Communist intelligentsia in particular, people began to make critical analyses of the economic, socio-political, technical-scientific and cultural conditions. This is where the roots of the reform movement are to be found. In the history of the various reform movements in the communist countries, Czechoslovakia was the one where economic and political change was demanded simultaneously from within and from outside the Communist Party.

As to Slovak reformers, they were oriented above all to federalisation, fuelled by resentment about the asymmetry in Czech–Slovak relations, that is, because of the smaller population of Slovakia, which represented one-third of the population, the Czech majority dominated the Slovak minority in central organs. Among Slovaks, this reinforced the conviction that Slovak interests were being neglected as all decisions were taken in Prague.[25] As observed by M. Londák and E. Londáková, the dissatisfaction over this situation famously came through in the speech by Alexander Dubček at the meeting of the Central Committee of the Communist Party of Czechoslovakia on 26–7 September 1967. Dubček was critical of planning that envisaged the mass migration of Slovak people, searching for work in the Czech Lands, because of investment decisions which were not to offer enough possibilities for placing them in jobs in Slovakia.[26] Nobody anticipated that this criticism of economic

---

[24] T. Judt, *Postwar. A History of Europe Since 1945* (London, 2005), p. 437. A balanced treatment of economic and social issues for this period is to be found in V. Průcha *et al.*, *Hospodářské a sociální dějiny Československa 1918–1992* [Economic and social history of Czechoslovakia], vol. II, *Období 1945–1992* [1945–1992] (Brno, 2009).

[25] This and the preceding paragraph draw on A. Teichova, *The Czechoslovak Economy 1918–1980* (London and New York, 1988).

[26] The relevant passage from the speech is cited by M. Londák, 'Ekonomický vývoj na Slovensku v rokoch 1960–1967' [Economic development in Slovakia in the years 1960–1967], in Londák, S. Sikora and E. Londáková, *Predjarie. Politický, ekonomický a kultúrny vývoj na Slovensku v rokoch 1960–1967* [Before Spring. Political, economic

matters affecting Slovakia was to set off a sequence of events which eventually led to the appointment of the then relatively unknown head of the Slovak Communists to the post of first secretary of the Communist Party of Czechoslovakia on 5 January 1968.

Covered by J. Žatkuliak and M. Štefanský, the rest is history, as the well-worn phrase has it: the Prague Spring, the entry of military units of five Warsaw Pact states, 'normalisation', the Velvet Revolution and the demise of Czechoslovakia as the common state of Czechs and Slovaks. Its dramatic dimension is personified by Dubček no less strikingly than by Husák, who replaced him as the first secretary of the Communist Party of Czechoslovakia in April 1969. Dubček's revolutionary pedigree is impeccable. His father was Štefan Dubček, a founding member of the Communist Party of Czechoslovakia (1921) and co-founder of the third illegal Central Committee of the Communist Party of Slovakia in July 1942. Shortly afterwards, he was arrested, imprisoned and, in early February 1945, transported to the notorious Mauthausen concentration camp in Austria. Meanwhile Alexander Dubček, with his brother Julius, joined the partisan movement. They became combatants in the largest Slovak partisan detachment (up to 1,600 participants) operating in west-central Slovakia. It is worth noticing that it carried the name 'Jan Žižka', the renowned blind Czech Hussite military commander. Whereas Julius was killed in January 1945, Alexander – wounded in the right foot – survived. He became full-time Party worker, advancing steadily when he was appointed first secretary of the Communist Party of Slovakia in 1963, and first secretary of the Communist Party of Czechoslovakia in 1968, as noted.

As is his wont, Eric Hobsbawm considers in a stimulating way the role of personality in history in an article on the possibility of writing the history of the Russian Revolution:

In spite of a lot of general political and ideological waffle, individuals do not always make all that much difference in history. For instance, the USA has actually lost seven presidents before the end of their term by assassination or otherwise since 1865 but, seen in the century's perspective, it doesn't seem to have made much difference to the shape of US history. On the other hand, sometimes individuals do make a difference, as in the case of Lenin and Stalin, or, for that matter, in the last years of the USSR.[27]

This also applies to the input of Husák and Dubček into the post-war history of Slovakia/Czechoslovakia – with all due deference to historical,

and cultural development in Slovakia in the years 1960–1967] (Bratislava, 2002), p. 246, n. 243.
[27] E. Hobsbawm, 'Can We Write the History of the Russian Revolution?', in his *On History* (London, 1997), p. 243.

geo-political and personal dissimilarities. But each man has had a different impact when the place of the Prague Spring in history is reflected upon in domestic and global terms. What the Prague Spring was all about is encapsulated perhaps most succinctly in the phrase 'socialism with a human face'.[28] The replacement of Dubček by Husák as first secretary of the Communist Party of Czechoslovakia put paid to any attempts to give a profounder meaning to democracy under socialism than that sanctioned in Soviet-type states. Husák – originally a reformist – transformed into a zealous Moscow loyalist, despite his previous personal experiences of Moscow-inspired repression. Indeed, this made him most acceptable to the Soviet leadership whereas Dubček – a symbol of the Prague Spring at home and abroad – had to go.[29]

Dubček was criticised within the Party for being both insufficiently and excessively reformist. The anti-communists found that his reformism was merely window-dressing. Possibly, it was in the Czech Lands rather than in Slovakia that Dubček enjoyed more popular trust, indeed affection, in the period before the overthrow of what the Prague Spring stood for. These feelings endured until his re-emergence 'from two decades of obscurity' which 'had opened the possibility that he might be chosen to replace Husák as President'.[30]

VII

The compromise – Dubček was elected chairman of the Federal National Assembly, whereas Havel became president – awaits a serious full-scale historical analysis.[31] So do the other landmarks in Czechoslovak/Slovak history after the tragic Munich Agreement (1938): the Communist takeover (1948), the 'Prague Spring' (1968), the demise of Czechoslovakia (1990–1992). Here one should recall what was stated in 1977 in a *samizdat* analysis of the Prague Spring: 'The Munich period

---

[28] The phrase originated with Eduard Goldstücker (1913–2000), transmitted in a Prague radio programme in late February/early March 1968. A native of Slovakia and veteran Communist, Goldstücker was imprisoned on trumped-up charges in the 1950s. Rehabilitated, he held the chair in German literature at Charles University in Prague and became internationally known as an authority on Kafka. At the time of the Prague Spring, he was chairman of the Czechoslovak Writers' Associations.

[29] After giving a lecture to an academic audience at Nagasaki University in the 1990s, Alice Teichova was presented by a female colleague (the only woman present) with a silver coin carrying a portrait of Dubček.

[30] Judt, *Postwar*, p. 620.

[31] See A. Benčík, *Utajovaná pravda of Alexandru Dubčekovi* [The hidden truth about Alexander Dubček] (Prague, 2001). The accidental nature of the car crash (1 September 1992), as a result of which Dubček died (7 November 1992), has been the subject of speculation.

and the war years are also in my opinion the key to comprehending everything that has happened and the way it has happened from then to now'.[32]

It is fair to say that the majority of Czechs and Slovaks were doubtful if not against the separation. As for contemporary views, first let me quote a prominent Slovak participant in the 1989 events:

The disintegration of Czechoslovakia was not an inevitable consequence of the emancipation process in Slovakia, but rather the unintended consequence of actions by political elites. As such, the disintegration of Czechoslovakia may be 'authorised'. The historic responsibility will be borne by protagonists of non-political politics [V. Havel], economic pragmatism [V. Klaus] and national socialism [V. Mečiar].[33]

A more robust if at times clichéd explanation was offered by the former dissident and important political player P. Pithart:

Because I participated in the majority of the negotiations regarding the constitutional set-up and because I am convinced that an agreement was possible, in spite of the ill-preparedness of both sides and a whole series of mistakes committed not only by one side. In fact, we were only two steps away in the spring of 1992 [and] I contend that what finally prevailed was trivial selfishness on both sides. Of course, the selfishness attempted to disguise itself more credibly as defence of national singularity, identity and so on. The prevailing selfishness on the Slovak side was childish [pošetilé] and naïve with elements of idealism – idealism connected with nationalism often assumes very dangerous forms. The prevailing selfishness on the Czech side in the end was businesslike [věcné] and sober, not at all naïve, even though similarly shortsighted, certainly without any trace of idealism. The paramountcy of the economic motivation is obvious in view of the general embarrassment which accompanied the actual formation especially of the new Czech state – of course not felt by the responsible politicians. They had to pretend something like a solemn pathos. But in general the talk in this connection was about an 'unwanted child'.[34]

[32] P. Pithart, Osmašedesátý [The year 1968], 3rd edn (Prague, 1990), p. 44. Following the samizdat edition, the book was published in Cologne under the pseudonym J. Sládeček in 1980. Until 1968 the author taught constitutional law at Charles University in Prague. He was a signatory of Charter 77, and prime minister of the Czech Republic within the binational Federative State of Czechs and Slovaks (16 February–2 July 1992).

[33] F. Gál, 'Rozpad Československa v politickej perspektíve' [Disintegration of Czechoslovakia in political perspective], in R. Kipke and K. Vodička (eds.), Rozloučení s Československem [Goodbye to Czechoslovakia] (Prague, 1993), p. 162. Fedor Gál, who was born in 1945 in the notorious ghetto of Terezín (Theresienstadt), became chairman of the Movement against Violence which played in Slovakia a role similar to that of Civic Forum in the Czech Lands.

[34] P. Pithart, 'Paradoxy rozchodu. Filosofická a mravní hlediska a evropské paralely' [Paradoxes of the separation. Philosophical and moral points of view and European parallels], in Kipke and Vodička (eds.), Rozloučení, pp. 224–5.

The issue of whether the disbandment of Czechoslovakia was inevitable has been taken up by Czech and Slovak historians. Was it due to the 'artificialness' of the Czechoslovak state, imposed by the Treaties of Versailles and Trianon, as claimed by their critics? After all, it lasted for merely twenty years and, having been restored, for another forty-seven years before it fell apart again.

The inevitability of the establishment of the Republic of Czechoslovakia became the theme of the conference 'Czechoslovakia: contingency, or logic of history?' convened by the Institute of History of the Czech Academy of Sciences in Prague on 12 and 13 October 1993. In the publication of the conference materials, there are four Slovak contributions of which only that by D. Kováč addresses the issue of contingency/inevitableness in relation to the foundation, duration and disintegration of the Czechoslovak state:

The centralist model of Czech–Slovak statehood was historically inevitable but, for a durable living together of Czechs and Slovaks, it had little perspective ... after 1945, this model was counterproductive and became a source of tension between Czechs and Slovaks. Under the condition of totalitarian dictatorship, it was possible to suppress and curb it. After its demise, it [re]appeared on the political scene quite lawfully [*zákonite*].[35]

VIII

In view of the rebirth of democracy of which the Velvet Revolution was the harbinger, it was ironic, if not bizarre, that the split of the Czech and Slovak Federative Republic was truly engineered by two individuals in the absence of a democratic mandate: V. Klaus and V. Mečiar. They were the leaders of the victorious parties in the June elections of 1992 in the Czech Republic and Slovak Republic respectively. Whereas the Civic Democratic Party advanced liberal capitalist policies, the Movement for a Democratic Slovakia professed social populist beliefs.

Be that as it may, these and other concurring Czech and Slovak politicians – in thrall to the free market credo – had not envisaged the possibility of a future crisis in capitalist society. Twenty years after 1989 and five years after the coveted accession to membership of the European Union, as I write these lines, the difficulties befalling the eastern states have been highlighted in *The Guardian*, the renowned British daily, as follows:

[35] D. Kováč, 'Idea česko-slovenskej štátnosti a slovenský štátoprávny program' [The idea of Czecho-Slovak statehood and the Slovak constitutional programme], *Moderní dějiny*, 2 (1994), 37.

The eastern states had nothing to do with the reckless behaviour and regulatory failures that led to the international economic crisis. Their banks are owned by foreigners, and they are in any case relatively minor economic players. Yet, as the recession takes its toll, these countries could end up paying a higher price than the big nations whose bankers and financiers created the problem. The dangers to the EU's cohesion are obvious, given that eastern Europe's abiding experience is one of being let down by the west.

These nations are heavily indebted, and many of those debts are in foreign currency, which means that repayments in their own money are soaring. The relatively low-cost manufacturing sectors upon which they depend are all now in trouble as external demand dries up. Jobs are disappearing, bankruptcies rising and foreign direct investment falling. Political consequences are already apparent in a strengthening of populist, nationalist and Eurosceptic currents of opinion, and in street protests.[36]

The unexpected reality of the post-1989 slump, dramatically propelling to the fore the 'forgotten' questions of poverty and inequality, has a historical dimension. It is a big question about the historic reality of society, historical evolution of social systems, their relations and transformations, fashionably viewed as obsolete and irrelevant.[37] Among those who take a more balanced view is the Cambridge historian of political thought Gareth Stedman Jones, a critic of Soviet-type regimes, who writes:

Those who doubt the relevance of history because they believe that the world was made anew by the defeat of communism, the end of the Cold War, and the demise of socialism at the beginning of the 1990s do not escape its hold. They simply become the guileless consumers of its most simple-minded reconstructions.[38] Those who devised the new reform programmes of post-socialist parties, desperate to remove any residue of an old-fashioned and discredited collectivism, hasten to embrace a deregulated economy hopefully moralized by periodic homilies about communitarian sentiment. By doing this, they imagine themselves to be buying into an unimpeachable and up-to-date liberal tradition handed down in a distinguished lineage of economists and philosophers inspired by the *laisser faire* libertarianism of Adam Smith's *The Wealth of Nations* ... such assumptions are at best dubious and, for the most

---

[36] 'A Test of Solidarity', *The Guardian*, 24 February 2009.
[37] See Alice Teichová and Mikuláš Teich, 'Marx stále žije?' [Marx still alive?], in P. Paleček (ed.), *Exil a politika. Historici o nejnovějších dějinách a o sobě* [Exile and politics. Historians about most recent history and about themselves] (Tišnov, 2004), pp. 132–62; Alice Teichova and Mikuláš Teich, *Zwischen der kleinen und großen Welt Ein gemeinsames Leben im 20, Jahrhundert*, ed. by G. Dressel and Michaela Reischitz (Vienna, Cologne and Weimar, 2005) (consisting of recorded interviews).
[38] Famously Margaret Thatcher is reported to have said in an interview at 10 Downing Street: 'And who is society? There is no such thing! There are individual men and women and there are families and no government can do anything except through people and people look to themselves first'.

part, false. The free market individualism of American conservatives and the moral authoritarianism which often accompanies it are not the products of Smith (although they certainly draw selectively upon certain of his formulations), but of the recasting of political economy in the light of the frightened reaction to the republican radicalism of the French Revolution.[39]

The relevance of history has been of no particular interest to those who have come to power in the Czech Republic and the Slovak Republic after 1989/1992, unusually for politicians of two countries in which the actual (or imagined) past had exercised a powerful influence of the forging of national identities and politics. Congruently they had virtually no interest in making sense of the Communist era in Czechoslovak/Slovak history – apart from repudiating it all round.

As the late Czech medievalist František Graus observed pointedly: 'With history it is possible to do almost anything – only to elude it is not possible'.[40] Sooner or later, the Communist era will have to be seriously addressed by Czech and Slovak historiography. Was it an anomaly in Czechoslovakia or, for that matter, in Russia from which it cannot be separated? The problem of what is 'anomaly' and what is 'normal', in the context of Czech/Czechoslovak/European history, was raised by the Czech historian F. Šmahel with regards to the Hussite Revolution and (in passing) to the Prague Spring.[41] It also has underlain the historical question debated at the Prague conference referred to earlier.

IX

In conclusion, on a personal note, I come from Slovakia and felt, as if duty bound, to offer an opportunity for the English-reading audience to become familiar with the history of a country which, to all intents and purposes, became independent in 1992, and has become a member state of the European Union. The contiguity of *Slovakia in History* with *Bohemia in History* has been remarked on. Fortunately, Dušan Kováč, who had contributed the chapter 'Czechs and Slovaks in modern history', consented to co-edit the Slovak counterpart. He suggested the structure of the volume and the corps of authors. As a rule, there are difficulties with multi-authored collections. In the case of *Slovakia in History*, the translations of the original Slovak versions of chapters proved to be a particular headache. Martin D. Brown brought relief when he joined the

---

[39] G. Stedman Jones, *An End of Poverty? A Historical Debate* (London, 2004), pp. 2–3.
[40] F. Graus (ed.), *Naše živá i mrtvá minulost* [Our living and dead past] (Prague, 1968), p. 8.
[41] F. Šmahel, 'The Hussite Movement. Anomaly of European History?', in Teich (ed.), *Bohemia*, pp. 79–97.

editorial duo. His knowledge of and empathy with the history of the Czechs and Slovaks has been invaluable in the preparation of the finalised English text. In truth, there have been editorial disagreements regarding individual contributions that were addressed while leaving a range of interpretations open to discussion.

Inevitably, one's understanding of the history of one's country has to do with one's personal history. Mine began shortly before the death of Austria-Hungary, on 24 July 1918, in Košice. But this east Slovakian town, second in size to Bratislava, had no further bearing on my life, connected, as it was, with the central Slovakian Liptov region during the formative first twenty years. The important part played by the historically strongly evolved regionalism in the making of *Slovenskost'* (Slovakdom) has recently been called to mind by the distinguished Slovak journalist Juraj Charvát:

[It] feeds on a multitude of diverse sources. There were not only urban and village sources, but also ecclesiastical as well as class and also strongly regional ones. Geographical conditions in Slovakia produced natural conditions for the formation of regions, constituted into counties [*župy/stolice*] with borders unchanged for centuries. Thus highly distinctive models of living and survival were brought into being, with characteristic linguistic variations, sometimes bordering on understandability.[42]

The Slovak idiom in central Slovakia, it will be recalled, was regarded by Štúr to be the Slovak *lingua franca*. I well remember that, along with some of my school-friends, I prided myself on speaking *the* pure Slovak.

As Roman Holec puts it: 'Liptov – that was traditionally two towns: Liptovský Svätý Mikuláš and Ružomberok.'[43] It was from Liptovská Teplá, a village located between the two, that my parents moved to Ružomberok when I reached school age. It was a small industrial town with approximately 14,000 inhabitants, of various social classes. Thus early in primary and secondary schools, I took in that there are children who come from better-off and poorer families. This was acutely brought

[42] J. Charvát, 'Tri prúdy. Úvahy nehistorika k 90. výročiu 28.10.1918' [Three currents. Thoughts of a non-historian on the 90th anniversary 28.10.1918], *Listy*, 5 (2008), 7–15 (12). A sheep cheese, 'Liptovská bryndza', is an export article sold under the German name 'Liptauer Brimsen' (some of my relatives were involved in the trade), though it is not to be mistaken for a spread made of sheep-cheese mixed with butter and paprika, offered in cafés and wine gardens in Vienna and elsewhere as 'Liptauer', and known in Magyar as 'körözött liptói'.

[43] R. Holec, 'Liptovské nádeje a prehry na prahu 20. storočia' [Hopes and setbacks of Liptov on the eve of the twentieth century], in K. Dzuriak and J. Žatkuliak (eds.), *Prínos osobností Liptova pre históriu a súčasnosť* [Contribution by personalities from Liptov to history and the present] (Liptovský Mikuláš, 2000), p. 10. This collection contains papers on the occasion of the 'World Meeting of Liptáks 2000' at Liptovský Hrádok.

home to me when my father was declared bankrupt in 1930 – the crisis year in terms of the global depression. The problem of the social and inequality divide never stopped troubling me. I was alerted to politics early on, not least because my home town, where Andrej Hlinka was parish priest (1905–1938), was the centre of Slovak political Catholicism. There were other influences that catalysed my politicisation, notably, the Reichstag Fire trial (1934) and the outbreak of the Civil War in Spain (1936), in which five anti-fascists from Ružomberok – well known to me – with different social and religious backgrounds, were involved.[44] It was 'natural', when I started medical studies at Charles University in Prague (1936), to join the Bloc of Democratic Medics, an association of communist, social-democratic and left-leaning Catholic students. By the time Slovak autonomy was proclaimed in Žilina in early October 1938, I was ready to help with the production of a leaflet, warning the workers in the Ružomberok–Rybárpole textile mill to heed the danger of fascism – while acknowledging the right of the Slovaks to self-determination. As brought out in this volume, the clerico-fascist regime was to play a fateful role in Slovak history during the Second World War, including that of my family. In the aftermath of the foiled Slovak National Uprising in the autumn of 1944 the two good people who gave me life fell into the hands of occupying SS army units. Thereupon they were shipped to German concentration camps, Oranienburg and Ravensbrück, where they perished in April 1945.

---

[44] They are Jozef ('Jožo') Májek, son of a prison warden and Catholic youth activist. He lost his life almost immediately after arrival in Spain; Ladislav ('Laco') Holdoš, a bank employee, from a Protestant family, son of a forester. Bedrich ('Frico') Biheller, a full-time Communist activist, son of a Jewish lawyer; Helena ('Helenka') Petránková, a pharmacist from a modest Jewish background; and Alica ('Alinka') Kohnová-Glasnerová, a lawyer from a well-to-do Jewish background. The participation of volunteers from Slovakia in the Civil War in Spain in support of democracy has been virtually ignored by Slovak historiography.

Index

This index uses Slovak alphabetical order.

CPSIA information can be obtained at www.ICGtesting.com
Printed in the USA
LVOW091434180412

278179LV00004B/55/P